the road to disappearance

A HISTORY
OF THE
CREEK INDIANS

BY ANGIE DEBO

THE CIVILIZATION OF THE AMERICAN INDIAN SERIES

The Road to Disappearance

The Road t

A History of the Creek Indians

Disappearance

By ANGIE DEBO

"The Indian is now on the road to disappearance ... We ... are facing the evening of our existence and are nearly at the end of the trail ... In time, perhaps, our own language will not be used but that will be after our days."

—SIAH HICKS

NORMAN : UNIVERSITY OF OKLAHOMA PRESS

By Angie Debo

The Historical Background of the American Policy of Isolation
(with J. Fred Rippy) (Northampton, Mass., 1924)
The Rise and Fall of the Choctaw Republic (Norman, 1934; New
edition, Norman, 1967)
And Still the Waters Run (Princeton, 1940; New edition, Prince-
ton, 1972)
The Road to Disappearance: A History of the Creek Indians (Nor-
man, 1941; New edition, Norman, 1967)
Tulsa: From Creek Town to Oil Capital (Norman, 1943)
Prairie City: The Story of an American Community (New York,
1944; New edition, New York, 1969)
Oklahoma: Foot-loose and Fancy-free (Norman, 1949)
The Five Civilized Tribes of Oklahoma (Philadelphia, 1951)
A History of the Indians of the United States (Norman, 1970)
Geronimo: The Man, His Time, His Place (Norman, 1976)
Oklahoma: A Guide to the Sooner State (Ed., with John M. Oski-
son) (Norman, 1941)
The Cowman's Southwest, Oliver Nelson (Ed.) (Glendale, Calif.,
1953)
History of the Choctaw, Chickasaw, and Natchez Indians, by H. B.
Cushman (Ed.) (Stillwater, Okla., 1962)

To

Grant Foreman *and* Carolyn Thomas Foreman

whose work has pointed the way

Preface

TWO hundred years ago when the activities of the white man in North America were dominated by clashing imperial ambitions and colonial hardships and struggles, the great Creek Confederacy rested in savage contentment under the reign of native law. The dwellers in this happy land looked out on life and found it good. They joined in community labors with singing and laughter, they shared the aspirations of religious ceremonials, and they entered joyously into recreational experiences. No one in their whole world could do them harm. Their warriors made safe and profitable forays against their enemies and returned with scalps and celebration; and they welcomed the slight white men who came with gifts and promises to the exuberant hospitality of their invincible towns.

The reputation of the Creeks as warriors and native diplomats extended to the most distant reaches of the Indian country, and the lonely settler hated them with a ferocity inspired by fear; but secure in their careless strength, they had no guile to match that of the white man, and no disciplined courage to oppose his ruthlessness. They met encroachment with angry and sporadic reprisals, but in the main they were held in check by specious arguments and pledges of friendship until their power was worn down and their savage spirits tamed. Piece by piece their land was wrested from them, and they submitted with grumbling, always believing that *this* time the treaty would be kept. In the Red Stick War and again in their desperate resistance to removal their smoldering resentment flamed up in brief revolt, but it was quickly stamped out. In the end they were dragged from their ancient homes and flung down upon a raw western frontier to conquer it or die.

In the West the Creeks gathered their forces again for constructive growth. Once more they found prosperity and undisturbed security, their influence spread to the most remote tribes of this wild region, and they even found that some of the white man's ways were worth adopting. But they were still too peaceable for the white man's warfare and too guileless for his diplomacy, and the Civil War left them broken and despoiled. They tried to rebuild their shattered institutions, they recovered their economic well-being, and they made a more earnest effort to acquire the white man's culture; but their progress was hindered by their own spiritual disintegration, the growing negro power in their midst, and above all by the encircling menace of a new frontier. Blindly and instinctively they clung to their heritage, and their educated leaders tried to hold back the white invasion until they should be prepared to meet it; but the end came too soon, and they were left to grope in helpless bewilderment through the complex order of a white man's world.

Although the Creeks attained a measure of what the white man defines as "civilization," their greatest strength always lay in their native steadfastness. They could—and did—change their style of dress, they were quick to see the advantage of planting peach trees around their dwellings or buying an ax from a trader, they were glad to substitute the convenience of owning domestic animals for the uncertainties of the chase, they even established schools as a measure of self-defense, and they found in Christianity a compensation for the loss of their ancient faith; but the attempt to replace their group loyalties with the white man's individualism brought a spiritual collapse from which they never fully recovered. After all the "civilizing" work of their missionaries and agents, they remained to the end essentially unchanged, and their hope of survival still rested upon the unyielding tenacity of their native traits.

But in spite of their tragic sufferings and final defeat one must agree with their greatest educated chief that the Creeks "have not lived for naught." Their influence upon the history of the white man has been profound and permanent. In his weakness he modified his ambitions at their demands, in his need he borrowed from their institutions, in his strength he struggled with his own conscience and made decisions affecting his own character in his contest for their possessions, and in his philosophic moods he may appraise his own civilization and see a reflection of his own problems and failures in the history of their tiny republic.

Many descriptions of early Creek life have been preserved in the accounts of travelers, and John R. Swanton and other ethnologists have brought all the resources of modern scientific thought to the study of their primitive institutions. Their history in the East should be as fully known, but it is apparent from the works of standard historians that it has never been objectively presented. The Removal and the incidents of their settlement and early development in the West have been revealed through the scholarly works of Grant Foreman, and the Civil War period has been definitively portrayed by Annie Heloise Abel. But for the sake of organic unity the author has included this portion of Creek history in the present work, shifting the emphasis somewhat to focus it upon the internal life of the tribe.

The history of the Creeks since the Civil War has been almost a complete blank. Indian agents, journalists, and travelers all centered their attention upon the more "progressive" Indians, and historians in the absence of convenient data have observed the same bias. The story of their life has remained hidden in the tribal records, the obscure newspapers published in their country, the reports of government agents, and the memories of the older Indians. The messages and letters of their chiefs, the proceedings of their courts, the original manuscript acts of their Council, and the reports of their diplomatic representatives were removed from their capitol at the close of the tribal period and deposited with the Union agency. Some of these documents still remain with the Superintendent of the Five Civilized Tribes at Muskogee, Oklahoma, and the rest have been removed to Oklahoma City and catalogued and calendared by the State Historical Society. Incomplete files of the newspapers are also in the possession of the Historical Society and in the office of the *Muskogee Phœnix*. The reports of the Federal agents may be found at Washington in the files of the Indian Office or in process of removal to the government archives. The reminiscences of the old-time Creeks have recently been recorded and preserved through a Works Progress Administration project under the direction of Grant Foreman. The importance of this last source can hardly be overestimated, for although the Creeks have no connected idea of their own history, their testimony is valuable for purposes of interpretation.

In exploring these sources the author has become deeply indebted to the archivists, clerks, and librarians in charge of historical collections and government documents; to Mr. Frank Phillips of Bartlesville for the creation of an important reference collection at the University of Oklahoma; to Mr. Paul Bruner of the *Muskogee Phoenix* for unlimited access to old newspaper files; and above all to the Social Science Research Council for a grant-in-aid without which the book could not have been completed.

ANGIE DEBO

Marshall, Oklahoma
June 1, 1941

Twenty-five Years After

NOBODY WRITES A BOOK except for the hope that it will be read. It is therefore a frustrating experience when it goes out of print and an occasion of gratitude when the publisher decides to make it available again. My relationship with the University of Oklahoma Press during the writing and publication of *The Road to Disappearance* was a happy one, and I am proud to see it go out once more under the same imprint.

It has a special place on my personal shelf, for it is the product of my most difficult research. Unlike more articulate tribes, which figured in the news and about whose history the salient facts were already known, the Creek Indians were a conservative people who lived their own lives and kept their own counsel, and their inner history was hidden until I uncovered it. Most of my findings have stood the test of time and subsequent research, but I welcome this opportunity to correct some errors.

On page 85 I located the Withington mission station on the Chattahoochee. I found this statement in contemporary accounts, but I have come to believe that it is an error, resulting from the general lack of information about the Creeks, and that the correct location was Tuckabatchee. A scholarly article by Carolyn Thomas Foreman about this mission may be found in *The Chronicles of Oklahoma*, Vol. XLII (1964), 291–99.

My account of Opothle Yahola's movements during the fall of 1861 was based on a contemporary map which, in common with other historians, I accepted without question. Further research has shown beyond doubt that it was inaccurate. The Union leader collected his people on the North Canadian a few miles above Thlobthlocco and Greenleaf towns on the western Creek frontier in the vicinity of the present Okemah. Cooper reached their camp and found it deserted, with "a large trail" leading towards the northwest. He believed they were on their way to Kansas, but actually they were circling the Confederates to join Union Cherokees with whom they were in communication. He followed their trail and overtook them near the Twin Mounds sixteen miles east of Stillwater; and here the Battle of Round Mountains or Round Mountain was fought. I have recorded my findings in *The Chronicles of Oklahoma*, Vol. XLI (1963), 70–104.

I cannot cite a faulty map to excuse an additional error in my account of this campaign. Opothle Yahola, circling to the north and east, effected his junction with the Union Cherokees. Cooper came up with him again, and the Battle of Caving Banks was fought on Bird Creek north of Tulsa. But Cooper, to his chagrin—and to mine, when I discovered what I had done—was not present at the third battle. The defection of the Cherokees was so alarming that he retreated to Concharty, and sent an urgent request for help to Colonel James McIntosh (a white man unrelated to the Creek McIntoshes) at Van Buren, Arkansas; and it was McIntosh and his white soldiers who, without waiting for Cooper to join them, defeated the Union Creeks in the Battle of Chustenahlah. It was only after this rout that they left the Cherokee Nation and fled to Kansas. Cooper arrived two days later and pursued them almost to the Kansas line.

ANGIE DEBO

Marshall, Oklahoma
May 12, 1966

Preface to Third Printing

THIRTEEN YEARS AGO I welcomed the opportunity to correct some errors in my account of the elusive history of the Creek Indians. Now I am glad to correct an even more serious error. In the records available to me during my research in the 1930's, I found the names "Big Warrior" and "Menawa" applied to the same person. Now with the emergence of additional contemporary records I find that they were separate individuals. Menawa may well have been the "Big Warrior" (Tustennuggee Thlocco, the ranking military officer) of his town, and the use of this title may have confused white men unfamiliar with the Creek government. But the Big Warrior who was the most influential leader in Creek affairs during that period was the "speaker" or head chief of the Upper Towns. I have made numerous changes in Chapter 3 to distinguish the separate actions of these two persons.

Angie Debo

Marshall, Oklahoma
March, 1979

Contents

Illustrations

The Road to Disappearance

CHAPTER I

In Savage Power

WHILE the ancestors of white Americans were establishing a precarious foothold along the Atlantic seaboard, a large and fertile area in the Gulf region was occupied by a powerful native Confederacy. These people were sometimes called Muskogees[1] from the name of their dominant tribe; but possibly because of the many streams that watered their country, and upon which they built their clustered towns, they were more often known by the English name of Creeks. Their domain comprised a large portion of the present states of Alabama and Georgia; it was bounded on the north by the lands of the Cherokees, on the west by the Choctaw and Chickasaw nations, on the east by the English settlements, and on the south by the Spanish and French outposts and the broken tribes of the Florida peninsula. Their number was variously estimated at from eleven to twenty-four thousand, grouped in fifty to eighty towns with outlying villages. Most of them belonged to the great Muskhogean linguistic stock, which received its name from the leading tribe in their Confederacy—and included the Choctaws and Chickasaws and many other Indians of the Gulf region.

The early history of the Creeks is lost in legend; but with the Muskogees proper there is a constantly recurring tradition of a western origin with huge mountains forming "the backbone of the world," a migration toward the sunrise, the crossing of a great and muddy river, and the occupation and conquest of their eastern home. These accounts are detailed and circumstantial,

---

[1] The origin of the name is obscure. James R. Gregory, a prominent Creek of the late nineteenth century, attempted to identify it as Is-te-cm-us-suk-c-kee, or People of the Holly Leaf Confederacy, from the Gulf holly used in their ceremonials.—James R. Gregory, "Early Creek History," *Sturm's Statehood Magazine,* I (1905), 86. John R. Swanton believes it to be an Algonquin term, probably meaning "swamp" or "wet ground."

and the towns were grouped in traditional friendships because of incidents on this mythical journey.

The Confederacy probably originated before the coming of the white man, but it increased in power and extent during the period of European colonization. It had two distinct divisions, the Upper Towns on the Coosa and Tallapoosa, and the Lower Towns on the Flint and Chattahoochee, but they usually acted in concert. It appears from their legendary history that one body of Muskogees migrated from the West and separated to form the Lower Towns of Cusseta and Coweta, and a close union of these two settlements may have been the beginning of the Confederacy. During the legendary period they were also associated with Arbeka and Coosa, Upper Towns of Muskogee stock with a tradition of western origin, and with Hoithle Waule (Thlewarle), one of the oldest of the Upper Towns. Apparently a little later they were joined by Tuckabatchee, which seems to have migrated independently. Most of the Muskogee towns in the Confederacy were descended from these six groups, but a few others seem to have joined separately. It soon became the habit of the Creeks to annex the tribes they conquered in war; and when the white men began to drive out the Indians in the neighborhood of their settlements, these refugees also were incorporated into the Confederacy. In this way they received the Alabamas, the Koasatas, the Hitchitees, and the Tuskegees very early in their history. These tribes were not Muskogees, but they all belonged to the Muskhogean stock. A still more distinctive tribe was the Natchez, a distantly related Muskhogean people with an elaborate system of sun worship, a hereditary nobility, and a royal family of divine attributes and prerogatives. They were almost exterminated in warfare with the French in Louisiana, but a few survivors fled to the Creek country, formed a town on the Coosa, and became incorporated eventually with the Arbekas. The Euchees, an alien people who had formerly been hostile to the Creeks, were crowded by the English, and they too joined the Confederacy, forming a strong settlement on the Chattahoochee. They spoke a distinct language unrelated, so far as is known, to that of any other Indian tribe, and they showed a marked clannishness in their social relations, but they followed the Confederacy in peace and war. A considerable number of Shawnees also lived in the Creek country, detached bands from their tribe which by this time was living on the Ohio. Although they were an Algonquin people, they were bound to the Tuckabatchees by strong ties of traditional friendship. They formed temporary towns in various places, but they showed a tendency to settle among the Euchees, so that traders often made the mistake of classing them as a kindred tribe. The Creeks also received individual accessions from the Catawbas, a Siouan people of the Carolina region, who had been almost exterminated in wars with other Indians, and the Biloxis, another Siouan tribe from southern Mississippi. Detached bands of Chickasaws also settled temporarily in the Creek country, attracted apparently by a legendary friendship for the Cussetas.[2]

An early characterization of this foreign policy is found in a dictatorial message sent the Lower Creeks in 1725 by the Senecas of the redoubtable Iroquois Confederacy of central New York. The Senecas scornfully rejected a Creek offer of mediation in a war they were waging against the Cherokees, warned the Creeks to fight the Cherokees and trust the English, and advised them to strengthen themselves as follows:

"As to the Indians that Lives to the Southward of you make a peace with a many of them as you please But Take Care That you oblige all Such as you make a peace with That they Imediately Remove and Setle near To oppose your Enemies[.] That is the Method that We Take and we would have you do the Same."[3]

But the English agents scheming to combat Spanish influence incited the Creeks to make war on the tribes to the south. The Indians of northern Florida had been Christianized by Jesuits and Franciscans, and they were living in thriving towns around the missions. The Creeks laid waste this country and almost

[2] For the earlier migration myths see John R. Swanton, "Social Organization and Social Usages of the Indians of the Creek Confederacy," *Forty-second Annual Report,* Bureau of American Ethnology, 33-77; for modern versions see United States Works Progress Administration Project S-149, D. W. Benson, Samuel Checote; for the history of the various Creek towns see John R. Swanton, *Early History of the Creek Indians and Their Neighbors, Bulletin No. 73,* Bureau of American Ethnology.

[3] Journal of Tobias Fitch, 21 f.

exterminated the inhabitants. Some of their bolder spirits then moved down and occupied this region, at the same time following the usual custom of incorporating into their own group members of the shattered tribes they found there.[4] These native frontiersmen thus received the name of *Seminoles* from a Creek word meaning "wild" or "people who camp at a distance." During the eighteenth century they joined irregularly in the councils of the Lower Creeks, but eventually they came to be regarded as a distinct people. The separation was brought about mainly by the extension of white spheres of influence; when English and later United States agents labored to bring the Creek Confederacy under their control, the people living in Spanish territory proved to be beyond their reach, and it became customary to disregard them in negotiating with the tribe.[5]

The gradual alienation of the Seminoles indicates the casual relationship that existed between different parts of the Confederacy; but nevertheless, on the whole it acted with surprising unanimity. Matters of war and peace were concluded and the fate of public offenders was decided at general councils composed of the head men from the different towns; and a certain amount of legislation was enacted, in the sense of adopting uniform customs throughout the Confederacy. These councils rarely embraced the whole nation, but concerted action was secured by messengers who came from other sections to deliver the views of their towns and to carry back the decisions of the assembly. The Creeks invested all deliberative bodies with such portentous significance that the Confederacy was united more closely by these councils than might be inferred from their irregular and regional character.

The Creeks recognized peace and war as separate governmental functions, and the towns were classed as White or Peace towns and Red or War towns. These distinguishing colors were painted on buildings and ceremonial articles and used in bodily decoration. Each group regarded its members as "people of one fire" and devel-

---

[4] It is possible that this was not a new movement among the Creeks, for some of their migration legends represent them as settling in the Florida peninsula and expanding toward the north.

[5] *Indian Record*, August, 1886; Journal of Tobias Fitch, 29 f., 42-57; *American State Papers, Indian Affairs*, I, 78 f.; 20 Cong., 2 sess., *House Ex. Doc. No. 91;* Henry Rowe Schoolcraft, *Archives of Aboriginal Knowledge*, V, 259 f.

oped a feeling of rivalry that was almost hostile toward even the most closely related towns of the opposing group. Councils were held at the White towns for the conclusion of peace, the adoption of conquered tribes, and to a certain extent the enactment of laws and the regulation of internal affairs. The leading White towns were cities of refuge and no blood was supposed to be spilled there, but it is said that enemies who fled there for protection were sometimes dragged out and killed. Most of the alien towns that came into the Confederacy were admitted as White towns, probably because their adoption was a function of peace. The Red towns took the initiative in declaring war and planning military expeditions, and apparently the councils involving war, diplomacy, and foreign relations were held there.

There was no fixed capital of the Confederacy. The councils met in the leading Peace or War town according to the nature of the business. Leadership depended partly upon legendary prestige and partly upon size and importance; the "mother" towns held a traditional ascendancy, but like a modern convention city the meeting place was usually a town with adequate public buildings and abundant food supply. There had once been a great town named Okmulgee on the river of the same name, and the site was hallowed in tradition as the first settlement made by the Muskogees when they arrived after the long journey from their far western home and as the place where Cusseta and Coweta had formed the league that was the basis of the Confederacy; but the spreading fields and great terraces had been abandoned before the historic period, and a later town of that name was a Hitchitee town of no particular importance. Among the Lower Creeks the powerful War town, Coweta, kept the primacy from 1700 on in negotiating with the whites, but the great Peace town, Cusseta, showed a jealousy that indicates a former ascendancy. Apalachicola or Tulwa Thlocco (Big Town), a Lower White Town of Hitchitee origin, was the meeting place of peace councils and was known by the whites as the "capital" of the Confederacy, but it began to decline before the 1770's, and by the end of the century it had become an insignificant and poverty-stricken village. The Creeks attributed its misfortunes to the fact that in a general massacre of English traders its people had disregarded the law of sanctuary and killed several that sought refuge there. Coosa had once been the leading Peace town of the Upper Creeks, but after 1700 its greatness was only a memory. The English agent, James Adair, who spent most of his time among the Indians from 1735 to 1768, characterized it as "a small ruinous village, . . . which is still a place of safety for those who kill undesignedly." Its daughter towns, Okfuskee and Tallasi (variants, Tulsa and Tullahassee), succeeded to its importance as council centers. Arbeka (Arbekoche) also was an important White town, and some of the most important customs and laws of the Confederacy were said by the Creeks to have originated there. Thlewarle seems to have been at one time the leading Upper Red Town with the right to declare war for the Confederacy, but it was succeeded by Tuckabatchee, which became the most important town of the Upper Creeks. There was also a tradition that Artussee had once been the leader among the Upper War Towns, and its prestige continued for some time after its decline. Existing data are not sufficient to explain the changes in the leadership of the Confederacy, but there is some indication that during the period of greatest expansion and prosperity and the annexation of native tribes, the White towns and the idea of peace were in the ascendant, and that the Red towns later became dominant as the fighting spirit of the nation was aroused by the aggressions of the white man.

The councils were impressive in the grave earnestness of the speakers and the rich and colorful symbolism of the ceremonials. They often continued in session throughout the day and night. The chiefs remained in their places, eating and sleeping at intervals, and the necessary food, ceremonial objects, etc., were brought to them by attendants. The whole town throbbed with activity during one of these great councils—women preparing food, men hurrying on errands for the chiefs, and young people dancing for the entertainment of the visitors.

The representatives from some of the towns enjoyed a traditional prestige—the chief of a certain town, for example, might be automatically recognized as the head chief of all the Lower Towns, all the White towns, etc. Others rose to leadership because of individual prowess in war and wisdom in council. No exact description of the organization is available, but it is clear that these distinctions of rank were rigidly observed in the seating and the deliberations. Although the most important decisions were made in a small conclave of the leading chiefs and communicated to the assembly by an official known as the speaker, popular sentiment had great weight in the formulating of these policies.[6]

Ultimately the strength of the Confederacy rested upon the vigorous and satisfying communal life of the towns. Every town was a center of free, abundant living—of toils shared in careless fellowship, of feasting, dance, and frolic, of sin and retribution and moral aspiration—all directed by the grave voice of the men in council. The town was always situated on a river or creek, for game was abundant there, timber and water were convenient, and the soil was rich. Sites were occasionally abandoned because of the exhaustion of the fields, the outbreak of a pestilence, etc., and the relative size and importance of the towns was constantly changing. There was a tendency for villages to form around the larger towns, and some of these became important enough to set up independent councils and ceremonials and branch off as separate towns. Some towns like Natchez and Euchee Town retained the names of alien tribes that entered the Confederacy; others were named from historic events, as Nuyaka (often spelled New Yorker) received its name when some of the chiefs signed a treaty at New York; but most of them, like Concharty (red earth), Wewoka (barking or roaring water), and Tallasi (old or abandoned town), adopted names descriptive of the location. The private dwellings of each town were grouped around a public place consisting of three units known as the *chunkey yard,* the *chokofa,* and the *square.* These were laid out with ceremonial exactness and were swept and kept in order by persons appointed for the purpose.

The chunkey yard was a level, sunken area forming an exact rectangle two or three hundred yards in length, surrounded with banks for the seating of spectators. It derived its name from the chunkey

[6] *American State Papers, Indian Affairs,* I, 18, 78 f., 672; Benjamin Hawkins, *A Sketch of the Creek Country in the Years 1798 and 1799,* 33, 42, 65; William Bartram, *Travels,* 387-89; Journal of Tobias Fitch, 9 f., 31, 40-42, 51 f.; James Adair, *History of the American Indians,* 159; John R. Swanton (editor), "Notes on the Creek Indians," *Bulletin No. 123,* Bureau of American Ethnology, 124 f.; Swanton, "Creek Social Organization," 310-15.

game, in which the contestants hurled poles at a swiftly rolling stone disc; the stones used in this game were so highly prized that they were kept from generation to generation as town property. In the center of the yard on a low, circular mound was a tapering pole thirty to forty feet high bearing the skull of an animal or other conspicuous object. This was used as a target for arrow shooting and as a goal in a scrambling, hilarious ball game in which the

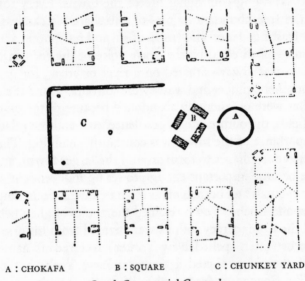

A : CHOKAFA   B : SQUARE   C : CHUNKEY YARD

Creek Ceremonial Ground
showing relation to private dwellings
(*After Bartram. Courtesy Bureau American Ethnology*)

men and the women played as opponents. At one end of the yard were two smaller poles from which enemy scalps were usually fluttering, and it was said that in earlier days it had been the custom to tie and torture captives there. The chunkey yard was used also for the informal dancing with which the Creeks enlivened the summer evenings.

The chokofa, sometimes called the "hot house" by the traders, in the older towns stood on a mound nine or ten feet high, but during the eighteenth century the custom of constructing mounds was generally discarded. It was a circular building often forty or more feet in diameter, with walls about six feet high and a cone shaped roof coming to a high point in the center. The frame was strongly and ingeniously constructed of concentric circles of posts driven into the ground and plates and rafters of poles bound to them and to each other with splints. The wall, following the outer circle of posts, was made of clay, and the roof was covered with bark and plastered with clay. The space between the outer wall and the inner circle of posts was divided into compartments by transverse walls and reserved for the ceremonial seating according to rank of the town officials and warriors; it was usually built in three concentric banks, rising toward the outer wall, and it was carpeted with mats woven of reeds and splints. In the center of the building a fire of dry canes or finely split pine furnished heat and light, without too much smoke, for the assembly, and the large open space around the fire was reserved for dancing. The building had no opening except from a portico that curved around the wall for five or six feet before it entered the house. This was the great meeting place of the Creeks in inclement weather; the men met there for their interminable councils, the entire town assembled there while the young people sang and danced through the long winter evenings, and the old and indigent found it a welcome shelter during the cold nights.

The square, also called "big house" or "town house," was the political and ceremonial meeting place of the Creeks during the summer. In the older towns it also was built on a mound. Its sides were formed by four buildings or sheds facing each other to form a hollow square with an entrance at each corner. The buildings were made of posts driven into the ground supporting slab roofs, with clay walls on three sides and an open side facing the square. Each was divided transversely by clay walls into three compartments and lengthwise to form two or three benches rising in tiers toward the back, and each savage freeman sat or reclined in his proper place. One of these sheds was occupied by the town officials, and there the councils were held and the public business transacted; the others by a system that varied from town to town were assigned to warriors, young men, spectators, etc. Ceremonial objects belonging to the town were religiously guarded in the chief building, and

the posts and walls were painted and carved with legendary and
sacred symbols. According to a visitor to Artussee in the 1770's,
"the pillars and walls of the houses of the square are decorated
with various paintings and sculptures; ... but they are extremely
picturesque or caricature, as men in variety of attitudes, some ludi-
crous enough, others having the head of some kind of animal, as
those of a duck, turkey, bear, fox, wolf, buck, etc., and again those
kind of creatures are represented as having the human head. These
designs are not ill executed; the outlines bold, free and well pro-
portioned. The pillars supporting the front or piazza of the council-
house of the square, are ingeniously formed in the likeness of vast
speckled serpents, ascending upwards."[7]

The leading men of the town assembled every day in council,
either at the square or the chokofa. Here they made decisions involving war and peace, planting and hunting, disputes between
citizens, the maintenance of order, the punishment of offenders,
the care of the public buildings and grounds, the ceremonials and
amusements—all that made up the bustling, pulsing life of these
thriving communities.

At the head of the government was the *micco,* called "town king"
or "town chief" by the white men, who was often known as Coweta
Micco, Tuckabatchee Micco, etc., after the name of his town. He
owed his position partly to descent and partly to an intricate elective system which varied from town to town, and he held office for
life unless recalled. He presided over the council and greatly
influenced its decisions, he received ambassadors and represented
his town in the councils of the Confederacy, and he was at the
head of the civil administration. With the approval of the council
he often appointed a second chief (*micco apotka* or "twin chief"),
who assisted him if he was old or infirm, took his place when he
was absent, and exercised a general control of matters within the
square. The chief's council was composed of a considerable body
of lesser *miccos,* who seem to have shared his minor administrative
duties; the *"beloved men,"* a very influential group, apparently

[7] John R. Swanton (editor), "The Green Corn Dance" (description by John Howard
Payne, 1835), *Chronicles of Oklahoma,* X (1932), 176 f.; Swanton, "Creek Social Organization," 174-91, 466-70.

made up of those who had formerly distinguished themselves in war and council but were too old for active leadership; and the *henehas,* who had the direction of public works and conducted the important ceremonials. One of the henehas, chosen for his eloquence, served as the chief's *speaker,* making his announcements and expressing his official sentiments on ceremonial occasions. Although the micco and his councilors had risen to their position largely through their prowess in war, their duties were mainly civil and their influence was usually for peace.

The war officials sat in another part of the square or chokofa. They were grouped according to their rank as *little emarthlas, big emarthlas,* and *tustennuggees.* Promotion from a lower grade to a higher was the reward of individual achievement, and the degrees were conferred with savage ceremonials of rejoicing after a successful military expedition. These warriors were sometimes called over to the chief's section to join in important councils, but their main duties were to act as enforcement officers in carrying out the sentences of the council against offenders, to arrange the formal ball games with rival towns, and to represent the tribe in war. Their leader was known as the *tustennuggee thlocco* or "big warrior"; he was selected from the tustennuggees by the micco and the beloved men. He had the command of military expeditions and general executive direction of the warrior group. The warriors also had a speaker, whose duties corresponded to those of the chief's speaker.

The common warriors sat apart from these leaders. In general they were young men who had taken part in military expeditions but had not yet distinguished themselves by individual exploits. They did not participate in the government. Naturally the aspiring members of this group thirsted fiercely for military honors as the only road to advancement among their people.

It was inevitable, therefore, that conflicting policies should develop between the warriors and the civil officers. In declaring war the decision lay with the chief and his council, but it was the tustennuggee thlocco who "lifted the hatchet." The two sets of officials were seldom ready for peace at the same time, and when the civil authorities attempted to negotiate and stop hostilities the tustennuggee thlocco and his eager followers often continued their raids. Their opposing functions were analogous to those of the Red and White towns in the Confederacy.[8] This two-fold division was also related in some obscure way to clan groupings.

The entire population of the Confederacy was divided into clans. Each clan cut across town and family life and natural friendships, and bound all its members in ties so close that it regulated the most casual and the most intimate detail of their social intercourse. The Wind Clan was the most important; its members were found in all the towns of the Confederacy, and they enjoyed the special privileges of an aristocratic caste. Other important clans were the Bear, Bird, Beaver, Raccoon, Alligator, Aktayatco (possibly water moccasin), Deer, and Tiger (panther). In addition there was a large number of smaller clans, known only in certain towns or certain racial groups. All members of a clan were regarded as close relatives with an unlimited claim upon each other's services even though they might be complete strangers from widely separated towns; and marriage within the clan was strictly prohibited.

The small clans were grouped around the larger ones to form phratries, and the members of these related groups treated each other with careful friendliness and respect, and refrained from intermarriage. In some cases this grouping was uniform throughout the nation, but with some clans it varied from town to town. The clans were all classified as *Hathagalgi,* or White People, and *Tcilokogalgi,* or People of a Different Speech. The White were peace clans, while the Tciloki were concerned with war, although the adjective *Red* was not usually applied. With a few exceptions the chiefs of the White towns were chosen from the White Clans and those of the Red towns from the Tciloki; the henehas, whose position was traditionally that of peace, were almost universally White; and the war officials, especially in early times, seem to have been selected from the Red Clans. But the members of the White Clans were, of course, not expected to refrain from fighting, and their advancement in civil rank was largely dependent upon military distinction.[9]

[8] Swanton, "Creek Social Organization," 276-98, 426-29; Swanton, "Notes on the Creek Indians," 132-36, 139-41; Hawkins, *Sketch,* 68-72.

[9] Swanton, "Creek Social Organization," 107-71; Swanton, "Notes on the Creek Indians," 136.

The lively fancy of the Creeks invented legends to account for these complicated clan relationships. According to one typical story, in remote ages a mighty fog descended upon their ancestors, and for a long time they wandered about in darkness. Families were separated, and fear fell upon all. When one chanced to touch another, the two held fast, and in this way groups were formed, which eventually grew into large bands. The animals also wandered about uttering various cries, so tame from terror that they, too, joined the groping bands of people. Finally a wind came from the east and swept the fog away. The band that was on the east and first came out of the fog became the Wind Clan. It had no animal near it, but because it first saw the light it was recognized as the leading clan. The other bands all took the names of the birds or animals that were found with them when the fog broke. All agreed never to desert their clans even for the sake of blood relatives, but to treat all members as "people of one flesh."[10]

During the great religious ceremonials of the town it was customary for each clan or set of related clans to meet privately for moral instruction, and the "clan uncle"—the oldest or most revered man of the group—exhorted the members to good conduct, praised those who had behaved well, and reprimanded or even punished those who had behaved badly. Clan descent was reckoned from the mother, although a man always treated his father's clan with respect. The children, of course, belonged to the mother, but in a larger sense to the clan; and their upbringing and discipline were in the hands of the mother and the old man who presided over the clan councils. Except in the case of great public offenders, whose fate was determined in council, punishment of crime was in the hands of the aggrieved clan and was carried out after solemn deliberation by the leading men. The fundamental idea regarding punishment was that it cleansed the criminal from all guilt, and he became thereafter as honorable as any other man in the community. Murder, death by witchcraft, and even accidental killing was commonly expiated by the death of the offender; but if the culprit was a man of recognized value to the community the aggrieved clan might adopt him in place of their lost kinsman, or they

[10] *Indian Journal,* July 5, 1877, and July 12, 1877.

might allow him to atone by the performance of some heroic deed against a hostile tribe, or they might inflict the death penalty upon one of his less important relatives. Stealing was rare except in the highly commendable form of robbing hostile tribes, but when it did occur the culprit's clan made restitution, and if it was an aggravated case they turned him over to the injured clan for whipping or other penalty. Sexual irregularity before marriage was not condemned, but adultery was severely punished. The clan relatives of the injured husband beat both culprits into insensibility, cut off their ears and sometimes their noses, and cut off the woman's long hair and fixed it in some conspicuous place in the square. A woman so punished was cast off by her husband, but if she and her paramour chose to continue their relationship, they were recognized as husband and wife. Incest—i.e., sexual relations within the clan or related clans—was punished by an ugly cut along the backbone and down the legs to the feet, or in aggravated cases, by death. Children were punished for their misdemeanors by scratching them deeply with gars' teeth, but this operation was also performed at intervals, with no idea of punishment, to let out the blood and make the muscles supple.[11]

Hospitality was largely a clan matter. The family dwelling belonged to the wife; she referred to it as "my home," but she used the same expression of any house belonging to a woman of her clan. When a man said "my home," he referred not to the house in which he lived with his wife and children, but to the house of his mother or any other woman of his clan. When a stranger from another town arrived, the men of his wife's clan would say, "Come to your home," and he was privileged to remain there as long as he chose. Indigent old men often spent their time traveling from town to town, sure of finding a "home" everywhere they stopped.[12]

Marriage was sometimes arranged by the clan without consulting the principals, but it seems to have been more general for the man to take the initiative. When he selected his own wife, he sent his

11 Swanton, "Creek Social Organization," 338-58, 363-66; Swanton, "The Green Corn Dance," 183; Swanton, "Notes on the Creek Indians," 137 f., 145-49; Albert James Pickett, *History of Alabama and Incidentally of Georgia and Mississippi from the Earliest Period*, 470.
12 Swanton, "Creek Social Organization," 171.

sister, mother, or other female relative to the women of the girl's family, and the latter referred the question to her brothers and maternal uncles. Sometimes her father was consulted as a matter of courtesy, but he had no real authority. If the men of her family approved, the answer was relayed in the same manner back to the prospective husband. He then sent presents by the women of his family to the female relatives of the girl, and if the presents were accepted the marriage was consummated. There was usually some trifling ceremony by the principals, such as sticking two reeds into the ground and then exchanging them, which gave the girl a chance to express her choice. The girl remained with her parents and the man went to her home and lived with her as his wife, but the marriage was not considered permanent until he had planted and gathered a crop, brought her a supply of game, and provided her a house. The construction of the house, like nearly every labor performed by the Creeks, was a communal enterprise; the matter was taken up in the council, and the work was done by the town under the direction of the officials. Obviously since the period of incomplete marriage depended upon the growing of a crop, it always lasted for some months; and the union could not be made final until after the corn harvest. During this time "the woman was not bound," as the Creeks expressed it; she could not be punished if she proved unfaithful, and the couple could separate at will. There was also a feeling that if a man neglected to work in her corn-field during each succeeding year a wife was released from her marriage obligations.

Polygamy was common. The plural wives usually lived in sep-arate houses, with no evidence of ill feeling; but often they lived together, especially if they were sisters, and were the best of friends. The husband, however, had to secure the consent of his first wife before choosing another, or she and her clan could punish him and the interloper for adultery. It was understood, however, that if she took such action she resigned him to her supplanter. Divorce could be secured at the wish of either party, but it was not common in families with children. In case of divorce the children and the property remained in the possession of the wife. A divorced man could remarry at once, but a woman, except during the incomplete marriage described above, was required to wait until after the annual corn harvest celebration.

When a man died, the women of his clan inducted the widow into a mourning period of solitary confinement in a separate house, with uncombed hair, unwashed clothes and body, and dismal wailing. If she married during this time, she was punished for adultery. This mourning period normally lasted four years, but it might be shortened if the man's clan relatives chose to be merciful or became convinced of the sincerity of her grief. At the expiration of her sentence they dressed her in her accustomed finery and conducted her to a dance and assisted her to secure a husband, usually the brother of the dead man. The mourning rites of a widower were similar except that they were shorter, in most cases only four months. The dead were usually buried under the earthen floor of the house.[13]

A woman also retired to a separate house during her menstrual periods. Before her return she bathed and washed her clothes, and the dishes she had used were either broken or left in the house to be used during her next retreat. A similar separation was observed at the time of childbirth, and she was expected to absent herself from her husband and from public company for four months. A man also was subject to numerous taboos during the period of his wife's pregnancy and for some time after the birth of the child.[14]

The family life of the Creeks was happy. The importance of the clan did not diminish the father's interest in his children. Husbands and wives did not have many points of mutual interest and companionship, for the group activities of the town obscured the social and recreational features of family life; but if a Creek's affection for his wife was somewhat casual, he always felt a strong responsibility to protect and provide for the women and children of his

[13] *Ibid.*, 368-84; Swanton, "Notes on the Creek Indians," 142-45; Hawkins, *Sketch*, 6-8.

[14] WPA Project S-149, Margaret Sains, Winey Lewis, Agnes Kelley, Mary Grayson; Frank Gouldsmith Speck, "Ethnology of the Yuchi Indians," *Anthropological Publications of the University Museum*, Vol. I, No. 1 (1909), 91-93, 96 f.; Frank Gouldsmith Speck, "The Creek Indians of Taskigi Town," *Memoirs of the American Anthropological Association*, Vol. II, Part 2 (1907), 116; Grant Foreman, *A Traveler in Indian Territory*, 130 f.; Adair, *History of the American Indians*, 124; H. F. and E. S. O'Beirne, *The Indian Territory: Its Chiefs, Legislators, and Leading Men*, 21.

tribe. The division of labor between the sexes was the same as that of the white people. The women performed the household tasks, which consisted of preparing the food, caring for the children, and making the clothing, pottery, baskets, and mats; the men supplied most of the food and the material for the clothing, made the implements of agriculture and the chase, built the houses, carried on the government, and fought the wars. When the tribe began to discard the native manufactures for European products, it was the men who procured the peltries used as the medium of exchange.

The dwellings of the Creeks were placed with some semblance of a street arrangement around the public buildings and grounds. Each dwelling consisted of from one to four separate buildings according to the wealth and size of the family, and this unit formed a little square similar to the town square. One building served as cook room and winter lodging house, another was the summer lodging house, one was a granary, and so on. They were rectangular in shape and strongly made; the frames were of poles, the walls were plastered with mud mixed with straw, and the roofs were shingled with cyprus bark. All the men of the town working together systematically could construct one of these substantial houses in one day. As Adair expressed it, "They first trace the dimensions of the intended fabric and every one has his task prescribed him after the exactest manner."[15]

Close to each dwelling was a small private garden plot, where the women of the family tended corn, beans, tobacco, etc., but the main food supply was grown on a large field belonging to the town. A tract of rich alluvial land was selected, preferably on a bend in the river so it would be protected on three sides from animals. The site chosen was as close to the town as possible, but frequently it lay across the river, and sometimes it was as much as two miles distant. It was divided into family plots by narrow strips of grass or some other boundary.

The planting was done the first of May. Early in the morning a conch shell was blown, and all the people hurried to the square

[15] Swanton, "Creek Social Organization," 171-73, 179 n., 371, 403; Bartram, *Travels,* 386 f., 394 f.

with their farm implements and went together to the field. They worked, not on the individual plots, but together, beginning at one side of the field and working across until it was finished. They used stone, wood, and bone implements, or hoes and axes purchased from the traders. They worked in high spirits to an accompaniment of songs and jokes and humorous tales. The chiefs worked side by side with the other men, and shirkers were fined or compelled to leave the town. The cultivating was done in the same way. During the growing season the children, under the supervision of some of the old people, watched the fields and drove off the birds, and at night the men took turns in patrolling them to keep out the bears, raccoons, and deer. When it was time to harvest the crops, the town turned out together as usual, but this time each family gathered the produce from its own plot and placed it in its own storehouse. Each family also contributed at will to a public store, which was kept in a large building in the field; and this supply was used, under the supervision of the micco, to accommodate strangers and travelers, to provision the men who went on military expeditions, to assist families whose own supply had given out, and to fill any other public need.[16]

The Creeks raised a plentiful supply of corn, beans, squashes, pumpkins, and melons, and they picked an abundance of wild fruits. Rice was grown extensively in the Lower Towns. They also gathered immense quantities of hickory nuts and acorns. The women pounded these in a mortar, sifted out the shells in a basket sieve, stirred the pulverized nut meat in boiling water, and skimmed off the oil, which they used in much of their cookery, especially in their hominy and corn cakes. Their principal source of meat supply was the deer, but the bear was highly prized for his fat, which was rendered and stored in deerskins. Each town had its own game preserves, and the hunters were very careful not to trespass upon the rights of other towns. The use of the game was carefully regulated by the town council, even to the extent of observing closed seasons. Good fishing places also were the property of particular towns. Hunting and fishing, like agriculture, were

---

[16] Adair, *History of the American Indians,* 406-409, 430; Bartram, *Travels,* 191 f., 509-11; Hawkins, *Sketch,* 35.

largely community enterprises—and were preliminary to the usual dancing and feasting.[17]

In addition to the shared experiences of these communal labors, the Creeks were bound together by the great unifying force of ceremonials. New towns that joined the Confederacy either adopted these observances or modified their own to conform with them. The greatest was the annual celebration at the beginning of the corn harvest. It was generally referred to by the whites as the busk, a corruption of *boosketah,* a fast. It was held the last of July or the first of August, upon a day selected by the micco and his council. Nobody was supposed to taste new corn until the conclusion of this ceremonial.

The whole town worked in preparation for this great occasion. The women made new clothing for the family and new pottery and other household furnishings, and swept and cleaned their houses and yards. The men cleaned the square and sprinkled it with fresh sand, and new mats were placed in the buildings that framed it. The rubbish, the old clothing and pottery, and all the stored food left over from the preceding harvest were heaped in a great pile and burned. The men laid four logs in the center of the square, with their ends together and radiating outward to form a cross.

The celebration lasted four or eight days. The sequence varied in different towns, but the essential features were the same. In the center of the square at the axis of the four logs a "new fire" was kindled by the archaic method of rubbing sticks together. The men fasted and drank "medicine" prepared from the yaupon or Gulf holly (*Ilex vomitoria*), which the Creeks called "ussi"; the red willow or "micco hoyanidja" (king of purgers); the button-snake-root (*Eryngium yuccaefolium*) or "passu"; and other plants of lesser sacramental importance—all of which induced the most profuse vomiting. Dances were performed at intervals, and there were bathing in the river and ceremonial handling of ashes and corn and the flower of a small, sacred tobacco. The men were required to remain in the square during most of the celebration. At times the

[17] Bartram, *Travels,* 38; Benjamin Hawkins, *Letter* (*No. 1 of Documents Accompanying the President's Communication to Congress the 8th Day of December, 1801*), 8; Hawkins *Sketch,* 33, 54, *et passim; American State Papers, Indian Affairs,* I, 79; Adair, *History of the American Indians,* 402–405.

women were admitted and joined in the dancing, but most of the time they and the children were rigidly excluded. All the fires in the town meanwhile had been extinguished and the hearths swept and sprinkled with clean sand; and the women now came to the square and received the "new fire" and carried it to their houses. The culmination of the festival was a great feast of green corn prepared by the women and carried to the square.

Every part of this sacred observance was fraught with deep moral and religious significance. The ritual was followed with the most painstaking exactness. The dances portrayed the town's whole collective experience—war, the chase, the group loyalties and beliefs, the mystic relationship between man and nature. Moral lectures were given by the leading men and were received with respectful attention. The people were profoundly stirred by the whole celebration; they entered it with an air of deep solemnity, which broke into rejoicing over the harvest and their own happy sense of security and power. It was a period of general amnesty when all crimes but murder were forgiven. Adulterers and other offenders who had managed to hide from their avengers could now return to their homes without fear or loss of prestige. It was the beginning of the new year, the convenient period for reckoning marriage, divorce, and the termination of widowhood, and the time for conferring war names upon the young men.[18]

But the busk was only the greatest of a series of ceremonial observances. The Creeks found many things to celebrate, and the season from April to October was filled with festivals. In some of these the recreational element was predominant, but there was usually a religious meaning in the background. Even the informal councils and desultory conversation that took place almost daily in the square or chokofa were dignified by the important ceremonial of the "black drink."

This was the yaupon tea, used also in the green corn festival. It was called "black drink" by the traders on account of its color, but the Creeks themselves called it "white drink" because of its sacred

18 John R. Swanton, "Religious Beliefs and Medical Practices of the Creek Indians," *Forty-second Annual Report*, Bureau of American Ethnology, 546-614; Swanton, "The Green Corn Dance"; Adair, *History of the American Indians*, 430; *Indian Journal*, August 7, 1879.

properties. As one observer expressed it, "... they have a religious belief ... That it purifies them from all sin, and leaves them in a state of perfect innocence; that it inspires them with an invincible prowess in war; and that it is the only solid cement of friendship, benevolence, and hospitality. Most of them really seem to believe that the Great Spirit or Master of breath has communicated the virtues of the black-drink to them, and to them only ... and that it is a peculiar blessing bestowed on them his chosen people."

The same writer described the ceremony. "The warriors and chiefs being assembled and seated, three young men acting as masters of ceremony on the occasion, each having a gourd or cala-bash full of the liquor, place themselves in front of the three great-est chiefs or warriors, and announce that they are ready by the word choh! After a short pause, stooping forward, they run up to the warriors and hold the cup or shell parallel to their mouths; the warriors receive it from them, and wait until the young men fall back and adjust themselves to give what they term the *yohullah,* or black-drink note. As the young men begin to aspirate the note, the great men place the cups to their mouths, and are obliged to drink during the aspirated note of the young men, which, after exhausting their breath, is repeated on a finer key, until the lungs are no longer inflated. This long aspiration is continued near half a minute, and the cup is taken from the mouth of the warrior who is drinking at the instant the note is finished. The young men then receive the cups from the chiefs or head warriors, and pass it to the others of inferior rank, giving them the word choh! but not the yohullah note. . . .

"It is generally served round in this manner three times at every meeting; during the recess of serving it up, they all sit quietly in their several cabins, and amuse themselves by smoking, conversing, exchanging tobacco, etc., and in disgorging what black-drink they have previously swallowed."[19]

All of the towns had sacred objects which they handled with reverent awe. The most celebrated of these were the seven mys-terious copper and brass plates of the Tuckabatchees. The copper plates were strips of metal, spatulate at one end, the largest about

[19] Caleb Swan in Schoolcraft, *Archives of Aboriginal Knowledge,* V, 266 f.

eighteen inches long by seven wide. The brass plates were circular, the largest about a foot and a half in diameter, and one of them was stamped with the diphthong Æ. According to one Tuckabatchee legend these hallowed objects were received from the Shawnees, but in general it was believed that they had been bestowed by the Master of Breath and that the welfare of the town depended upon their safe keeping. They were carried in solemn procession during one of the dances of the green corn festival, but the rest of the year they were kept closely guarded from profane eyes in a compartment of the chiefs' building in the square.[20]

Each town had priests, who cared for the sacred objects and were expected by their incantations to prosper the public enterprises in peace and war. These officials were selected from a group who had gone through a protracted course of instruction in magic formulas and initiation by fasting and drinking the sacred medicines. The graduates of these primitive schools were theoretically able to cure diseases and control the elements, and might be tempted upon occasion to practice witchcraft. Their magic, like the great public ceremonials, was related in some dimly defined way to the benevolent guardianship of the Master of Breath (Esaugeta Emissee) and various lesser deities. Creek ceremonials in general were directed to points of the compass—four was a sacred number, and east was a sacred direction. Certain animals, especially the wolf and the rattlesnake, were treated with anxious reverence, as were various mythical creatures such as the great horned snakes, the horns of which were greatly prized as charms in hunting and war, and the "tie snakes," which lived under water in organized towns and sometimes tied themselves around men and conducted them to their squares for a friendly visit.[21]

The success of a war party was supposed to depend mainly upon fasting and the drinking of medicine in the chokofa or a temporary enclosure in the forest, the carrying of charms and sacred objects, and the observance of strict taboos; but these measures were reinforced by infinite patience and skill in stalking the enemy, and individual bravery received punctilious recognition. The entire Con-

20 Swanton, "Creek Religion and Medicine," 503-10, 570, 575.
21 *Ibid., passim;* Swanton, "Notes on the Creek Indians," 154-59.

federacy rarely or never took concerted action against a common enemy; but the individual towns usually confined their private raids to recognized enemies like the Cherokees and the Choctaws, against whom it was nearly always legitimate to wage war, and more ambitious designs were determined upon at regional councils, from which red clubs were sent as symbols to member towns. The object of war was retaliation for injuries and the winning of personal distinction; hence the Creek warrior had no intention of dying for his country, but of returning home with scalps and glory. Prisoners were at the disposal of the individual captor; warriors were usually killed, but women and children were adopted into the tribe.[22]

A young man was not allowed to take part in the rites of the square until he had participated in a military raid, or, in rare cases, had distinguished himself in hunting or priestcraft. A war title was then conferred with great ceremony and the casual clan or family name or nickname which he had carried since childhood was discarded. Additional titles were given as he rose in war honors or official position. The usual title consisted of two parts: first was the name of his clan, his town, or another town; then came his official designation as *Micco, Tustennuggee, Emarthla,* or *Heneha,* or the arbitrary distinctions *Harjo* ("recklessly brave," usually translated as "mad" or "crazy"), *Fixico* ("heartless," literally "without feelings"), or *Yahola* (from the mystical cry given in the black-drink ceremony). In extraordinary cases distinctive names were given descriptive of some individual exploit. Girl children were given conventionalized names that had originally had some such meaning as "Getting-very-near-the-enemy-by-stratagem" or "Two-returning-wounded," and they carried these throughout life.[23]

The fierce contest of the ball game was substituted for war between the towns that joined the Confederacy. It was known as "the brother of war" and was preceded by a like ceremonial discipline. The game was similar to that played by other southeastern Indians; a level stretch of prairie was selected, a goal was erected at each end, and the players of each side tried to throw or carry the ball to their

[22] Swanton, "Creek Social Organization," 405-43.
[23] *Ibid.*, 97-107, 420; Swanton, "Notes on the Creek Indians," 138, 141 f.

own goal by means of long sticks looped back at the end and
webbed across the loop to form a sort of racket. It was played with
incredible speed and skill; and with the savage background of
fervent spectators and the distant view of peaceful fields and tim-
bered stream and pointed chokofa rising high above the clustered
town, it presented a strange and beautiful sight. Red and White
towns always played as opponents in matched games, and Tciloki
and White clans played against each other during informal games
within the town.[24]

The whole extent of the great Confederacy thus rested under
a savage peace. To other Indians the Creeks offered war or friendship with proud indifference. To the whites they showed a sturdy
sense of equality and independence, tempered by a genuine appreciation of European goods. They understood the advantages of neutrality, and during most of the eighteenth century they held a balance of power between the English at Charleston, the Spanish at
Pensacola, and the French at Mobile.

De Soto made his dark trail of rapine and plunder across their
country in the summer of 1540,[25] but he left no permanent impression. When the Spanish settled Pensacola a century and a half later,
the Creeks entered into trade and diplomatic relations with them,
but they never came under their influence. They received Spanish
envoys and listened to Spanish offers, but they destroyed the Florida
Indians at the instigation of the English, and at one time they
attacked Pensacola.

The French settled at Mobile Bay in 1702. There was some fighting between them and the Alabamas, who had several strong
towns on the Alabama River just below the junction of the Coosa
and Tallapoosa, but the able Bienville managed to make peace.
Permission was granted the French to establish a fort in the Creek
country to protect their trade, and each side promised to punish
any of its people who should commit depredations on the other.
Bienville accordingly went up the Alabama in the summer of 1714
and built Fort Toulouse at Tuskegee Town on the lower Coosa,

[24] Swanton, "Creek Social Organization," 297, 458-66.
[25] Edward Gaylord Bourne (editor), *Narratives of the Career of Hernando de Soto,*
I, 59-87; II, 13-16, 91-116.

in a rich and beautiful region surrounded by populous and thriving towns. While it was under construction, he visited Tuckabatchee and then crossed the country on foot and visited the Lower Creeks at Coweta and Cusseta, exchanging courtesies, giving presents, and trying to detach the Indians from English influence. But as the English paid more for peltries and charged less for goods than the French, they were able to trade even with the Alabamas under the very guns of the fort. Father de Guyenne, a Jesuit, started missionary work among the Lower Creeks, but the English stirred the Indians against him and he was forced to retreat to Fort Toulouse. Father Moran was at Fort Toulouse for several years and lived occasionally at the neighboring town of the Koasatas, but his work was without result and he was eventually recalled. The English even managed at one time to incite the garrison to mutiny, but the Creeks assisted the French to hold the post and it was reoccupied.[26]

In the meantime the French had provoked the Natchez to war, and in 1732, they overwhelmed and destroyed them with a ferocity that shocked all the Indians of that region. The English tried to use this circumstance to incite the tribes to a general war of extermination against the French. The Chickasaws joined them, and the Choctaws were divided between a pro-English and a pro-French party, but although the Creeks welcomed a miserable remnant of the Natchez into their Confederacy, they declined to fight the white man's battles. In 1747 Adair, the ablest and most unscrupulous of English agents, did manage to persuade a Creek war party to join the Chickasaws in a raid on the French settlements, but the Confederacy as a whole remained at peace. The French then tried to effect the punishment of the raiders through the action of chiefs they believed friendly to their interest. But the Creeks called a council and sent the defiant message that they were all people of one fire and would stand together; and unless the French should cease their evil design to foment a civil war among them as they had among the foolish Choctaws, their garrison would be wiped out and the river would carry their blood down to Mobile.[27]

[26] Pickett, *History of Alabama,* 160-270.
[27] *Ibid.,* 279-303; Adair, *History of the American Indians,* 320 f.

The colony of South Carolina controlled the English relations with the Creeks. A Commissioner of Indian Affairs under authority of the Assembly granted licenses to trade and kept the traders under close supervision. It was the object of the colonial officials, by a combination of intrigue, bullying, and the sale of manufactured goods, to get control of the Indians' foreign relations, undermine their independence, and reduce their country to a protectorate. The reports of George Chicken, Commissioner of Indian Affairs, who went to the Cherokee country in the summer of 1725, and Tobias Fitch, who was sent to the Creeks at the same time, present an illuminating picture of English treachery and the conflicting imperial influences that were brought to bear upon the Confederacy.

The Cherokees and Upper Creeks as usual were raiding each other's settlements, and this time the Chickasaws had joined the Cherokees. In the course of one of these raids the Creeks had wounded and robbed an Englishman, apparently a trader, who was living among the Cherokees. Some of the border Creek towns had become tired of the war and sent a messenger from Coosa to offer peace "for the Summer gone, the Winter coming and the Spring following." At the same time the Spanish had brought the Yamassees of Florida under their influence and were working actively among the Lower Creeks, and the French were hand and glove with the Spanish. It was the object of Chicken and Fitch to drive out the Spanish agents and incite the Creeks against the Yamassees, to counteract the French influence, to discourage the Creeks from fighting the Cherokees and Chickasaws, and to bring the Cherokees under their control and stir them up against the Creeks. Both men were in constant communication with Arthur Middleton, the president of the Council of South Carolina.

Fitch traveled back and forth across the Creek country holding councils in the leading towns. He conducted himself with studied insolence, and, if his account can be believed, the Creeks were courteous to the point of servility. Apparently they were anxious to retain their trading privileges, and they may have felt the force of his argument when he said, "I must tell your Young Men that if it had not Been for us, you would not have known how to Warr Nor yet Have any thing To Warr with[.] you have had nothing But

Boes and Arrow's To kile dear; You had no hoes or Axes then What you made of Stone[.] you wore nothing But Skins; But now you have Learn'd the use of Firearm's as well to Kill Dear and other Provissions as To War ag^{s}t your Enemies; and yet you Set no greater Value on us Who have Been Such good Freinds unto you, Then on yr greatest Enemies[.] this all that are old men knowes to be True And I would have you make your young men Sensable of it."

Of the Upper Creeks he demanded a great indemnity in furs for the harm done to the Englishman, and he managed to turn back some of the war parties that started against the Cherokees. When he was not able to prevent one expedition, he reported to Middleton, and the latter forwarded the report to Chicken advising him to warn the Cherokees of the impending attack. Chicken immediately convened the Cherokees in council and tried by mingled taunts and flattery to incite them to fall upon the advancing war party. But the Cherokees declined to abandon the safe Indian method of fighting. They strengthened the fortifications of their frontier towns and remained behind their defenses. When the Creeks found them on guard, they accused Fitch of betraying their plans, and for a time his life was in danger, but he lied so convincingly that they promised to collect the indemnity and allowed him to depart unharmed.

Fitch also visited Cusseta, Coweta, and Apalachicola and met the Lower Creeks in council. He accused them of treachery because they were too friendly to the Yamassees, the allies of the Spanish and the enemies of his king. He found "Old Briminus" of Coweta willing to accept the dignity and emoluments of English vassalage, and desirous of a commission for Sepe Coffee, his son, to serve as his assistant. Fitch accordingly procured the desired commission "to King Sepe Coffee to be Comander in Chief of this Nation under his Father Emperour Brimin's Derections the meaning of which Comission is to Take all orders that shall Come from my King to hear no talk But What Comes from him, and to be sure to put all his orders in Execution, and that all men in this Nation is to pay the Said Sepe Coffee due obedience as there King dureing the Time that Sepe Coffee Continues to be True and Trusty to my King and no Longer." This high-flown language, of course, had no particular

meaning except to indicate that two Creek leaders would probably
work for a time in the English interest.

Sepe Coffee at once set out on an expedition against the Yamassees, but the French at Mobile sent a negro who persuaded seventy
of the war party to turn back, and an influential Lower Creek chief,
whom Fitch called Squire Mickeo, sent a warning to the Yamassees
and they took refuge in their fortified towns. The war party returned without scalps and with several of their own men missing
on the same day that Fitch had convened a great council of all the
Lower Creeks at Coweta. Fitch reminded them that their losses
had resulted from the advance notice the Yamassees had of their
designs, and he made the helpful suggestion that among the English a man who would betray military plans would be tied to four
mad horses and torn to pieces. But Squire Mickeo, who was sitting
in the council, remained unmoved and it is not recorded that he
suffered dismemberment.

While Fitch was in the Lower Towns, two Spaniards arrived
from St. Augustine with a negro interpreter. They distributed two
kegs of brandy at Coweta, "which soon put the Town in a Confusion." Fitch seized the negro as a runaway slave, but Squire
Mickeo effected his escape. Fitch captured another negro and held
him bound in Apalachicola, but one of the head men of the town
cut the ropes and threw them into the fire. He also found a captive
English girl at Apalachicola. He warned the Indians that if they
desired the friendship of his king they would return the captive
and pay for the two negroes; but although Sepe Coffee expressed
some courteous sentiments it was apparent that the Indians were
undisturbed by the king's long-distance vengeance. Fitch also went
to the Alabama towns and claimed the negro who had turned back
part of the Yamassee war party, and he took occasion to taunt the
Alabamas with being slaves of the French, compelled to purchase
their goods in a dear market. He sent a defiant message to the commander at Fort Toulouse and carried off the negro, only to lose
him again before he had finished his business in the Creek country.

Fitch then received word from Chicken that the Creeks had
killed a Chickasaw only thirty miles from the Carolina settlements,
and he returned empty-handed to the colony. Although he reported

that he had browbeaten the Indians, reduced the two Spaniards to abject submission, and intimidated the French commander, the indemnity was unpaid, the negroes were at large, the white girl was still a captive, the Creeks were still at war against the Chickasaws and Cherokees, and the Yamassees were unharmed. It is also fairly clear that in spite of the efforts the English had made to create a party in the Lower Towns, those Indians were intriguing with the Spanish. The Creeks valued English trade and were willing to listen to a certain amount of bullying and make a few good promises to retain it, but they made no real concessions. They did eventually destroy the Yamassees, but they had no intention of subordinating their own interests to English imperialism.[28]

The English continued to look with apprehensive eyes upon the savage might of the Confederacy. Adair said about 1770 that the Creeks were unquestionably the most powerful Indian nation known to the English, and that they had doubled their population during the preceding generation partly by natural growth and partly by their "artful policy" of adopting other tribes. By this time they had reduced the Cherokees to a perpetual state of defense and attacked the Choctaws with such fury that it was believed to be only a question of time until that peaceable and populous tribe would be reduced to dependence. Adair claimed considerable credit for fomenting war between the Creeks and Cherokees, "well knowing that one pack of wolves, was the best watch against another of the same kind"; and he had no words strong enough to express his disgust when Governor James Glen of South Carolina tried to induce the head men of the two nations to come to Charleston to make peace. Some of the Creeks used the same argument. They were enjoying the war and had no desire to end it. Lachlan McGillivray, a Scot who owned a great trading establishment on the lower Coosa, used all his influence to induce them to negotiate. At a council where he had made an earnest speech in favor of peace, an old war leader told him, "You have made yourself very poor, by sweating, far and near, in our smoky town-houses and hot-houses, only to make a peace between us and the Cheerake, and thereby enable our young mad people

[28] Journal of Tobias Fitch; Journal of the Commissioner of Indian Affairs.

to give you, in a short time, a far worse sweat than you have yet had, or may now expect. But forasmuch as the great English chieftain in Charles Town, is striving hard to have it so, by ordering you to shut your eyes, and stop your ears, lest the power of conviction should reach your heart, we will not any more oppose you in this mad scheme." But Glen's efforts were successful, and the Creeks and Cherokees made a precarious peace.[29]

The Creeks at this happy period were not aware of the relentless force that was moving toward them—the expansion of the white man's frontier. This influence had been introduced by the establishment of Georgia in 1733, but it did not at once become apparent. When they first encountered the white man's land hunger, it was a vexatious local circumstance; they did not foresee that it would become the dominant fact in their history.

When Oglethorpe came up the river with his settlers, he stopped at the present site of Savannah at the establishment of John Musgrove, a wealthy trader with a Creek wife. The Indians of the vicinity were captivated by Oglethorpe's sincerity and courtesy of manner, and they welcomed him with ceremonials and gifts symbolic of peace and friendship. He decided to build his city there and to protect it by a fort against the Spanish. He sent runners to Cusseta and Coweta and called a council and made a treaty with the Lower Creeks. They gave him permission to establish his settlement and promised "to give no encouragement to any other white people but themselves [the English], to settle amongst us, and that we will not have any correspondence with the Spaniards or French, ... and do firmly promise to keep the talk in our hearts, as long as the sun shall shine or the waters run in the rivers." The English thus scored against their European rivals; and the Creeks, not knowing that Oglethorpe's grant from the king contemplated the absorption of all their territory, supposed that they had secured friendly neighbors and a convenient market for their produce.[30]

The Georgians immediately began laying out plantations on the

[29] Adair, *History of the American Indians*, 258-61, 270, 278-81; Bartram, *Travels*, 390.
[30] S. G. McLendon, *History of the Public Domain of Georgia*, 9-11; Pickett, *History of Alabama*, 261 f.; Charles C. Royce, "Indian Land Cessions in the United States," *Eighteenth Annual Report*, Bureau of American Ethnology, Part 2, 634 f.

Creeks' lands and turning their cattle loose to graze on their cornfields. The Creeks complained to Oglethorpe, and Oglethorpe
tried to restrain his settlers. In 1739 he attended a great council
at Coweta, where he was received with the exuberant and beautiful Creek ceremonies of welcome. From Coweta he visited the
neighboring towns, sitting in their squares, smoking their tobacco, drinking their black drink, making friends everywhere
he went. Another treaty was signed limiting the Georgia settlements to a narrow strip extending into the interior between the
Savannah and the Ogeechee and another strip meeting it at right
angles and lying along the coast as high as the tidewater between
the Savannah and the St. Johns, and shutting out Spanish colonization in all the region north of the St. Johns and Apalachee
Bay; and Oglethorpe left a paper with the Creeks warning English subjects not to trespass on their lands.[31]

The first Protestant missionary work was begun among the
Creeks with the establishment of Georgia. A colony of Moravian
Brethren, who settled there in 1735, began preaching to the Indians
and started a school for them on an island in the Savannah. But
although these pacifists had secured legal exemption from military service before they came, the Georgians were so exasperated
at their refusal to fight the Spanish that in 1739 they were forced
to abandon their work and move to Philadelphia. This ended the
attempt to influence the Creeks by missionary and educational
efforts.[32]

But a profitable trade connection was soon established between
the Creeks and the Georgians. Augusta, which was settled soon
after Savannah, became the chief center of this commerce. Some
of the traders became very wealthy. George Galphin, in particular,
operated a great trading establishment at Silver Bluff, a few miles
below Augusta on the South Carolina side of the Savannah River.
He also owned trading houses in Savannah and Augusta, and
his influence was felt as far as the Mississippi. From these centers
trains of pack horses with half savage drivers went out over well-

[31] Pickett, *History of Alabama*, 266-68; Royce, "Indian Land Cessions," 635 f.;
McLendon, *Public Domain of Georgia*, 11-13.
[32] John Holmes, *Historical Sketches of the Missions of the United Brethren for Propagating the Gospel Among the Heathen from Their Commencement to the Year 1817*, 122 f.

defined trails carrying guns, ammunition, hatchets, knives, cooking pots, articles of clothing etc., and bringing back skins and other native products. Nearly every Creek town had its local English trader—usually living with an Indian wife—who managed the retail end of this important commerce. The traders had no extra-territorial status—it was not uncommon, for example, to find traders who had sacrificed their ears to the Creek law against adultery—but travel and trade were usually safe in the Creek country. The Indians were rapidly abandoning their native manufactures, and this traffic had become an important part of their economic life. For a long time, however, they remained indifferent to the white man's firewater. They had been occasionally treated to the strange drink as a mark of special favor, but they were uncontaminated by its influence. The English government tried to restrain the traders from selling intoxicants, and when these regulations were violated the Creeks had been known to splinter the kegs with their tomahawks and spill the contents untasted.

The influence of the traders was especially noticeable in their dress. They purchased cloth of the brightest colors and combined it with their native fashions according to their own picturesque ideas of personal adornment. The women wore a short dress of calico or printed linen decorated lavishly with feathers and beads. They wound their heavy black hair around their heads and fastened it with a silver brooch, and from this knob a profusion of silk ribbons of various colors streamed down on every side almost to the ground. The men wore a ruffled shirt, a breech-clout with fringed ends hanging from the belt, and leggings decorated with lace, beads, or silver bells. The shirt was belted in at the waist with a woolen sash ornamented with tassels and beads, and a tobacco pouch was held in place by a broad beaded band over one shoulder. They wore a scarlet or blue blanket with lace or fringe or little bells around the border, or a short cloak ingeniously woven of gay feathers. A large silver gorget hung from a cord around their necks, and silver bells ornamented their arms. Waving heron plumes stood up from a richly beaded band around their temples, and the rim of their ears was cut loose and stretched to form a large elastic circle, which moved with every motion of the body. Both sexes continued to wear soft deerskin moccasins elaborately embroidered with beads.

The French tried to break this English influence, especially during the French and Indian War. At that time the English settlers and soldiers committed atrocities against the Cherokees and drove them into hostility, and the Creeks, now at peace with the Cherokees, raided the Georgia and South Carolina frontiers. They also attempted a general massacre of English traders; a number were killed, others had hairbreadth escapes, and some were saved by their Indian wives. But when Spain surrendered Florida to England and the French withdrew from the whole Gulf region at the close of the war, English commercial prestige was almost unchallenged.[33]

England had tightened her imperial control during the war and appointed special Indian administrators. In general these officials attempted to define the boundaries of the settlements and prevent encroachments beyond these limits; but John Stuart, Southern Superintendent, assisted Georgia to secure her first great land cession. The Georgians were still confined to a narrow strip along the coast and the lower Savannah, and they coveted the fertile valleys of the Broad and Little rivers. The Creeks had become indebted to Galphin and other traders, and Stuart and Sir James Wright, the royal governor, called a great council at Augusta in 1773 to demand a land cession in payment. The Cherokees also had been invited, for the colonial officials recognized them as the owners of the upper part of the tract. The Georgians negotiated with them privately and then announced the cession to the council as *fait accompli*. The Creeks immediately fixed accusing eyes upon the Cherokees and began to upbraid them as old women, whom they had long forced to wear the petticoat. They informed the Georgians that it was *their* land, and they would leave the council unless the Cherokee treaty was annulled; but they finally ceded about two million acres on the upper Savannah. The "New Purchase" filled rapidly with settlers. Then disputes arose

[33] Bartram, *Travels*, 446 f., 471, 490 f., 499-502, *et passim;* Adair, *History of the American Indians*, 246-66, 280 f.; Pickett, *History of Alabama*, 263 f., 422-24.

over the execution of the treaty, the Creeks began raiding, and for a time the colonists abandoned the new frontier and retired to the old settlements on the lower Savannah. Stuart and Wright tried to bring the Indians to terms by an embargo on English trade, but the American Revolution broke out shortly after, and before the year 1775 was over, Wright was a refugee at St. Augustine.[34]

Upon the whole the Creeks had profited from their association with the white man. The use of European goods had relieved them of much of their toils—the painful chipping of stone implements, the careful molding of pottery, the slow preparation of skins for clothing, the patient stalking of game with bow and arrow—and the ruthless march of settlement had weakened their rivals and increased their importance. They possessed their whole rich country in security and plenty. Their towns swarmed with people, and their storehouses bulged with food. Their necessary labors were lightly undertaken and soon ended, and they spent their days in games and ceremonials and their nights in dancing. They feared no foe, either Indian or white, but their trails were safe for the traveler, and they welcomed him with proud friendliness to the free but ordered life of their towns. But with the beginning of the American Republic an unreckoned force had come to influence their destiny.

[34] Bartram, *Travels*, 33 f., 39 f., 321 f., 483 f.; Pickett, *History of Alabama*, 329 f.; McLendon, *Public Domain of Georgia*, 14 f.; Walter H. Mohr, *Federal Indian Relations 1774-1788*, 11-23.

CHAPTER 2

The Making of a Protectorate

WHEN the imperial administration collapsed at the outbreak of the Revolution, the Continental Congress and the individual states immediately attempted to take over Indian affairs. By July, 1775, the Charleston Committee of Public Safety had appointed three men to superintend Indian administration; and on July 12, Congress created three Indian departments, of which the Southern included the Creek country, and commissioners were appointed to treat with the tribes. It was the object of the revolutionary government to hold the Indians neutral, regulate their trade, and expel British agents and pro-British traders. George Galphin and several other traders joined the patriots and worked actively in this cause.

In the meantime Stuart was attempting to direct Indian affairs from Pensacola. He was assisted by the traders in the Indian country who had remained loyal to England. He was able to pose as the protector of the Indians against the land hunger of the settlers, and he had the additional advantage of more ample funds than the Congressional agents. In September he received a letter from General Gage at Boston directing him to enlist Indians in the British service. He immediately sent an agent with a supply of ammunition to arouse the Creeks and Cherokees. The Cherokees began raiding the frontiers; but although the Creeks were in a bad humor because of difficulties growing out of the land cession of 1773, they were inclined at first to balance the offers of England and the revolutionary government.

But the British eventually won some of the Creeks, especially in the Upper Towns, to their cause. By the summer of 1778 they were raiding the outlying settlements, and their attacks soon became so serious that they affected military movements on the coast. With other southern Indians they coöperated actively with the British by attacking the frontier when the borderers were fighting the battle of King's Mountain, and when Wayne's army was besieging Savannah, a party of several hundred Creek warriors came to the assistance of the British garrison and made a furious assault on the besiegers. Creek participation in the war also helped to protect Mobile and Pensacola from attacks similar to George Rogers Clark's expedition against Vincennes and the Northwest.[1]

The Creeks' confident assumption that they were an independent people carried no weight with the diplomats who signed the peace treaty of 1783. England returned Florida to Spain and ceded the rest of the Creek territory to the United States. As an afterthought she notified her savage allies that the war was over, but several complications hindered the return of peace. Georgia under her colonial charter still claimed the land back to the Mississippi; but her settlements were restricted to a long narrow strip extending from the coast up the Savannah and Tugaloo rivers, and her people were clamoring for more Creek cessions. The United States tried to make peace with the Creeks and at the same time to secure the best terms possible for Georgia, but the government was too weak to take the initiative. The boundary between the United States and the Spanish possessions was unsettled, and Spain planned to bring the Creek Confederacy under her influence, thus creating a buffer state against the advancement of the Georgia frontier. But the Creeks were still strong, and their designing neighbors were relatively weak; moreover their destiny was directed at this time by one of the most remarkable men in their history.

In the 1730's young Lachlan McGillivray had run away from his wealthy parents in Scotland and settled among the Upper Creeks. He established a trading house at Ochiapofa or Hickory Ground Town (also known as Little Tallasi), close to the present Wetumpka, Alabama, and he owned plantations well stocked with negroes on the Savannah River, and warehouses bulging with Indian goods in Savannah and Augusta. He married Sehoy (Two-kept-on-after-the-enemy) Marchand, the young daughter of a former French commander of Fort Toulouse and a fullblood woman of the Wind Clan. His daughters married white men; some of their descendants

[1] Mohr, *Federal Indian Relations*, 20-60.

rose to leadership in the Creek Confederacy, and others became the founders of the most prominent families in Alabama. His son, Alexander, was endowed with remarkable powers of mind and capacity for leadership. With the consent of Sehoy he attended school at Charleston and acquired the white man's tricks of learning, but in spite of his white blood the Creeks were his own people and his proper career lay with them. During the Revolution the powerful McGillivray family had worked actively in the British interest, and Alexander had received the rank and pay of lieutenant colonel. Like other Tories they were ruined by the defeat of the British cause. Lachlan sailed for home, hoping Sehoy and her children might be allowed to keep the property he left in Georgia, but the Georgians confiscated everything but a few negroes who fled to Sehoy's establishment on the Coosa.

With his important family connections and his native gifts Alexander McGillivray soon rose to supreme power in the Confederacy. His people felt that he alone understood the white man's treacherous ways, and they were willing to entrust their foreign policy to his leadership. No warrior himself, he seems to have elevated the tustennuggee thlocco at the expense of the micco in the various towns, thus building up a strong military organization subservient to him. Apparently he introduced some innovations into the civil administration; the profitable custom of raiding the white settlements had brought about a certain amount of horse stealing within the tribe, and he is said to have established the principle that "if an Indian steals a horse, he is liable . . . to return him, or another of equal value, and pay a fine of thirty chalks, or fifteen dollars; if he is unable to do so, he may be tied and whipped thirty lashes by the injured party." He kept the traders completely under his control, and he held the towns in obedience by threatening to deprive them of their traders. During his leadership the Confederacy for the first time had a unified foreign policy and a centralized administration. At the same time the terms "dictator" or "emperor," which the white men applied to him, were hardly accurate, for his authority rested wholly upon his personal influence.[2]

[2] Pickett, *History of Alabama*, 346, 366 f.; Swanton, "Creek Social Organization," 99; Schoolcraft, *Archives of Aboriginal Knowledge*, V, 281 f.

The Georgians took the initiative in the diplomatic contests that followed the peace with England. Opothle Micco of Tallasi, one of the prominent elder chiefs of the nation, had been friendly to them throughout the Revolution. They induced him and the chief of another friendly town, probably Cusseta, and some Cherokees to come to Augusta, May 31, 1783, and sign a "treaty" deeding away a favorite hunting ground of the Creeks between the Tugaloo and the upper Oconee. A council of the whole nation at Tuckabatchee refused to ratify the cession and sent a strong "talk" to the Georgians warning them not to claim the land; but the Georgians treated this notice with contempt and began to divide the tract into counties and open it up for settlement. The Confederacy was so loosely organized that there was no law to punish a chief for unauthorized commitments, but when Opothle Micco returned home he found that his house had been burned during his absence and his corn and cattle destroyed.[3]

McGillivray then attended a general congress of Indian nations at Pensacola in 1784 and made a treaty with the Spanish on behalf of the whole Creek-Seminole Nation. In return for Spanish trade and protection he pledged the Creeks to obey the orders of the captain general at Havana and to admit no white person to their country without a Spanish license. In the way of general conciliation they also agreed that they would make peace with the Chickasaws, Choctaws, and Cherokees; that they would abandon the custom of taking scalps in their wars; and that they would deliver up all citizens of the United States that they held as captives. McGillivray was appointed as "commissary of the Creek nation" and paid a salary by the Spanish government.

Most of the Creek trade was in the hands of Panton, Leslie and Company of Pensacola. William Panton was a rich Scottish trader, whose estates like Lachlan McGillivray's had been confiscated in the Revolution. When the Spanish recovered Florida, he continued to import British goods under a Spanish license. He had some kind of understanding with McGillivray by which he advanced money

---

[3] Mohr, *Federal Indian Relations*, 141-43; *American State Papers, Indian Affairs*, I, 18-23; Schoolcraft, *Archives of Aboriginal Knowledge*, V, 281.

to the crafty mixed blood for private and governmental purposes, and the latter furthered his trade with the Creeks.[4]

McGillivray's commitments with the Spanish hindered him somewhat in his subsequent negotiations with the United States, but the Creeks as a whole did not take them seriously. From the time of De Soto they had been given words expressing allegiance to various mythical kings across the water, words strangely satisfying to the white men, but carrying no meaning to the Indians other than a courteous expression of good will. They understood the significance of land cessions and always insisted upon strict fulfillment of the terms of such treaties, but the white man's system of protectorates was beyond their experience.

Creek councils continued without effect to disavow the fraudulent treaty of Augusta. They finally began to send out scouting parties with orders to remove the settlers and their effects, peaceably if possible, defending themselves only in case of attack. At the same time McGillivray informed the Spanish officials of Georgia's encroachments, reminded them of their pledges of protection, and expressed the hope that the Spanish government would not treat with the United States in a way that would strengthen her pretensions. The United States Congress was too feeble to assume much responsibility for Indian administration, but commissioners were finally appointed, March 15, 1785, to negotiate with the Creeks. They were instructed to notify the state officials of their intentions and apply to them for the necessary military protection and funds. The Georgians tried to forestall them and secure a confirmation of the grant before their arrival, but the Creeks refused to enter into separate negotiations. It was accordingly decided to hold the council at Galphinton in October.

McGillivray wrote a very able letter in answer to the overtures of the United States commissioners. He had expected, he said, that as soon as peace was made with England the United States would take immediate steps to settle the differences with the Creeks and confirm them in their territory. The United States was the natural ally of the Creeks, and he regretted the aggressions of Georgia that had

---

[4] Pickett, *History of Alabama,* 367, 385-96; John Walton Caughey, *McGillivray of the Creeks,* 75-77.

forced them to accept the protection of Spain. The Creeks desired only to be secure against encroachments on their hunting grounds; "they have been ours from the beginning of time, and I trust that, with the assistance of our friends [the Spanish], we shall be able to maintain them against every attempt that may be made to take them from us." The Creeks had been attempting in as peaceable a manner as possible to clear their land of the intruders, but to show his good faith he had "taken the necessary steps to prevent any future predatory excursions of my people against any of your settlements." He would be glad to meet the United States commissioners, and he was confident that every difficulty would be adjusted in a spirit of justice and liberality worthy of the glorious defenders of liberty and independence.

But when the time for the council arrived, the chiefs and warriors of the two friendly towns were there as usual, and McGillivray and the other Creek leaders did not appear. The United States commissioners therefore explained in very conciliatory terms the Indian policy of the new government and adjourned the council. The day after they left, the state commissioners made a "treaty" with the few Indians who were still present, confirming the Augusta cession and ceding another large tract between the Altamaha and the St. Marys. The legislature then passed a resolution commending the state commissioners for their vigilance and patriotism and instructed their delegates in Congress to insist upon the abolition of the United States commission.

But the indignant Creeks resumed their raids, and the Georgians were too weak to defend the territory they had seized. In 1786 they tried to make an alliance with the turbulent settlements in western North Carolina—the so-called "State of Franklin"—and they sent agents to the Choctaws, Chickasaws, and Cherokees to induce those tribes to fight their battles against the Creeks. In October they called another council at Shoulderbone Creek on the Oconee, giving the Indians the most binding promises of safe-conduct. Most of the Creeks again stayed away, but the friendly chiefs of Tallasi and Cusseta found Colonel Elijah Clarke there with a body of Georgia militia. These rough frontier soldiers surrounded the chiefs, brandishing their swords and threatening to kill them; they forced them to confirm the former illegal grants, and they seized a number of the friendly Cussetas and carried them to Augusta to be held as hostages until the Creeks should kill certain traders and McGillivray and several other leading chiefs. Opothle Micco was completely disillusioned by the treachery of these white men he had trusted, and from that time on he became one of the most uncompromising enemies of the frontier.[5]

At the same time, the Creeks were trying to drive back the settlers that were coming into the Cherokee country and threatening them from the north. In 1785 the Georgia legislature established a county called Houston, taking in all the territory north of the Tennessee in what is now the state of Alabama. Commissioners were sent to open a land office and organize the government, and settlers went out and tried to hold the land, but the Indians drove them off and the movement collapsed. But white men were settling on the Cumberland in the present state of Tennessee, and the Cherokees and Upper Creeks were not able to dislodge them.[6]

As soon as the Georgians had secured the "treaty" of Shoulderbone, the governor wrote to his agents and his prospective allies that his objectives had been accomplished and that it was no longer necessary to stir up a general war of Indians and frontiersmen against the Creeks. But Congress had become concerned at the increasing restlessness of the Creeks and Cherokees, and at the very time when the Georgians were bullying the friendly Creeks at Shoulderbone, James White, Superintendent of the Southern District, was instructed to investigate the causes of the difficulty. White communicated with McGillivray and met the Creeks in council at Cusseta the following April. He asked them to ratify the illegal treaties and to make arrangements for running the boundary around the ceded territory. They firmly refused. Yahola Micco, of Coweta, an influential chief whom the whites called the Hollowing King, expressed the unchanging sentiment of the Indians toward their land: "our lands are our life and breath; if we part with them we part with our blood." McGillivray then made an

[5] Mohr, *Federal Indian Relations*, 139-55; *American State Papers, Indian Affairs*, I. 16-23; Hawkins, *Sketch*, 26 f.

[6] Pickett, *History of Alabama*, 372-88; *American State Papers, Indian Affairs*, I, 17 f.

interesting proposal to the Superintendent. He had been forced into
the alliance with Spain, he said, only to resist the greedy encroachments of the Georgians, and if Congress would form an Indian
state south of the Altamaha he would be the first to take the oath
of allegiance. To compensate Georgia for yielding her claim on
this territory he would persuade his people to surrender the lands
on the Oconee where the state had "deluded people to settle under
pretense of grants from the Indians."

White reported to Secretary of War Henry Knox. He said the
Georgians had made a mistake in taking hostages from the Cussetas, for the only effect had been to anger the friendly Indians; but
they had finally liberated all the captives except one boy who had
killed himself because of "his impatience of confinement." He
warned Knox that in the event of a Creek war the Confederacy had
six thousand warriors and plenty of Spanish arms and the Spanish
territory to fall back on in case of defeat, while Georgia was having
serious currency troubles and could not be expected to furnish any
financial assistance. The Georgians, however, had resumed the
efforts of the previous year to stir up a general war, and they worked
on Congress to provide the funds. They also tried to detach the
Lower Creeks from the Confederacy, to bribe McGillivray by a
tentative offer to return his father's estates, and to secure a promise from the Spanish officials that they would refuse to furnish
supplies to the Indians while the war was going on.

The appeal to Spain was the most successful. Governor Miro
notified McGillivray that the supply of ammunition would be cut
off the following November, and he advised the Creeks to settle
their differences with Georgia and the United States. But the
Franklin movement collapsed about this time, and Georgia's other
recruits were not forthcoming. Congress, moreover, was in no
mood for war, and it was the opinion of Secretary Knox that a
military expedition sufficient to break the power of the redoubtable
Confederacy would require twenty-eight hundred men for a nine
months' campaign at a cost of $450,000. Meanwhile the Creeks
raided the disputed territory at will, burning the towns, killing the
settlers, and carrying home white and negro captives and plunder.

Under these circumstances Georgia was ready by the beginning of 1788 to coöperate with the United States in seeking a peaceable settlement, but before a council could be arranged, the state was so completely bankrupt that it could not even carry on the negotiations. The impending change in the United States government formed a convenient pretext for postponing the treaty making, and McGillivray consented to wait until after the inauguration of the Federal government under the new constitution. The Creeks and Georgians proclaimed a truce, which the Indians observed better than their antagonists; the Creek raids had been directed to a specific purpose, and McGillivray could restrain his warriors, but the frontiersmen were subject to no law and there was no power on earth that could hold them within bounds.[7]

George Washington took the oath of office as President of the United States on April 30, 1789. The War Department was created August 7, and Henry Knox was reappointed to the new position. Commissioners were immediately chosen to treat with the Creeks, and on August 29 Washington and Knox furnished them with detailed secret instructions. These instructions are immensely significant, not only as the basis of the pending negotiations, but as the foundation of subsequent Indian policy.

The commissioners were to ascertain whether or not the Georgia treaties were valid, but in any event they were to secure the land, for "on your success materially depends the internal peace of Georgia, and probably its attachment to the General Government." They were authorized to spend twenty thousand dollars on the negotiations and an additional twenty thousand for the purchase of land, but they were to take into consideration the money that Georgia had already spent and the fact that the land, having been "entirely despoiled of its game by the settlements," was now of no value to the Indians. In addition to a cash payment they were to offer the following inducements: a seaport between the Altamaha and the St. Marys; "gifts in goods, or money to some and, if necessary, honorary military distinctions to others, of the influential chiefs"; a commission to McGillivray a grade higher than his Spanish commission if he could be induced to resign the latter, and

---

[7] Mohr, *Federal Indian Relations*, 155-67; *American State Papers, Indian Affairs*, I, 18-30.

the "assurance of such pecuniary rewards ... as you may think reasonable, consequent on the evidence of his future favorable conduct"; and "a solemn guarantee of the United States to the Creeks of their remaining territory, to be supported, if necessary, by a line of military posts."

If the Creeks would not accept these offers, the commissioners were to present plans to Washington and Knox for an offensive and defensive war to protect the frontier. They were also to collect all kinds of statistical information about the Creeks: population, number of towns, government, trade, the character of the country between the Georgia settlements and the Mississippi, the navigability of the rivers, the nature of the Creeks' and especially McGillivray's relations with Spain, etc. Regarding the navigability of the rivers, "the accurate knowledge of this subject is of considerable importance, but the inquiries thereto should be circuitously conducted." They were to try to secure permission for missionaries to live in the nation to inculcate "religion and morality ... and a friendship and attachment to the United States"; to establish the principle that the Creeks living in the United States acknowledged the protection of the United States and no other sovereign; and to demand that the raids on the Cumberland settlement should cease immediately. Finally they were to remember in all their negotiations that the "Government of the United States are determined, that their administration of Indian affairs shall be directed entirely by the great principles of justice and humanity."[8]

McGillivray was unaware of the ominous strength of the new government and its deep-laid designs against the cherished independence of his people. He was very well satisfied with himself that summer. Just a few days before Washington and Knox prepared these instructions he wrote an adroit letter to William Panton, bidding for Spanish support. He boasted that he had forced the United States to sue for a conference—"to bend and supplicate for peace at the feet of a people whom shortly before they despised and marked out for destruction." He was ready to treat now, but he was going to limit the agenda to settling the boundary and securing a recognition of Creek independence. The latter, he said,

[8] *American State Papers, Indian Affairs,* I, 65-68.

was very important, for the Americans "pretend to a territorial claim and sovereignty over us" because of the terms of the peace treaty with England. The commissioners, he knew, would offer trade concessions, but he would refuse; Panton by the favor of Spain could supply goods as cheaply as Georgia, and he preferred Spanish trade. The arms and ammunition furnished the Creeks by the king of Spain would strengthen them in the negotiations; he was sorry, however, that the guns were of such poor quality, for his people were accustomed to the best make of British guns. The commissioners had informed him that they wanted a private conversation with him before the council. He knew what they would say; they would offer to restore his father's property. He was undecided. What would Panton advise? He realized he had put Panton to heavy expense for years, and he hated to continue under such an obligation. Why were the Spanish so niggardly in their dealings with a man of his station? He closed with the suggestion that Panton might send a copy of the letter to the Spanish governor.[9]

The commissioners sailed from New York, at that time the Federal capital, with abundant presents for the Creeks. The meeting was held in September at Rock Landing on the Oconee. This council did not represent the submission of a few tame chiefs; it was an imposing demonstration of the power and might of the great Confederacy. McGillivray was there at the head of two thousand chiefs and warriors. They conducted themselves with grave dignity and received the white men with a proud and gracious courtesy. The first two days were spent in private conferences with McGillivray. Then the council opened with the mystic ceremony of the black drink. The commissioners presented a draft treaty ratifying the land cessions, acknowledging the sovereignty of the United States, granting a free port on the Altamaha, and providing for the return of captives and property carried off by the Creeks. That night McGillivray and his chiefs went into a grand private council. The next morning he formally rejected the terms, but promised to keep his warriors from hostile acts that winter. The

[9] Pickett found this important letter with some papers filed in the district court of Louisiana in a suit between the McGillivray and Panton heirs.—*History of Alabama*, 391-95. Caughey found the more cautiously worded copy in the Spanish archives.—*McGillivray of the Creeks*, 245-49.

commissioners tried vainly to persuade him to continue the nego-tiations. The presents remained undistributed, and the Creeks calmly broke camp and returned home. Obviously it was not going to be easy to cajole or intimidate the assembled rulers of the nation.

The commissioners had entered frankly into conversations with the governor of Georgia and had received his version of the controversy. Their final judgment, expressed in their report to Washington, deserves to be quoted as a classic; they found that the negotiations at Augusta, Galphinton, and Shoulderbone "were all of them conducted with as full and authorized repre-sentation, with as much substantial form, and apparent good faith and understanding of the business as Indian treaties have usu-ally been conducted." No historian can question the essential truth of this guarded conclusion. But they went on then to the obvious misstatement that after the land was ceded, the Georgians held and cultivated it for a number of years "without any claim or molesta-tion by any part of the Creek nation."

They did not recommend further negotiation; a Federal agent should be sent with an ultimatum, and if the Indians should refuse to accept it, "the arms of the Union should be called forth for the protection of the people of Georgia, in the peaceable and just possession of their lands." They presented a plan of attack, with such statistical information as they had been able to collect regarding the Confederacy. The Creeks, they said, were armed with good rifles, which they had obtained by gift or purchase from the Spanish. They hunted, raised corn and potatoes, and owned cattle and horses and a few slaves. Lately in some instan-ces they had introduced the plow. They took about £10,000 worth of fur every year, which they sold to Indian traders in the nation for exportation through Spanish ports; and they con-sumed annually about £12,000 worth of European goods, mostly furnished by the Panton firm. The commissioners were hopeful that the United States might capture this commerce. They advised the appointment of a Federal agent to regulate and encourage the trade in the Indian country, and they suggested that such an official might be able to influence the Choctaws and the Chickasaws to join in a war against the Creeks.[10]

Washington decided to make one more effort before risking the expense and danger of a Creek war. In the spring of 1790 he sent Colonel Marinus Willett on a confidential mission to induce McGillivray to come to New York. McGillivray conducted Willett through a rich and beautiful country exuberant with prosperity and power; populous towns welcomed him with speeches and ceremonials, entertained him with dancing, feasted him on fish, venison, strawberries, and mulberries. McGillivray sent out "broken days"—bundles of sticks from which one was removed each day— to summon the chiefs to council. The Lower Creeks assembled at the Red town, Osochee, and the Upper Creeks at Tuckabatchee. Willett told them that his Great Chief had invited McGillivray and their other leaders to New York to sign with his own hand a treaty of peace "as strong as the hills and lasting as the rivers." He assured them that the United States had no desire to take their land, but would secure them in their possessions and open a profitable commerce with them. The Indians deliberated and decided to treat; and the cavalcade set out for New York—twenty-six of the Indian dignitaries riding in three wagons and four on horseback.

To the chiefs the journey was as strange and interesting as Willett had found his travels through the Creek country. As they moved north, their progress became a triumphal procession. Richmond, Fredericksburg, Philadelphia, New York—all turned out to do them honor, and Washington and Congress received them with a pomp and dignity equal to their own. The Spanish officials at Pensacola and New Orleans were thrown into consternation. They sent an agent to New York ostensibly to buy flour, actually to buy McGillivray, but Washington guarded his guest from disturbing influences.

Secretary Knox carried on the negotiations with the chiefs. They refused absolutely to ratify the cession of the land south of the Altamaha, which they treasured as their best winter hunting ground. They consented to surrender the land on the Oconee, but

[10] *American State Papers, Indian Affairs*, I, 66-79.

the Federal officials insisted on using the Apalachee fork as the boundary in spite of McGillivray's warning that he did not believe he could persuade his people to accept that interpretation. The Federal officials also placed an article in the treaty guaranteeing the return of the captured negroes, although McGillivray protested that the slaves had changed hands so often since their capture that the Creeks would never consent to return them.

In spite of these reservations the treaty was signed on August 7 in behalf of the "Upper, Middle, and Lower Creeks and Seminolies, comprising the Creek nation of Indians." Besides the land cession and the promise to return the slaves, it provided for the surrender of white captives and gave the desired recognition of United States sovereignty. The new boundary was to be surveyed and marked by a line of felled trees where it crossed the upland; and the United States guaranteed the remaining Creek territory from encroachment and granted permission to the Creeks to punish white trespassers at will. No inhabitant of the United States was to enter the Creek country without a passport from the governor of a state or a Federal official. Creeks committing crimes against United States citizens were to be delivered for punishment, but white men who committed crimes against the Creeks were to be punished by the state or district of their legal residence. The United States would pay for the Oconee cession by turning over the goods still stored in Georgia and an annuity of fifteen hundred dollars a year; and would aid the Creeks in civilization by gifts of live stock and farm implements.

The Creeks for the first time thus surrendered their independence. Obviously the unilateral provisions of this treaty were not meaningless phrases of allegiance to some distant king, but the expression of a policy dictated by a determined and growing power that would eventually be able to enforce them. The only solid advantage which the Creeks gained by their concessions was the guarantee of their remaining territory, and the sequel was to show that such promises were the most brittle of all commitments made by the United States. There was also McGillivray's warning that even as the treaty stood two of the stipulations could not be enforced. An even more ominous threat for the future was suppressed by Washington and Knox, the fact that no words or engagements or plighted faith of nations was strong enough to hold back the resistless movement of the frontier.

Many years after the treaty was signed, the indefatigable Alabama historian, Albert James Pickett, uncovered a significant document among some dusty court records in Louisiana. It was a secret treaty engrossed on parchment and signed by Washington and Knox and McGillivray and the other chiefs; and it provided that McGillivray should be recognized as the agent of the United States with the rank of brigadier general and a salary of $1,200 a year, and that six other chiefs—Opothle Micco, of Tallasi; Efa Harjo (Mad Dog), of Tuckabatchee; and the chiefs of Okfuskee, Coweta, Cusseta, and the Seminoles—should each receive a handsome medal and an annual stipend of one hundred dollars. The treaty also provided that after two years the commerce of the Creek Nation should be diverted from its existing channels and carried through United States ports.[11]

McGillivray received one half of his "salary" in advance before he left New York, and subsequent payments to him and the other chiefs were carefully kept up. When Efa Harjo died in 1812, at least two of his colleagues—Opothle Micco and a chief of the Cussetas whose identity is difficult to discover—were still living and receiving their stipends. Obviously Washington and Knox had carried out their intention to bribe the chiefs, but subsequent events were to show that the money did not purchase their subservience, and it is impossible to determine to what extent it induced them to sign the treaty. Even McGillivray's experience had been limited to the frontier, and the honors the chiefs had received and the cumulative impressions of the white man's power and wealth probably overawed them more than the financial reward influenced them to make their first real submission. None of the Federal officials ever understood that the Creeks had a case, and they regarded McGillivray simply as an unprincipled adventurer who would sell his influence to the highest bidder; but the Creeks' foreign policy, so far as they understood it, was directed to the preservation of their inde-

[11] *Ibid.*, I, 80-82, 127, 255, 315 f., 840; Pickett, *History of Alabama*, 399-407; Charles J. Kappler, *Indian Affairs, Laws and Treaties*, II, 25-28.

pendence and their territorial integrity, and McGillivray, for all his self-seeking, was trying to accomplish that end. The bribes certainly oiled the wheels of diplomacy, but they hardly affected the result.

The Georgia senators, dissatisfied with the extent of the land cession, voted against the treaty, but it was ratified by the United States. Early in 1792 James Seagrove was appointed as superintendent of the Creeks and sent to Rock Landing, and the government erected a fort there and put in a strong garrison. But the Creeks, as McGillivray had predicted, refused to surrender the negroes or accept the Apalachee fork of the Oconee as the boundary. The Federal agents attributed some of the blame to William Augustus Bowles, an adventurer living among the Lower Creeks. It was said that Bowles even committed piracy against Panton's trading vessels in the Gulf, and by opening this desirable field of plunder he became very popular with the more turbulent of the Lower Towns and began to break down McGillivray's influence.

McGillivray apparently did not try to reconcile the Creeks to the Treaty of New York. His position with Spain had been strengthened rather than weakened by his dealings with the United States. He called on the governor and received the title of Superintendent General of the Creek Nation, with a salary of $3,500 a year, and obtained a promise that led to Bowles' eventual capture and transportation in chains to Madrid. Captain Don Pedro Olivier (or Olivar), a Frenchman in the Spanish service, was stationed at Hickory Ground to advance Spanish interests.

Knox suspected these intrigues, but the Federal government was not strong enough to dictate to the Creeks. A similar condition of fraudulent land grants and aggressions of frontiersmen had driven the Indians north of the Ohio into hostility, and in the fall of 1791 a military expedition sent against them under Major General Arthur St. Clair had been almost annihilated. There was grave danger, of course, that the Creeks might join the hostiles; and such a general war, with the possibility of European interference, might have jeopardized the very existence of the young Republic. To prevent their joining the enemy, Knox offered to enlist one or two hundred Creek warriors, keeping the number as low as he dared and yet trying to give them the feeling of participation. He wrote to McGillivray with apparent frankness as to an ally, admitting the seriousness of the military disaster but expressing confidence in the outcome of the campaign. He explained that the United States "require no lands from the Indians; they require nothing of them but what shall tend to their own happiness"—a policy, in fact, "so replete with kindness to them that all good men [including McGillivray] ought to delight in forwarding" it.[12]

The Creeks had stopped their organized efforts to clear the Georgians from the disputed territory, but a desultory warfare continued all along the border. It is apparent even from the prejudiced sources available that the Georgians were the chief aggressors. Adventurous and lawless spirits among the Creeks delighted in raiding the settlements and stealing live stock, but the sober chiefs made an honest effort to restrain and punish them. On the other hand lawless white men crossed into the Creek country, sneaked up and murdered one or two peaceable Indians, and dashed back across the border, and no attempt was ever made to deter them. The Creeks showed surprising restraint in such cases; but as their reasonable requests for satisfaction were invariably ignored, they sometimes avenged the murders by their old law of retaliation upon the first innocent white man they encountered, and these instances of savage justice went to swell the Georgians' list of "Indian depredations." White thieves also stole horses from the settlements and drove them into the Creek country. The town chiefs voluntarily returned many of these animals, but some were purchased from the thieves and retained by covetous members of the tribe. The chiefs vainly asked the white men to keep these renegades out of their country, but this request was disregarded and the stolen horses were added to the list. The Georgians, of course, held the Creeks accountable for all depredations on the territory they claimed under their fraudulent treaties; and during the whole period they drove large herds of live stock into the territory that was indisputably Creek and held the Indians responsible for all losses that occurred. At the same time they swarmed into the Creek country with packs of dogs and slaughtered the game

[12] *American State Papers, Indian Affairs,* I, 126, 246-55, 315 f.; Pickett, *History of Alabama,* 408-13.

thirty or forty miles back from the border. When their economic resources were destroyed, the Creeks were as disturbed as a civilized farmer would be by the confiscation of his crops, or a modern industrial state by the seizure of its petroleum fields. After the Indian habit of conferring humorous nicknames they called the frontier settlers *Econnaunuxulgee* (People-greedily-grasping-after-land); William Blount, territorial governor of the Tennessee region, received the name of *Tuckemicco* (Dirt King); and the governor of Georgia was dubbed *Econnaupopohau* (Always-asking-for-land).

During 1792 both the Creeks and the Georgians denied the validity of the Treaty of New York, and neither would consent to a survey of the boundary. The Federal officials suspected that Spanish agents, especially Olivier, were encouraging the Creeks and arming them in preparation for war; but negotiations were then in progress at Madrid for the settlement of the international boundary and other questions in dispute between the United States and Spain. Secretary of State Jefferson finally asked the representatives of the Spanish court to state the policy of their government toward the Creeks. They showed him a letter from the governor of Louisiana expressed in the most insulting language possible under the courteous usages of diplomacy. The governor asserted that the Treaty of New York was "null in effect" because it had been rejected by the Creeks and because it was in violation of the Creek-Spanish treaty of 1784; the pending negotiation in Madrid, however, "has engaged me to restrain the hostilities which the Creek nation had resolved to commence against the State of Georgia, to recover the lands which it had usurped from them"; but he was giving the United States "an amicable pre-admonition" that any attempt to run the boundary would probably "kindle a very bloody war."

About all the United States could do was to distribute presents to the Indians. In August, Knox sent Seagrove—who by this time had retired to the St. Marys—12 pairs of silver arm bands, 4 silver medals, and 132 sets of "nose and ear jewels" to be given to the subservient "as an earnest of future rewards." In the fall, goods, corn, and money to the amount of $13,314.61 were sent by Knox for distribution to a "council" of about one thousand men, women, and children assembled on the St. Marys. An ominous circumstance, almost unregarded at the time, was the fact that the Lower Creeks were seriously in need of the food and clothing they received here. There had been a severe drought, but a more important cause of their distress was the constant turmoil that had interrupted their labors, and no doubt the destruction of game was having its effect. It was a new experience for these prosperous Indians to receive relief from the white man, but from this time on it was apparent that the native economic system was disintegrating before the advancing frontier. Knox began to talk of introducing "artificers, husbandmen, and physicians" to help them over the transition; the alternative to civilizing them, he said, was a protracted war to drive them across the Mississippi, a measure cruel to them and unnecessary to the United States.[13]

Matters were in this unsettled state when death ended the troubled career of Alexander McGillivray. He died February 17, 1793, at the home of his wife, the daughter of a French Huguenot named Joseph Cornell. He left a son and two daughters, and his property consisted of sixty negroes, three hundred cattle, and many horses. A letter from Panton carried the news of his death across the water to old Lachlan, who must have marveled at the strange career of the man who had been his son. He has been characterized as the ablest man ever born on the soil of Alabama. Certainly he was more than a crafty intriguer. He understood the treachery of his white opponents, and he sought to defeat their schemes and obtain an advantage for himself and his people with a perfidy that matched their own. It might have been wiser to submit, but nature had denied to his restless genius the gift of foresight.[14]

The border difficulties increased after the death of McGillivray. Shawnees from the Northwest were known to be working among the Creeks, boasting of their victory over St. Clair the previous fall, showing the scalps they had taken, and urging the Creeks to join them in a general war. There were strong reasons influencing

[13] *American State Papers, Indian Affairs,* I, 139, 256-70, 292-97, 304-22, 362; *American State Papers, Foreign Relations,* I, 139; Hawkins, *Sketch,* 9 f.
[14] Pickett, *History of Alabama,* 431 f.; Hawkins, *Sketch,* 40.

the Creeks to accept the invitation. Besides the standing irritation against the Georgians and the pleasurable excitement of warfare, there was a tradition of Creek-Shawnee friendship going back to the dim days of their legendary history. The alarmed Seagrove sent letters to be delivered to the leading chiefs by trusted traders, saying that the Great Father would send an army and destroy the Shawnees as soon as the snow should melt, and offering a packload of goods for every Shawnee they would deliver to him at Rock Landing and half a packload for every Shawnee scalp.

All the leading chiefs except the embittered Opothle Micco worked for peace. More humane than the superintendent, they suppressed his offer to pay for Shawnee captives or Shawnee hair, but they asked the northern visitors to leave their towns as soon as hospitality would permit. Among the Upper Towns only Tallasi, the town of Opothle Micco, and Coolome, an important town on the Tallapoosa, "took the war talk." The Lower Creeks were more responsive. The settlers—not satisfied with the Oconee boundary, which the Indians had not yet conceded—had already crossed that river and built several houses on the Creek side, and great herds of cattle ranged twenty miles into the interior; and the Shawnees pointed to these intrusions to illustrate the futility of boundaries and guarantees. The Cowetas took the war talk, partly through the influence of John Galphin, a white man who had gained an ascendancy in their councils.[15] They were joined by Broken Arrow (Thikachka), a daughter town, by Osochee, the former residence of Bowles, and by some warriors from Chiaha and the main town of the Euchees. On March 11, a war party of about thirty of these hostiles led by Galphin plundered a trading post owned by a brother of Seagrove at Traders Hill on the St. Marys. In this raid they killed six or possibly seven persons and brought back a gratifying number of horses, cattle, and negroes.

Seagrove demanded that the Creeks make restitution by the surrender of seven of the hostiles, including Galphin, and the return of the property. The friendly chiefs tried to comply. Their action

---

15 He was commonly referred to as a white man. George Galphin's will mentioned a half-blood son named John, but if the two John Galphins were identical the fact was not commonly known.

brought some internal dissension, but the unifying forces among the Creeks were still too strong for the Confederacy to break up in a civil war. They held a council at Tuckabatchee in June and decided to surrender Galphin and another white man, appointed men to kill five of their own raiders, and made preparations for the return of the property. They drew up very conciliatory letters to Seagrove notifying him of this decision and sent them by young David Cornell, the cousin of a friendly mixed-blood chief of Tuckabatchee named Alexander Cornell or Oche (from the Hickorynut Clan) Harjo. As Cornell with a young boy and two other Indians, all unarmed, approached Colerain on the St. Marys, a detachment of Georgia militia learned of their presence, met them ten miles out, murdered Cornell and the boy and drove off the others, and returned in triumph with the packhorses and baggage. The Creeks were deeply stirred by this outrage. Even Governor Telfair admitted that it was "unfortunate," and Seagrove promised them that the murderers should be punished.

While these events were happening in the Creek country, the St. Marys raid had repercussions on the white man's side of the line. Washington took decisive steps to protect the state against invasion, but still hoping to prevent a war with the whole Confederacy, he did not order an expedition into the Creek country. Governor Telfair decided to take matters into his own hands. Just a few days before the council at Tuckabatchee entrusted the dispatches to the unfortunate Cornell, seven hundred Georgia militiamen invaded the Creek country, marched forty miles to the Ocmulgee, mutinied, and then—to use the governor's own words—"from circumstances of their provisions being nearly exhausted, many horses tired, and other adverse events, they returned." The inability of the Georgia militia to fight was a constant temptation to the Creeks, but Seagrove explained this particular misadventure by telling the Indians that their benevolent Great Father, to give them a few days' more time to make restitution for the St. Marys raid, had turned the Georgians back.

These disturbances were aggravated by the presence of Spanish agents, who worked actively throughout the Creek country during 1793. Panton was at the same time supplying the Creeks with ammunition and working against the commercial plans of the United States. Early in the year the Chickasaws declared war on the Creeks, but the fighting was not very brisk, and the Federal officials believed that Panton's intervention had stopped this highly desirable conflict. To add to the general confusion Genet came to Charleston as an emissary of the Revolutionary French Republic and began to give commissions to the frontiersmen to drive out the Spanish. Major General Elijah Clarke of the Georgia militia was his most influential assistant.

But the leading chiefs remained friendly to the United States. They invited Seagrove to their country, and a council was called to meet in September on the Ocmulgee. Feeling ran so high in Georgia that it was with some hesitation that he notified Telfair of his plans. As he approached the frontier, he met with such insults and threats from the Georgians that it was necessary for a detachment of Federal troops from Fort Fidius, the garrison on the Oconee, to escort him to the border. As soon as he arrived on the Oconee, he found that parties of militia were frequently making raids into the Creek country, murdering and scalping any unprotected party of Indians they could find. Bands of these ruffians now crossed over with the avowed intention of breaking up the council. One band seeking revenge for a horse-stealing expedition from Coweta went to Little Okfuskee on the Chattahoochee, one of the most friendly towns in the nation, murdered and scalped six men, plundered and burned the houses, and carried back eight women and girls as captives.

Seagrove then received an ultimatum from Telfair entitled, "Conditions that will be required on the part of the State of Georgia, on the establishment of peace between the United States and the Creek Indians." The Creeks were to surrender all captured property and prisoners and carry out all individual contracts with Georgians, to hand over thirteen of their men accused of murder, and to deliver ten of their head men from the Upper and Lower Towns to be held as hostages. Finally Georgia would recognize no settlement unless her commissioners participated in the negotiation. At the same time Galphin sent a defiant offer of peace from a council of the Cowetas to General Jared Irwin of the Georgia

militia. The Creeks would accept a boundary "fairly agreed upon
... by the legislative body of the nation, and not a clandestine
bargain, with a few chiefs." Meanwhile he had ordered his warriors to commit no depredations beyond the Oconee; he hoped
Irwin would give his people similar orders, for "we still have warriors sufficient to stain your land with blood."

All these events occurred while Seagrove waited on the Oconee.
Under the circumstances he decided not to cross the river, and the
council was postponed. He still worked for peace, however. He
even tried to turn the "horrid affair on the Oakfuskee village" to a
"pleasant issue": the Cowetas, he told the friendly Creeks, were
really to blame, for they had angered the Georgians to commit the
depredations; hence the relatives of the victims should attack the
Cowetas. Telfair, meanwhile, had called a council of general officers and planned to raise five thousand men to march in October
against the five hostile towns. It was expected that the Federal
government would pay this army, but Knox notified him that the
President "utterly disapproves the measure," and that only Congress had the power to declare war. This decision cooled the military ardor of the Georgians, and in November Seagrove was permitted to enter the Creek country.

He had a promise of safe-conduct from the Creeks, but thirteen
mounted militiamen accompanied him as far as the Ocmulgee to
protect him from attacks by lawless Georgians. Here 130 chiefs and
warriors were waiting to receive him. He dismissed his escort and
went on to Cusseta, where he was received in the square with great
ceremony. Next he visited Tuckabatchee. His reception there was
courteous, but less cordial than at Cusseta, and it was apparent that
the Upper Creeks were divided in their sentiments toward the Federal government and its representative. The estranged Opothle
Micco was hostile as always, and the family of the murdered
Cornell was distinctly sullen. There was also a tendency to hold the
United States responsible for the Cherokee–Upper Creek war with
the Cumberland settlements. In September General Sevier with
four hundred Tennessee militiamen had started out to invade the
Indian country; he had defeated the Indians in a battle at the forks
of the Coosa and Hightower and had gone down the Coosa and

destroyed a number of towns. The son and three other relatives of White Lieutenant, the friendly mixed-blood chief of the Okfuskees, had been killed in this raid, but he remained loyal to the United States. At one time Opothle Micco stirred up the Indians to kill Seagrove. The superintendent was forced to take refuge in a swamp, and his life was saved only through the interposition of White Lieutenant.

In spite of these inauspicious circumstances Seagrove's mission was a success. A full representation of the Upper and Lower towns met for two days and nights in a continuous council, and terms of peace were unanimously adopted. Seagrove again promised that Cornell's murderers would be punished, and that the women and children taken from the Okfuskee village would be restored— a condition that the governor subsequently refused to carry out. The Creeks promised to cease their depredations on the Georgia frontier, to restore all prisoners, negroes, and live stock captured during the preceding twelve months, and to kill two or more of their hostiles. They appointed White Lieutenant, Efa Harjo, and Yahola Micco to carry out this decision. Seagrove remained among the Creeks until the following May.[16]

While Seagrove was in the Creek country, Fushatchee Micco (known as White Bird King or Bird Tail King by the white men) of Cusseta, who had always been friendly, was hunting on his own ground between the Ocmulgee and the Oconee, when a party of Georgians attacked him with no provocation whatever and killed two of his men. He went immediately to Fort Fidius and complained. The commander promised that the murderers should be punished and managed to pacify the injured chief. Meanwhile the heads of the nation delivered the captives and were collecting and preparing to deliver the stolen goods. In May the superintendent and a delegation of six leading chiefs went to Augusta and had a very satisfactory interview with Governor George Mathews. About 150 of their people accompanied them as far as Fort Fidius and camped on their own side of the river. While they were there, a report came that two members of the Georgia militia had been

16 *American State Papers, Indian Affairs*, I, 269 f., 305-472, 621-23; Pickett, *History of Alabama*, 438-40.

killed on the northern frontier, apparently by Cherokees. Major Adams, who commanded a body of militia men not far from the fort, thereupon swore loudly that he was "going to have hair," and attacked the camp of the unsuspecting Creeks. Several were murdered, but the rest fled. Some sought protection in the fort, and the militia then threatened to attack the garrison. To avoid trouble the commander slipped the Indians out in the dead of night, hoping they might be able to find their way home in safety. Adams then threatened to murder the chiefs who had gone to Augusta, and Governor Mathews had to send them back under a strong military escort. Seagrove was at the end of his patience. He notified Mathews that he had made peace and he was done; if the Georgians could not be restrained, the Indians had no alternative except to defend themselves, and the state could choose between punishing the militia officers and fighting the whole Creek Nation.

The long-suffering Creeks still did not declare a general war. Their opportunity soon passed, for that summer Wayne administered a crushing defeat to the Indians north of the Ohio. The same summer of 1794 they witnessed the first attempt of the state government to restrain its turbulent citizens. General Elijah Clarke attempted to set up an independent state just beyond the Georgia frontier. He built a blockhouse and laid out a town across the Oconee opposite Fort Fidius, and people rushed there and began feverishly to erect houses. After repeated warnings to the settlers Mathews finally sent the militia against them and burned the town. The Creeks were touchingly grateful for this action. Not realizing that it had been taken to protect the territorial integrity of the state against secessionist movements, they accepted it as an evidence of good faith on the part of the white chiefs.

In December the legislature authorized the settlement of the land south of the Altamaha, claimed under the fraudulent treaty of Galphinton, and appropriated twenty thousand dollars for extinguishing the Indian title "should any there be" to the land between the Oconee and the Ocmulgee. The United States was invited to negotiate for the new cession, but a commission was appointed to represent the state. In the meantime the white men's position was strengthened when the United States and Spain settled their differences by the Treaty of San Lorenzo in 1795 and agreed upon a boundary following the present southern line of Georgia and extending west on the parallel of 31° to the Mississippi. But at the very time this treaty was signed one Benjamin Harrison and some fellow cutthroats disturbed the peace of the frontier by murdering twenty or more peaceful Creeks who were hunting on their own land and mutilating their bodies with a ferocity that shocked even the Georgians. The Creeks were aroused and retaliated by killing some innocent Georgians, but the legislature unanimously passed a resolution condemning Harrison, and he and his accomplices were placed in prison to be tried for the novel crime of murdering Indians. Under these circumstances the Creeks consented to negotiate.

The council was held at Colerain, May 26, 1796. Seagrove attended as Creek superintendent, and Lieutenant Colonel Henry Gaither, who had commanded the garrison at Fort Fidius, was present to maintain order. Colonel Benjamin Hawkins, of North Carolina; George Clymer, of Pennsylvania; and Andrew Pickens, of South Carolina, constituted the Federal commission. Hawkins was the most active member. The commissioners treated the Indians with a fairness unique in Indian negotiation: they assured themselves that the assembled chiefs really had authority to treat for the nation; they were careful to explain every detail, so that there would be no possible misunderstanding; and they did not resort to bribery or intimidation. The Creeks were represented by about four hundred chiefs, headmen, and warriors. Fushatchee Micco was spokesman. They conducted themselves with firmness and dignity, and their feeling of solidarity, their intelligent conception of issues, and their grave sense of responsibility were impressive indications that even after twenty years of war and disintegrating influences the great Confederacy could gather its forces for a supreme effort of self-preservation. The Federal commissioners did not know that they had cached great quantities of dried meat, carefully wrapped in skins, at various places in the forest along a possible line of retreat to the safety of their guarded towns. They were courteous to the white man, but they did not trust his promises of safe-conduct.

This fear of treachery was not ill-founded, for the Federal commissioners learned that the Georgians planned to introduce armed militia into the council. They accordingly drew up rules providing that the superintendent should camp with his charges, forbidding armed men to approach the Indian camp, and prohibiting anyone from selling intoxicants to the Indians or conversing with them except by permission. The Georgians soon arrived with a schooner loaded with goods and guarded with militia. They found a sentinel posted on the river to keep armed men from landing. They were deeply incensed. They said they were expecting some of their citizens from the frontier to attend the meeting, and of course they would come armed; now they were forbidden even to speak to the Indians. The Federal commissioners courteously offered half of their tents to the state commission, agreed to make arrangements to accommodate the unexpected guests from the frontier, and informed them that their guard could be quartered with Gaither's men; but they declined to modify the regulations. The Georgians angrily refused their hospitality and maintained their headquarters on the schooner.

Most of the meetings were held at a square, called Muskogee Hall by Seagrove, which the Indians built in their camp. The chiefs were received with great formality by Hawkins and his colleagues, and they responded by the eagle tail dance, the smoking of the pipe, etc. The state commissioners delivered a "talk" at the beginning of the negotiations. They expressed deep regret for the atrocities committed by Harrison, but they blamed the Creeks for not observing the treaties of Augusta, Galphinton, and Shoulderbone, and they presented a list of depredations running back to the outbreak of the Revolution—89 negroes, 825 horses, 1159 cattle, and 495 hogs taken, and 115 houses burned, representing a value of $70,000 before the Treaty of New York and $40,000 since. They had shown their good faith by removing Clarke from the Creek land, but they wanted to purchase the tract between the Oconee and Ocmulgee. The Georgians were numerous; "They are like a river, so very full that its banks cannot contain it, so that it overflows the neighboring grounds. . . . We have not land enough to raise corn for all our people. No red man would refuse a white man something to eat, if he came hungry to his cabin; and yet a refusal of this land will be like a denial of bread to many hungry families, who want to raise corn on it to feed themselves." They had a vessel yonder in the river filled with goods that would comfort the Indians' women and children more than many years hunting on the Oconee-Ocmulgee tract.

For the most part the Indians listened in silence to this communication, but their disapproval was apparent. When the Treaty of Galphinton was mentioned, they asked who signed it. When the hogs were mentioned in the list of stolen property, they laughed. After the council adjourned, some of the chiefs dined with the Federal commissioners and talked freely with each other of the speech. The tustennuggee thlocco of Cusseta asked if the commissioners could supply a roll of paper bigger than the Georgians had used for their depredations, for the Creeks could easily fill it up. Another asked how the Georgians could tell whether Indians or bears had destroyed their hogs; "the Georgians have done us much evil, but we never blamed them for the hogs we lost." They met in their own square and prepared a formal answer. Probably John Galphin was the one who rendered their arguments in the white man's form of speech; for because of the failure of the various peace agreements, that adroit adventurer still lived and was allowed as an adopted "Indian" to remain in the camp with his tribesmen.

The Creeks pointed out that they had never accepted the three treaties claimed by Georgia. The Treaty of New York was legal except that they had never consented to the Apalachee boundary. As for depredations, they had occurred on both sides; and even then the whole upper country between the Oconee and the Ocmulgee was filled with trespassers. If the whites were given the land to the Ocmulgee, they would drive their cattle across that river and allow them to range to the Flint. "The land belongs to the Indians and they wish to keep it, ... and hope the white people ... will ... keep their goods for other purposes."

The Federal commissioners tried without success to break their resolution. They were determined, however, to secure the ratification of the Treaty of New York. The Creeks pleaded desperately for the upper fork of the Oconee. The Apalachee crossed the very heart of their hunting grounds, it was too small a stream to hold back the Georgians' cattle, etc. Hawkins and his colleagues refused to bargain on that point, and the Indians finally yielded, although they said "it was like pulling out their hearts, and throwing them away." The Federal representatives then asked permission to establish military and trading posts in their country. At first they refused, but after considering the plan in council they decided that they liked it very much, that the Federal garrisons would protect them from the encroachments of frontiersmen. It was apparent throughout the negotiations that the main advantage they expected to derive from the treaty was the protection of their remaining territory. They were still grateful for the breaking up of Clarke's fort two years before; and during the council they received a very favorable impression when the Secretary of War sent the commissioners a copy of the Indian Intercourse Law recently enacted to protect the Indian country against intruders.

Mindful of their duty to civilize the Indians, the Federal commissioners tried to secure their consent to the establishment of schools, but the subject was "received with so much dislike . . . that it was postponed." Cusseta Micco said that educated Indians invariably turned out to be worthless characters, who involved the two races in difficulties. They did consent to accept the services of two blacksmiths with "strikers," and goods amounting to six thousand dollars was distributed.

Amnesty was declared on both sides for all crimes except that Harrison and his associates should stand trial in the state courts. The Indians consented to this provision with great reluctance. The tustennuggee thlocco pointed out that the murder of Cornell was still unavenged. The relatives of Harrison's victims had come with the pleasurable expectation of seeing the murderers hanged at the council after the speedy manner of Indian justice, and they were deeply disappointed to learn of the slow and uncertain processes of the white man's jurisprudence. In theory the Creeks were willing to substitute legal proceedings for their old law of retaliation, but they doubted that a white man would ever be punished for a crime against an Indian.[17]

[17] *American State Papers, Indian Affairs,* I, 472-87, 495-501, 551-60, 589-616; Pickett, *History of Alabama,* 438-50; Kappler, *Laws and Treaties,* II, 46-50; Hawkins, *Sketch,* 62 f.; *Niles' Weekly Register,* LIII (1837), 66 f.

The Treaty of Colerain was the first settlement to which the Creeks had freely consented since the outbreak of the Revolution. It had been demonstrated that they would not yield what the Georgians wanted except through fraud and violence, but this was the problem of the future, and for the time a condition resembling peace settled upon that troubled frontier. The Upper Creeks continued to assist the Cherokees in their war with the Cumberland settlers, but they were gradually restrained through the influence of Benjamin Hawkins.

Hawkins was appointed as agent to the tribe soon after the council at Colerain. He was the ablest man that ever represented the United States among the Creeks. It was frankly his purpose to "civilize" his charges by bringing them under submission. As he expressed it, "The men are bred in habits proudly indolent and insolent; ... and they will reluctantly and with great difficulty be humbled to the habit of national life." If it did not occur to him that he might destroy what was best in the Creeks by this "humbling" process, it is to his credit that he worked with singleness of purpose without seeking to enrich himself or to gratify the frontiersmen at their expense. An interested student of their institutions, he compiled a grammar of their language; and he made an inventory of their natural resources, not for the guidance of the land-grabbers who schemed to dispossess them, but for the use of the civilized and disciplined Creeks of the future that he hoped sometime would develop their rich heritage. His reports are unique among Federal Indian documents for their freedom from boasting, their frank statement of difficulties, and their accurate portrayal of conditions.

In 1798 he persuaded the chiefs in council to pass a law to punish those who committed depredations against the whites. A year later he was able to report that it had been "carried into effect, in a few instances" where his influence had been "greatly exerted." The most important test came when the international commission attempted to run the boundary under the Treaty of San Lorenzo. The surveyors began at the west and ran the line through the Choctaw country. Then they held a council and obtained the consent of the Creeks, but they were stopped at the confluence of the Flint and Chattahoochee by Opothle Micco and his irreconcilable Tallasis and the warriors from Eufaula Town on the Chattahoochee. The Creeks did not know that this survey would divide their country into two parts, each under the protection of a different power, but they were suspicious of the white man's custom of marking their land. Hawkins asked the chiefs to call out their warriors and punish Opothle Micco and his associates, and after repeated urging he finally saw the law enforced in an "exemplary manner." But this humiliation did not destroy the influence of the independent old chief, and the survey was still uncompleted. The surveyors finally went around to the St. Marys and raised a mound to mark the place where the eastern end of the line would strike that river and abandoned their attempt to run the boundary.

While this experience was fresh in the minds of the Indians, Hawkins called a council of the chiefs at Tuckabatchee and persuaded them to adopt a new plan of government. The Upper Towns were divided into eight groups, and one man (in some cases two men) was selected from each group to superintend the execution of the law in that division. The distinctive functions of Peace and War towns were abolished; "towns of the same fire" were grouped together, but it was "unanimously agreed that the E-tall-wau, *white towns,* should be classed as warriors" in their relation to the Confederacy. The same council adopted the principle that when a man was put to death according to law, it was the law that killed him, and no man or family was to be held accountable. It was decided that white "mischief-makers" in the Indian country were under the authority of the agent, who might bring in soldiers or call out Creek warriors to arrest them.

With the law enforcement under his control Hawkins also labored to bring the council under subjection. Once a year he invited each town to send a deputation of not more than five or six members to comprise the National Council. At this meeting he reported the state of the nation, recommended legislation, and applied for compensation and satisfaction for depredations on the frontier. The Council elected a speaker—using the term in a new sense—to preside over the deliberations. This official was recognized as the head chief, and it was still customary for him to employ

a "speaker" or orator to make announcements and express his sentiments to the assembly. Efa Harjo was elected to the new office,
and Tuckabatchee thus became the meeting place of the Council.
Hawkins hoped to centralize the government at the expense of the
town and the clan in order to "civilize" the Creeks "and give the
United States a more commanding influence over them." He eventually brought the Lower Creeks into his organization. Each division had its own council and speaker, but there was a head chief,
or speaker, of the nation, whose town became the seat of the united
council.

Hawkins also worked out a system for checking the depredations
on the frontier. When a hunting party went out in the fall for the
great winter hunt, one of its members was appointed as chief, to be
responsible for the conduct of the party. This chief was supposed
to report to Hawkins and receive a certificate recommending him
to the friendly attention of the whites. Creeks with horses to sell
were required to report to Hawkins and obtain a certificate guaranteeing the title; but the Cumberland settlers had no scruples
against buying horses stolen from the Georgia frontier, and with
this encouragement the depredations continued to a certain extent.
Hawkins also used the fifteen hundred dollar annuity, paid under
the Treaty of New York, to increase the Creeks' dependence. He
paid a reward of $2.50 for each stolen horse delivered to him by
any Indian except the thief, and $12.50 for every fugitive negro
when it was proved that the Creeks had been responsible for the
escape. He also paid the warriors who went on his messages to the
Seminoles to keep in order that turbulent portion of the Creek
tribe living in Spanish territory.

Hawkins maintained his own residence at Coweta, and he had
a subagency at Tuckabatchee under Alexander Cornell. The public
blacksmiths furnished under the Treaty of Colerain were located
at these two places, and each establishment had also a model farm,
a garden, and a nursery. Hawkins tried to show the Indians the
value of fencing to protect their fields, and he distributed peach
trees throughout the nation. He discouraged the communal system
of agriculture and the habit of sitting around in the squares, and
influenced the more "progressive" Indians to leave the compact

towns and settle out in villages, where they might practice the white man's individualism. He distributed a number of plows, gifts of philanthropic Quakers, and by careful demonstration he persuaded a few of his budding agriculturalists to use them. A few Indians, probably mixed bloods, began to plant small patches of cotton, and a little was sent to market. He found the greatest success in his efforts to encourage stock-raising. The Indians were beginning to feel the loss of their game and were rapidly acquiring domestic cattle as a substitute; they were raising hogs, but they allowed them to run in the woods where many were destroyed by wild animals; and horses of a small and comparatively worthless breed were in general use. Slaves were becoming numerous and were greatly valued. It was apparent, in fact, that the unaccustomed labors of the new order were performed mainly by slaves and mixed bloods.

The trading business had declined with the scarcity of pelts and the disruption of industry caused by the war then raging in Europe, and the traders with their numerous mixed-blood offspring were engaged in farming and stock-raising. A United States "factory" was maintained to sell goods to the Indians. This was apparently a demoralizing influence, for they were allowed to purchase on credit and by 1802 they had run up bad debts amounting to ten thousand dollars.

Hawkins encouraged the women in the production of nut oil and found a market for it at Mobile and New Orleans. He employed a young man from an English manufacturing town to make spinning wheels and looms, and he secured the services of a woman to teach the Indian women to spin and weave. A few of them, especially the mixed bloods, became greatly interested in the new way of making clothing. The chiefs at first feared that if the women learned to clothe themselves by their own efforts they would become independent of their husbands, but this primitive feminism did not develop; as Hawkins said, the marriage "link is more firm, in proportion as the women are more useful, and occupied in domestic concerns."

The effect of this economic transition and the white man's depredations was apparent in the changing fortunes of the towns.

The great leading towns of the preceding century were rapidly
declining from the exhaustion of their fields, losses in war, and the
general demoralization. The old site of Coweta, now known as
Coweta Tullahassee, was almost abandoned, and the inhabitants
had moved to a new location two and one-half miles away, or were
living in villages. Cusseta was still one of the most populous towns
in the nation, but its great thousand-acre field was almost exhausted
and its people had barely enough for food. The Cussetas had become badly demoralized through their friendship with the frontier
whites, but some of the villagers were more enterprising. It was
evident that Okfuskee would soon be an "Old Town," but its
numerous inhabitants were spreading out in thriving villages. Artussee was a small and poverty-stricken place. Tallasi was almost
deserted, but its people were moving up the creek and forming
new settlements. Tuckabatchee had lost a number of its people in
wars, but several of its villages had recently built squares and
chokofas and were branching off as separate towns. The friendly
village that received the name of Nuyaka after the Treaty of New
York had once been on the Chattahoochee, but its people in fear
of Georgian vengeance had fled to the Tallapoosa in 1777 when
their neighbors joined the British. The survivors of Little Okfuskee
had fled to the Tallapoosa and rebuilt their town on that stream
when the Georgians had made the unprovoked attack on them in
1793. Padgeliga (Pigeon Roost) had once been a prosperous village
on the Flint, but sixteen of its warriors had been among Harrison's
victims, and after that horrible experience most of its people had
built a new town under the protection of the Tuckabatchees. Oconee,
a thriving town on the Flint, was composed of the people who had
lived on the Oconee before that region was occupied by the whites.
A number of the Koasatas had even crossed the Mississippi; with
some of their Alabama kinsmen they eventually settled in Texas,
and they sent back glowing reports of the fresh unspoiled country
and the abundance of game.[18]

In general the Upper Creeks, who had suffered less from white

[18] *American State Papers, Indian Affairs*, I, 647 f., 676-79; Hawkins, *Sketch;* Hawkins, *Letter;* Jedidiah Morse, *Report to the Secretary of War of the United States on Indian
Affairs*, 147; Pickett, *History of Alabama*, 451-59; Kappler, *Laws and Treaties*, II, 58 f.

encroachment, were more prosperous than the Lower. But the Creek country was no longer a place of peace and security and overflowing abundance; and Hawkins reported that its population was declining or at a standstill. Almost without their knowledge the power and independence of the Creeks had been completely undermined. Their diplomacy had failed. England and Spain had professed friendship and then forgotten them, Georgia had crowded them with brutal and unashamed violence, but it was the United States that had held them in check by bribery and humanitarian pretensions and betrayed them into submission. Perplexed and baffled, subdued but still untamed, they entered upon a way beset with difficulties where the assertion of their old spirit would bring disaster.

CHAPTER 3

The Destruction of a Nation

THE Creeks were soon asked to make further land cessions. General James Wilkinson, who was in military command of the Southwest, Benjamin Hawkins, and Andrew Pickens were appointed to negotiate. Secretary of War Henry Dearborn instructed them to try again to secure the Altamaha–St. Marys and the Oconee–Ocmulgee tracts, and to effect the capture of Bowles, who had escaped from prison and returned to his former occupation of inciting the Indians.

The council opened May 24, 1802. It was held near Fort Wilkinson on the Oconee. The Creeks were represented through the artificial government Hawkins had created, and Efa Harjo acted as spokesman. Wilkinson took the lead in the negotiations. He began in an arrogant tone to upbraid the Creeks, charging them with murders and depredations; this, he explained in his report, was calculated "to excite a strong sense of humiliation and dependence." He demanded a land cession as an indemnity, and he argued that their game would "soon be entirely destroyed" and urged them to protect themselves against "poverty and wretchedness" by accepting an annuity. Moreover their compliance would "ensure the remainder of their wide extended nation forever."

The Creeks also presented a list of depredations and pointed to the unavenged murders of Cornell and others of their people. They complained that the Cumberland settlers were destroying their game and that the Georgians had penetrated to the Ocmulgee and were cutting cedars on that stream. They had a new grievance in the development of a third frontier; for settlers were coming by way of the Gulf and clearing land, cultivating fields, and building houses on the Tombigbee and the Alabama. This was a portentous circumstance; the Creeks were being hemmed in on three sides by settlements, and the Choctaws lay on their western border. It was apparent, however, that they had suffered encroachments with comparative meekness since the Treaty of Colerain. Hawkins and the chiefs had done their best to restrain the warriors. Since they had inaugurated their new government they had put one of their men to death for the unprovoked—but not fatal—scalping of a white woman, and whipped twenty-five for committing depredations on the border.

The chiefs expressed an awakening interest in the white man's "civilizing" agencies; some of them had tried out their plows and found them useful, they requested additional blacksmiths, and two chiefs wanted women to come to their towns and show their young women how to weave. They asked for forts in their country to protect them from the depredations of the frontiersmen, and (apparently as an afterthought) to restrain their own lawless spirits. In reporting the conference Wilkinson recommended this measure to Dearborn as an excellent device for the absorption of the land up to the forts. Truly they had no weapons against the white man's treachery.

They showed an accurate knowledge of the resources and value of the land they were asked to cede, and the prospect of an agreement seemed hopeless. As the days dragged on past their planting time, they became increasingly anxious to return home. Eufaula Harjo said, "I have to regret that our women, with the hoes, are behind us; that they and their children are likely to have poverty and hunger for their lot. . . . I think I have done all in my power to save my land. I want in three days, at farthest, to try to set out, that we may not entirely lose our crops, and all suffer with hunger."

Finally to the surprise of the Federal commissioners the chiefs suddenly held a private council, decided what land to sell, and sold it quickly without bargaining. They ceded the Altamaha tract and a portion of the land lying between the Oconee and the Ocmulgee. The United States agreed to pay them a perpetual annuity of $3,000; salaries totaling $1,000 yearly for ten years to the chiefs who should administer the government; goods valued at $10,000, which were distributed at the council; an appropriation of $10,000 to satisfy debts due the United States factory from Creeks and whites living among the Creeks; a sum of $5,000 to satisfy claims for property taken by Creeks from United States citizens subsequent to the Treaty of Colerain; and two additional blacksmith shops for a three-year period. The chiefs also prepared a "talk" to the Seminoles, asking them to end their warfare against the Spanish, and sent it by trusted messengers. Bowles was subsequently captured at Tuskegee and turned over to the Spanish officials. This time he remained in Morro Castle until he died.

The year that this treaty was signed Congress strengthened the Indian Intercourse Acts against trespassing on Indian land. The same year an agreement of great import to the Creeks was made between Georgia and the United States. The Federal government purchased the state's claim to all the territory embraced by the present Alabama and Mississippi, except that portion lying south of the international boundary, and agreed to extinguish for the benefit of Georgia the Indian title to all land within the present limits of the state as soon as it could be done "peaceably and upon favorable terms." Dearborn was optimistic about securing these "favorable terms," for when he reported his Creek cession to Congress he stated that he expected to get more land from the same tribe before the end of 1803.

President Jefferson appointed William C. C. Claiborne as governor of the territory relinquished by Georgia, and settlers began to flock in. The purchase of Louisiana from Napoleon in 1803 increased this southwestern movement. In most cases these people settled beyond the Creek country, but they threatened the Creeks and their Choctaw neighbors from a new frontier along the Mississippi. Settlers also occupied the region along the Gulf south of the parallel of 31°, and this territory was soon wrested from Spain. The next demand was for a Federal road across the Creek country for the convenience of these settlers on their southern frontier.[1]

In 1805 the Federal officials called a picked delegation of chiefs to Washington and secured another treaty. The remainder of the Oconee-Ocmulgee tract was ceded to Georgia, and the United States obtained permission to construct a horse path from the Oc-

[1] Pickett, *History of Alabama*, 462-71; *American State Papers, Indian Affairs*, I, 651, 678-83, 853; Kappler, *Laws and Treaties*, II, 58 f.

mulgee to the Alabama, with the right to regulate the inns and ferries and the conduct of travelers along the trail. One of the signers of this treaty was young William McIntosh, the son of a roistering Scot and a fullblood woman of Coweta. He was soon to rise to an unhappy eminence among the Creeks.

The highway was laid out by a detachment of Federal troops. It was constantly crowded from end to end by emigrants hastening to the magic West; and the inevitable quarrels resulted over the mutual depredations of lawless travelers and the irresponsible element among the Creeks. The Secretary of War next instructed Hawkins to secure permission for the Tennessee settlers to navigate the Coosa on their way to market at Mobile. In 1811 the Creeks considered this proposition in council. The irreconcilable Opothle Micco had become the speaker of the nation, and it was he who announced their decision:

"I am glad the President has asked us without doing it first—we must know and I know we have some young people and they will mix to the disadvantage of one another—I have a little path here that the white people makes use of and my people are so mischievous that I have continued complaints of my people interrupting of them you ask in addition a water path and road to the right of this If we give it it will be much worse that way than this—I have a large family of people in the Country and cannot govern all so as to preserve a good understanding—what land we have left is but large enough to live and walk on. The officers must not be going through our lands to hunt paths I spoke last summer to you Col. Hawkins and to the President about paths through our Country I told you no, and the President no ... the great god made us and the lands for us to walk on. I hope the great father our President will feel for us and pay attention—we hope he will pity us and not take from us our rights—when friends ask for property we must tell him straight words—if he asks for the waters of Coosa or by land my Chiefs and warriors now present will never say yes—I hope it will never be mentioned to us again—"

But Hawkins did mention it two years later—April 24, 1813. He made his request of Alexander Cornell, who was still his interpreter and assistant agent; William McIntosh, who was by that time the speaker of the Lower Towns; and Big Warrior (Tusten-nuggee Thlocco) of Tuckabatchee, the speaker of the Upper Towns. These leaders were earnestly trying to keep the peace, but they were not subservient to Hawkins. They answered that they had recently killed some of their people for murdering settlers, and like Opothle Micco they declined to increase the occasion for friction.[2]

Neither Hawkins nor these chiefs perceived that the Creeks were in the midst of the greatest catastrophe in their history—the terrible Red Stick War of 1813–14. Tecumseh had been in their country preaching his pan-Indian crusade; and among his converts was Menawa, the second chief of the Okfuskee towns, a mixed blood who had won an enviable reputation for his raids on the Cumberland frontier. Now he owned great herds of live stock, operated a store, and carried on an important fur trade with Pensacola. Tecumseh had sought him out and enlisted his support when he came to the Creek country in 1811, and other Creeks had been swayed by the appeals of this Northern visitor, who had a special relationship with their people.

It is said that the parents of this great Shawnee were born at Sauvanogee, a Shawnee town on the Tallapoosa, which was at one time a member of the Confederacy. They removed to the Ohio region, and Tecumseh was born in the North, but after the friendly Indian manner he had made long visits to the Creeks and had joined in their hunts and festivals. He had greatly distinguished himself in the Shawnee wars against the United States and was no less admired for the zeal of his ceremonial observances. When he conceived his great project of uniting all the Indians to stand in the strength of their primitive customs against the encroachments of the white man, he began to visit the Creeks, urging them with all the force of his passionate eloquence to enlist in the cause. He taught them the "Dance of the Lakes," using his magic Red Stick that would point out the direction of his enemies and confound and overwhelm them. Creek converts accompanied him to the North and returned to their country to teach their people the use of the new incantations. When war broke out between the United States and England

[2] *American State Papers, Indian Affairs,* I, 840-43; Kappler, *Laws and Treaties,* II, 85 f.; Pickett, *History of Alabama,* 476-80, 510; United States Archives, Division of Department of the Interior, Office of Indian Affairs, Original Incoming Letters, Creek—Chattuck-fau-Co Hoboheithlee Micco, May 15, 1811.

in 1812, he was able to promise the mundane assistance of British guns and military support.

The Creeks were deeply stirred by the dramatic power of his appeal. Eyewitnesses have described one of these occasions when Hawkins had called the Creeks in council at Tuckabatchee in the fall of 1811. The news had spread abroad that Tecumseh would be there, and it is said that five thousand people from all parts of the nation crowded the great war capital. Hawkins delivered his usual report and recommendations to the council. At the conclusion of his address Tecumseh and his Shawnees marched into the square. Their painted bodies were entirely naked except for their breech-clouts and ornaments, eagle feathers rose defiantly from their heads, and buffalo tails stood up from bands around their arms and streamed behind them from their belts. They exchanged civilities with the chiefs and seated themselves in silence. Every day they entered in this manner, but every day Tecumseh delayed his "talk."

Finally after eight days Hawkins finished his business and departed for the agency at Coweta, confident that the Creeks would not break their peace with the United States. That night a great council was held in the chokofa, and Tecumseh delivered his message. He urged his hearers to destroy their live stock, abandon their plows and looms, and return to the old ways. The white man would turn their beautiful forests into fields, muddy their clear streams, and reduce them to slavery. The king of England would help them to expel these enemies. Those who joined in this holy war would be invulnerable; the unseen powers would lead the white men into quagmires and drive them back to the Savannah.

The friendly chiefs tried to combat his influence, but everywhere he went he made converts. The supernatural forces seemed to be on his side—a comet, a shower of meteors, even an earthquake. The Creeks never forgot the last of these portents. He had said that when he returned to the North, he would stamp his foot and the earth would tremble. Later when the houses began to shake and the pottery knocked together, only a skeptic could have doubted. The sequence of these events is uncertain, but with the tendency of primitive people to run dates together the Creeks soon believed that the signs had appeared in exact fulfillment of his predictions.

The venerable Opothle Micco became the leader of the hostiles. The disaffection spread through the Upper Creek country. The war began in February of 1813 when a small party on the way back from a conference with Tecumseh killed seven white families near the mouth of the Ohio. Possibly two or three others were killed on the Tennessee and Georgia frontiers. Tennessee immediately took steps to call out ten thousand militiamen to "exterminate the Creek nation." Hawkins told the chiefs they could avert destruction only by punishing the murderers. Big Warrior dreaded the conflict with his own people, but he and McIntosh sent a party and killed about eleven of the offending warriors. This summary law enforcement took place during April 16-26, 1813, and it was to these events that the chiefs referred when they refused to grant the navigation of the Coosa. But it is plain that they considered the incident closed and were wholly unprepared for the conflagration that followed.

The hostiles began to kill the members of the enforcement party, and they threatened to kill Big Warrior and Tustennuggee Hopoie, the son of Efa Harjo.[3] Apparently the Alabamas first took the war talk, and the red clubs traveled from town to town and bundles of red sticks set the day for a general attack. The squares vibrated to the wild rhythm of the Dance of the Lakes, and the air was filled with incantations and portents of miracles to come. The war party began to kill the live stock and fowls and destroy the industrial implements of the progressives. By the middle of the summer the civil war that the whites had tried so many years to ignite was sweeping over the Creek country.

The Red Stick party was in the minority. Most of the Lower Creeks remained friendly to the United States, and they began to ask Hawkins for ammunition to put down the hostiles. The Upper Towns were more evenly divided. Tuckabatchee and Kialigee tried to remain neutral, and the Red Sticks attacked and completely destroyed those ancient settlements. It was a new experience for the Creeks when the unwalled towns that had rested so many years in proud security from the attacks of alien enemies began to

[3] It will be remembered that Efa Harjo had died the year before.

fall before the ravages of civil war. The Tuckabatchees hastily buried their sacred plates and with the Kialigees fled to Coweta.

Menawa immediately joined the hostiles and became one of their ablest leaders. The McGillivray family like many others was divided; but William Weatherford or Red Eagle (Lumhe Chati), the son of a white trader and Alexander's sister Sehoy, cast his lot with the Red Sticks. Resolute, daring, honorable in his fierce way, his name has passed into a legend. William McIntosh and Timpoochee Barnard (Barnett), the son of a white trader and a Euchee woman, became active allies of the white men.

The Red Sticks made their first concerted attack on the settlements August 30, 1813, when Weatherford and several hundred followers fell upon Fort Mims, a few miles above Mobile. The place was crowded with men, women, and children who had come from their exposed plantations for protection. Owing to the criminal negligence of the commander the attack was a complete surprise. The yelling warriors rushed in through the open gate, and when the savage din died down, 107 soldiers, 160 civilians, and 100 negroes were lying dead, and their bloody scalps were dangling from the belts of their exulting foes. Seventeen or eighteen people managed to escape. They spread the alarm throughout the countryside, and within a short time the river was covered with boats as the settlers streamed from their homes and sped down the river to Mobile. The long dreaded Creek war had at last struck. It must be counted to the success of the white man's tortuous diplomacy that it was only a minority faction of a distracted and weakened people that set itself to check the growing power of the young Republic.

When the news of Fort Mims spread through the settlements, the rage of the white men knew no bounds. Tennessee raised a large force under Andrew Jackson and another body of militia under James White. While these invaded the Creek country from the north, the Georgia volunteers under John Floyd attacked from the east, and Federal troops came in from the south. Friendly Creeks served in these armies, and did most of the fighting in some of the battles. The Choctaws, who had steadfastly rejected the appeal of Tecumseh, also furnished a large body of warriors under the great

Pushmataha; and a few Cherokees joined the Tennessee volunteers.

These invasions of the Creek country took place during the winter of 1813-14. The Creeks, who had known only the quick foray against the enemy and the triumphant retreat to their invincible towns, were now subjected to a pitiless extermination in the heart of their own country. In most cases they stood with desperate courage and fought to the death, neither expecting nor asking quarter.

White went against the spreading villages that comprised Hillabee Town, routed the defenders in a stubborn fight, and burned the houses. Later Jackson defeated the surviving Hillabee warriors and other Creeks in a furious battle at Talledaga Town. Floyd and his Georgia militia, accompanied by McIntosh with the Cowetas and Tustennuggee Hopoie with the Tuckabatchees, found the warriors of eight towns assembled at Artussee. Here on this "beloved ground," dedicated from ancient times to the sacred arts of war, the Red Sticks believed they would be invulnerable. But no miracle occurred to confound the white man, and they were finally routed. Floyd burned Artussee and Tallasi and retreated hastily from the enemy country. He estimated that he had destroyed four hundred houses, "some of a superior order for the dwelling of savages, and filled with valuable articles." Later the Red Sticks rallied and attacked his camp, but with the help of Barnard and his Euchees he managed to repulse them. Brigadier General F. L. Claiborne with Federal troops and Pushmataha and his Choctaws marched up the Alabama to the towns of the Koasatas and Alabamas. Here the Red Sticks under Weatherford had built a stronghold since the beginning of the war and stocked it with provisions. They had named it Holy Ground, and again they expected their desperate valor to be reinforced by supernatural agencies, but again they were defeated.

The final catastrophe came March 27 at Horseshoe Bend on the Tallapoosa. Here Menawa and about a thousand Red Sticks from Okfuskee, Nuyaka, Hillabee, Fish Pond (Thlothlagalga), Upper Eufaula, and other towns had taken a strong position on a peninsula almost surrounded by the river and built a breastwork of logs across the narrow isthmus. Their women and children they had carefully hidden in a swamp down the stream. Jackson with his frontiersmen and some supporting Cherokees and Creeks attacked this stronghold. The defenders fought like demons until they were annihilated. Toward the last a few tried to escape by swimming, but Jackson's Indian allies cut them off before they reached the bank. When the slaughter was over, 557 dead warriors lay in heaps on the peninsula and an unknown number had fallen into the reddened stream. Jackson believed that not more than ten had escaped, but seventy miserable survivors, of whom all but one were wounded, finally dragged their way to the women's hiding place. Jackson was not boasting when he reported that the power of the Creeks was broken forever.

Menawa was sorely wounded, but he managed to hide under water, and when night came he painfully made his way to the swamp where the women lay hidden. There he and his shattered warriors held a "silent council" for three days, neither eating nor drinking nor permitting their wounds to be dressed. At the end of that time they decided to return home and submit to the victors, every man making his separate peace. The women then dressed their wounds and they strengthened themselves with food and dispersed as soon as they were able to travel. Menawa did not recover sufficiently to leave the retreat until after the close of the war.

So strong was the faith of the Red Sticks in the supernatural forces they had invoked, that now after the lapse of a century and a quarter they remember these tragic events not in the light of their suffering and defeat but in terms of miraculous escapes. As a present-day Creek expresses it, "those old Indian chiefs and warriors knew how to make the bullet from a gun go around them or glance from them. If they were wounded they blamed themselves for neglecting their medicine, although they were never wounded much." The Tuckabatchees, on the other side, preserved a legend of their deliverance by tie snakes. For three days the Red Sticks besieged their square, shooting so furiously that the arrows lay three inches deep over the ground, but nobody was injured. Finally the chief sent his fourteen-year-old son up the river for help, but the lad was dragged under water by the tie snakes and carried to a square where the posts and seats, even the floor of the square itself, were made of the living reptiles. The chief of these friendly beings promised to aid the beleaguered town, instructed the boy in the necessary formulas, and sent him back to his father. The Tucka-batchees followed his directions, and in the morning they found their enemies lying apparently dead about the town. When they ventured out to investigate, they found them alive but helpless, bound hand and foot by tie snakes.

At the time, however, the spirit of the Red Sticks was completely broken. By May they were coming down the Alabama and passing through the white settlements on their way to Pensacola. The British, whose controlling influence in Spain at that time will be remembered by the historian, soon landed a large force in Florida and began to arm the refugees. From this retreat about one thousand sent a despairing message to Hawkins that they would never surrender. "We have lost our country and retreated to the sea side, where we will fight till we are all destroyed." This challenge was not accepted, and they continued to live in Florida, where they formed an important element in the Seminole tribe.

By July, however, Hawkins was able to report that hundreds of the Red Sticks *had* surrendered. The story of Weatherford's submission has become famous in Alabama legend. He came into Jackson's camp, walked directly up to that dauntless Indian-fighter and said, "I am alone; do with me as you please; I have done the white people all the harm in my power, and, if I had any warriors left, I would still fight and contend to the last." "Old Hickory" was moved to generous admiration; he restrained his rough soldiers, who thirsted to avenge the blood of Fort Mims, and treated the fallen warrior with all respect as a prisoner of war. The McGillivray descendants still hold a tradition that while the whole frontier clamored for Weatherford's blood, he was kept hidden for several months in Jackson's home. He afterwards returned to Alabama and became a prosperous plantation owner, dying peaceably in 1824.

In August, Andrew Jackson summoned thirty-five chiefs to Fort Jackson, on the long-abandoned site of Fort Toulouse, and dictated a treaty of peace. All but one or two of this group belonged to the majority party that had fought so valiantly for the United States throughout the war, but they were required to subscribe to a confession of war guilt and to cede twenty-two million acres of land as an indemnity. The Upper Creeks, including the Red Sticks, were permitted to retain the territory conquered by the United States between the Coosa and Tallapoosa, but the ceded territory comprised an immense tract in central Alabama and a wide belt stretching across southern Alabama and Georgia. Jackson took the land in southern Georgia upon his own initiative as a military measure to cut the Creeks off from the Spanish by a wide belt of white settlement and to make a permanent separation between them and the Seminoles. When the friendly Creeks who lived in the region protested that they had fought in his army, he explained that he had taken it to balance the land left to the Red Sticks, whose whole territory had been subject to forfeiture.

The United States made the usual guarantee of the contracted domain remaining to the tribe, but the Creeks gave permission for the establishment of military and trading posts and roads and for the navigation of the rivers. The tribe received no payment for the ceded land, but the friendly faction did obtain partial compensation for their immense property losses at the hands of the Red Sticks. Federal agents estimated the damages at $195,417.90; and Congress made an appropriation of $85,000 in 1817, and the remainder was paid in 1853. During the next forty years the Federal treasury realized more than eleven and a quarter million dollars from the sale of the ceded land, and there was the immeasurably greater gain of individual United States citizens who were using these immense natural resources. From the white man's point of view it had been a very satisfactory war.

The United States and England made peace before the end of 1814. The treaty provided that both countries would make peace with all the Indian nations with whom they might be at war and restore "all the possessions, rights and privileges" which they had enjoyed in 1811. This provision hardly applied to the Creeks, who had already made their hard peace with the United States; but Colonel Edward Nicholls, a British adventurer, collected a motley force of British, Indians, and runaway negroes at Pensacola and urged the Creeks to resist the land cession. The Creeks did for a time prevent the survey of the new boundary, the settlement of the ceded tract, and the passage of travelers through their country. By the fall of 1815 four thousand soldiers were stationed there to keep them in order, but no outbreak occurred and they sullenly submitted. The next year McIntosh with five hundred Creek recruits joined a United States force and attacked a fort where Nicholls had established himself with about three hundred negroes on Apalachicola Bay. They killed about one hundred negroes and captured the rest and turned them over to their masters in Georgia.[4]

After the Red Stick War the Creeks submitted to wrong in silence, but they were a dispirited and broken people. Their isolation had ended. White people were crowding them from all sides and their trails were filled with emigrants on their way to the ceded land. The scattered refugees gradually stole back and tried to rebuild their ruined homes, but the towns never regained their former importance. With the destruction of game and the disintegration of community agriculture, an increasing amount of labor and hardship fell upon the women and they became bent and worn from unrelieved drudgery. Drunkenness had been apparent in the Creek country since the beginning of the century, but with the general apathy and hopelessness and the greater opportunity to secure intoxicants, it became a destructive influence. A few individuals, mostly mixed bloods, began to establish farms after the white man's custom, and some of the chiefs entered into partnership with white men to establish inns along the trails, but the tribe as a whole was in a state of economic degradation. It was impossible for the Creeks to return to the old way of living, and with a few exceptions they had not learned any other.

They finally gave a grudging consent to the establishment of schools in their country. They had been approached many times since the council at Colerain, but their prejudice against the white man's institutions still held. The Brethren's Society in North Amer-

[4] *Niles' Weekly Register*, III-XI (1812-16); Draper Collection, Tecumseh Manuscripts, Phillips Collection, University of Oklahoma; Pickett, *History of Alabama*, 510-14; WPA Project S-149, Sebron Miller; *American State Papers, Indian Affairs*, I, 837-61; Kappler, *Laws and Treaties*, II, 107-10; Thomas L. McKenney and James Hall, *History of the Indian Tribes of North America*, I, 106-11; 32 Cong., 2 sess., *House Misc. Doc. No. 10;* J. J. Methvin, "Legend of the Tie Snakes," *Chronicles of Oklahoma*, V (1927); Grant Foreman, Copies of Manuscripts and Newspapers, article by Marion Elisha Tarvin.

ica, with the cordial encouragement of Hawkins, had even established a mission station on the Flint in 1803, but the Indians had
shown little interest and the work had been abandoned because
of the war. But in 1822 the Baptists secured Big Warrior's consent to
the establishment of a school, provided they would refrain from
preaching to adults; and they began their work at a station later
called Withington at Tuckabatchee. The same year the South Carolina Conference of the Methodist Church secured similar permission from a council, and the Asbury Manual Labor School was
accordingly established near Fort Mitchell on the Alabama side of
the Chattahoochee. It was difficult to interest the carefree young
savages in the manual labor features of these institutions, and the
adults regarded the venture with distrust. "Their firm attachment
to the customs of their fathers, their extreme mental apathy and
physical indolence, their mutual quarrels and bitter animosities ...
the disastrous influence of liquor-dealers and other designing
whites, and the depressing state of their relations with the Government of the United States"—all made the work of the missionaries
difficult and uncertain. A few of the leading chiefs, however, subscribed in theory to the principle that only the acquisition of the
white man's culture would save the Creeks from extinction.

Big Warrior was still the head chief, or speaker, of the Upper
Towns, but Little Prince, an aged chief of Broken Arrow, was recognized as speaker of the nation. McIntosh as head chief of Coweta was
the most influential leader of the Lower Towns, but he was subordi-
nate to Little Prince. Broken Arrow, as the residence of the speaker,
had succeeded Tuckabatchee as the meeting place of the Council. Various laws and regulations that the Creeks had been persuaded to
accept during the preceding generation were reduced to writing by
McIntosh and formally adopted by the Council in 1817. This code
became the basis of Creek law. Stealing had increased to the extent
that it was a recognized crime; it was punished by whipping for the
first offense, loss of ears for the second, and death for the third.
Adultery was still punished by the clan. Murder was punished by
death; private retaliation was gradually dying out, and the town
officials held a brief trial and imposed the penalty immediately.
Murderers of white people were punished in the same summary

manner, for the Indians did not wish to repeat the mistake of the Red Stick War.

White people continued to murder Indians with impunity. The Territory of Mississippi, comprising the present states of Mississippi and Alabama, in its law code did not admit the testimony of an Indian against a white man. In 1817 the Territory of Alabama was created with its present limits, including the Upper, and part of the Lower, Creek towns, and in 1819 it was admitted to the Union. The new state never developed the savage hostility to the Creeks that had been shown by Georgia, but local prejudice always ran too high to punish a white man for a crime against an Indian.[5]

The white man's desire for land increased with this rapid development of the country. The first cession was obtained in 1818 by Daniel B. Mitchell, who became agent when Hawkins died soon after the Red Stick War. The Creeks gave up two small tracts in Georgia—one between the Apalachee and the Chattahoochee, and the other south of the Ocmulgee and the Altamaha—and they received $120,000 over a ten-year period. In 1821 by the Treaty of Indian Springs they ceded five million acres in Georgia between the Ocmulgee and the Flint for $450,000, of which $200,000 was paid to them over a period of fourteen years, and the remainder was reserved to pay depredation claims of citizens of Georgia. State commissioners had been present at the negotiations and had presented a bill for the whole $450,000, even charging the Creeks for all negroes carried off by the British in the late war and all who had taken refuge with the Seminoles. The claims were audited by a special commission appointed by President Monroe. No allowance was made for counterclaims, claims based on the three fraudulent treaties were freely admitted, and the hearings were held in the interior of Georgia with no opportunity for the Creeks to be present. Even so, a considerable balance of the $250,000 was left after all the claims had been allowed; but nothing was said about return-

[5] *Niles' Weekly Register*, XI (1816), 142; XII (1817), 399; XVI (1819), supplement, 100 f.; XXI (1821), 272; XXII (1822), 361; XXXIV (1828), 379 f. Foreman, *A Traveler in Indian Territory*, 149; Joseph Tracy and others, *History of American Missions to the Heathen from Their Commencement to the Present Time*, 394 f., 537; McKenney and Hall, *Indian Tribes of North America*, I, 281 f.; Holmes, *Missions of the United Brethren*, 216; Adam Hodgson, *Letters from North America*, I, 117-39; *Indian Journal*, August 7, 1878.

ing this amount to the Indians, and it remained in the Federal treasury.[6]

McIntosh was the spokesman of the Indians during the negotiation of this treaty. He argued ably against the unconscionable padding of the claims, but in other respects he was subservient to the white man. His prestige at this time was very high; the whites appreciated his services in the Red Stick War, and his own people were inclined to follow the leader who had known how to choose the winning side.

The white men had become dissatisfied with the gradual absorption of Indian land, and the idea of removing the tribes to the West was steadily gaining favor. In 1817 the Cherokees had purchased a tract of land in this wild region beyond the Mississippi, and a number of their people had emigrated. The remainder under the leadership of the great John Ross were resisting the attempt to seize the rest of their country and force them to that remote frontier. McIntosh now began to advocate an emigration policy for the Creeks. He was probably attracted by the possibilities of this unspoiled region, but additional light is thrown on his motives by a letter he wrote to Ross in 1823 suggesting that bribes would be paid to the Cherokee leaders for land cessions.[7] Ross proved to be incorruptible, but McIntosh continued in a receptive mood and was greatly commended by the frontiersmen for his "progressive" policy. His white admirers did not realize that the Creeks had passed a law in 1811, upon the advice of McIntosh himself, imposing the death penalty upon any chief who should subscribe to an unauthorized sale of land.

From this time on, Cherokee influence was noticeable in the Creek councils. Both tribes were fighting the same battle. The Cherokees hoped to strengthen their own position by united action, and the bewildered Creeks were ready to accept advice from a tribe that had begun to acquire the white man's useful learning. The old way of trusting in dancing and incantations and miracles had brought disaster; perhaps the Cherokee way was best—to learn the

[6] Kappler, *Laws and Treaties*, II, 155 f., 195-97; 20 Cong., 2 sess., *House Ex. Doc. No. 91*; 30 Cong., 1 sess., *Sen. Misc. Doc. No. 147.*

[7] Annie Heloise Abel, *The American Indian as Slaveholder and Secessionist*, 236-37 n.

white man's arts and thus strengthen themselves to hold their ancient heritage.

In May, 1824, the Creeks met in council at Tuckabatchee and drew up a careful declaration of future policy. It was probably reduced to writing by John Ridge and David Vann, young educated Cherokees, but there is little doubt that it represented the considered judgment of the council. It began by a nostalgic reference to the past greatness of the Confederacy, when the Creeks had "never met a nation that was equal to us in warfare." But "our crazy young men" had gone to war against the United States, and defeat and land cessions had resulted. They could support themselves in their restricted limits only by agriculture and civilization, and they resolved to acquire these skills and remain in their ancestral homes; "and, on a deep and solemn reflection, we have, with one voice, [decided] to follow the pattern of the Cherokees, and on no account whatever will we consent to sell one foot of our land, neither by exchange or otherwise. This talk is not only to last during the life of the present chiefs, but to their descendants after them." As for the white man's system of individual ownership, "we want the talk to be straight, that the land is to remain as it is, in common, and as it always has been." This declaration "is to remain for our rising generation to see, that they may know what their fathers said before them. We do most earnestly enjoin on our rising generation to be honest and to do harm to no person whatsoever, but to remain in honesty and in industry. We recommend that our laws may be kept in writing, in order that our chiefs may keep in mind what laws have been passed. We are Creeks; we have a great many chiefs and head men but, be they ever so great, they must all abide by the laws. We have guns and ropes: and if any of our people should break these laws, those guns and ropes are to be their end." Finally they appealed to the white people "to treat us with tenderness and justice." The declaration was signed by Little Prince, Big Warrior, and twelve other leading chiefs.[8]

Later in the year John Crowell, who had succeeded Mitchell as agent, summoned the chiefs to meet United States commissioners

[8] *Niles' Weekly Register*, XXVII (1824), 225.

at Broken Arrow to make a new land cession. The leading chiefs then assembled at Pole Cat Springs. They reënacted the law against unauthorized land sales, and in a style unmistakably Cherokee they drew up an appeal to the conscience of "our christian brothers, the white people" against attempts to dispossess them. This protest was signed by Little Prince, Big Warrior, and fifteen others. Among the latter were Etommee Tustennuggee, of Coweta, and Opothle Yahola, a brilliant young Tuckabatchee, said to have been a son of David Cornell.

Duncan G. Campbell and James Meriwether were appointed as the Federal commissioners. They held their council at Broken Arrow in December and received an unqualified refusal. They then summoned a few picked chiefs to meet them in February at Indian Springs, which was near the home of McIntosh. McIntosh, of course, was present, and so was Etommee Tustennuggee, whom he had won to his support; all the other leaders were absent except Opothle Yahola, whom Big Warrior had sent to watch the proceedings. When the draft treaty was presented, Opothle Yahola solemnly warned McIntosh and the commissioners of his fate should he "sign that paper." The next morning he left the council and returned to Tuckabatchee. But the commissioners promised the protection of the United States, and the names of McIntosh, Etommee Tustennuggee, thirteen lesser chiefs, and about fifty men of no rank whatever were affixed to the fatal document. It purported to carry the assent of all the chiefs of the nation except those of Tuckabatchee to a cession of all the Creek land in Georgia and a portion in Alabama in exchange for a tract in the present state of Oklahoma. Two days later a supplementary treaty was signed by which McIntosh was to be paid $25,000 for his residence and 1,640 acres of improved land in the ceded tract.

Crowell had tried to protect the Creeks from the treachery of the commissioners, and he protested to the President against the ratification of the "treaty." Probably John Quincy Adams, who came into office a few days later, did not even see this protest; he accepted the statements of Campbell and Meriwether that the treaty was genuine and submitted it to the Senate. The ratification was proclaimed March 7.

In the meantime the Creeks held a council, pronounced a sentence of death against McIntosh and his associates, and directed Menawa to execute the law. Menawa collected one hundred Okfuskees and proceeded stealthily to the home of McIntosh. They surrounded the house just before daylight. The doomed chief and his family, two white men, and Etommee Tustennuggee were inside. Menawa called to the white men and the women and children to leave the building. They passed through the cordon unhurt, and Chilly, the son of McIntosh, who also had signed the treaty, managed to escape because of his light complexion. When the two guilty chiefs were left alone, the avengers set fire to the house and shot them as they came out of the door. They also shot the cattle and destroyed the other property of McIntosh. About noon of the same day Sam Hawkins, a mixed blood who had married the daughter of McIntosh, was hanged in the square of one of the Lower Towns. The next day Ben Hawkins, his brother, who was also a son-in-law of McIntosh and a member of the treaty party, was shot and wounded by a party of Hillabees; but he managed to escape, and he settled eventually with a band of Cherokees in Texas.

Chilly McIntosh and other adherents of the fallen chief fled for protection to the settlements. The Georgians could find no words strong enough for their condemnation of the "atrocious murders," and they appealed to the governor and the President to protect them against a Creek invasion. But the chiefs in council issued a formal statement through Crowell, explaining that they were only enforcing their own laws and that no white person would be harmed. For their own guidance they resolved to refuse all payments under the illegal treaty, to refrain from war against "those who should be sent to take their land from them," and to "die at the corners of their fences, ... rather than ... abandon the land of their forefathers." Except for the punishment of the three apostates, no disturbance of any sort took place, and travelers continued to follow the trails through their country with perfect safety.

Meanwhile Chilly McIntosh had hurried to Washington to lay his case before James Barbour, Secretary of War. He urged the punishment of his father's "murderers," and he tried to get control of the annuity due under former treaties, saying that his party needed it to pay the expenses of removal to the West. Special agents sent out by President Adams investigated the whole affair and persuaded the Creeks to declare an amnesty and agree to reimburse the McIntosh family for its property losses. When Adams understood the fraud practiced in the negotiations, he decided to make a new treaty.

An authorized Creek delegation was then called to Washington in the fall. Big Warrior had recently died, and Opothle Yahola, Menawa, and Charles Cornell, a chief who had actively opposed land cessions, headed the party, and somewhat to Barbour's displeasure, John Ridge and David Vann served as secretaries. A new treaty was signed the following January. The chiefs had refused to negotiate until the McIntosh treaty was specifically repudiated, and they did secure improvements in the manner of execution, but in view of the temper of the Georgians they had no choice but to accept a land cession. They surrendered all of their land in Georgia but a small tract north of the Chattahoochee for $217,600 in cash and a perpetual annuity of $20,000. They promised to make financial restitution to the McIntosh party according to the findings of a special Federal agent. The United States undertook to finance the removal of the McIntosh faction, subsist them for one year in the West, and pay them $100,000 or less according to the size of the emigrating party. The Creeks were to give possession of the ceded land by January 1, 1827, and the United States as usual guaranteed their remaining territory against aggression.

The legislatures of Georgia and Alabama protested against the ratification of this treaty, and the Senate withheld its consent. Finally Barbour induced the chiefs to surrender the tract north of the Chattahoochee for an additional $30,000, and the Senate then gave its approval. This was supposed to complete the expulsion of the Creeks from Georgia, but the western boundary of the state had never been surveyed, and it was afterwards found that a small area had been omitted. When Congress took up the appropriation of the cash payment another bitter fight arose. It had become known that $159,700 of the amount was to be distributed as follows: to each of the two Cherokee secretaries, $15,000, and to Major Ridge, a prominent Cherokee, the father of John, $10,000; to Opothle Yahola,

Menawa, and Charles Cornell, $10,000 each, to Mad Wolf, $6,000, and $5,000 each to the seven remaining members of the delegation; and to chiefs who were not present, amounts varying from $10,000, the share of Little Prince, to $1,000.

The righteous indignation of the Georgia delegation against such "fraud" and "villainy" was increased by their chagrin over the repudiation of the McIntosh treaty, but it was brought to the boiling point by their hatred of all Cherokees. Congress finally made the appropriation with the qualification that the $217,600 should be paid "under the direction of the Secretary of War, in a full council of the nation convened upon notice for that purpose." This safeguard probably did not prevent the contemplated division. The chiefs had come to expect these special grants as the prerogative of office; and they used the money to purchase adherents, to carry on the legitimate expenses of their government, and to feed and clothe the needy members of their tribe. They had never developed a sense of accountability in the handling of public funds, but they did feel a patriarchal responsibility for the welfare of their people. As for the employment of the young Cherokees, they really felt the need of educated agents of their own race; for the most benevolent of Federal officials was as much their enemy as the most brutal frontiersman on the border.

The annuities, as usual, were under the control of the agent. By citing Ridge and Vann, whom he privately detested, as shining examples of educated Indians, Barbour had already secured the consent of the chiefs to spend $24,000 of the money they received from their supplementary cession, to educate Creek boys at the so-called Choctaw Academy in Kentucky.[9]

Many disputes followed the attempt to carry out the treaty. George M. Troup, a virulent Indian-hater, who ironically enough was a distant relative of McIntosh, was governor of Georgia. Obviously the state had attained its object, but Troup felt compelled to uphold the sanctity of the former negotiations by overbearing conduct toward the Creeks and loud threats against the United

[9] *Ibid.*, XXVII-XXX (1824-26); McKenney and Hall, *Indian Tribes of North America*, I, 281-85, 308-12; United States, *Statutes at Large*, IV, 187 f., 191; Kappler, *Laws and Treaties*, II, 214-17, 264-68, 1034 f.

States. But apparently his boastful language was intended mainly to impress his constituents, and the details of the cession were conducted by President Adams under the legal agreement.

Much discontent developed also among the Creeks. It irked them to see the agency moved to their restricted limits west of the Chattahoochee and to observe the granting of licenses for stores and public houses within their nation. They had never understood the commitments they had made regarding the reparations to the McIntosh party. When the special agent came out to assess the damages, they "explained the law" under which the chiefs had been punished, and naïvely they supposed that ended the matter. They expressed their perplexity by confused complaints against Crowell penned by John Ridge, and contradictory expressions of confidence in the agent.

The trouble came to a head when Crowell called them in council at Wetumka Town in June, 1827, to receive their annuities. When they arrived, he asked them to cede the small tract they still held in Georgia. They indignantly refused. Then they found that the indemnity to the McIntosh party had been fixed at about $25,000 and deducted from their payment. They declined to touch the rest of their money, and the council broke up in confusion. They got John Ridge to express their sentiments to Barbour—"we never expected this; and we always thought every nation had a right to administer their laws in their own way ... We thought that you very well knew the penalty was death, by our laws, if any man, without the consent of the nation, should sell any portion of our lands." They demanded control over their own finances; the agent should "pay the money over to us in full council, and let the chiefs apply it to suit the nation. ... We cannot consider our money safe in his hands; and we particularly deny his authority to acknowledge claims against our nation. Because he can very easily acknowledge bad ones." This last complaint was certainly inspired by Ridge. The Federal officials had good cause to hate this gifted Cherokee, not for his exploitation of the Creeks, but for his ability and independence.

Thomas L. McKenney, who held a position corresponding to that of the present Commissioner of Indian Affairs, visited the

Creek country in November to obtain the rest of the Georgia land. According to his own sanctimonious account he tried first to win Opothle Yahola, who was by this time the real power in the Creek government. Opothle Yahola finally consented to call a council at Tuckabatchee but, fearing that some trick would be played in the wording of a treaty unless Ridge and Vann should be present to read it, he delayed the meeting until their arrival. Then the council opened with the "disgusting" ceremony of the black drink and decided to reject McKenney's proposal. A messenger was then sent to conduct the commissioner to the assembly.

In some way he learned of the action already taken by the council. He immediately concluded that Ridge and Vann had persuaded Opothle Yahola to sell no more land until the Creeks could obtain control of their finances under a written constitution similar to one recently framed by the Cherokees; and he was equally sure that one of these young men was scheming for the office of treasurer. He decided to use these suspicions to destroy Opothle Yahola. With this intention he walked into the council and presented his offer of purchase. When his proposal was rejected by the unanimous voice of the chiefs, he "boldly disclosed" the imaginary Cherokee plot. His scheme worked, and for a time Opothle Yahola's life hung by a thread. With a final threat to appeal to Little Prince, he left the council. He found the aged chief lying on a blanket under a tree with a fire burning near and his provisions hung on a bough over his head. He related to him also the story he had constructed of the Cherokee intrigues. The old man listened without comment, and McKenney went to the agency at Fort Mitchell to spend the night. The next day Little Prince came to the agency and affixed his mark to a paper prepared by the commissioner warning the Cherokee Chief that the young men would be killed if they should attempt again to enter the Creek country. McKenney then prepared the treaty and it was subsequently accepted by the Creeks in council.

By this agreement the Creeks ceded the rest of their land in Georgia. They received $27,491 in cash, $5,000 in blankets and other goods, and $10,000 to be devoted to educational and industrial purposes. The last was to be apportioned as follows: $5,000 for Creek boys at the Choctaw Academy, $1,000 each for the Withington and

Asbury schools, $2,000 for the erection of four mills, and $1,000 for cotton cards and spinning wheels. The expulsion of the Creeks from the soil of Georgia was now complete. Less than a century had passed since they had welcomed Oglethorpe to the gracious abundance of their towns.[10]

The members of the McIntosh party meanwhile were preparing for their long journey to the West. Early in 1827 a delegation went out to explore the country, and with the assistance of a Federal agent they selected a location in what is now the eastern part of Oklahoma, near the "Three Forks" of the Arkansas, Verdigris, and Grand rivers, and close to Fort Gibson, which had been established near the mouth of the Grand in 1824. They were welcomed by the wild Osages, who inhabited that region, and by the Cherokee emigrants, and they received emblems of friendship to carry back to their people. When they returned, Crowell called a council at the Upper Creek Town of Wewoka on August 1. They made a favorable report on the land, timber, soil, game, etc., and took formal leave of their former opponents with mutual expressions of friendship and good will.

The following February 780 men, women, and children were brought up the Arkansas and Verdigris in the steamboat, *Fidelity*, and settled in their new home. About thirteen hundred had arrived before the year was over. In general they were prosperous mixed bloods, who began with their slaves to lay out plantations along the rich river valley. They suffered the losses and hardships incident to the settlement of a remote frontier, but they soon began to prosper.[11]

The less progressive inhabitants of the ceded territory crossed the Chattahoochee and joined their brethren in Alabama. An English traveler who visited the new agency at Fort Mitchell in the spring of 1828 gave an unforgettable description of "those miserable wretches who had been dislodged from their ancient territory" and

[10] 19 Cong., 2 sess., *House Ex. Doc. No. 76*; 20 Cong., 1 sess., *House Ex. Doc. No. 248*; Kappler, *Laws and Treaties*, II, 284-86; McKenney and Hall, *Indian Tribes of North America*, I, 285-92; *Acts of the General Assembly of the State of Georgia, 1826*, 227-37; *Niles' Weekly Register*, XXXI (1826), 130; XXXII (1827), *passim*.
[11] *Niles' Weekly Register*, XXXII (1827), 420; XXXIV (1828), 108. Grant Foreman, *Pioneer Days in the Early Southwest*, 69; 30 Cong., 1 sess., *Sen. Misc. Doc. No. 147*.

were "wandering about like bees whose hive has been destroyed." Crowell was distributing clothing and food, but many had starved to death.

A great contrast to these despairing refugees was presented by the enterprising settlers who hastened to occupy the territory they had abandoned. Georgia had disposed of the land by lottery in the summer of 1827, and the speculative fervor of her citizens was raised to fever pitch. A townsite on the Chattahoochee had been reserved for the future city of Columbus, and it was planned to advertise the lots to prospective buyers throughout the United States. Four months before the time set for the lot sale, this English visitor found about nine hundred people assembled on the site hoping to secure an advantage through possession. One of these "inhabitants" proudly conducted him over the "city." As they followed the "principal street"—a lane cut through the living forest—they heard anvils "ringing away merrily at every corner; while saws, axes, and hammers were seen flashing amongst the woods all around." Many of the houses were built on wheels to be moved to a permanent location as soon as the lots should be offered for sale. Another English traveler who visited the place a bare two years later found a thriving town of fifteen hundred people, three churches, a post office, several brick buildings, and many comfortable frame houses. Truly the American frontier was an irresistible force rolling on to destroy the Creeks.[12]

Events moved rapidly after the removal of the McIntosh party. By the fall of 1828 Alabama was threatening to extend her laws over the Creeks, and the Federal officials were urging them to emigrate. A delegation of four accordingly went out with an exploring party of Choctaws and Chickasaws conducted by the great Baptist missionary, Isaac McCoy. They reached the McIntosh settlement in November. McCoy had feared that the old feud would appear, but the meeting in the wilderness was pleasant to both parties. The settlers held a council and prepared a cordial message inviting the rest of their people to join them in the new land. It was estimated

---

[12] *Niles' Weekly Register*, XXXII (1827), 405; James Stuart, *Three Years in North America*, II, 130; Basil Hall, *Travels in North America in the Years 1827 and 1828*, II, 288 f.; III, 280-86.

that between two and three thousand Creeks had settled on the Verdigris by 1830.

Conditions became so disturbed in Alabama that both the Methodists and Baptists decided in 1829 to close their missions. The two schools had been conducted under discouraging conditions, and the results of their work were not apparent. In 1827 the Baptists had seen "evidence of piety" in two of their pupils—a fullblood boy whom they called John Davis, and a young girl—and had taken them into the church. Several negro slaves of the Indians had been baptized, but the Indians were so hostile that the missionaries had seen some of these converts terribly whipped for attending the services. The Methodists also reported a few Indian and colored members, and the school enrollment in 1829 was twenty or twenty-five. Among their pupils was a quiet, intelligent, ten-year-old boy from Sawokla of the Hitchitee towns. He was a member of the Checote Clan, a small clan related to the Toad People; hence he received the name of Samuel Checote.[13]

In 1829 Andrew Jackson came to the presidency with the announced intention of driving the Indians across the Mississippi. The same year the state of Alabama divided the Creek land and added it to organized counties and placed the Creeks under the jurisdiction of the local courts. This policy exactly suited Jackson's purpose, and he sent a communication to the Creeks urging them to preserve their political autonomy by removing beyond the limits of the state. The Creeks met in council in June and rejected his overtures. Their reply, as reported to the press, was probably prepared by John Ridge and placed in the mouth of an imaginary chief named Speckled Snake. It was a complete answer to Jackson's benevolent professions, and it portrayed with accuracy but with devastating sarcasm the whole history of Creek-frontier relations since the establishment of Georgia.[14]

Secretary of War Eaton had already sent General William Car-

[13] Stuart, *Three Years in North America*, II, 153 f.; Tracy, *History of American Missions*, 395, 537 f.; *Niles' Weekly Register*, XXXV (1828), 123, 151; *Missionary Herald*, XXV (1829), 41 f.; Isaac McCoy, *History of Baptist Indian Missions*, 337, 349, 366.

[14] *Niles' Weekly Register*, XXXV (1828), 123; XXXVI (1829), 182, 257 f., 274 f. *Laws of the Colonial and State Governments Relating to Indians and Indian Affairs from 1633 to 1831, inclusive*, 243 f.

roll and General John Coffee to influence the Creeks and Cherokees in favor of removal. He instructed them to conceal the official character of their mission and "to engage in this work of mercy to the Indians" by working on the chiefs privately in their homes. They were to point out the Indians' former strength and their present decline and degradation, the inability of the United States to protect them from state jurisdiction, and the fertility and opportunities of the West. If this argument should fail they were to resort to bribery. But the commissioners found the Indians aware of their official character; hence they decided "to treat them in an open and candid manner." Disturbing reports came from the Creek country that summer—rumors of secret councils, of runners to other tribes, of plans to kill Crowell, exterminate the settlers, and retire to the swamps to die. In August the chiefs issued a public appeal—again in eloquent Cherokee English—to the citizens of Georgia and Alabama; and in the fall they held a full council and voted to remain in their ancient homes and submit to the state laws.[15]

Little Prince by this time had died, and Eneah (Grease, his clan?) Micco had become the head chief of the Lower Towns. He was unalterably opposed to removal. Menawa was inclined to surrender, but he was no longer active among the Upper Creeks. Opothle Yahola, the recognized leader of the nation, opposed removal at first, but he came eventually to see that it was inevitable. Early in 1831 a delegation of the Lower Towns went to Washington and pleaded their love for their homeland, but Eaton only advised them to prepare to emigrate. In December Eneah Micco sent a list of fifteen hundred intruders who were in the Lower Creek country, laying out homesteads, etc. Eaton again advised that such evils could be remedied only by emigration. Finally Opothle Yahola and other Upper Creek leaders went to Washington and signed the famous Removal Treaty of March 24, 1832.

By this agreement the Creeks surrendered all their land in Alabama; but they were privileged to select homesteads to which they would receive patents in fee simple at the end of five years' residence, and twenty sections were to be reserved for the benefit of

[15] *Niles' Weekly Register*, XXXVI-XXXVIII (1829-30); Commissioner of Indian Affairs, *Annual Report*, 1829, 178-83.

their orphan children. They were to receive: $210,000 to be paid according to their own laws over a period of fifteen years; two blacksmith shops after their arrival in the West, and an educational annuity of $3,000 for twenty years; and $100,000, representing the value of their improvements, to be used for the payment of their debts and the relief of their destitution. The chiefs who negotiated the treaty were to receive a compensation of $16,000, and three of the Lower Creek chiefs including Eneah Micco were to be paid small salaries for life. The United States was to supply a rifle and ammunition and a blanket to every warrior who would emigrate, pay all expenses of emigration, and subsist the emigrants for one year in the West; "Provided, however, that this article shall not be construed so as to compel any Creek Indian to emigrate, but they shall be free to go or stay, as they please."

The article that the Creeks never forgot was the pledge of future autonomy: "The Creek country west of the Mississippi shall be solemnly guaranteed to the Creek Indians, nor shall any State or Territory ever have a right to pass laws for the government of such Indians, but they shall be allowed to govern themselves, so far as may be compatible with the general jurisdiction which Congress may think proper to exercise over them."[16]

Elbert Herring, who was then Commissioner of Indian Affairs, characterized the removal policy as a "magnanimous act of inter-position" to save the Indians "from approaching destruction. . . . Founded in pure and disinterested motives, may it meet the approval of heaven, by the complete attainment of its beneficent ends!" But the "beneficent ends" attained by this treaty were the white man's objectives. The Federal officials began in a leisurely way to carry out its provisions. A census was taken and for the first time the population of the tribe was ascertained; 14,142, including 445 negro slaves, were enrolled in the Upper Towns, and 8,552, including 457 slaves, in the Lower. The ceded land measured about 5,200,000 acres, of which the Indians were entitled to select about 2,187,200 acres as their individual homesteads. The survey was to be completed by the end of 1833 so that they could make their selections.

[16] Kappler, *Laws and Treaties*, II, 341-43.

The whites, of course, should have been kept off the land until these selections were made and the remainder entered into the possession of the United States to be sold to settlers; but as soon as the treaty was signed, land-grabbers flooded the Indian country. Such feeble efforts as the government made to remove these intruders were resisted by mob violence and the connivance of the local courts. These ruffians drove the Indians from their homes, burned their houses, stole their live stock, and destroyed their crops. The Indians, of course, did not understand deeds, contracts, and other legal papers, and even before they selected their allotments under the treaty, swindlers obtained contracts of sale by misrepresentation, the use of intoxicants, the misuse of notary seals on blank instruments, impersonation, forgery, and dishonest probate procedure in the courts.

The dispossessed Indians wandered about the country, hopeless and utterly demoralized. Such small sums of money as they obtained through the distribution of treaty payments they quickly spent on intoxicants. But starving and destitute as they were they still refused to leave the neighborhood of their homes. About twenty-five hundred drifted into the Cherokee settlements in Georgia and Alabama. The people of both states were absolutely savage toward these last unfortunates, and they demanded that the government hunt them down like wild beasts. About 630 finally enrolled for transportation and began their journey in December, 1834.

After shocking losses from the terrible winter journey, the survivors finally reached the Verdigris. A year later Benjamin Marshall, a prominent mixed blood, organized a small party, which was conducted to the same location. At the same time Opothle Yahola announced that the Tuckabatchees, Kialigees, Thlopthloccos, Thlewarles, Autaugas, and Artussees, "who all burn the same fire and talk with the same tongue," were preparing to start. "We shall at that time take our last black drink in this nation, rub up our tradition plates, and commence our march." He had prepared his "marching physic" and was "preparing his traveling clothes, and will put out his old fire and never make or kindle it again, until he reaches west of the Mississippi, there never to quinch it again."

In the meantime starving Indians, honest agents and army officers, and decent citizens of Alabama had implored the Federal officials to stop the land frauds; but Lewis Cass, who was now Secretary of War, comfortably assumed that they were beyond the reach of Federal authority. Finally the scandal reached such monstrous proportions that during 1835-36 he undertook an investigation. Some of the land-grabbers became alarmed at the prospect that there might, after all, be a penalty for forgery and theft and arson even when committed upon Indians.

A "Creek war" seemed a happy solution. The Indians had endured their sufferings with the apathy of despair, but a few, especially the starving Euchees, had stolen some food. Now in May, 1836, a few towns were stirred up by their white exploiters to commit desperate acts of hostility. Cass immediately stopped the investigation and ordered the whole tribe removed as a military measure. The governor of Alabama issued a proclamation that all Creeks who should not help in putting down the uprising would be treated as enemies. The whites did very little of the fighting. Opothle Yahola, with the subservience that had become the curse of the Creeks, placed himself with a force of 1,806 warriors under the command of General Thomas S. Jesup to subdue the "hostiles." The Creeks were once more plunged into civil war. The hostiles were led by Eneah Micco, Jim McHenry, the son of a Scotch father and an Indian mother, and Eneah Emarthla, a grand old man of eighty, who had fought the United States in the Red Stick War and had lived for a time among the Seminoles. These leaders with their bands were all captured before the summer was over. The men were placed in irons, and with their wailing women and children— a total of 2,495 people—were forcibly removed to the West. They were in the most appalling destitution; literally naked, without weapons or cooking utensils, they were set down on their bare new land to live or die.

The resident Creeks were alarmed at the arrival of these wronged and desperate people. Roley McIntosh, a half-brother of the dead chief, was at the head of the western settlement. They held a council at Fort Gibson, and he informed the newcomers that they were welcome to stay if they would submit to the existing government. Eneah Emarthla, who was recognized as the leader of the hostiles, was in no position to contend for supremacy; he answered mildly that he supposed the western Creeks had organized their government for their own good and that he was willing to obey its officers. Opothle Yahola and large detachments of his party also arrived in a short time; most of them settled in the fertile valley at the junction of the North and South Canadian. Altogether 14,609 Creeks including the hostiles emigrated during 1836.

A chief named Tustennuggee Emarthla or Jim Boy remained behind with 776 warriors to assist Jesup in subduing the Seminoles, who also were resisting removal. The Federal officials promised to protect their families during their term of service and to discharge them early in 1837 so that they could emigrate in good season. But Jesup kept them seven months beyond the appointed time, and in the meantime their defenseless families, who were kept in concentration camps, were mobbed by Alabama and Georgia militia, and it was necessary to rush them down the Alabama for their own protection, leaving all their property behind them. They were held for months at Mobile Point and Pass Christian, suffering greatly from sickness and despondency, until their men joined them in the fall and the survivors were removed by steamboat around to New Orleans and up the Mississippi. The greatest single loss of life occurred when a large boat, the *Monmouth*, sank in the Mississippi and more than three hundred were drowned.

In the spring of 1837 about 543 Creeks were hunted out from among the Cherokees and dragged to their new homes, but a number remained and emigrated with the Cherokees the next year when that tribe also was driven West. They were adopted as Cherokee citizens and formed a compact settlement in the Illinois District of the Cherokee Nation. About eight hundred who had fled to the Chickasaws were compelled to remove with that tribe in 1838. They remained a short time with the Chickasaws in the West, but most of them soon joined their own people. Other Creeks drifted into Texas, where the Alabama and Koasata colony had settled so long before, but they eventually found their way north to their own country. Of the few remaining in Alabama several were hanged under the forms of law for participating in the "uprising" of 1836, and others were reduced to slavery. Small parties continued to emigrate until about 1850. Wealthy mixed bloods who had intended to remain as citizens of Alabama, finding it impossible to hold their farms or protect their property with the courts in the possession of the land speculators, sought the untrammeled opportunity of the new land. Lost and helpless full bloods who had been left behind were often sought out and ransomed by their people in the West. Ward Coachman (Co-cha-my), a mixed-blood Alabama, returned and rescued about sixty-five of these unfortunates, but he stated at the time that about one hundred, whom he had not been able to liberate, were still held in slavery.

The Creeks were at last cleared from the path of the white man, but the eager settlers who plowed their fertile fields and built rich cities along their streams never understood the cost of their expulsion. A tenacious people in their own way, they had none of the daring hardihood of the frontiersman, his burning zest for adventure, his ruthless acquisitiveness, his adaptability and resourcefulness. Reckoned by other Indians as a warlike people, they lacked the cruel, driving ferocity of the white man, and when they were driven from their homes they knew nothing but to die of hopeless grief along the trail. Inarticulate and beaten, they had no champion to tell the story of their wrongs, but the mute evidence of their census statistics stands as an everlasting refutation of the white man's professions of benevolence. A population of 21,792 Creeks was enrolled under the Treaty of 1832, which with the McIntosh emigrants brought the number accounted for by name and town well above twenty-three thousand. No subsequent enumeration was made until 1859 when the Indians had partially recovered from the terrible losses of the journey; but a careful census taken that year showed a population of 13,537. Obviously not more than half the Creeks who were uprooted from the loved soil of Alabama ever lived to thrive again in the rude land into which they were transplanted.[17]

The memories of these experiences have never been blurred by

[17] Grant Foreman, *Indian Removal*, 107-90; 50 Cong., 1 sess., *Sen. Ex. Doc. No. 198; Cherokee Advocate*, March 9, 1883; Foreman, Copies of Manuscripts and Newspapers, 113-16; Commissioner of Indian Affairs, *Annual Report*, 1832, 160; 1833, 185; 1836, 382. McKenney and Hall, *Indian Tribes of North America*, I, 111-15, 292-94; II, 71-74. United States, Superintendent for the Five Civilized Tribes, Files, Creek Per Capita Roll, 1858-59; Swanton, "The Green Corn Dance."

the lapse of time. The present-day Creek speaking only from tradition remembers circumstantial details that fit in surprisingly well with the account written by Grant Foreman, the historian of the Removal. The quiet pathos of these accounts presents a strange contrast to the fulminations of contemporary white men against the hated redskins.

Mary Hill, a middle-aged Okfuskee woman, tells the story related "many years ago" by her grandmother. "A council meeting was mostly composed of men, but there were times when every member of a town (tulwa) was requested to attend the meetings. Many of the leaders, when unrest was felt in the homes, visited the different homes and gave encouragement to believe that Alabama was to be the permanent home of the Muskogee tribe. But many different rumors of a removal to the far West was often heard. The command for a removal came unexpectedly upon most of us. There was the time that we noticed that several overloaded wagons were passing our home, yet we did not grasp the meaning. However, it was not long until we found out the reason. Wagons stopped at our homes and the men in charge commanded us to gather what few belongings could be crowded into the wagons. ... We were taken to a crudely built stockade and joined others of our tribe. Even here, there was the awful silence that showed the heartaches and sorrow at being taken from the homes and even separation from loved ones.

"Many of us had not foreseen such a move in this fashion ... but times became more horrible after the real journey was begun. Many fell by the wayside, too faint with hunger or too weak to keep up with the rest. ... A crude bed was quickly prepared for these sick and weary people. Only a bowl of water was left within the reach, thus they were left to suffer and die alone. The little children piteously cried day after day from weariness, hunger, and illness. ... They were once happy children—left without father and mother—crying could not bring consolation to these children. The sick and the births required attention, yet there was no time or no one was prepared. Death stalked at all hours, but there was no time for proper burying or ceremonies. My grandfather died on this trip. A hastily cut piece of cottonwood contained his body. The

open ends were closed up and this was placed along a creek. ...
Some of the dead were placed between two logs and quickly covered by shrubs, some were shoved under the thickets, and some were not even buried but left by the wayside.

"There were several men carrying reeds with eagle feathers attached to the end. These men continually circled around the wagon trains or during the night around the camps. These men said the reeds with feathers had been treated by the medicine men. Their purpose was to encourage the Indians not to be heavy hearted nor to think of the homes that had been left."

Willie Harjo, an elderly Indian of Wewogufke Town, remembers a swamp crossed by his father. "He said it was not only he and his father that had to wade through the swamp but also men, women, boys, girls, old or young. He said it wasn't anything like crossing a small sized swamp for it took them six days before they ever set a step on dry land. Knolls, higher levels of ground or small hills were sought out for sleeping places for there the places were a little drier than the swampy bottom lands. My father even told of the time that he once had the luck to find a bone which was the large shoulder blade of some large animal and this he used for a rest for his head. It was not only a journey through swamp but there were deaths and there were burials. It was at that time as my father said that my grandfather gave out from old age and exposure and fell on the way. His grave was a small brooklet which was chosen because it was rather deep and narrow. My grandfather's body was placed in this and the dirt picked with axes from along the banks were then heaped over the body."

Elsie Edwards, aged daughter of Tustennuggee Emarthla, heard the story from an old woman, possibly her mother. "When the events, with never no more to live in the east, had taken place, she too, remembered that she had left her home and with shattered happiness she carried a small bundle of her belongings and reopening and retying her pitiful bundle she began a sad song which was later taken up by the others on board the ship at the time of the wreck and the words of her song was: 'I have no more land, I am driven away from home, driven up the red waters, let us all go, let us all die together and somewhere upon the banks we will be there.' "

Siah Hicks, an old time Indian, describes the native attempt at interpretation. " 'The Indians will vanish' has been the talk of the older Indians ever since the white people first came to mingle among them ... and when their removal to a country to the West was just beginning, it was the older Indians that remarked and talked about themselves by saying, 'Now, the Indian is now on the road to disappearance.' They had reference to their leaving of their ways, their familiar surroundings where their customs were performed, their medicine, their hunting grounds and their friends. When they had reached their new homes ... they said, 'We ... are facing the evening of our existence and are nearly at the end of the trail that we trod when we were forced to leave our homes in Alabama and Georgia. In time, perhaps, our own language will not be used but that will be after our days.' ... When those old men met, they would talk about their old days with tears in their eyes and cry for the children that were to come, with the belief that they would be treated just as they had been treated."

Others than Mary Hill remember the ceremonials that guarded their sorrowful march. Trusted officials of the Tuckabatchees walked in single file in advance of the town carrying the sacred plates. The Cowetas brought the large conch shells which they had used in the black drink ceremonial from time immemorial. Many Indians relate how the town fire was carried from the old hearth and used to found the new settlement. Some of them insist that it was kept alive throughout the journey and used to start each night's campfire; others say that only the dead ashes were brought from the old square. Two picked men under the direction of the town chief were entrusted with this sacred task. They observed the strictest taboos regarding women, refusing even to drink out of a cup a woman had used; and they ate only White Food (humpeta hutke), hominy made from white corn with no seasoning or flavoring. When the new site was selected, the whole town watched while the chief established the communal hearth. One Indian describes the rites conducted by the leader of Okchiye Town. "After the ceremony had been completed, Hotulke Emarthla said,

'My town (tulwa) shall not go any further West, but this marks the end of our journey.' " It remained now for the shattered fragments of this once great people to gather themselves together and rebuild a nation in a new and untried land.[18]

[18] WPA Project S-149; Foreman, *A Traveler in Indian Territory*, 128; Pickett, *History of Alabama*, 83.

CHAPTER 4

The Conquest of a Frontier

MANY problems faced the Creeks when they arrived, most of them naked and famished and empty-handed, on their raw western frontier. It was a region of rich soil, fine timber, and luxuriant grass, but it required great labor before it could be brought under cultivation. It abounded with game, and to the west lay the wide grassy reaches of the buffalo plains, but it was the home of the wild Osages and the buffaloes were the special property of the mounted nomads of the Southwest. The climate was one of extremes, with violent rains and burning droughts, and the broad, low-banked, treacherous rivers were shallow ribbons of water weaving over dry beds or raging torrents tearing across the flooded valleys.

Not understanding the vagaries of western streams, they settled as usual along the banks, only to find their houses swept away, their crops destroyed, and their live stock drowned. Worst of all, they found the climate unhealthful. Neither they nor their white agents and teachers understood the cause of malaria, and as the summer streams shrunk to noisome, mosquito-breeding pools, "billious and intermittent fever" took a terrible toll of the population. The mild, sunny days of the winters alternated with short, sudden periods of intense cold, new to the experience of these southern people, and as they shivered under rude shelters and inadequate clothing great numbers died of pneumonia. As the bones of their unburied dead whitened on the prairie, the sick and despairing survivors were ready to flee from that pestilential land to their brethren in Texas, but better seasons came and they remained.

They had to clear land and place it under cultivation without farm implements, to cut timber and build houses without tools, and to hunt game without ammunition, for the government failed to supply them with the expected assistance. The subsistence promised them until they could raise their first crop proved inadequate, for it was furnished by corrupt contractors, who cheated them on measurements and delivered decayed food. Even the money to be paid under the treaties was withheld in some cases for many years.[1]

Fortunately the Creeks were industrious—more industrious than the gifted Choctaws, who were settling across the Canadian to the south, or the proud and valiant Cherokees, whose homes were on the east. As soon as the people of a town selected their location and established their fire, they began to construct crude dwellings and clear the lands for crops. As one aged Creek remembers it, the old people said that their first temporary shelters were made of deerskins and elm bark. Lizzie Winn (or Wynn), who was born in 1849, can still give a graphic account of the building process as she heard it from her uncle. They had no nails, and no tools except "little tomahawks—hatchets with hollow top and handle for smoking—that were made of steel and sharpened by rubbing a certain way on the rocks." They set a post to form each corner, and the rest of the wall was made of peeled saplings stuck upright in the ground and tied with grapevines. Bark was used for shingles, and the wall was daubed inside and out with mud. "The house had no chimney or fireplace and of course they had no stoves so they made the only stove they knew how to make. Wet mud was put in the middle of the room about three feet in diameter but it was nearer round than any other shape. When that wet mud or clay got dry more was added on top of it, leaving an opening at one side to put the wood in and a hollow place for the fire. It was made up about two and a half feet high for the stove, then went on up to the roof to let the smoke out. No cooking was done on this stove; it was just to heat the room. The cooking was done outside and at first everything was roasted. Then they made mud bowls and pots and cooked them until they were hard."[2]

The land selected by the delegation sent out by the McIntosh

---

[1] The whole sordid story of the swindling contractors is told by Grant Foreman, *The Five Civilized Tribes*, 147-62. See also Foreman, *A Traveler in Indian Territory, passim.*

[2] WPA Project S-149.

Creeks in 1826 had not been surveyed or patented, and in 1828 it was sold by the government to the Cherokees. The Creeks were highly indignant at abandoning the farms they had so hardly won from the wilderness, but Federal commissioners called the leaders of both tribes in council at Fort Gibson in 1833 and succeeded in making a compromise. The eastern boundary was fixed so that the Creeks retained all of the Arkansas valley above the Three Forks and most of the Verdigris, their northern boundary cut the Arkansas near the mouth of the Cimarron, and their land extended on the south to the Canadian and west to the hundredth meridian. For their compliance they were promised an additional blacksmith, a wheelwright, four grist mills, twenty-four crosscut saws, and an annuity of one thousand dollars for education.[3]

As the McIntosh settlers were reinforced by later immigrants, mostly from the Lower Towns, they cleared the heavy timber and spread across the two rivers and up the valley between them as far as the mouth of the Cimarron. Some of the mixed bloods and inter-married whites in this group had brought large numbers of slaves and the white man's standards of living. Even during the first hard years they raised a surplus of corn, which they sold to the garrison at Fort Gibson and to the contractors who supplied the later immigrants. Soon they had great plantations and ranches, each a busy industrial unit providing for the needs of a large body of workmen and producing corn and cattle to be shipped to distant markets. The slaves raised cotton and carded, spun, and wove the material for their own clothes; they prepared cowhide by removing the hair with ashes and tanning it with bark, and they made harness and shoes; and they raised rice in the swampy land along the rivers for their food. The plantation owners lived in large, comfortable dwellings, usually double log houses with spreading verandas, and they had rich and elegant furniture which was shipped in from the outside world. Among this wealthy group were Benjamin Marshall, who is said to have owned a hundred slaves; several members of the McIntosh family, especially Roley and Jane, the widow of Sam Hawkins; and Benjamin Perryman and his numerous descendants. But with the exception of these mixed bloods the people in this

3 Kappler, *Laws and Treaties*, II, 388-91.

settlement were less thrifty and prosperous than the Upper Creeks on the Canadian. There were more cases of extreme poverty and more drunkenness and general demoralization. The relaxation of town control by this more "progressive" group had been disastrous to the less acquisitive members of the tribe.

The densest population of the Upper Creeks was clustered in the triangle formed by the confluence of the North and the South Canadian; the settlements extended up these two rivers and the Deep Fork, reaching the mouth of the Little on the main Canadian, with an isolated colony about fifty miles farther upstream. These people still worked their communal fields, and the few axes and hoes they had at first were usually the property of the town.

By 1843 in the rich valley of the main Canadian they had one tract three miles wide and eight miles long that was one continuous field of growing corn. The Tuckabatchee Micco told Ethan Allen Hitchcock in 1842, "When we order out the people to make a public fence (There is a public field for every town, besides each one's own field) if they don't turn out we send and take away their gun, or horse; or something else to punish them." He also explained that when there were widows or orphans with nobody to care for them he "turned out his people" and built a house, made a fence, and planted their private field. Pleasant Porter, the great mixed-blood chief at the end of the nineteenth century, also described this early care of dependents: "Now ... the custom of the Creeks was that everybody had to work or live on the town, and the town had taskmasters who took care of him and saw that he worked. There was not a skulker or one who shirked amongst us then ... If anyone was sick or unable to work, the neighbors came in and planted his crop, and they took care of it—saw that the fences were all right— and the women took care of the garden, and wood was got for him, and so on. In fact, everything was done under the care of the people —they did everything and looked after the welfare of everything." As these excerpts indicate, the custom of planting individual fields grew up alongside the communal agriculture; and there was an increasing tendency for each family to establish its domicile in the midst of its own fields. From these separate farms the people gathered to attend the necessary town meetings, but they often had to travel as much as twenty miles to reach the community center.

The McIntosh Creeks had been able to bring their live stock, but the main body of immigrants had been forced to abandon all their property at the Removal. Under a treaty made in 1838 at Fort Gibson the United States now paid them $50,000 in stock animals to be distributed according to their losses, $21,103.33 to pay additional claims of the McIntosh party, and $10,000 in stock animals to starving "hostiles" of the "uprising" of 1836. A fund of $350,-000 was created, the interest of which was paid to the holders of lost property claims until the principal was distributed under a treaty made in 1854. The acquisition of live stock was slow at first, but by 1845 nearly every family had one or two cows and ponies and a few hogs. From that time on their herds increased rapidly. They fenced their patches of corn, and their live stock ran almost wild in the woods.

At first they depended upon hunting for their meat. Until they could secure guns and ammunition they revived their forgotten skill with the bow and arrow. Besides the game they killed in the vicinity of their homes, they took regular trips to the buffalo range for the winter's supply of meat. They gathered nuts for cooking oil, and they sent thousands of bushels of pecans down the Arkansas to market.[4]

The commerce between the Creek country and the outside world was carried on mainly by small, sturdily constructed steamboats that ran up to the vicinity of the Three Forks. Their trips were usually confined to the season of the spring freshets, and their schedules were subject to interruption by submerged rocks, uprooted trees, sandbars, and low water; but they managed to carry a considerable amount of produce from the Creek country to be exchanged for manufactured articles at New Orleans.

The most important trail was the Texas Road. This great highway gathered up several streams of traffic from Kansas and Missouri and crossed the Cherokee country; it entered the Creek

[4] Commissioner of Indian Affairs, *Annual Reports*, 1839-60; Foreman, *A Traveler in Indian Territory*, 116, 127 f., 151-57; Josiah Gregg, *Commerce of the Prairies*, II, 304; George Catlin, *North American Indians*, II, 139 f.; WPA Project S-149; Walter N. Wyeth, *Poor Lo*, 69; *Niles' Weekly Register*, XXXV (1828), 58; 59 Cong., 2 sess., *Sen. Rep. No. 5013*, I, 624; Kappler, *Laws and Treaties*, II, 524 f., 647.

Nation from the northeast, crossed the Arkansas in the vicinity of the Three Forks, and continued through the eastern edge of the Creek domain until it reached the Canadian; then it passed through the Choctaw Nation and crossed the Red River into Texas. It was continually crowded with covered wagons pointed south on their way to Texas. The California Trail became important from the time of the California Gold Rush of 1849. It started at Fort Smith and followed up the Arkansas and Canadian rivers on the way to Santa Fe; one branch ran for a distance on the north side of the Canadian and thus traversed the southern portion of the Creek country.

Trading posts were established at various places to supply the needs of the Creeks and the emigrants that traversed the California and Texas trails. The most important trade centered at the agency, which was located successively at three places in the vicinity of Three Forks. Here were the convenience of river transportation and all the manifold financial activities of annuities, removal, subsistence, etc. Even in the first difficult years the full bloods came bringing their meagre farm produce to sell for cloth, ammunition, and agricultural implements, and as the country prospered it became the center of an important commerce. A post office was established there in 1843. Another trading post was established at Honey Springs close to Elk Creek on the Texas Trail, about halfway between the Arkansas and the Canadian. Here William F. McIntosh, the son of Chilly, built a toll bridge for the use of the travelers, and the Indians came to furnish them with corn, meat, and fruit. Farther south on the Texas Trail, North Fork Town grew up in the dense Upper Creek settlement between the two Canadians. It was only a small village, but the California Trail also passed through it, and several of the mixed bloods from the Arkansas settlement moved there and established stores. The post office of Micco was opened there in 1853.

Farther up the Canadian the California Trail passed through Edwards' Trading Post, which was located at the mouth of the Little. Fort Holmes had been erected here in 1834 to protect the Creeks from the Plains Indians, but it had been abandoned almost immediately and a quiet agricultural Creek community had grown up to form the background of a vigorous commercial intercourse with the wild tribes. A few trading houses were established at remote places in the interior of the Creek country; one of the most important was at Shieldsville, close to the Deep Fork about thirty miles above its junction with the main Canadian. A few of the traders were mixed-blood Creeks, but most of them were white men licensed by the Commissioner of Indian Affairs upon the recommendation of the agent.[5]

The Creek women made part of the clothing for their families from gay-colored cloth purchased from these traders. The small farmers, especially the thrifty full bloods on the Canadian, also planted little patches of cotton, and the women picked out the seeds by hand and spun and wove material for their clothing. The fullblood men, especially among the Upper Creeks, disdained trousers as a badge of servility to the white men. Washington Irving described them in 1832. "They dress in calico hunting-shirts of various brilliant colors, decorated with bright fringes, and belted with broad girdles, embroidered with beads; they have leggings of dressed deerskins, or of green or scarlet cloth, with embroidered knee bands and tassels; their mocassins are fancifully wrought and ornamented, and they wear gaudy handkerchiefs tastefully bound round their heads." Among the wealthy mixed bloods the women dressed in rich silks and muslins made according to the fashions of their white sisters, but the men combined with the sobriety of conventional coats and trousers the gay ruffles of the hunting shirt.[6]

The annuities, especially for the first few years, were paid mainly in goods, but the supplies were almost entirely worthless—trinkets of no value and a few agricultural implements so carelessly packed that many were lost in transit. Individual Creeks formed the habit of selling them in advance at a great discount so that they might

[5] James H. Gardner, "One Hundred Years Ago in the Region of Tulsa," *Chronicles of Oklahoma,* XI (1933), No. 2; Grant Foreman, *Fort Gibson;* WPA Project S-149; Commissioner of Indian Affairs, *Annual Report,* 1845, 522; 1847, 760-62. Balduin Möllhausen, *Diary of a Journey from the Mississippi to the Coasts of the Pacific . . .,* I, 73 f.; Grant Foreman, "Early Post-Offices of Oklahoma," *Chronicles of Oklahoma,* VI (1928), No. 1; Grant Foreman, *Down the Texas Road;* Washington Irving, *A Tour on the Prairies,* 12 f., 134.

[6] WPA Project S-149; Irving, *A Tour on the Prairies,* 13, 21; Foreman, *A Traveler in Indian Territory,* 111 f.; Catlin, *North American Indians,* II, 139 f.

have a little cash to spend for ammunition and tools and clothing. The government made only a belated and feeble attempt to construct the mills promised by the treaties. It was also very slow in furnishing the blacksmiths and wheelwrights, but the shops were finally established and were very useful to the Creeks. The Indians themselves were not mechanically inclined; hence white men, or more often slaves or free negroes, were employed as blacksmiths.

Except on the plantations of a few mixed bloods, slavery rested very lightly upon the Creek negroes. The easy-going Indians found the possession of slaves a great convenience, but they saw no reason to adopt the white man's ruthless system of exploiting and degrading them. The slave was usually expected to perform a certain amount of work for his master and to support his own family by the labors of his free time. Many employed their own time so well that they were able to accumulate property and purchase their freedom.

The Indians credited the negroes with understanding the white man's unpredictable ways, and they rewarded them accordingly. A present-day negro, whose father was a Creek slave, explains the system. An Indian would often take a slave along "as an interpreter when he would go to trade with horse-traders ... because the negro could talk English and also knew the value of an animal and would save his owner from buying a poor or no-good animal. His owner would give him a colt or calf or maybe money. He would have his freedom in mind and would save the money and raise the animals to sell for more money. In that way, he would finally get enough to buy himself and he knew how to support himself as well. ... I've heard of a slave owner borrowing from his slave."

According to a statement made by Chilly McIntosh a negro named Governor Nero, who died about 1854, had bought the "first set" and the "second set" of his children; he had "needed help to finish paying for one" child and had borrowed three hundred dollars from an "old woman" and given her his note; and had owned a wagon, three or four head of oxen, and ten ponies, which his children inherited after his death. Under such conditions free negroes were numerous in the Creek country. Except for a few of the mixed-blood aristocrats the Creeks had little prejudice against intermarriage with them, and the children of such marriages were accepted without prejudice as members of the tribe.[7]

Creek economic development was paralleled by the growth of education and the acceptance of Christianity; there was the same difficult beginning, followed by a period of rapid expansion. The Creeks still felt a deep distrust of the white man's culture, and the inherent difficulties of a language handicap and an unaccustomed discipline were intensified by the adherence of the Creeks to their ancient ceremonials and the bitterness of the Removal experiences.

Young John Davis had come west to the Arkansas-Verdigris settlement in 1829. He began talking informally to his people in their homes, and in 1830 the Baptist denomination allowed him an annual stipend of two hundred dollars to pay his expenses. Early in 1830 he and two other young Creek men entered Union Mission, which the American Board of Commissioners for Foreign Missions had recently established among the Osages a few miles north of the Creek settlement. Before the end of the term twenty Creek young people were enrolled there. At the same time missionaries from Union, using Davis and other students as interpreters, preached regularly to small gatherings in the Creek country; and in September, 1830, they organized a Presbyterian Church of thirty Indian and negro members, part of whom had been Baptist or Methodist converts in the East. A few converts from Asbury Mission also carried on individual work similar to that of Davis.

In 1832 the Baptists sent a missionary to reside in the Creek Nation, and on September 9 McCoy visited the station and organized the Ebenezer Baptist Church. At this time Davis, after some diffident hesitation, received a license to preach. The same year one of the American Board missionaries from Union settled in the Creek country. By the end of the year the Presbyterians reported eighty-one members, the Methodists two hundred, and the Baptists sixty-five. The majority of the members were negroes, but a number of young Creek men were actively assisting the missionaries,

[7] WPA Project S-149; Creek Nation, Tribal Records, 29197-29219; Foreman, *A Traveler in Indian Territory*, 151 f.; Commissioner of Indian Affairs, *Annual Report*, 1857, 200.

and it was believed that the old hostility was rapidly disappearing.

A certain amount of school work was carried on in connection with the missionary activities. Davis had from the first devoted part of his time to teaching the children, but most of the schools were conducted by the missionaries' wives, who sank rapidly under the strain of household duties, teaching, and childbearing. The attendance of the children was irregular because of lack of interest, insufficient food and clothing, and the appalling unhealthfulness of the climate. But the language difficulty was the most serious, and the missionaries soon became convinced of the failure of the English schools.

John Fleming, of the American Board, managed with the help of young James Perryman, a student of Union, to reduce the Creek language to writing. In 1835 his *I stutsi in Naktsokv* (*The Child's Book*) was published by the recently installed printing press at Union Mission. This attractive little illustrated volume was probably the first publication in the present state of Oklahoma. Fleming and Perryman also prepared a Creek book of hymns, which was published at Boston in 1835, and another primer, which was published the next year by the Union Press. At the same time the Baptists sent Davis to the Shawnee Mission in Kansas, where they had set up a printing press, and with his assistance prepared a primer and St. John's gospel in the Creek language. As soon as the new books were available, the missionaries of both groups opened Creek language schools, but considerable bad feeling developed between them concerning the accuracy of the translations.

By 1836 several churches of the three denominations had been established in the Arkansas-Verdigris settlement, and Davis upon the advice of the Baptist board had located among the Upper Creeks, who were then beginning to settle on the Canadian. But when two thousand sullen and desperate "hostiles" were turned loose on the settlement that year, and it was known that ten thousand more of the conservative Opothle Yahola party would arrive shortly, the presence of the misionaries presented an unwelcome complication. At the same time a missionary sent out by the Methodists was charged with serious misconduct; and although the missionaries had refrained from expressing abolition sentiments, some of the Indian slaveholders resented their work among the negroes. In the council held at Fort Gibson between the McIntosh party and the hostiles it was decided to expel them. Acting Superintendent William Armstrong willingly gave the order; it was feared that the hostiles might incite the frontier to a general Indian war, and upon the whole the sacrifice of the missionaries seemed the cheapest method of propitiating the Creeks for the crimes of the Removal policy. One of the Baptists gave a moving account of the grief of his converts and his own distress "at leaving his little flock a prey to wolves in that howling wilderness." Except during one short visit to the community the following year by one of the Baptist missionaries the only preaching services were conducted by Davis at North Fork and a few ignorant negroes in the Arkansas settlement.

The chiefs in council imposed a penalty of fifty or one hundred lashes upon anyone who should attend Christian services. This punishment was frequently inflicted upon slaves and Indian men and women, but the converts endured the persecution with unflinching steadfastness. Small earnest groups met secretly, sang negro spirituals and the portions of Creek hymns they could remember, and listened to the instruction of ignorant slaves. Davis was not molested, but in the absence of his missionary friends he suffered much from loneliness and discouragement. His young wife died in 1837 and a niece, who had come to care for his motherless children, died within a year. In 1839 he wrote to the mission board, "Since, some of my family have been afflicted and some have died. And because of my being placed in the midst of superstitious and benighted men of my nation, and having been often reproached by notional and self-confident brethren, I have almost, some days, sunk into oppressed feelings."

About fifteen young Creeks were maintained in the Choctaw Academy by the $3,000 set aside for education under the Removal Treaty and the $1,000 provided by the Treaty of 1833. Some of these returned students eventually became leaders of their people but at this time they were regarded with prejudice and suspicion and they suffered tragic disillusionment. After the expulsion of the missionaries the Creeks finally consented to use a portion of this money for the employment of "government teachers" in their own country. Davis for a time taught one of these schools at North Fork, but for several years the only one was conducted at the agency by a roving white man who was afterwards sent to prison as a counterfeiter.

The Creek agent had become convinced that the English day schools were a failure, but the Creeks had begun to insist that all their school money be spent at home; hence he urged them to contract with missionary societies for the establishment of boarding schools in their own country. In the fall of 1841 the Presbyterian mission board sent young Robert M. Loughridge, a recent Princeton graduate, to investigate. He rode six hundred miles on horseback from his home in Alabama and presented a proposition to the council. The chiefs answered that they were opposed to preaching because it broke up their busks, ball plays, and dances, but they consented to the school upon condition that he would confine his preaching to the mission buildings. He rode back to Alabama and returned by steamer the following February with his courageous young bride. They began their work in a log cabin at the center of the Coweta settlement. He spent his time in constructing buildings and preaching, and his wife opened the school. At first they boarded several of the children in their own family, but as other missionaries were sent to assist them, they soon had a boarding school with forty students. The girls were instructed in housework and the boys in farming and stock raising; and they received the fundamentals of an English education.

Some of the chiefs abandoned their hostility to Christianity about 1842, and the converts of the native preachers multiplied. The Baptist missionaries began to hold services on the Cherokee side of the boundary and in the edge of the Choctaw country. The Creeks flocked to these meetings, and a number were baptized. By 1845 Baptist and Methodist missionaries were openly working in the Creek country, and the next year Loughridge persuaded the chiefs to lift the ban on his preaching. But although the white missionaries were not molested, in 1845 the council imposed a fine upon all who should neglect the black-drink ceremony, and the whipping of converts was still a frequent occurrence.

The official opposition to Christianity ended in 1848. Chilly McIntosh and several other prominent chiefs united with the Baptist Church at a great camp meeting that year, and a Baptist missionary was even invited to address the council. At that time the Baptists had eight preachers—one white, four Indians, and three negroes—seven churches, and 550 members. The same year the Methodists reported 592 members—524 Indians, 39 negroes, and 29 whites. The Presbyterians had fewer members, but they were the most effective in education.

In 1847 two more boarding schools were authorized by contracts with the Methodist and Presbyterian mission boards. The Methodists located their school near North Fork Town and named it Asbury after their old mission in the East; the Presbyterians chose a site in the Arkansas settlement and gave the school the old Creek name of Tullahassee. Both plants were completed by 1850. Each accommodated from eighty to one hundred pupils.

Tullahassee was the greatest of the three Creek boarding schools. Loughridge was transferred from Coweta to take charge. The principal was young W. S. Robertson, who had recently married Ann Eliza Worcester, the daughter of the great missionary to the Cherokees. Loughridge and Mrs. Robertson revived Fleming's language studies and published readers, tracts, and portions of the Bible in Creek. The teachers were young men and women of superior culture, and the graduates of this wilderness school were distinguished throughout their lives for high intellectual attainments. The list of students reads like a roll call of the future leaders of the tribe.

In general, however, it was only the mixed bloods that attended the boarding schools, and their training therefore increased the cleavage that was already apparent within the nation. Several small day schools were conducted in the heart of the fullblood settlements by Methodist and Baptist missionaries, whose salaries were paid by the Federal government out of the Creeks' educational annuities; but the native language project was not revived, and the instruction in English proved to be beyond the capacity of children who spoke only Creek at home. In 1856 the Creeks sold a portion of their land to the Seminoles and thus secured large additional annuities and complete control of their educational funds. They immediately established seven day-schools under the administration of a native superintendent in each of the two settlements, and several graduates of Tullahassee received appointments as teachers. They now had a national system of education with a possibility of bridging the gap between the progressive and conservative members of the tribe.

The missionaries used all their influence in developing a spirit of national unity. Loughridge, the Robertsons, and Americus L. Hay, the leading Baptist missionary of the period, were especially successful in identifying themselves completely with the Creeks. They were of course unsympathetic toward the native ceremonials and "superstitions," but they instilled a patriotism that was purely Creek, and unlike the government officials, who constantly schemed to bring the Indians under subjection, they encouraged them to protect their own interests. They had no desire to "Americanize" their charges except in the way of fitting them economically and intellectually to cope with the white man.

Denominational rivalry still continued, but each group found a distinctive place in the life of the tribe. While the progressive leaders of the next generation were receiving their intellectual training from the Presbyterians, the full bloods at remote settlements were converted at Baptist camp meetings. Less cultured than the Presbyterians and less dogmatic than the Baptists, the Methodists held a sort of intermediate position in educational and evangelistic work. By 1853 most of the Methodist and Baptist churches were served by native pastors. Davis had died, but James Perryman, Chilly McIntosh, William F. McIntosh, and others carried on his work as Baptist preachers. Among the Methodists Samuel Checote, who had never forgotten his early training in Alabama, was rapidly advancing in religious leadership, and Jim McHenry, upon whose head a price had once been placed by the vindictive Alabamans, was greatly loved for his earnest piety. It was the Presbyterian method to prepare their native preachers by the slow process of boarding school training, but in 1860 two of their mixed-blood graduates were in the field: the brilliant David Winslett, who was soon to die in the Civil War, and earnest, studious young Joseph M. Perryman.

A certain amount of opposition to Christianity continued, but it was individual and sporadic. Most of it was based upon a well-founded distrust of the white man. The religion itself was attractive to the Creeks. The adversities of the preceding years had weakened the influence of the moving native ceremonials and had broken up the moral solidarity of the town and clan. It was impossible to return to the old loyalties, and the new faith appealed to the same deep ethical and religious sentiment. But in spite of this stabilizing influence, the moral recovery of the Creeks was very slow.[8]

Drunkenness was a serious evil. The Creek country was flooded with intoxicants from Arkansas. The Intercourse Acts forbade the sale of liquor to Indians, but little attempt was made to enforce them. From 1840 on, the Creeks were influenced by their agent to pass laws to punish their own citizens who engaged in the traffic; but it is clear that they resented the idea that they should be tee-totalers when soldiers, government officials, Arkansas settlers, traders, Texas and California emigrants—all the white men they knew except the missionaries—considered strong drink one of the necessities of life. Their busks were marred by drunkenness, their councils sometimes degenerated into orgies, and the "drunken frolic" was one of their main diversions. But this condition was only a symptom of the moral breakdown that followed the decline of the towns.

Few of the towns ever erected public buildings on an important scale in the new country. The Tuckabatchees alone at their seat on the main Canadian about twelve miles from North Fork Town constructed their square and its four enclosing buildings with the old loving craftsmanship; and their great chokofa, sixty feet in diameter and thirty feet high, rising above the unfamiliar wilderness brought to those strange surroundings a feeling of home. In 1842 the Tuckabatchee Micco explained to Hitchcock through a

[8] Tracy, *History of American Missions, passim; Missionary Herald,* XXVI-XXXIII (1830-37); McCoy, *Baptist Indian Missions, passim;* Carolyn Thomas Foreman, *Oklahoma Imprints,* 1 f.; Wyeth, *Poor Lo,* 74-81, 154-57; John Fleming, *I stutsi in Naktsokv;* Commissioner of Indian Affairs, *Annual Reports,* 1836-60; Creek Tribal Records, Checote Manuscript; Foreman, *A Traveler in Indian Territory,* 109 f., 115 f., 127, 148, 260-62; *Indian Record,* October, 1886—February, 1887; H. F. Buckner, *The Gospel According to John,* notes; Methodist Episcopal Church, Minutes of the Indian Mission Conference; O'Beirne and O'Beirne, *The Indian Territory,* 475-81; John D. Lang and Samuel Taylor, Jr., *Report of a Visit to Some of the Tribes of Indians Located West of the Mississippi River,* 40.

negro interpreter the building of this chokofa. He "cut sticks in miniature of every log required in the construction of the building, and distributed them proportionately among the residents of the town, whose duty it was to cut logs corresponding with their sticks, and deliver them upon the ground appropriated for the building, at a given time. At the raising of the house, not a log was cut or changed from its original destination; all came together in their appropriate places, as intended by the designer. During the planning of this building, which occupied him six days, he did not partake of the least particle of food."[9]

The decline of the towns was imprudently hastened by the various United States agents, who worked constantly to force the Creek government into the pattern of the American state. The Treaty of 1832 had specified that the annuities would be paid "as the tribe may direct," and the money was accordingly placed in the hands of the town chiefs for distribution. The agents tried to break their financial control so that the money could be paid out in per capita shares to the "head"—meaning the husband and father—of each family. No doubt some greed and selfishness and more caprice and despotism did enter into the native financial administration, but the town was fundamental to Creek life and it could not be torn apart without weakening the whole structure of society.

Chiefs, henehas, warriors, medicine men, etc., still discharged their official duties according to the complicated system of precedents observed by each individual town. In their relations with the central government they were loosely classified as (1) chiefs and (2) "lawmakers" or "councilors"; each town had a chief, one or two second chiefs, and from four to forty or forty-five lawmakers. The chiefs and one or two of the lawmakers represented the town in council.

The Arkansas and Canadian settlements were still referred to as the Lower and Upper Towns respectively, although there had been considerable interchange of populations. Roley McIntosh continued as the head chief of the Arkansas District. In the Canadian District Little Doctor, Opothle Yahola, Tamarthla Micco, Tucka-

9 Swanton, "Creek Social Organization," 179 n.; Swanton, "Notes on the Creek Indians," 132; Foreman, *A Traveler in Indian Territory*, 113-37, 157 f.

batchee Micco, and Echo (Deer) Harjo served successively as chief, but Opothle Yahola's influence was supreme during the whole period. Each division had its own council, and the two settlements were virtually independent until 1840, or possibly 1839, when a General Council was created. Both chiefs presided at the General Council, sitting side by side, but McIntosh was entitled to the precedence. Sometime during the period the office of second chief developed in each district. This official served in case of the absence or disability of the head chief.

As soon as the two districts were united, a tree-clad hill about midway between them was selected as a council ground. Near the summit was a beautiful, clear spring falling into a fern-fringed basin of rock, and the place accordingly received the name of Wekiwa Hulwe or High Spring. Here the tribal legislators camped with their families under the trees, sent their boys to carry water for their horses from the spring, and deliberated gravely in the log council house which they constructed in 1840. They were very anxious for the establishment of the Federal agency at the same location, but the desired action was never taken.

In 1859, or possibly 1858, the Creeks adopted a short written constitution and undertook to make their tribal officers elective. This brief document mentioned only five officials: a principal and a second chief for each district, and a national speaker. The chiefs were to be elected "by the People or Voice of the Office Holders that may be present," and the speaker was to be appointed by the principal chiefs. The term of office was four years. In the election held under this constitution the members of the Council formed in lines behind their respective candidates to be counted. Motey Canard (or Kennard) and Jacob Derrisaw, both mixed bloods, were chosen as principal and second chief of the Lower Creeks, and apparently it was understood that Canard should be entitled to precedence as principal chief of the nation. Echo Harjo and Oktarharsars (Sandy Place) Harjo were elected by the Upper Creeks. Both Canard and Echo Harjo had previously served as second chief. In 1860, or possibly 1859, the Creeks at the urging of their agent went through the form of adopting an artificial constitution that entirely ignored the towns and the native political customs and created an elaborate system of courts; but they never troubled to put it into operation.

The Council really enacted legislation during this period, and the services of the clerk or secretary—a mixed blood who had been to school or even an intermarried white man—became very important. In 1826 the Lower Creeks had adopted a code based upon McIntosh's earlier compilation of 1817. The Opothle Yahola party began reducing their laws to writing soon after their arrival. These laws were collected into a uniform code for the nation and adopted by the General Council of 1840. As soon as the town chiefs returned home from the Council it was their custom to call their people together and tell them orally what laws had been passed. A brief digest was prepared from time to time and kept in manuscript in the care of the two principal chiefs.

By 1861 the Creeks had a fairly complete criminal code. Rape had been added to the list of crimes; it was punished by fifty lashes for the first offense, one hundred lashes and the loss of an ear for the second, and death for the third. The old law against murder had been modified: accidental killing and self-defense were excepted; in playing ball unintentional killing was not murder, but killing with "a stick or stamp" carried the death penalty. Liquor dealers were subject to fine, and "if any person in an intoxicated state becomes troublesome or otherwise he or she may be confined by tying or otherwise." Marriage between persons "descended from the same woman" was punishable by fifty lashes. Women who used drugs to cause abortion were to receive fifty lashes.

Civil laws were enacted in keeping with the advancing economic individualism of the Creeks. A horse trade could be annulled if one of the parties was intoxicated. Stray horses and cattle were to be advertised, and if not claimed they were taken to the Council and sold to the highest bidder. A Creek could collect damages done to his crops by live stock only if his field was enclosed by a nine-rail fence "staked and ridered." Unlike their white sisters, women had complete independence in the ownership and control of property. Curiously enough, husbands and wives did not inherit from each other; in case of death the property was divided among the children, or if there were no children, among the nearest blood relatives of the deceased. Wills, either oral or written, were recognized.

The Council also legislated for the towns. They were forbidden to suspend a law enacted by the Council; their members were made subject to fine for failure to assist in the town labors; there was the law of 1845 prescribing a fine for absence from the town ceremonials; and a town was liable to a fine of fifty dollars for using ineligible players in a matched ball game. In 1840 the Council tried to restrict the widow's mourning period to four months, but the law aroused so much popular opposition that it was repealed the next year. Later a law was enacted providing that "no town or towns person or persons shall have power to keep any woman widowhood exceeding twelve monts from the death of her husband," and that "no mail should be kept in widowhood exceeding two months from the death of his wife."

The Council finally took over the control of the annuities formerly distributed to the town officials. In 1855 the office of national treasurer was created, and the number of chiefs and lawmakers was reduced to five hundred. By a treaty with the United States the next year the Creeks secured control of their educational annuities and "civilization" funds; and the Council passed a comprehensive school law and drew up regulations for four public blacksmith shops in each district. It was probably at this time that the office of district treasurer was created. Appropriations were to be made only by the General Council and no money was to be paid out except upon a warrant signed by the principal chief of the district.

The Council also adopted a slave code, which increased in severity as the aristocratic mixed bloods sought to change the easy and tolerant slavery of the primitive Indian to the real servitude practiced by the neighboring states. The first law, apparently passed some time after 1842, was concerned mainly with the protection of property in slaves. If a slave killed an Indian, he suffered death; if an Indian killed a slave, he was forced to pay the owner or suffer death; if one slave killed another, the murderer received one hundred lashes and his owner was forced to pay one-half the value of the dead negro.

A later law sought to protect the Creeks against negro influence.

Freed negroes were allowed to remain in the nation, but they were subject to a poll tax and a property tax; intermarriage between negroes and Creeks was punished by whipping both parties; and fine and whipping was imposed upon any Creek or negro who should assist a fugitive slave. A still later law provided that a citizen might free his slaves if he would take them outside the limits of the nation. A law, apparently of a still later date, prohibited slaves from owning property and provided for its confiscation and sale. The school law passed in 1856 forbade the superintendents to employ abolitionists as teachers. On May 8, 1859, the Council enacted a savage slave code designed to keep every slave on his master's premises and forbidding slaves the use of their free time; but some sections were not to go into effect until 1861 and it is probable that it was never enforced. Like so much Creek legislation it seems to have represented wishful thinking on the part of their agent and the attempted leadership of a small group that had come under the white man's influence.

The crude, simple laws that the whole Creek people approved and understood were quickly and drastically enforced. At first the council of the district sat as a rude court to try murder, theft, etc., and the penalty was inflicted by some of its members detailed for the purpose or by a special group of enforcement officers known as lighthorsemen. After the union of the two settlements in 1840, the General Council took over the main judicial functions. Each principal chief might call a council of his district to try cases, but an appeal was allowed to the General Council.

The Creeks of their own accord seemed to be developing a court out of the judicial functions of the Council. At some undetermined date they created a "judicating commity" of six men from each district, "seperate and distinct from the Kings and Warriors," to "be prompt in attention to every and all General Councils," and to decide difficult and complicated lawsuits. A law was passed at some time during this period for a jury trial in murder cases, but it is probable that this white man's device for securing justice was not used.

The Council heard some civil cases, probably as a court of last resort, and decided on claims to be paid by the nation out of the annuities. The lawmakers of the town decided most civil cases, especially probate matters, in a town council and executed their own judgments or entrusted the execution to the lighthorse. Appraisements of damages were made by disinterested parties appointed for the purpose. Private debts were collected by the lighthorse, probably after a decision by the lawmakers. A great number of usages and customs that had never been reduced to statute were enforced by the towns, and the punishment of adultery was still left to the clan relatives.

The creation of a separate "judicating commity" illustrates a tendency the Council had shown since earliest times to divide according to the rank of its members into specialized functions. The most marked division seems to have been between the chiefs and lawmakers or warriors, and a bicameral council was apparently in process of development. Hitchcock reported in 1842 that the Council proper was composed of the two principal chiefs and the town chiefs, and that the lawmakers and one "judge" from each district formed a separate assembly known as the Committee. It can be determined from their appropriations that by the close of the period the Creeks recognized four classes of Council members: "Frst Class Committee Men," "2 Class Committee Men," "52 Second Chiefs, Head men or Town Chiefs," and "45 First Class Town Chiefs." In 1865 the "Committee" was exercising important legislative and executive functions.[10]

After they settled in the West, the Creeks resumed their ancient practice of incorporating alien tribes within their nation, and some of them were admitted to their Council. Several broken bands, wanderers who had left their eastern homes to escape the advancing frontier, or victims of the Removal policy, were permitted to settle in the Creek country. There were large and prosperous Shawnee and Delaware villages on the South Cana-

[10] Isaac McCoy, *The Annual Register of Indian Affairs Within the Indian Territory*, No. 3 (1837), 18; No. 4 (1838), 51. Gregg, *Commerce of the Prairies*, II, 315 f.; Thomas J. Farnham, *Travels in the Great Western Prairies, the Anahuac, and Rocky Mountains*, I, 129 f.; United States Archives, Creek 1866/H78, 1868/B636, S639, 1873/C278; Commissioner of Indian Affairs, *Annual Reports*, 1840-60; Phillips Collection, University of Oklahoma, Pamphlet No. 166, 48; Foreman, *A Traveler in Indian Territory*, 93, 111-23, 149; Five Tribes Files, No. 52, 56-58; *Indian Journal*, April 12, 1877, and July 26, 1877; Creek Tribal Records, Checote Manuscript; WPA Project S-149.

dian near the mouth of the Little and farther up the stream. These Indians were thrifty farmers and stockmen, shrewd and intelligent traders, and the most skilled and adventurous scouts on the border. They traveled the southwestern prairies for an incredible distance, exchanging calico, ammunition, and other goods for peltries taken by the wild tribes, and mules and specie from the Mexican settlements. The brave Kickapoos, who had come originally from Wisconsin; the peaceable, agricultural Piankashaws, a subtribe of the Miamis; and the impoverished Quapaws, a Siouan tribe forced from its home in Arkansas, also lived above the mouth of the Little on the Creeks' southwestern frontier. All of these Indians purchased Mexican children from the wild Comanches; many of these captives came into the possession of the Creeks as half-slaves, half-adopted children, and through the tolerant native process of assimilation became members of the tribe. For at least part of the time the Piankashaws shared in the Creeks' annuities, and their chiefs were admitted to the Council. If the other alien settlers did not receive similar privileges it was because the Creeks did not trouble to define their status.[11]

Strangely enough the kindred Seminoles were not able to settle with the Creeks on satisfactory terms, and one of the favorite projects of the Federal officials was thereby defeated. In 1833 they had been tricked into signing such an agreement, but it was many years before they could be surrounded in their inaccessible swamps, hunted down with bloodhounds, and dragged to the West; and when they arrived, naked, starving, but still untamed, they refused to place themselves under Creek jurisdiction.

A large portion of the tribe was composed of Red Sticks, who had not forgotten that Creeks had marched with Floyd and Jackson against their Alabama homes and forced them to flee to the tangled Everglades; there was the more recent memory of the Creeks who had enlisted with Jesup to force them from this retreat; and there was a long and involved controversy with the Creeks over the owner-

---

[11] Creek Tribal Records, 35403; Foreman, *A Traveler in Indian Territory*, 256 f.; Commissioner of Indian Affairs, *Annual Report*, 1840, 313 f.; 1845, 508; 1851, 386 f.; 1860, 124. Möllhausen, *Diary*, I, 69-74; 33 Cong., 2 sess., *House Ex. Doc. No. 15*, 13-15; WPA Project S-149; Five Tribes Files, No. 63, 445 f., 467-69; United States Archives, Creek 1871/C205.

ship of the Seminole negroes. They remained for a long time in the vicinity of Fort Gibson, and when they were finally induced to enter the Creek country they erected a council house and continued under their own government. One party even crossed the vast southwestern prairies and settled on the Mexican side of the Rio Grande.

Finally the Federal officials were forced to admit that amalgamation of the two tribes was impossible. Moreover, some of the Seminoles still remained in Florida fighting desperately against removal; and the Seminoles in the West managed to convince their agent that they could end the war and persuade their brethren to join them if only they had a national home. Delegates from both tribes were accordingly called to Washington, and this and other long-standing disputes with the United States were settled by the Treaty of 1856.

The Creeks ceded to the Seminoles a separate tract of land between the two Canadians, beginning about forty miles above the mouth of the Little and extending west to the limits of the Creek country. Each tribe was given the right of self-government within its territory and full jurisdiction over all people within its limits except white persons who had not been adopted as citizens; but they agreed upon the mutual extradition of criminals, the right of their people to settle in either tribe with "all the rights, privileges, and immunities" of citizens except participation in the annuities, and the use of their courts by the citizens of either nation.

The Creeks also quitclaimed all their land east of the Mississippi, thus surrendering a claim for compensation for the land taken by Andrew Jackson from his allies at the close of the Red Stick War. For this and the cession to the Seminoles they received one million dollars: $200,000 to be invested as an educational endowment; $400,000 to be paid per capita under the direction of the General Council, except that $100,000 might be reserved by the Council for some national object; $200,000, of which $10,000 was to be used to indemnify Creeks who had failed to receive reservations under the Treaty of 1832, $120,000 to compensate those who had removed before 1832 and had thereby lost their opportunity to secure reservations, and $70,000 for individual claims to be passed upon by the Council; and $200,000 to be retained by the United States until the removal of the remaining Seminoles from Florida.

The Creeks were given the right to employ their own teachers and mechanics, and the control of their remaining annuities as soon as the Council should request it.

Other provisions of this treaty stood throughout the tribal period as the basis of all subsequent relations between the Creeks and the United States. The United States undertook to remove from their country, with the aid of the military if necessary, all persons not members of the tribe except Federal employees and their families, persons traveling through the country, licensed traders, and people permitted by the Indians to reside among them. Licensed traders were to pay a moderate annual compensation to the Indians for the use of their land and timber, the amount to be fixed by the tribal authorities with the approval of the agent. The United States promised to protect the Creeks against domestic strife, hostile invasion, and aggressions by other Indians and white people, and undertook to indemnify the tribe for all injuries committed upon them. The tribe granted the right of the United States to establish military posts, roads, and agencies, and the right of way for railroads and telegraph lines. Finally amnesty was granted for all offenses committed east or west of the Mississippi.

Forty Seminoles and six Creeks subsequently went to Florida and effected the emigration of 239 of the intrepid people that had withstood the whole military force of the United States. This ended one of the most costly, most prolonged, and most cruel of all Indian wars. The Seminoles slowly left the Creek country and moved to the West, and an agency was constructed for them on their own land. The government's policy had been a costly mistake; it had all but destroyed a hardy and heroic tribe, and it had added to the gigantic problems that confronted the Creeks.[12]

The Creeks were more successful in their relations with other tribes. For a time they were in real danger from the wild Osages, whose hunting trails to the buffalo plains lay across their territory; the Kiowas, Comanches, and other tribes of the Southwest, who liked nothing better than to harry the border; and predatory bands

[12] Creek Tribal Records, Checote Manuscript, 20; Commissioner of Indian Affairs, *Annual Reports,* 1839-60; 33 Cong., 2 sess., *House Ex. Doc. No. 15;* Foreman, *A Traveler in Indian Territory,* 111-13; Foreman, *The Five Civilized Tribes,* 223-78; Kappler, *Laws and Treaties,* II, 344 f.

of Pawnees from the distant Platte. The Creek country, moreover, was the favorite battleground and horse-stealing range of the Osages and their plains enemies, the wily Kiowas and the swift-riding Pawnees. The Little River frontier was protected to a certain extent by the friendly tribes that had settled there, but the Creeks observed a wary alertness on their trips to the buffalo plains; they punished Comanches and Pawnees for raids on their settlements; and they had many unrecorded battles with the Osages. The present-day Creek can point out the site of many such encounters. In the kindly haze of tradition they are all seen as Creek victories, but there is no doubt that the Creeks were feared and respected throughout the West for their formidable reputation as warriors. At the same time they entered into native councils with a zest and seriousness foreign to the more educated and supercilious Cherokee and the quiet and clannish Choctaw. The same combination of prowess in war and tolerant internationalism that had created their Confederacy made them the leading peace influence on all that wild frontier. They were also the most active in councils of the "Five Civilized Tribes," as they and their Cherokee, Choctaw, Chickasaw, and Seminole neighbors soon came to be called.

When the first Creeks and Cherokees settled in the vicinity of the Three Forks, the government officials called several councils to secure the consent of the Osages, and beads and expressions of friendship were exchanged. Finally at the request of Roley McIntosh and other Creek chiefs a special commission was created to settle intertribal questions growing out of the Removal policy. The able Montfort Stokes, of North Carolina; Rev. John F. Schermerhorn, of New York; and Henry L. Ellsworth, of Connecticut, were appointed as commissioners.

Ellsworth arrived in time to join a ranger expedition from Fort Gibson to the West in 1832. This *Tour on the Prairies* has become celebrated because of the lively account written by Washington Irving, who accompanied the expedition. The rangers were irregular frontier troops, who enlisted for short terms and supplied their own mounts and equipment. They were supposed to penetrate to the Red River, but they were satisfied with a short journey west through the Creek country to the buffalo plains. As soon as they left the Creek settlements, which at that time were confined to the Arkansas-Verdigris region and a few scattered cabins to the west, they were in supposedly dangerous Indian country; but they straggled off in pursuit of game and lost members of their party, allowed their horses to wander away or rode them to exhaustion, ran out of food, established disorderly, unguarded camps, and flew into helpless panic at Indian rumors. They met only a few friendly Osages, to whom Ellsworth addressed some futile admonitions to observe the peace. The Osages listened with grave courtesy, but the interpreter heard them remark to each other that they had better steal as many horses as possible from the Pawnees before this peace should be proclaimed.

Ellsworth's colleagues arrived during the winter, and it was this commission that settled the Creek-Cherokee boundary dispute and arranged for the Seminoles to locate with the Creeks. Before the end of 1833 they had called several tribes to Fort Gibson for friendly conferences and had held an important council with the Creeks, Cherokees, Choctaws, Osages, and Pawnees. In the summer of 1834 General Henry Leavenworth led a dragoon expedition to the plains of the Southwest to hold conferences with the Kiowas, Comanches, and Wichitas. Leavenworth and more than one hundred of his men died of a fever on this journey, but the southwestern tribes were induced to meet the Osages and the immigrant Indians in a great council at Fort Gibson in September. Here many beads were exchanged, much tobacco was smoked, and many speeches were delivered by the Indians; and many flags and medals were presented by the Federal officials.

The next year an important council was held in the Creeks' territory on the eastern border of the vast prairies stretching beyond their western settlements. The site selected was on the Canadian at a place known as Camp Holmes, where the intrepid Auguste Pierre Chouteau afterwards built a stockade and carried on a trade with the western tribes. Here the Comanches, Wichitas, Osages, Senecas, Cherokees, Choctaws, and Creeks signed a treaty of peace and friendship with each other and the United States. The Federal officials had been successful in bringing these unrelated tribes into a semblance of friendly intercourse.

The next important council was called by Stokes upon the initiative of the Cherokees for the purpose of making an Indian league. A garbled rumor of the approaching meeting spread to the settlements, and some of the western army officers hastily concluded that the tribes were planning to unite in a general war against the whites. They began to rush troops to the Cherokee country and called on the governors of Tennessee and Arkansas for volunteers. The chagrined Stokes managed to send back the soldiers, and in the summer of 1839 eleven tribes, including some recently arrived Seminoles, met in the vicinity of Tahlequah, where the Cherokees had established their council ground. Cherokee influence was supreme. A permanent organization was effected with Cherokees filling most of the offices and Roley McIntosh serving as second chief. This organization, of course, represented nothing more binding than a friendly feeling on the part of the participating tribes, but there is no doubt that this friendly feeling was increasing.

But the wild tribes still raided the Creek settlements, and the Osages and their enemies of the plains raided each other across the Creek country. In 1842 the Creeks called an intertribal council near the mouth of the Deep Fork for the purpose of checking this evil. Here the delegates of seventeen tribes made their camps, turned their horses out to crop the rich grass, feasted on the Creeks' beef, and gathered for solemn speeches and ceremonials. Several Federal officials were present, but the Creeks assumed the leadership. An atmosphere of great good will prevailed. The Osages voluntarily delivered about twenty stolen horses, and in the presence of the other tribes the Creeks warned them against such raids in future; but as soon as the council broke up, the same party went out to the plains on their buffalo hunt and stole about thirty horses and mules from the Kiowas. The Kiowas asked Chief McIntosh for redress, and he forced the Osages to surrender the captured property. The Creeks, in fact, not only protected their own frontiers, but by this time held a sort of balance of power between the various wild tribes. The Mexicans also tried to enlist them against the Texans, and Sam Houston intrigued at the same time for their support; but they refused the overtures of both sides and advised the wild tribes to observe the same neutrality.

While the Creeks were extending their influence over the wild tribes, the Cherokees pursued their favorite policy of organic union. They sent wampum tokens of invitation to thirty-six tribes of Indians throughout the whole area between the Mississippi and the Rocky Mountains, and in 1843 a great council convened at Tahlequah in the midst of the beautiful wooded hills that surrounded the wilderness capital. John Ross presided. Delegates of eighteen tribes were present—the agricultural Cherokees, Creeks, Chickasaws, and Seminoles, the partially tamed Osages, broken bands driven from the East, and visitors from distant Iowa — but the plains tribes did not attend. The happy confusion of a great Indian encampment, the picturesque contrast of paint and feathers and civilized elegance, the esoteric symbolism of speeches and ceremonials blended with the earnestness of Christian prayer—all created a strange and beautiful spectacle. With all their ancient mystical love of hearth and homeland, and the white man's borrowed weapons of law and logic, the exiled tribes were conquering that strange wilderness and gathering their forces to preserve the integrity of their race.

They drew up a compact which began as follows:

"Whereas the removal of the Indian tribes from the homes of their fathers, east of the Mississippi, has there extinguished our ancient council fires, and changed our position in regard to each other: And whereas by the solemn pledge of treaties, we are assured by the Government of the United States that the lands we now possess shall be the undisturbed home of ourselves and our posterity forever: Therefore, we, the authorized representatives of the several nations parties hereunto, assembled around the great council fire kindled in the west at Tahlequah, in order to preserve the relations between our several communities, to secure to all their respective rights, and to promote the general welfare, do enter into the following compact:"

The convention then provided for intertribal naturalization, the requisition of criminals, and the jurisdiction of the local courts over resident Indians of another tribe. It condemned the use of intoxicants as "a fruitful source of crime and misfortune" and recommended the suppression of the traffic. It declared that to promote agriculture and industry and "the comfort and happiness of our women and children a fixed and permanent location on our lands is an indispensable condition"; and it pledged the signatories not to cede any of their land to the United States without the consent of the other parties. This compact was ratified by the Creeks, Cherokees, and Osages and became the basis of all their subsequent intercourse. Only the article dealing with land cessions was disregarded, mainly because the Indians never surrendered any of their land except in response to superior force.

During succeeding years the Creeks acted as hosts to numerous councils which they called in the interest of peace between various wild tribes, especially the Osages and Pawnees. In 1845 they themselves were subjected to the novel experience of an "Indian scare." A great war council of the wild tribes had been called to meet on the Great Salt Plains northwest of the Creek settlements as soon as the grass should be "grown a foot high"; and it was known that the purpose of the meeting was to plan some form of redress against the immigrant Indians, especially the Creeks, for establishing farms and destroying the buffalo range.

Before the council met, there was a skirmish between the Creeks of the Little River settlement and a wandering band of Pawnees, and several of the marauders were killed. The Creeks, fearing a general attack by the wild tribes, began to move in from their exposed settlements to Edwards' Trading Post and called on the Creeks of the Arkansas District for help. Roley McIntosh and Jim Boy collected a number of warriors and went to their assistance. Rumors soon reached the Arkansas Creeks that this force had been repulsed, that the Little River Creeks had been annihilated by Pawnees, and that the Osages were planning to fall upon the exposed Cimarron and Verdigris frontier. The settlers in panic gathered up their children and their movable property and streamed across the river to Fort Gibson. Troops from the fort were rushed toward Little River, but they returned when they met McIntosh and Jim Boy coming back from the "war" without having seen an enemy.

The Creeks then planned to neutralize the approaching council by calling a meeting of their own on the Deep Fork. Echo Harjo and five other Creeks were sent to invite the southwestern tribes, but the Comanches curtly informed them that they were planning to attend the Salt Plains meeting and held them for a time as captives under sentence of death. The Pawnees also refused the invitation. It was attended, however, by the Osages, the Civilized Tribes, several of the broken bands from the East, and the Caddoes from the Southwest. Tuckabatchee Micco as Chief of the Upper Creeks assumed the leadership. He announced that the purpose of the meeting was to reopen the White Path that had been stained by the blood of the slain Pawnees, and he entrusted some white beads to the Delawares to be delivered to the Pawnees with a Creek message of peace. Other "talks" and tokens were prepared by the Creeks to be communicated to the Pawnees by the Caddoes and to the Comanches by the Osages at the approaching Salt Plains council. The hostile tribes were won by the deep emotional appeal of these messages and symbols, and they were impressed by a warning from the Osages that the Creeks were a dangerous people to arouse. The Comanches sent a "talk" by the Wichitas inviting the Creeks and Cherokees to make a treaty of friendship with them; and when the Creeks called a council of their own on the Salt Plains in the fall, the Comanches and many other wild tribes accepted the invitation.

From this time on the Creeks held many meetings on the plains with their wild brethren of the buffalo range, and they engaged to an increasing extent in the Indian trade of the Southwest. Their primitive admirers even credited them with understanding the strange ways of the white man and began to ask for their advice and intercession in their troubles with the Texas settlers. The Creeks counseled them to abandon their wandering lives, make peace with the white man, and settle down as farmers. In 1855 several thousand Comanches from a great camp far up the Arkansas sent word to the Federal officials through Tuckabatchee Micco that they had seen the prosperity of the Creeks and wished to imitate it, and that they wanted a separate tract of land where they might become an agricultural people. Thomas S. Drew, Southern Superintendent, advised compliance with their request, but no action was taken.

But while the Creeks were gaining this moral ascendancy over

the wild tribes, they became the leaders in councils of the civilized
Indians. The intertribal law code drawn up at Tahlequah in 1843
was clarified and strengthened by a compact adopted by the Five
Tribes at Asbury Mission at North Fork Town in 1859. The Cherokees and Choctaws probably supplied the legal knowledge, but
it was the all-embracing internationalism of the Creeks that furnished the atmosphere of the negotiations. It may not have been
formally ratified, but all subsequent intercourse between the Creeks
and their civilized neighbors was carried on according to its provisions.[13]

The compacts of 1843 and 1859 comprised the answer of the
Indians to a favorite project of the white man—the creation of an
Indian territory or state in the area belonging to the Five Civilized
Tribes. Sincere friends of the Indians like Isaac McCoy believed
that such a strong union of the tribes would enable them to contend
with the white man on equal terms; ardent patriots, stirred by the
sight of star after star added to the flag, dreamed of the day when
the glorious sisterhood would include the Indians also; and, above
all, land-grabbers knowing the inability of Indians to hold their
farms under the white man's tenure schemed to force them to
accept statehood and United States citizenship and individual allotments so that they might dispossess them. In 1832—the very year
he induced the Creeks to surrender their eastern homes upon a
promise of future autonomy—the unprincipled Herring piously
lamented the limitation to Indian progress in the power of their
chiefs and their system of land holding. From that time on, territorial bills were frequently introduced in Congress, and territorial
plans were repeatedly offered to the Indians. The relationship between these projects and the land hunger of the frontier settlers
was plainly apparent when Major Elias Rector, of Arkansas, was
appointed to the Southern Superintendency in 1857.

Rector filled his official reports with glowing descriptions of the

---

[13] Commissioner of Indian Affairs, *Annual Reports,* 1839-59; WPA Project S-149;
United States Archives, Creek 1861/G382; Grant Foreman, *Advancing the Frontier,* 131-
38, 168 n., 195-237; Foreman, *Pioneer Days in the Early Southwest, passim;* Foreman,
A Traveler in Indian Territory, 69 f., 243 f.; Kappler, Laws and Treaties, II, 435-39;
Irving, *A Tour on the Prairies; Niles' Weekly Register,* XXXV (1828), 58; 49 Cong., 1
sess., *Sen. Rep. No. 1278,* 350 f.

fertility and undeveloped mineral wealth of the country belonging to the Five Tribes—an area generally known as the "Indian Territory," embracing all the present Oklahoma except the "Panhandle." The Indians, he said, did not use one acre in a hundred, and he predicted the great benefits that would accrue to them if they could be induced to exchange their petty nationality for the glorious privileges of United States citizenship and accept their land in severalty. They might then retain a portion of these individual tracts under inalienable tenure and sell the remainder to honest and thrifty whites, who would influence them in civilization; and they would live under the beneficent influence of the white man's courts and law. As for the inconvenient guarantees in the Removal Treaties, "necessity is the supreme law of nations . . . and before its stern requisitions every other consideration will give way."

The Five Tribes stood as a unit against this policy. The Creeks fought their battles with less legal skill than their Cherokee and Choctaw neighbors, but they never forgot their experience with individual land tenure and the white man's courts in Alabama. Their mixed bloods knew that they held their land under a patent given by Millard Fillmore in 1852 in fulfillment of their Removal Treaty—"to have and to hold the same, unto the said tribe of Indians, so long as they shall exist as a Nation, and continue to occupy the country hereby conveyed to them." Their simple-minded full bloods based their claim to perpetual tenure upon a silver medal given to Opothle Yahola, and they developed a mystical love for their new homeland. A present-day Creek remembers the exhortations of the medicine man at the ceremonials of Locker Poker (Lutcapoga, Place of Terrapins) Town, a branch of Tallasi; "the mountains and hills, that you see, are your backbone, and the gullies and the creeks, which are between the hills and mountains, are your heart veins." Their great missionary, Loughridge, warned the Federal officials that the destruction of their land tenure would reduce them to homeless wanderers and pleaded for time for education and undisturbed development.

In 1859 the Commissioner of Indian Affairs sent a formal request to the Creeks urging them to accept a survey of their land and the allotment in fee simple of as much as should be necessary for their actual occupancy. The Creeks in council drew up a decided refusal. "We have had some experience in sectionalization, under the treaty of 1832. . . . The results were evils and evil continually, the misery and punishment endured by our people growing out of sectionalization as above stated is fresh open our minds. Hence there is no consideration that can induce us to try the experiment again."[14]

In matters less vital to their existence the Creeks showed a surprisingly conciliatory spirit toward the United States. They listened to their agent with courtesy if not with subserviency. They were genuinely glad of the protection offered by Fort Gibson, which was not abandoned until 1857, and by several forts to the southwest of their country. As their educated mixed bloods gained in legal knowledge, they learned to claim their rights, and their treaties after 1833 were increasingly favorable.

By their removal they had won comparative freedom from the presence of white men. In 1842 their agent reported twenty-two living in the nation with Indian wives, and six licensed traders. Some of these intermarried white men had been adopted as citizens, but as soon as the Treaty of 1856 gave the Creeks a certain control over white immigration they passed a law providing that in the future no white man should be adopted, directing the principal chief of each district to furnish the agent with the names of intruders for their expulsion from the nation, placing a tax of one hundred dollars a year on traders and three dollars a day on peddlers, and permitting citizens to employ white mechanics under contract for a limited time. The Federal officials gave the required consent to the tax law. This policy of refusing citizenship to intermarried whites, requesting the removal of intruders, taxing traders, and granting permits to laborers was followed by the Creeks throughout the rest of their tribal existence.

In the fall of 1860 the Council directed Samuel Checote, a prominent mixed blood named John G. Smith, and the two principal

<hr/>

[14] Commissioner of Indian Affairs, *Annual Report,* 1832, 163; 1836, 383-90; 1857, 201 f.; 1858, 6 f., 126-28; 1859, 181 f.; 1860, 14. WPA Project S-149; Creek Tribal Records 29689; *ibid.,* Checote Manuscript, 3; United States Archives, Creek 1860/G127.

chiefs to go to Washington on special business. These delegates informed the Commissioner that there was "a very great transit" from Missouri and other states to Texas, and that the emigrants were tempted to linger or even settle in the Creek country with their cattle. Licensed traders also were establishing farms and raising live stock. The Creeks wanted an explicit definition of the Treaty of 1856 and the Intercourse Laws, so they would know the exact status of a white man in their country. They also wanted an opinion from the Commissioner regarding the justice of increasing the traders' tax. This early attempt of the Creeks to protect their range from intruding cattlemen and licensed traders was also to continue throughout the rest of the tribal period. The delegates referred these matters to the Commissioner in January, but the peril of the times delayed their consideration.[15]

By this time the Creeks were once more prospering and happy. They had composed their differences and become a united people, they had tamed the wilderness and learned to love it as their home, they had gained a moral leadership in Indian councils throughout the Southwest. Although a conservative people, they were acquiring such of the white man's ways as seemed necessary for their survival—his more effective farming methods, his skills of learning—and they were replacing the lost loyalties of their ancient faith by the steadying influence of Christianity. Some of their "progress" had been artificially imposed from without but there was a strength in their native steadfastness and promise for the future in a genuine natural advancement. But just as they had painfully reached this hopeful stage in their development, they were thrust again into abject misery by the horrors of the white man's war.

[15] Commissioner of Indian Affairs, *Annual Reports*, 1842-59; Creek Tribal Records, Checote Manuscript, 16; United States Archives, Creek 1861/G382, K33.

CHAPTER 5

The White Man's War

THE white man's Civil War was also a civil war among the Creeks. The full bloods with characteristic conservatism and loyalty stood by their old commitments, but they had no avenue of communication with the Federal government. Their agent, William H. Garrett, of Alabama, was an ardent secessionist; and Southern Superintendent Rector, from his office at Fort Smith, Arkansas, worked actively with his cousin, the governor of the state, to bring them to the Southern side. The educated mixed bloods entered enthusiastically into the treaty making, conventions, and diplomatic opportunities of a new political alignment, and an alliance with the Confederate States was manipulated without the real consent of the tribe.

Early in 1861 the educated leaders took steps to protect the tribe in the impending crisis. The delegation mentioned in the preceding chapter, apparently inspired by Garrett, who seems to have joined them in Washington by this time, inquired how their landed interests would be protected during "the commotion now shaking the United States" and "earnestly" requested that their annuities, unpaid for the past year, should be placed in Garrett's hands for distribution. In the general confusion little attention was paid to their requests, but it was decided to withhold the annuities because of the danger of their falling into Confederate hands.

At the same time the Chickasaws requested the Creeks to call a council of the Five Tribes to renew the harmony established by the Asbury Mission Compact and enter into a further agreement to protect them "in the event of a change in the United States." The Creeks called the meeting for February 17 at their council ground, but only the Cherokees and Seminoles joined them there. John Ross through the Cherokee delegates used his influence in favor of neutrality, and it was decided "simply to do nothing, to keep quiet, and to comply with our treaties." The utmost harmony prevailed, and it was felt that whatever exigencies should arise in the future "we will be found acting in concert and sharing a common destiny."

It was probably while the Creeks were assembled at this meeting that they convened their own General Council and passed a law calculated to force their free negroes into temporary slavery. These negroes were required to choose an Indian owner before March 10 or to be sold for a twelve months' period to the highest Indian bidder; but their new owners were forbidden to dispose of them to non-citizens under pain of a fine equal to two times the value of the negro, one hundred lashes, and the loss of one ear. This law was enacted February 29, and in the absence of the principal chiefs, who were still in Washington, it was approved by Derrisaw and Oktarharsars Harjo.

Soon after this meeting adjourned, three commissioners from Texas came to the Arkansas settlement. Here H. F. Buckner, a Baptist missionary, "did us great kindness and showed us eminent service"; and they enlisted the support of Chilly McIntosh, Benjamin Marshall, and Daniel N. McIntosh, a younger half brother of Chilly. Through these leaders the commissioners prevailed upon Chief Canard to call a council of the Five Tribes at North Fork Town April 8. The Choctaws and Chickasaws were kept from this meeting by high water, but delegates were present from the Creek, Cherokee, Seminole, Sac and Fox, and Quapaw tribes. Canard was elected chairman. One of the Texans addressed the meeting. They reported that they found the Creeks "Southern and sound to a man." The council adjourned to meet May 1, and it was apparently this later meeting that appointed delegates to confer with the Confederate government. They did go to Montgomery, only to find that the capital had been removed to Richmond.

During this same April and May, Texas troops occupied all the military posts in the Indian country to the southwest, and the garrisons hastily retreated across the Creek Nation to Fort Leavenworth, Kansas. Fort Gibson, it will be remembered, had been abandoned four years before. The Federal government was not able even to send an agent to the Creeks, and William G. Coffin, who had been appointed to Rector's place as Southern Superintendent, was forced to remain in Kansas. William P. Dole, Commissioner of Indian Affairs, sent a message of encouragement to Canard and Echo Harjo, but it failed to reach them. The Indian country, surrounded on three sides by Texas and Arkansas, was completely cut off from the United States. At the same time Albert Pike, of Arkansas, was appointed by the Confederate Secretary of State to negotiate treaties with the tribes.

In June, Oktarharsars Harjo and other fullblood chiefs were sent to a great council of the plains Indians. As soon as they were out of the way, an important council of Choctaws, Chickasaws, Creeks, and Seminoles was held at North Fork Town. Most of the delegates were wealthy and educated mixed bloods, and they represented the leading Southern sympathizers within their tribes. James M. C. Smith, who had served as superintendent of schools for Canadian District; Timothy Barnett, the able and educated grandson of Timpoochee Barnard; George W. Stidham, an intelligent mixed blood who owned a trading house at the agency; Samuel Checote; D. N. McIntosh; and John G. Smith were among the Creek delegates. Robert M. Jones, the richest plantation owner and most militant secessionist in the Choctaw Nation, was made president. Pike, who had come to negotiate treaties with the delegates, probably worked in the background.

On July 1 this council drew up a constitution creating an Indian confederacy to be known as the "United Nations of the Indian Territory." Its legislative body was a Grand Council, composed of six delegates from each member tribe, meeting annually at North Fork Town. Each principal chief was to attend these meetings to report on conditions in his nation and recommend needed legislation; all laws passed by the Grand Council required the approval of a majority of the principal chiefs; and any principal chief might call the Grand Council in special session. The Grand Council was given authority to call on the member nations for troops to repel the "invading forces of Abolition hordes under Abraham Lincoln"—the irony was unconscious—and free passage was granted the armed forces of the Confederate States. The Cherokees and the

Caddoes eventually accepted this compact, and the Grand Council met, under Southern auspices, throughout the war. Meetings may have been held for the first two years at North Fork Town; but after Southern military reverses, which occurred in 1863, at least one session was held at Tishomingo, the Chickasaw capital, and the regular place of assembly was at the Choctaw capital of Chahta Tamaha.

A few days after this constitution was drawn up, Pike negotiated a treaty with a Creek delegation consisting of Motey Canard, Echo Harjo, Chilly McIntosh, D. N. McIntosh, and other leaders. Oktarharsars Harjo later summarized his arguments. "That man told Indian that the Union people would come and take away property and take away land—now you sleep, you ought to wake up and attend to your own property. Tell them there ain't no U. S.—ain't any more Treaty—all be dead—Tell them as there is no more U. S. no more Treaty that the Creeks had better make new Treaty with the South and the Southern President would protect them and give them their annuity—Tell them if you make Treaty with southern President that he would pay you more annuity and would pay better than the U. S. if they the Indians would help the Southern President—Mr. Pike makes the half breeds believe what he says and the half breeds makes some of the full blood Indians believe what he says that they (the Indians) must help the secessionists." The main trouble with this reasoning was that so far as the Indians could see it was all true. It proved expedient, however, to bribe Canard, and he was made a colonel of cavalry for life and promised a uniform, a sabre, a Maynard rifle, and ammunition to maintain his new state. This provision was made in a secret article, and apparently was never suspected by any other Creek leader. The treaty was finally signed on July 10.

It was more favorable to the Creeks than any treaty they ever made with the United States. The protectorate relationship was clearly and exactly defined; there were explicit guarantees against territorial government and allotment; the annuities formerly paid by the United States—now totaling $71,960 since the Treaty of 1856— were assumed by the new government; and slavery was expressly legalized and placed exclusively under Creek jurisdiction.

The Creeks agreed to furnish alone or with the Seminoles a regiment of mounted men to serve in the Confederate army with the same pay as other soldiers; and the Creeks and Seminoles together were entitled to a delegate in the Confederate Congress.

Unlike most treaties made with the United States—even the liberal Treaty of 1856—this compact was not to go into effect until ratified by the Creeks. When Oktarharsars Harjo and his party returned from the West, the General Council had already been called to take this action. These conservatives refused to accept Pike's reasoning; as Oktarharsars Harjo expressed it, "as for himself he dont believe him yet. Then he thought the old U. S. was alive yet and the [old] Treaty was good. Wont go against the U. S. himself." His party withdrew from the Council, and the treaty was ratified July 20. Jacob Derrisaw and a number of other chiefs affixed their signatures, and it was witnessed by Garrett, who apparently had been present during the whole proceedings. The names of at least three of the "Loyal" party were affixed without their consent.

While Pike was at North Fork Town, he also negotiated a treaty with the Choctaws and Chickasaws. The Choctaws were overwhelmingly Southern in their sympathies and the Chickasaws entered into relations with the Confederacy without serious difficulty. He then went on west and met the Seminoles at their agency. He found them disunited and distracted, but with the help of Canard and other Southern Creeks he managed to secure a form of agreement with them. With a large mounted escort of Creeks and Seminoles he then proceeded to the plains and obtained treaties with bands of the wild Indians. John Jumper, of the Seminoles; Elias Rector, who was still using his influence to bring the Indians into the Confederate service; Motey Canard; and Chilly McIntosh all signed the Comanche treaty. Pike then returned to the Cherokee Nation in the fall and persuaded that tribe to abandon its neutrality. At the same time he secured treaties with the Osages, Quapaws, and Senecas.

Meanwhile affairs in the Creek country were falling rapidly into chaos. The Presbyterian missionaries had hoped to keep the boarding schools running, but on July 10—the very day the treaty was signed—Motey Canard and Jacob Derrisaw gave orders for them to vacate the Coweta and Tullahassee properties. The children packed their little bundles, bade their teachers a tearful farewell, and scattered to their separate homes, the first victims of a desolation that was soon to engulf the nation. The missionaries made their perilous way to their people, North or South, Loughridge going to Texas and Robertson to Kansas. The Asbury Mission was closed also, but possibly because it belonged to the Southern Methodists one of the missionaries remained as custodian of the building.

On August 5 the Loyal Creeks met in council, declared the treaty illegal and the office of chief vacant, and authorized Oktarharsars Harjo—or Sands, as he was usually called by the white men—to act as principal chief. The Confederate party then placed a bounty of five thousand dollars on his head. Apparently it was at this time that Opothle Yahola came out for the Federal cause. His previous actions are difficult to ascertain. There seems to be no record of his participation in any of the councils, but the present-day Creeks have a confused tradition of dramatic meetings and Olympian quarrels between him and the other Creek leaders, and—most persistent of all—of an immense treasure that he had buried. All that is known with certainty is that by August 15 he and Sands were writing to President Lincoln for the protection promised by the Treaty of 1856.

"Now I write to the President our Great Father who removed us to our present homes, & made a treaty, and you said that in our new homes we should be defended from all interference from any person and that no white people in the whole world should ever molest us ... and should we be injured by any body you would come with your soldiers & punish them. but now the wolf has come. men who are strangers tread our soil. our children are frightened & the mothers cannot sleep for fear. This is our situation now. When we made our Treaty at Washington you assured us that our children should laugh around our houses without fear & we believed you. . . . Once we were at peace. Our great father was always near & stood between us and danger.

"We his children want it to be so again, and we want you to send us word what to do. We do not hear from you & we send a letter, & we pray you to answer it You[r] children want to hear your word, & feel that you do not forget them.

"I was at Washington when you treated with us, and now white people are trying to take our people away to fight against us and you. I am alive. I well remember the treaty. My ears are open & my memory is good."

This letter did not reach Washington for nearly a month. As the Confederates began to collect their forces, part of the Loyal Creeks moved to the Little River. From there they called a great Indian council. The Choctaws, who had entirely gone over to the South, failed to attend, but members of the other Civilized Tribes, the broken tribes living in the Little River region, and several bands of plains Indians decided to remain loyal to the United States. They sent Micco Hutke (White Chief), Bob Deer, and Joe Ellis, their interpreter, through that bandit-infested border to Kansas to carry the letter of Opothle Yahola and Sands and an oral message from the council.

These messengers finally reached the Shawnee Agency, and Agent James B. Abbott forwarded their communications to Washington. They notified the government that "our people are in great distress. Men have come among us, who claim to represent a New Government, who tell us that the Government represented by our Great Father at Washington, has turned against us and intends to drive us from our homes and take away our property. they tell us that we have nothing to hope from our old Father and that all the Friends of the Indians have joined the New Government. And the New Government is ready to make treaties with the Indians and do all and more for them than they can claim under their old treaties. they ask us to join their Armies and help sustain the Government that is willing to do so much for us. But we doubted their statements and promises and went to talk with the Agent and Superend which our father has always kept among us. but they were both gone. and then some of our people began to think that our Great Father had forsaken us and a very few joined the Army of the New Government." They went on to say that their country was full of Confederate agents, and they earnestly requested that some Federal official be sent to meet representatives of the Loyal party at some place in Kansas.

Tentative plans were made for this council, but it proved impossible for the Indians to attend. Sands, Micco Hutke, Bob Deer, and a few Seminoles and Chickasaws finally reached Leroy, Kansas, in November. Here for the first time in many weary months they found a Creek agent, Major George A. Cutler. Sands told him the whole story of his opposition to the Confederate treaty, his continued loyalty, and his perplexity and helplessness. "Never knew that Creek have an agent here until he come and see him and that is why I have come among this Union people. Have come in and saw my agent and want to go by the old Treaty. Wants to get with U. S. Army so that I can get back to my people as Secessionists will not let me go. Wants the Great Father to send the Union Red people and Troops down the Black Beaver road and he will guide them to his country and then all his people will be for the Union . . . At the time I left my union people I told them to look to the Beaver Road until I come. . . . The way he left his country his people was in an elbow surrounded by secessions and his people is not strong enough against them for Union and that is the reason he has come up for help—" They wanted ammunition, clothing, and tents, and they were in need of their annuities. The mixed bloods, he said, had joined the South, but twenty-seven towns with 3,350 warriors were loyal and were willing to fight for the Union.

The Federal officials then sent these chiefs to Washington in order that they might see the military preparations around the capital—an inexpensive way of showing them the Great Father's protection. "On arriving there, face to face, we informed our Great Father of the situation that our country was in, and were informed by our Great Father that our treaties were and should be respected; and we were further assured that he would send us help as soon as he could."

That same fall of 1861 Garrett wrote from the Creek Agency to the Confederate Commissioner of Indian Affairs, giving a careful estimate of the Creek situation. There were 1,650 warriors among the Lower Creeks, of whom 375 were unfriendly to the Confederacy; and 1,600 warriors among the Upper Creeks, of whom only 400 were friendly—a total of 1,575 Northern Creeks and 1,675 Southern. Of the Southern Creeks 1,375 were already enlisted in the Confederate army, and most of them had been furnished with arms; they were organized into a regiment under Colonel D. N. McIntosh, a battalion under Lieutenant Colonel Chilly McIntosh, and an independent company under Captain James M. C. Smith.

The Confederate government had created the Department of the Indian Territory and placed Pike in command; but Pike was still in Richmond with his treaties, and Douglas H. Cooper, former Federal agent to the Choctaws and Chickasaws, was in charge. By a sort of natural leadership Opothle Yahola began to direct the movements of the Loyal Creeks. They prepared stores of food, collected their property, and gathered for protection in a great camp near the junction of the North Fork and the Deep Fork; and a number of Seminoles, Kickapoos, Shawnees, Delawares, Wichitas, and Comanches joined them there. Conditions were ready for a repetition of the terrible tragedy of the Red Stick War.[1]

Cooper with a force of Indians and Texas cavalry prepared to attack this refuge. Opothle Yahola broke camp November 5 and attempted to conduct his people, with their horses and herds and wagons, to safety in Kansas. Cooper reached the deserted camp ten days later and started in pursuit. On the night of November 19 he overtook them at Round Mountain near the confluence of the Cimarron and the Arkansas. An indecisive battle was fought here, and Opothle Yahola slipped away in the darkness and crossed into the Cherokee Nation.

Cooper was delayed some time by conflicting orders from his superiors and the defection of his fullblood Cherokees; but he came up with Opothle Yahola's people again on Bird Creek, and the Battle of Caving Banks was fought December 9 at the Bird Creek crossing. In the absence of uniforms and other insignia the Loyal warriors decorated themselves with corn-shuck badges. The attackers were beaten off and again Opothle Yahola slipped away and

[1] James M. Matthews, *Statutes at Large of the Provisional Government of the Confederate States of America,* 232, 289-303; Commissioner of Indian Affairs, *Annual Report,* 1861, 9 f., 34-39, 41-49, 171-74; 1862, 138; 1865, 328 f.; 1869, 80 f. WPA Project S-149; United States Archives, Creek 1861/G382, B484, B787, K33; 1865/G146. *Indian Record,* March, 1887; Creek Tribal Records, Checote Manuscript, 30; *War of the Rebellion, Compilation of the Official Records of the Union and Confederate Armies,* First Series, Vol. XXXIV, Part 2, 958; Choctaw Nation, Tribal Records, 17708; Annie Heloise Abel, *The American Indian as Participant in the Civil War,* 66-248; Abel, *The American Indian as Slaveholder and Secessionist,* 66-67 n.

continued his orderly retreat to Kansas. Cooper waited until he received white reinforcements; then he pursued Opothle Yahola again and overtook him in the rocky gorges and deep recesses of the Osage Hills. Here on December 26 the Battle of Chustenahlah was fought. Opothle Yahola's ammunition failed and he was completely routed. His terrified followers abandoned everything—wagons, bed coverings, camp equipment, food—and fled wildly through the night and the following day, never stopping until they reached refuge in Kansas. The weather was intensely cold, the ground covered with snow, and a bitter wind blowing from the northwest. Many froze to death and their bodies were devoured by wolves. Children were born on the naked snow and died of their terrible exposure.

Present-day Creeks remember how each family prepared for the journey, storing their food, burying their valuables, leaving their homes; they know the location of various local camps where their people collected before they joined the main body; and they can tell incidents of the retreat. James Scott, of Greenleaf Town, was about ten years old when the flight took place. He is entirely unfamiliar with published accounts, but he remembers many details of the journey. "Opuithli Yahola's heart was sad at all the war talk. He visited the homes of his followers or any of the Indians and gave them encouragement to face all these things, but above all things to stay out of the war. It was no affair of the Indians."

When Larney's parents began to prepare for the journey, "I did not fully realize or understand why I was given orders to round up the cattle. I wondered at the vast amount of cattle being killed and the meat being dried, the pork being cooked down, and all the other numerous preparations. At all the homes of neighbors, I saw all sorts of preparations with little knowledge of its meaning." This community gathered at Hillabee Creek on the western frontier. "We were joined by larger groups and we in turn joined other larger groups," and all moved east until they effected their junction with Opothle Yahola. "I was given the task to help drive the cattle, but I relinquished my job over to the older boys when we joined the main body." He gives a clear account of the first two battles and confused, flashing pictures of the flight. "One time we saw a little baby sitting on its little blanket in the woods. Everyone was running because an attack was expected and no one had the time to stop and pick up the child. As it saw the people running by, the little child began to wave its little hands. The child had no knowledge that he had been deserted."

The fugitives slowly collected on the upper Verdigris, where they huddled together for comfort. As soon as Coffin learned of their plight, he obtained supplies from General Hunter, who was in command of the Department of Kansas. By that time 3,168 Creeks, 53 Creek slaves, 38 free Creek negroes, 777 Seminoles, 136 Quapaws, 50 Cherokees, 31 Chickasaws, and a few Kickapoos and others had assembled. New refugees were constantly arriving, but many died by the roadside before they reached that meagre solace. Conditions in the camp were wretched beyond description. Indian-like they tried to construct shelters, where white people under similar circumstances would have wrapped themselves in whatever rags they could find. Men, women, and children lay on the frozen ground with only the snow-encrusted prairie grass for a bed and scraps of cloth—handkerchiefs, aprons, anything—stretched on saplings for their sole protection against the blizzards. An army surgeon who reached the camp early in February counted seven children who were entirely naked. He found Opothle Yahola, once a rich man in the careless Indian manner, lying ill of a fever. His tent had been made by stretching a narrow blanket on a switch ridge pole, but the sides failed by two feet to reach the ground. Many had worse shelters; few had better. More than one hundred frozen limbs had to be amputated.

By April there were 7,600 refugees in the camp. Coffin soon had them removed to the Neosho, and the Creeks were quartered near LeRoy under the care of their agent. Congress by a resolution of February 22 had authorized the Secretary of the Interior to use the unpaid annuities for their support. Obviously this provision was insufficient—a food allowance of only fifteen cents a day would have required a yearly expenditure of nearly $400,000, and there was the terrible need for medicine and clothing—but through the dishonesty that seems inseparable from Indian contracts even this meagre sum was wasted on damaged flour and inferior meat.

The men were impatient to enlist in the army. With rations and ammunition and white support they believed they could clear their country of Confederates and conduct their women and children home. After many disappointments they were finally organized under white officers to form the First Regiment of Indian Home Guards. On June 28, having been armed with worthless guns discarded by white men and having taken their bullet-proof medicine and danced their war dance, they started with high hopes toward the Indian Territory. Colonel William Weer was in command, and white troops from Wisconsin accompanied them.

There had been considerable confusion and disorder in the Creek country, especially in the Canadian District, during that same winter of 1861-62. Not all of the Northern Creeks had left with Opothle Yahola. Malucy Bear, also of Greenleaf Town, remembers the experiences of those who stayed. She describes the departure of the neighbors to the rendezvous on Hillabee Creek. It must have been in the fall, she says, for the corn and sweet potatoes were ready to gather; but there was no one to gather them. The once happy community was a place of desolation. "We would see some lone cow that had been left. The roosters would continually crow at some deserted home. The dogs would bark or howl. Those days were lonesome to me, as young as I was, for I knew that most of our old acquaintances were gone." Men of the Northern and Southern factions killed each other on sight. Raiding parties stole everything and even burned the houses. The women and children hid in the thickets by day and returned to "what was left of our homes" at night.

But in comparison with the sufferings of the Loyal party the Southern Creeks possessed their country in comparative tranquillity during the winter of 1861-62. In December the Confederate Congress made the necessary appropriations under the Pike treaty: $71,960 in annuities, $750 to compensate the delegates who carried on the negotiations, and $240 to equip Motey Canard in the splendor promised by the secret article. Cantonment Davis was erected on the west side of the Arkansas just below the Three Forks, and the Creek troops were in their own country. Colonel J. J. Clarkson was in command of the Confederate forces north of the Canadian.

As Weer marched down through the Cherokee Nation, Clarkson with a Missouri battalion met him at Locust Grove July 3. The Creeks in the Union service bore the brunt of the fighting. The Confederates were defeated, and Weer went on to Fort Gibson. But the weather was hot, and the troops suffered for lack of provisions. Matters reached a crisis on July 18 when Frederick Salomon, colonel of the first brigade, arrested Weer, placed himself in command, and started back to Kansas with his white troops, leaving the disappointed Indians on the Verdigris to cover his retreat. Thus ended the first feeble attempt of the United States to recover the Indian Territory.

The deserted Indians became demoralized and some returned to the refugee camp. Others remained in the vicinity of Fort Gibson and Tahlequah and engaged in the guerrilla warfare that was now desolating the Cherokee Nation. The Southern Creeks at this time were operating in the West, trying with small success to hold that wild region for the Confederacy. The disheartened Creeks in Kansas settled down to another refugee winter. A census taken in September showed 416 men, 1,342 women, and 1,666 children at LeRoy; and 150 in a smaller camp on Walnut Creek—a total of 3,769 refugees besides about 800 warriors enlisted in the Union army. They were removed to the Sac and Fox Reservation, farther north in Kansas, where they settled for the winter.[2]

Colonel William A. Phillips had remained most of the time with the Indian troops ever since Salomon had abandoned them. Now he occupied Fort Gibson and carried on a constant skirmishing with the Confederate Cherokees in the vicinity. At the same time he sent messages to whatever Indians he could reach to detach them from the Confederate service; and a number of Creeks came into his camp with white badges on their hats and accepted this opportunity to change their allegiance.

But in spite of these defections, the Southern Creeks were still fairly unified. They maintained their governmental organization, and Canard and Echo Harjo served out their four-year terms as

[2] Commissioner of Indian Affairs, *Annual Report*, 1862, *passim;* 1865, 328 f. United States Archives, Creek 1865/G146; Matthews, *Confederate Statutes at Large*, 232; Abel, *The American Indian as Slaveholder and Secessionist*, 254-79; Abel, *The American Indian as Participant in the Civil War*, 22-228.

principal chiefs. The Council met to pass laws, but about half of its members had gone North and its sessions were usually held wherever the Southern soldiers happened to be stationed. Several important laws were passed in the early spring of 1863. Citizenship was granted to Frederick B. Severs, a young white man who had come from Arkansas to teach in the Creek schools and had enlisted in the Creek regiment at the outbreak of the war. It was provided that the property abandoned by the Loyal Creeks was to be confiscated and sold, and all free negroes who had followed Opothle Yahola were to be sold when captured; and the proceeds were to be turned into the public treasury. Since the schools were all closed, the educational annuities paid by the Confederate government were distributed per capita; and provision was made for the issuance of fractional currency or "shin-plasters" to the sum of twenty thousand dollars.[3]

The greatest battle fought in the Indian Territory during the war took place at Honey Springs in the Creek Nation, July 17, 1863. As the fall of Vicksburg and Lee's defeat at Gettysburg the same month marked the turning point in the white man's Civil War, this battle was decisive in Indian warfare. By this time there were two Creek regiments—the First still commanded by Colonel D. N. McIntosh, the Second by Colonel Chilly McIntosh. Cooper had concentrated his Indian forces—Choctaws, Chickasaws, Cherokees, and Creeks—at Honey Springs. He also had a squadron of Texas cavalry. He was waiting for reinforcements from Fort Smith, and when they arrived he planned to advance up the Texas Road and capture Fort Gibson. His plans probably would have succeeded, but the Federals advanced from Fort Gibson and struck before the Arkansas troops arrived. The Southern Indians fought bravely—especially the Creeks, who were defending their own country—but they ran out of ammunition and were finally routed.

The Federals now assumed an uncertain offensive. For a time they occupied the country between the Arkansas and the Canadian, and within six weeks they captured Fort Smith, which they held until the end of the war. The Confederates slowly withdrew to the Choctaw and Chickasaw nations, and the commanding officers of

3 Creek Tribal Records, Checote Manuscript, 31-35.

the Indian Territory were stationed there. The Creek forces at first retired to the west, but they gradually abandoned their own country and retreated to the south of the Canadian.[4]

After the Battle of Honey Springs, the families of the Southern Creeks fled to the Red River region and formed refugee camps in the Choctaw and Chickasaw nations and northern Texas. Many elderly Creeks, who were children at the time, remember this flight as it affected individual families. Elsie Edwards has a lively memory of details. "The neighboring people were so excited that they were just running around getting ready to go somewhere. Men folks were fixing up the wagons while the women folks were busy getting the quilts ready, gathering up pots and other cooking utensils, and loading up the wagons. Ropes were made of cow hides cut in long strips and these were used to tie small bundles. They loaded up the light articles . . . upon the horses and securely tied with the cow hide ropes." She remembers that Jim Boy, her father, placed her and another child on top of one of these packs, and that she rode there throughout the journey. "I remember that we made our camp across the Red River near a high hill. The people made shelter in any way and out of anything that could be used, but most of the people made their crude houses out of bark which was usually of hickory bark. Some covered their shelter with twigs and covered it over with cow hides. . . . The bark houses were arranged along a street-like clearing with the houses opposite each one and in the center of the street was dug a long ditch, running the length of the street, and this was used to build a fire in it and cooking was done over the fire in the ditch."

Lizzie Winn, the daughter of a Creek father and a Shawnee mother, was living in the Shawnee settlement on the Creek frontier. The family owned a few negroes, but "daddy said he guessed we would be safe if we just turned them loose." They started east, but while they were still in the Creek country her father became ill and they stopped at a vacant house. "The Northern soldiers came to the door and I was standing at the head of his bed. They told me to move but I thought that if I stayed there they surely wouldn't

[4] Abel, *The American Indian as Participant in the Civil War,* 243-311; Commissioner of Indian Affairs, *Annual Report,* 1864, 323; 1865, 285 f.

shoot him. They shot him and blood and brains spattered all over me." After the guerrillas left, "we covered daddy up and shut the doors and left him laying in the bed. There was a hill at the back of the house so we ran to it so that we could get away without being seen." After incredible hardships they reached the Chickasaw Nation, where "some soldiers from the south gave us some clothes from wagons and fed us" and conducted them to a camp on the Washita. She soon went into Texas to assist some white women who were making cloth for the refugees and the Southern soldiers. "I couldn't talk any English and they couldn't talk any Indian, so they just showed me how to do as they talked English and I learned to talk English." The young Indian girl enjoyed this association, and when the war was over, "it was a sad parting, everyone cried."

In spite of their hardships these refugees were never reduced to the hopeless demoralization of their relatives in the North. One of them said that the Choctaws "were always willing to give us a part of anything they had that we needed." The Creek government—meaning, of course, the Southern government, from which Opothle Yahola's faction had seceded—furnished them small amounts of food, and the Confederate government, in spite of its financial perplexities, carried on an organized system of relief. They were able to plant crops, and their men took time off from their military service and supplied them with meat. Some of the Methodist and Baptist missionaries, who because of their Southern sympathies had been able to remain with their flocks, ministered to them in the refugee camps. A few of them still held considerable property. A will made by Abram Foster in 1864 shows not only the orderly manner in which they still tried to transact their business, but the financial situation of these more fortunate citizens. He had with him $1,175 in gold, $1,300 in Confederate paper, 6 negro slaves, 9 horses, 3 yoke of oxen, and 2 wagons, and the Creek Nation owed him for 51 head of beef cattle. He also bequeathed "my stock of cattle in the Creek Country with my Buildings and Fields Should we ever be fortunate enough to regain the country My house hold goods, with any and all other property that may be here after recovered, belonging to me." He also made provision for a daughter who apparently was with the Northern refugees—"Should my daughter Sally ever return to our (the Suthren Creek people) or peace be made that She will again be united with her people (relatives). . . ." But in general the refugees were entirely without property; it was estimated in 1865 that there were 6,500 people in these Southern camps and that most of them were in a pitiable state of destitution.[5]

Not only in its provision for the refugees but in its diplomatic dealings the Confederate government showed more consideration for the Southern Creeks than the United States showed to the Loyal party. As their delegate in Congress the Southern Creeks had chosen Samuel Benton Callahan, a white man with a very little Creek blood, who had joined them in 1858; and at their request Israel G. Vore, who had served them in various capacities before the war, was appointed as their agent. The Southern soldiers also chose their own regimental officers, while the Creeks in the Northern army were commanded by white men. But the Confederate military administration of the Indian Territory was almost as bungling and inefficient as the Federal. Neither side recognized the importance of this distant frontier, and its command was dominated by sordid self-seeking, jealousy, political patronage, incompetence, and the subordination of Indian interests to those of the surrounding states. The Southern Creeks protested through their tribal officers and the Grand Council, but in the summer of 1863 they passed an act conscripting all men between the ages of eighteen and fifty.

At the same time the Loyal Creeks accepted the hard prospect of another refugee winter at the Sac and Fox Reservation. Their sufferings were not so severe as formerly, and the pay of their men in the army was of great assistance. About one thousand other Creeks, who had not gone north with Opothle Yahola, had gathered with about six or eight thousand Northern Cherokee refugees in the vicinity of Fort Gibson. Stand Watie, with the Confederate Cherokees, raided at will in the neighborhood of the fort and threatened and sometimes captured the supply trains. When the refugees attempted to raise food, he destroyed their crops, and once

5 WPA Project S-149; Commissioner of Indian Affairs, *Annual Report*, 1865, 255, 351 f.; Creek Tribal Records, 39508; Phillips Collection, Thomas Bertholf Manuscript, 2755/90; Five Tribes Files, No. 53, 64-73.

in the fall of 1863 his raiders dashed up and stripped off their clothes to supply their own naked women and children. Some of these refugees were reduced to picking up the corn that fell from the horses of the soldiers.

The concentration of the Creeks in refugee camps subjected them to the machinations of Federal officials and Kansas land-grabbers. In spite of their warlike reputation and their great ability as native diplomats, the Creeks had always been too trusting and too tractable to match the white man. Only their mixed bloods could have have protected them, and those leaders had chosen to bargain with Pike. They had been reduced to their present plight because of their childlike confidence in the Great Father, and that same uncritical faith exposed them to his designs.

It is probable that none of the Creeks would have joined the South if the United States had not entirely failed in its treaty obligations to protect them, and a similar condition existed among the Cherokees and Seminoles. The Federal officials, however, developed the thesis that their "rebellion" had absolved the United States from all commitments; and the Indian Appropriation Act of July 5, 1862, authorized the President to declare the abrogation of all treaties with Indians whose tribal organization was in hostility to the United States. The President did not take this action, but the Federal officials proceeded on the principle that the treaties *were* abrogated and the land subject to confiscation.

This theory opened up dazzling possibilities. If the United States should win the war, there would be millions of emancipated slaves to adjust in some way to a free society. Perhaps the Indian Territory should be used for their colonization. Or, it might be used for the concentration of all the Indian population of the United States. Kansas, especially, was full of these unwelcome occupants: broken tribes from the East had been removed only a generation before to that remote land, where they might remain undisturbed "forever"; and wild nomads roamed the prairies where they had hunted from time immemorial. Coffin opposed this plan, however. More greedy than his contemporaries, he was not willing that even the Indian Territory should be used exclusively by Indians; and he urged the United States to make new treaties abolishing the tribal govern-

ments, allotting farms to individual Indians, and opening the remainder of the country to white settlement. But Commissioner
Dole favored the removal of other Indian tribes to this land,
where he was willing to protect them to a certain extent against
white intrusion; and during the winter of 1862-63 Congress authorized him to carry out this policy. For a number of years, however,
the possibility of negro colonization was always kept open.

Dole and Coffin selected the helpless, starving Creek refugees as
their first victims. Stout-hearted Opothle Yahola insisted that the
old treaties were still in force, but Sands and the other chiefs were
ready to make a new agreement. Early in 1863 Coffin prepared to
secure a treaty with them that would serve as a model for negotiations with all the "greatly reduced and fragmented tribes" of the
Indian Territory. He found the intrepid old leader upon his death-
bed, still burdened with the plight of his people, but ready at last—
if the Superintendent's statement can be believed—to enter into
negotiations. On March 21 the chiefs signed a three-year contract
employing Major Perry Fuller, who had probably been recommended by the Federal officials, as their attorney. Opothle Yahola's
mark was affixed to this instrument. If this signature was genuine,
it was probably his last public act, for he died shortly after. It was
also signed by Sands, Micco Hutke, and several other leaders.

From this time on, there was a division among the Loyal Creeks,
which the Federal officials failed to observe or possibly chose to
ignore. Before his death Opothle Yahola conferred his succession
upon Ispokogee Yahola, of Tuckabatchee. The name of this leader
was deeply significant to the Tuckabatchees: the Ispokogees were
mythical beings who had taught them their ceremonials and presented them with the sacred plates; one of their most important
town officials was a special chief with priestly functions, who was
known as the Ispokogee Micco; and the people of the town itself
were known ceremonially throughout the nation by the esoteric
title of Ispokogees. The Tuckabatchees, after the self-sufficient
Indian fashion, did not at first dispute Sands' position as principal
chief of the tribe, but when they discovered the land schemes of the
Federal officials they claimed Ispokogee Yahola as their only leader
and clung to the old treaties with stubborn tenacity.

Sands and the other chiefs did not suspect the designs of the white men. They entered into the negotiations for other objects: they had long-standing claims against the United States, which had not been settled in 1856; they wanted the back annuities, which had been withheld or expended irresponsibly since the beginning of the war; they wanted compensation for the property they had lost because of the abandonment of their country by the United States; they were unalterably opposed to allotment, and they wished to be protected against this threat; their former treaties were "lame" on the subject of white immigration, and they wanted to strengthen them; and most of all they longed to return home. Even after Fuller went to Washington and returned with a draft treaty ceding as a home for other Indians two and one half million acres of the rich land formerly occupied by the McIntosh party, Coffin persuaded them to accept it. They hoped never to see their estranged brethren again, and the settlement of other tribes among them was in keeping with their tolerant hospitality. Dole himself came out to assist in the final negotiations; and Harry Island, a shrewd Creek negro, served as interpreter and apparently looked after the interest of his race. The treaty was drawn up and signed by Sands and other leaders at the Sac and Fox Agency September 3.

The Creeks accepted the justice of Lincoln's Emancipation Proclamation and agreed to colonize their negroes or—with the consent of their chiefs, any negroes—in a special section of their country, where they would remain under Creek law. They ceded to the United States the triangle of land between the Arkansas and their northeastern boundary; and for this cession and "their general good conduct" they were to receive annuities of ten thousand dollars a year. The United States promised to compensate them for their losses in the war according to the findings of a special commission. Finally they were free to take back the members of the Southern party "upon such conditions as said nation may impose," except that none of them should hold office in the nation unless he could prove to the satisfaction of the Secretary of the Interior that he had always been loyal to the United States.

In general the Loyal Creeks were highly pleased with this treaty, but in the spring of 1864 it was radically amended by the Senate;

one half of their land was to be taken for the colonization of Indians or negroes, and a grant of $120,000 was substituted for the obligation to compensate the Loyal Creeks for their losses. This was too much even for the trusting full bloods. They protested against the changes made by the "Great Council in Washington" and continued, in spite of Cutler's persuasion, to ask for another treaty. Once in the fall of 1866 Congress, in a state of absent-mindedness or with the deep-laid intention of tricking them into acceptance, appropriated $50,000 under its provisions, but they steadfastly refused to recognize it.[6]

The Northern forces in the Indian Territory were clearly in the ascendant during 1864. In February Phillips made a rapid march into the heart of the Choctaw country, hoping to detach the Indians from the Confederate alliance. As he passed through the Creek Nation on his way south, he sent his Creek soldiers in advance to secure their property and protect their families and friends if any still remained there. In general the whole country was deserted, but Major Willett made a rapid scout to the Little River and returned with fifty refugees who had remained in that vicinity. Except for a few skirmishes with Chilly McIntosh's soldiers, Phillips found his passage unopposed. He crossed the Canadian and penetrated almost to the Red River. On the way he sent copies of Lincoln's Amnesty Proclamation to D. N. McIntosh and the leaders of the other tribes, with a warning to accept this mercy before it should be too late. He then returned to Fort Gibson.[7]

A little later in the year Coffin undertook the return of all the Northern refugees to Fort Gibson. During the journey Ispokogee Yahola and his party of about three hundred traveled alone, refusing even to camp on the same side of the stream with the main body. The removal was effected without incident, but travel was necessarily slow, and the refugees did not reach their destination until the middle of June, when it was too late to plant crops. The

[6] Commissioner of Indian Affairs, *Annual Reports*, 1862-64; *War of the Rebellion*, First Series, Vol. XXII, Part 2, 1095 f., 1107 f., 1118 f.; United States, *Statutes at Large*, XII, 528; XIV, 272. United States Archives, Creek 1862/F31, O45; 1863/C240, C280, C608, O6; 1864/O23; 1865/O35; 1867/B94, I204. *Ibid.*, Treaty File, Treaty of 1863.

[7] Commissioner of Indian Affairs, *Annual Report*, 1864, 320 f., 328 f.; *War of the Rebellion*, First Series, XXXIV, Part 2, 190, 828 f., 994-97.

food situation became acute within a month, and it continued to grow worse. There were now six thousand Creeks and ten thousand other refugees in the neighborhood of the fort. The Creeks settled on the west bank of the Grand River, two or three miles from their own country, which was still held by Confederate guerrillas. Here within sight of the familiar outline of valley and stream and distant hills they were more homesick than ever. Worst of all they were forced to watch the systematic looting of their country by its supposed protectors.

Early in the war the plains Indians had begun to drive cattle from the Creek country to Kansas and sell them to army and refugee contractors, and of course a good many cattle had been used by the Confederate Creeks, but the country was still full of cattle at the beginning of 1864. By this time the stealing of cattle had become an organized business that involved Federal army officers, Indian service officials, and many of the most prominent citizens of Kansas. It was bad enough for the Creeks to starve while corrupt officials squandered their annuities; but it was worse for them to see their own cattle stolen, delivered to contractors who were implicated in the theft, charged at high rates against their annuities, and doled out to them as refugee rations. Their mild protests were ignored, and by the fall of 1864 their country was largely stripped of the herds that had constituted their main wealth before the war.[8]

During the winter of 1864-65 Sands and the other chiefs constantly appealed for military protection so that they might return home. In February they crossed the Verdigris and established themselves on their own soil in the neighborhood of Tullahassee Mission, where Phillips had stationed an outpost of his Indian soldiers. But Ispokogee Yahola and his irreconcilables settled on the Cherokee side of the Verdigris in order to avoid placing themselves under Creek jurisdiction. Lucy Scott, an aged Tuckabatchee woman, remembers how they "made little log houses and one hoe would have to do for the whole settlement." But by such exertions about half

[8] Commissioner of Indian Affairs, *Annual Report,* 1864, 303-20; 1865, 32-34, 252-79. United States Archives, Creek 1864/O23, 1867/B247; Annie Heloise Abel, *The American Indian Under Reconstruction,* 73-97.

the Creek refugees raised enough food to carry them through the succeeding winter. They were still almost destitute of clothing.

In spite of this division their habits of orderly government stood them in good stead during the years of their exile. Their town chiefs and lawmakers met in council to regulate internal affairs and decide on matters of policy in their relations with the United States. Sands, Micco Hutke, and other leaders assumed responsibility for the administration. These head chiefs even borrowed money on the authority of the Creek Nation; they secured $2,034.25 on December 30, 1864, possibly for the expenses of removal to their own country, from a once wealthy member of the Perryman family, and the loan was finally repaid by the Council in 1880.[9]

The Southern Creeks continued to carry on their government from their military camps. Samuel Checote, of the Arkansas District, and the venerable Tuckabatchee Micco, of the Canadian, were elected as their principal chiefs at the close of 1863 or the beginning of 1864. Tuckabatchee Micco died on the South Canadian, probably toward the close of 1865, and no successor seems to have been chosen. With him perished some of the ancient mysteries that had been handed down from generation to generation since the dim days when the inspired Ispokogees were supposed to have walked with men and instructed them in the sacred rites.

The Creek delegates—who were also the army officers—met frequently with the delegates of the other tribes at the Grand Council. Here they listened to messages from Confederate officials and military commanders, reaffirmed their allegiance to the Confederate government, and complained of the shortage of military supplies. In the fall of 1864 they sent messages to the Osages and all the other tribes in Kansas to meet in a great council on the western prairies of the Creek Nation. Coffin did all he could to prevent the meeting, and apparently he succeeded in part, but it was held at Camp Napoleon on the Washita, the following May. The peace pipe was smoked and the ceremonial tokens were exchanged between the Confederate Indians, consisting of the Five Civilized

9 Creek Tribal Records, 28973, 32656, 35144; Commissioner of Indian Affairs, *Annual Report*, 1865, 290 f.; United States Archives, Creek 1865/O33, O35, P358; 1867/B247. WPA Project S-149.

Tribes and bands of the Caddoes, Osages, and Comanches on the one side, and the plains tribes, consisting of the Kiowas, Arapahoes, Cheyennes, and Lipans, and bands of Comanches, Caddoes, and Anadarkoes on the other. By this time the collapse of the Confederacy was apparent, and what might have been intended as a military alliance, materialized as a league for peace. A compact was adopted May 26, or possibly May 24, enlarging the organization formed at North Fork Town four years before and pledging the member tribes to settle all future difficulties "without the shedding of any blood" and to stand united against white aggression.[10]

The Creeks needed all the moral support they could find in such action. On the very day that this compact was signed, E. Kirby Smith surrendered all the Confederate forces west of the Mississippi. The same month the United States demobilized the Indian Home Guard regiments. Two straggling bands of returning soldiers, three colonies of destitute refugees, and three fragments of governments were all that remained to the Creeks to rebuild their nation and defend their right to live and hold their land under the white man's overshadowing power.

A drastic territorial bill introduced by James Harlan, of Iowa, had passed the United States Senate during the session of 1864-65. It was an unfortunate day for the Indians when Harlan received appointment as Secretary of the Interior on March 9. In his official report of that year he deplored their "perfidous conduct" in making "unprovoked war upon us" in "flagrant violation of treaties which had been observed by us with scrupulous good faith." D. N. Cooley was appointed as Commissioner of Indian Affairs and Elijah Sells as Southern Superintendent; and both worked actively to promote Harlan's policy. J. W. Dunn was sent to Fort Gibson as Creek agent.

Cooley, Sells, and several special appointees were designated as a commission to make peace with the Confederate Indians. On August 16 Harlan drew up instructions to be used as the basis of the negotiations. They were to inform the Indians that all their

---

[10] *War of the Rebellion,* First Series, Vol. XXXIV, Part 2, 958-60; Vol. XLI, Part 2, 1035f. *Ibid.,* Part 4, 1039; Vol. XLVIII, Part 2, 1102 f. Commissioner of Indian Affairs, *Annual Report,* 1864, 306 f.; Creek Tribal Records, Checote Manuscript, 35, 41 f.; United States Archives, Creek 1866/1640; Swanton, "Creek Social Organization," 66.

money and lands were forfeit and their treaties abrogated; they were to create a territorial government, using the Harlan Bill as a model; they were to effect the emancipation and adoption of the slaves; and they were to obtain land for the use of other Indians, but they were to guarantee the Indian Territory against white immigration. The Indians, moreover, were expressly to agree that any amendment to the treaties subsequently made by the United States Senate "shall be as binding in every respect as if it had, after being made, been formally submitted to and ratified by the parties." Throughout this document were frequent tributes to the devotion of the Loyal Indians, and expositions of the humane and Christian purposes of the Federal Indian policy.

The Confederate Indians, for their part, took prompt and intelligent action. A special session of the Grand Council was held in June at Chahta Tamaha. Here the tribes reaffirmed the union established at Camp Napoleon and invited "the proper authorities" of the Cherokees, Seminoles, Creeks, and others allied with the United States to enter the Indian Confederacy and stand together in making peace. The regular session of the Grand Council would convene the first Monday in September at Chahta Tamaha, and they tried to persuade the Federal commissioners to meet them there.

If the commissioners had really wanted to make peace and establish a constructive Indian policy, this great gathering of civilized and wild tribes offered an unexampled opportunity. It also attracted a great deal of attention among white men, who hoped a few luscious plums in the form of railway and land grants might be picked there. An enterprising Kansan from the neighborhood of Kansas City wrote to his Representative in Congress, "White men from here and Kansas City will go along. Treaties will be made—railroad grants fixed up and things done generally . . . & we should have a hand in it." Obviously a council in the Indian country under Indian auspices would not be favorable to get the "things done generally," which constituted the real purpose of the negotiations; hence the commissioners summoned the tribes to meet them the first week in September at Fort Smith. Under these circumstances the tribes and factions of tribes allied with the United States, of course, did not attend the Grand Council; but, since the invitations had already gone out, the Southern leaders of the Five Tribes convened there with their Osage, Comanche, Caddo, and Arapaho friends, and then proceeded in a body to Fort Smith.

Meanwhile the Northern Creeks had taken some steps toward "Reconstruction." To these simple-minded full bloods the freedman problem proved easy of solution. Many of the negroes had fled north with Opothle Yahola, others had been taken south with their masters, and still others had remained in the Creek country; but during the latter part of the war they had been congregating with fugitive slaves from other sections around Fort Gibson. Now they settled on the rich Arkansas-Verdigris valley where they had formerly tilled the plantations of the wealthy mixed bloods and began to establish little farms of their own. By August 10—almost certainly on August 4—the Northern Creeks had passed a "law," probably upon the urging of Agent Dunn, recognizing them as members of the tribe.

Sands and the Southern leaders had also exchanged messages looking toward reconciliation, but apparently no meeting had been held. When Dunn shepherded his chiefs to the Fort Smith council, they looked forward to meeting their Southern brethren, and they supposed that the healing of their factional differences was the real purpose of the gathering.[11]

There were twenty-one or more members of the Northern Creek delegation. Sands was recognized as the principal chief. Fully as important was Micco Hutke, who served as spokesman, for he had been one of their most loved and trusted leaders during the entire period of the war. Cotchoche (Little Tiger) and Lochar Harjo (Crazy Turtle) were also prominent delegates, and they were destined to rise to greater leadership within the tribe. Most of the delegates were full bloods, but one of the members was young Sanford W. Perryman, a graduate of Tullahassee, who like many other Creeks had changed his allegiance from South to North

---

[11] Abel, *The American Indian Under Reconstruction,* is the main authority for this period; see especially 125-45, 164, 167 n., 169-70 n., 219-26, 243-67. See also 59 Cong., 2 sess., *Sen. Rep. No. 5013,* I, 697 f.; United States Archives, Creek 1865/S740; *War of the Rebellion,* First Series, Vol. XLVIII, Part 2, 1103 f.; Commissioner of Indian Affairs, *Annual Report,* 1865, iii, 290, 296.

when Weer marched through the Indian country. Perryman's literacy proved very useful to the Creeks. Harry Island was the interpreter, and it is possible that two or three members of the delegation were negroes.

The council opened September 8 with Cooley as president. The Southern leaders had not yet arrived from Chahta Tamaha, but many tribes were in attendance, for the Federal commissioners planned not only to dispossess the former owners of the Indian Territory but to make arrangements with other Indians to settle there. The various agents were present to exert their influence in behalf of the government's objectives. Lobbyists and land-grabbers hovered, not too inconspicuously, in the background.

After a prayer by a Cherokee delegate, Cooley addressed the assembly. In fulsome and pious language he informed these men, who had suffered more for their devotion to the Union than any white population in the United States, that their tribes had "rightfully forfeited" all their money and lands, but that the President was "willing to hear his erring children's extenuation of their great crime" and had authorized the commissioners to make new treaties with them. The Indians listened in consternation. Micco Hutke answered for the Creeks, "Our people at home supposed that we came to meet and come to terms with our rebel brothers, and we thought that was all we had to do at this council. . . . We expect to find out fully what the government wants us to do from your commission, and will then be able to answer."

Cooley enlightened them the next day by an ultimatum based on Harlan's instructions. Micco Hutke answered for the Creeks, "We have learned what the government wants us to do, but are not ready at this time to reply." Perryman presented a written argument three days later. He explained that by the Creek constitution a principal chief might be removed for misdemeanor and succeeded by the second chief; he gave an accurate summary of the Loyal Creeks' repudiation of the Pike treaty, their removal of Echo Harjo and the succession of Sands, the journey of their leaders to Washington—"and we think that all of the talk is on the record in Washington"—their flight to Kansas and their subsequent sufferings, and their enlistment in the Union army; and he "most respectfully asked" that they should "not be classed with the guilty." But after some hesitation they accepted a preliminary treaty renouncing the Confederate alliance, and acknowledging themselves under the protection of the United States; and later in the council they agreed to adopt their freedmen and they stated that they believed their people might be persuaded to make the required land cession, but they declined to surrender their tribal independence in favor of territorial government.

Only Loyal Indians had been present so far in the negotiations, but the Southern party arrived September 16. Their arrival was the occasion of much hand-shaking and the delivery of much good advice from a Quaker member of the Federal commission. D. N. McIntosh assumed the leadership of the Southern Creeks. They objected to the granting of citizenship to the negroes and asked that the two factions be allowed to form separate tribes. But the next day was Sunday, and during the recess the two groups of delegates composed their differences. When the council convened on Monday, the Southern members signed the preliminary treaty and the united delegation obtained permission from Cooley to withdraw from the council and return to their homes.[12]

As a result of the concord established at Fort Smith, the leaders of the two parties and the head men of the towns met in a council November 5 at "Scipio's place"—probably on the farm of a negro named Scipio Barnett. Here Checote surrendered his office, and Sands was recognized as principal chief of the united nation. Sands told the Southern leaders to return to their people on the Red River and the Washita and invite them back to settle on their own land. Most of them returned during the winter, and except for Ispokogee Yahola's irreconcilables, who still refused to leave the Cherokee Nation, the members of both parties began quietly establishing their homes in the desolate waste where they had once been so prosperous. They gathered and identified the few cattle that had escaped the thieves, reclaimed so far as possible their weed-grown fields, and built rude shelters where blackened chimneys and heaps of ashes marked the site of their former dwellings.

Many family reunions took place as they assembled. One present-

[12] Commissioner of Indian Affairs, *Annual Report*, 1865, 37, 297-351.

day Creek woman tells how her mother's people "went in all directions . . . Somehow they got mixed up and lost my uncle who was about seven and they didn't know what became of him until after the war." Another remembers that her father had two wives. One went with her husband to Kansas; the other fled south with her two little girls and died on the Red River. After the war the father managed to find his children and bring them home. The reunited neighbors were too happy in the knowledge that the long horror was over to waste their energy in recriminations; and each town had its own meeting, where—as a Greenleaf woman expresses it—"those Indians that had parted came together again and made peace among themselves." Here the communal hearth was reëstablished with the ashes the leaders had carried through all the deprivations of their exile.

In October Dunn removed his office from Fort Gibson to the site of the ruined agency. He distributed rations as needed to both the Northern and Southern factions; but in March he reported that all were "farming to the best of their ability and according to their teams and other means," and except in special cases the relief was discontinued at the end of June. During the winter Major General John B. Sanborn came out as a special agent of the government to investigate the status of the freedmen. He commended the Creeks for their readiness to accept the negroes as equals, but he proved to be a mischievous meddler in Indian affairs. He advised the destruction of the tribal nationalities, and as for the land, he recommended that small allotments should be made to the Indians and larger ones to the negroes, portions should be reserved for the colonization of other tribes, "liberal" grants should be made to railroads, and the remainder should be thrown open to white settlement.[13]

The negroes remained in the Arkansas-Verdigris valley. The Creeks even made some irregular agreement with them assigning this region to their exclusive use. The mixed bloods never returned to their old plantations. They were unwilling to live in a negro community, and they knew, moreover, that the Federal officials still

[13] *Ibid.*, 1866, 56, 283-87, 290; 1867, 330. United States Archives, Creek 1865/D944, 1866/S54, S228, S231; Creek Tribal Records, Checote Manuscript, 36-38; Five Tribes Files, No. 52; WPA Project S-149.

intended to take this region as a war indemnity. Except for the Perrymans, who remained on the upper Arkansas, most of this class settled in the vicinity of North Fork Town. As the full bloods gradually moved away from the agency and its rations, they withdrew after their manner to remote places and established their homes in the broken blackjack hills that stretched across their country to the west.

During this same winter of 1865-66 the Federal officials carried on negotiations for a definitive treaty with the Creeks. As they planned to punish the Indians for their "rebellion," they extended many favors to the Southern agents who had seduced them. In November Harlan submitted a copy of his territorial bill to Pike. The Southern leader, who had negotiated such favorable treaties with the Indians when he was bidding for their support, gave his unqualified approval to Harlan's plans and pointed out ways in which it should be amended to make it even more destructive of Indian nationality.

In December Sands, Coweta Micco, and Cotchoche were appointed as delegates by the Loyal Creeks. They reached Washington January 7 with the ever-trusted Harry Island as interpreter. The situation called for much tact on the part of the Southern Creek leaders. None knew better than they the diplomatic ineptitude of their Northern brethren, but their own position in the tribe was too precarious for self-assertion. They finally met in council with Checote as principal chief and Echo Harjo and Yahkinhar Micco as second chiefs, and chose D. N. McIntosh and James M. C. Smith to go to Washington and assist in the negotiations. Instructions drawn up by Checote January 17 directed them to coöperate with the Loyal Creeks in a spirit of "harmony and friendship and for the best interest of the whole without reference to former difficulties," and to follow their own judgment to secure the best possible terms with the United States. They reached Washington February 22, but the Federal officials did not recognize them as official delegates. Both sets of delegates employed attorneys; the contract of the Loyal Creeks with Perry Fuller had not expired, and McIntosh and Smith entered into a contract with Colonel J. B. Luce.

Cooley, Sells, and Ely S. Parker, an educated Seneca who had served on the Fort Smith commission, were the Federal commissioners. Sands and his colleagues were entirely helpless in their hands. Two weeks before the arrival of the Southern delegates they consented to a treaty adopting their freedmen, providing for the creation of a territorial government under the control of Congress, and ceding the western half of their territory for thirty cents an acre, of which $775,000 was to be used to compensate the Loyal Creeks for their losses in the war. McIntosh and Smith after repeated requests to the Federal commissioners were finally allowed to see a copy, but they were unable to persuade their deluded brethren to join them in asking for a modification of the terms. They then submitted a separate protest. It was expressed in the most conciliatory language—"We know our weakness, and the power of the United States and accepting the issues decided by the war, which we did in good faith, we throw ourselves upon the generosity and magnanimity of the Government." But they said they represented the majority faction of the tribe, and they asked to be recognized as delegates. They considered the amount paid for the land cession inadequate; and they objected to the use of the money to pay the reparation owed by the United States to the Loyal Creeks. They were willing to set aside a separate tract of land for their freedmen, but they were opposed to adopting them as members of the tribe. They also objected to the territorial proposal.

Three days after this protest was drawn up, the Federal commissioners concluded a treaty with the Seminoles. It was based on the same ungenerous principles, for the Loyal full bloods of that tribe had suffered as deeply as the Creeks and were as incapable of protecting their interests. This buffeted people ceded their entire domain for the colonization of Indians and negroes, and the United States promised to sell them two hundred thousand acres of the land ceded by the Creeks. These transactions were characterized by a thrift unique even in Indian land bargains; the United States agreed to pay the Seminoles fifteen cents an acre for their land and charged them fifty cents an acre for the tract which the Creeks had already agreed to sell for thirty cents. This treaty was eventually ratified by the United States and became the basis of subsequent relations with the Seminoles.

But although the Federal commissioners could take such action against the helpless Seminoles, the lucid protests of McIntosh and Smith received some consideration. The treaty was referred back to the Loyal delegates, but those bewildered full bloods still instinctively relied upon their Great Father and distrusted the educated members of their own race. On April 21 they wrote to Cooley protesting against the protest. They did not believe McIntosh and Smith were authorized delegates anyhow; Checote had abdicated to Sands, and they did not think he would appoint an opposition delegation. They did not need any help; they had seen Harlan, "and he and the Government made out the desires that he thinks will be satisfactory to us." McIntosh and Smith had no right to fight against their treaty; it suited them, all but one clause—"There where the land for the school houses the government wanted it and which we wanted to remain the same as in the old treaties other of our Treaty we want it to remain as we have made it and not a clause of it changed." They hoped Cooley would pay no attention to these objectors but "release us and let us go home for we are home sick and are suffering and want to go home ... The treaty we have made we think the best that can be made for our people which the best could not do any better."

While the Loyal Creeks were thus placing themselves more completely in the power of the United States, a surprisingly favorable treaty was concluded with the Choctaws and Chickasaws. The delegates of these tribes were educated and able and they represented a people that had supported the Confederacy as a unit throughout the war. In the apportionment of war guilt it seemed easier to punish the helpless, trusting Creeks, who had wandered all over Kansas in search of an agent before whom they might declare their allegiance, and had suffered the unspeakable horrors of the refugee camps. McIntosh and Smith pointed out this discrepancy and asked for similar treatment, and they objected to the Creek-Seminole land transaction. They did secure a diminution of the payment to the Loyal Creeks—a concession which at the time cost the United States nothing—and apparently they effected a modification of the territorial provisions. With these changes they were forced to be content, and the treaty was signed by the Federal commissioners and both sets of Creek delegates on June 14. It was approved by the Senate July 19, and proclaimed August 11.

It was designated as a "Treaty of cession and indemnity." Its preamble stated that the Creeks had "ignored their allegiance to the United States, and unsettled the treaty relations existing between the Creeks and the United States, and did so render themselves liable to forfeit to the United States all benefits and advantages enjoyed by them in lands, annuities, protection, and immunities"; and "in view of such liabilities the United States require of the Creeks a portion of their land."

It restored the annuities and the guarantees of previous treaties. It provided for the establishment of United States courts, with no limitation to their jurisdiction. It granted right of way to one north-south and one east-west railroad, and provided that the nation would sell to the United States or to the railway company a strip not more than six miles wide along the track, to be reconveyed only to Creek citizens. It granted one hundred and sixty acres of land to every religious society which had previously erected buildings for educational or religious purposes or should erect them with the consent of the tribe. It provided for the adoption of the Creek freedmen and free negroes who were living in the Creek country or should return within one year from the date of ratification; and it gave them equal property rights and placed them under Creek law. It contained elaborate provisions for a permanent council of the Indian Territory tribes under the supervision of the Federal officials.

The cession of the western half of the Creek domain for the use of Indians and—by implication—freedmen was confirmed. The amount was fixed at 3,250,560 acres, and the compensation of $975,168 was to be used as follows: $200,000 in cash, of which not more than $2,000 might be used to restore the ruined buildings at Tullahassee and Asbury, a sum agreed upon by the agent and the Council might be appropriated to pay the delegates, and the remainder should be distributed per capita; $100,000 was to be paid to the Loyal Creeks and negroes according to an investigation of their losses; $275,168 should remain in the United States treasury to draw 5 per cent interest; and the remaining $400,000 was a debt which would draw 5 per cent interest until it could be paid per capita to the Creeks as it accumulated in the Federal treasury from the sale of land to other tribes. Finally the Creeks confirmed the diversion of their annuities during the war and accepted the treaty as a full settlement of all claims growing out of the conflict.

Fuller and Luce received adequate compensation for their services from the cash payment under the treaty; but in addition both sets of delegates were induced to sign promissory notes for an additional $84,396 to each attorney. In view of the hard terms their clients had obtained from the United States in the negotiations, this provision was so excessive that it amounted to spoliation. If Luce had accomplished anything it was only for the Southern faction in securing a reduction of the indemnity to the Loyal party, and the legal services of Fuller are nowhere apparent.[14]

Only a few days after the Senate ratified the Creek treaty, Congress granted franchises to two railroads to cross the Indian Territory. One was to cross from Missouri and on to the Pacific coast, and it received a grant of every alternate section of public land in a strip forty miles wide along the right of way. The Indian Territory, of course, was not public land; hence the United States undertook to "extinguish, as rapidly as may be consistent with public policy and the welfare of the Indians, and only by their voluntary cession, the Indian title to all lands falling under the operation of this act and acquired in the donation to the road." The road was thus invited to intrigue with the Indians for a "voluntary" cession and with Congress for the extinguishment of their title. The other franchise held out a temptation to the railroad in even more definite terms. It granted the right of way across the Territory from Kansas to Texas with alternate sections in a twenty-mile strip "whenever the Indian title shall be extinguished by treaty or otherwise. . . . *Provided,* that said lands become a part of the public lands of the United States." The real forces that were at work in the Reconstruction Treaties may be seen more clearly in the light of these grants.[15]

[14] United States Archives, Creek 1866/D344, I640, M176, M245, M402, M525, S231, S250, S417, V77; United States Department of the Interior, Office of Indian Affairs, Files, 1889/L1797; Abel, *The American Indian Under Reconstruction,* 314 f., 327-37; Commissioner of Indian Affairs, *Annual Report,* 1866, 18; Kappler, *Laws and Treaties,* II, 910-15, 931-37.

[15] United States, *Statutes at Large,* XIV, 236-39, 294.

But punitive and confiscatory as was the Treaty of 1866, it did enable the Creeks to resume their relations with the United States under the old guarantees, and they remained under its provisions as long as they existed as a nation. With these relations defined, it remained for them now to perform the equally difficult task of healing their internal divisions and adjusting themselves to the changing conditions forced upon them by the white man's post-war development.

CHAPTER 6

Building Again

WHILE the treaty negotiations were in progress, the Creeks at home were holding "one continuous council," as their assistant agent expressed it, trying in their own way to reorganize their national affairs. After the selection of their delegates the Southern party continued to recognize Checote as chief, but the tribe, accustomed to a dual executive, accepted him and Sands without question. When the delegates returned with the treaty, Dunn called a council and explained its provisions, using as his interpreter David M. Hodge, an educated great-grandson of Benjamin Perryman who had fought on the Northern side. The council ratified the agreement, but the Loyal full bloods—as they afterwards asserted—believed that under its provisions the United States undertook to reimburse them for all their losses in the war. Dunn was probably not to blame for this misunderstanding; for five years they had been trusting to the justice of the United States in spite of all evidence to the contrary, and this was only another act of self-deception.

With the assistance of the town chiefs, Dunn prepared a roll for the per capita payment under the treaty. Ispokogee Yahola's band refused to be enumerated, but he listed 2,372 families and a total of 9,771 persons. The estimated number of the irreconcilables was 370; hence there was a total population of 10,141—a loss of 24 per cent since the census of 1859. Except for a few refugees still in the South, some of whom remained permanently with the Choctaws and Chickasaws, this terrible decrease in numbers represented the lives lost in the war.

The payment began March 14, 1867. Each Indian received $17.34, but the payment was made in currency, which at the time was greatly depreciated. Dunn had prepared a careful roll of the negroes entitled to citizenship and found the number to be 1,774; but without the knowledge of the Loyal Creeks, Checote prevailed upon the Commissioner to exclude them from the distribution. Harry Island and two other negroes, Ketch Barnett and Cow Tom, went to Washington to protest, and in 1868 Congress, with some expressions of indignation against the "rebel Indians," set aside $30,882.54 of the tribal annuities for them. The payment was made in the summer of 1869.[1]

Dunn tried to use the per capita payment as a lever to break the morale of Ispokogee Yahola's followers. He did persuade the Wewogufkees, who had been among the irreconcilables, to rejoin their people and accept their shares; but about two hundred Tuckabatchees withdrew farther into the Cherokee country, where they lived in the most abject poverty refusing to acknowledge the treaty by participating in its benefits. They finally abandoned their self-imposed exile during the winter of 1869-70 and permitted the agent to conduct them home. Ironically enough they had a stronger legal position than the Federal officials who had asserted so blatantly and inaccurately that all previous treaties had been abrogated by the war; but since the Creeks as a people had succumbed to Federal threats in their Reconstruction Treaty, this passive resistance served only to illustrate the stubborn constancy of the fullblood Creek. It was their fault to believe that the Great Father could never break his word.[2]

As the Creeks took root again in their own soil their missionaries returned to assist in the growth of the new society. In after years Alice M. Robertson, the daughter of the Tullahassee educators, gave a graphic picture of the conditions and problems that faced them. The family returned in December, 1866. As they came through the Cherokee Nation they saw "ruined chimneys, marking what had once been great plantation houses, prairie fires had swept through miles and miles of country killing orchards, burning fences, etc., all domestic animals had vanished, but the wild animal

[1] United States Archives, Creek 1867/B34½, B54, B212, B247, D1195, S228, W44, W427; 1868/I983. Five Tribes Files, Creek Roll of 1867; WPA Project S-149; *Muskogee Phœnix*, September 8, 1898; 57 Cong., 1 sess., *Sen. Doc. No. 420*, 12, 14.

[2] United States Archives, Creek 1867/B247, 1867/P104, 1868/W696, 1869/F115, 1870/F303.

denizens of forest and plain had increased alarmingly." On the border of the Creek country one of the children, who had been walking along by the wagon, came running with a human skull which she had picked up from a number lying on the prairie. They found a place to ford the Verdigris, and "following old, almost impassable, roads" they came at last to Tullahassee. "In the five years the formerly well-kept hedge surrounding the front yard had grown into a mass of tall trees,—in field, in yard, and everywhere weeds had grown so rank and large that the tall stalks had to be broken and chopped down to make a road for the wagons to enter, and to make room to pitch our tents and make our camp fires. A row of graves near by added to the gloom. The building was windowless and doorless, the large dining room had been used as a stable, and was deep with stable refuse; the kitchen wing in the rear had much of the wall torn down, its brick had been hauled over to Fort Gibson during the Federal occupation to make bake ovens for the troops."[3]

Men from both parties welcomed back the mission family. The educated mixed bloods longed to exert their statesmanship to extricate the nation from its difficulties; and with Robertson's encouragement they took steps to establish a more "progressive" government. In separate and joint councils the two factions labored throughout 1867 to reach a permanent agreement and build a united nation. Some of these important meetings were held at High Spring, but the council house like nearly everything else in the Creek country had been destroyed, and it was more convenient to meet at Black Jack Grove, a favorite council ground on the south side of the Deep Fork.

A solemn concord was established between the two factions in February; it was agreed—to quote Checote—"that the Muscogee people unite and live as one Nation and those who were North during the late war, were not to be called Northern peop[le] and those who were South, were not to be Southern people; in short there was to be no North and no South among the Muscogee people but peace and friendship." A resolution was adopted and approved February 11 by Sands and Checote that there should be one

[3] Alice M. Robertson, *Incidents of the Civil War*.

principal chief elected at a council in May, and that persons should be employed to build a council house. The next month this joint council, anticipating the resumption of annuity payments, established ten blacksmith shops in widely separated settlements, and made provision for the reopening of the neighborhood schools the following fall. It also passed a law to assist citizens in regaining possession of the farms and cattle they had abandoned during their exile.

The proposed election of principal chief did not take place in May, for by this time more fundamental governmental changes had been initiated. This movement culminated in a constitution and a code of civil and criminal law prepared by a committee, of which it is said that D. N. McIntosh, David M. Hodge, Sanford W. Perryman, Coweta Micco, James McHenry, and others served as members. In October this committee submitted its work to a full council of the nation at Black Jack Grove. It was a solemn and dramatic occasion. Graduates of the mission schools, impatient to use their borrowed learning for the advancement of their people; old time chiefs, strong in the memory of ancient customs; former opponents, trying after the forgiving Indian manner to heal the rankling feud of North and South, the division between Red town and White town, the dispute between progress and conservatism—all debated long and earnestly in council and gravely talked in groups far into the night around their campfires. Finally they decided to accept a new organic law as the basis of the post-war order; and on October 12 the constitution and code of laws for the united "Muskogee Nation" was unanimously adopted.

The constitution was very brief and very badly drafted. It began with a preamble copied after that of the United States. It created a legislature known as the National Council, composed of a House of Kings and a House of Warriors. The organization of the legislature, privileges of members, etc., were similar to the corresponding Anglo-American practice; and it was forbidden to pass laws impairing the nature of contracts or "laws taking effect upon things that occurred before the enactment of the law." Each town was entitled to one member in the House of Kings; and in the House of Warriors, one member and an additional member for every two hundred people. There was a principal chief, whose duties were similar to those of the governor of an American state, and a second chief to succeed him in case of his death, resignation, or impeachment. The principal chief was authorized to select a private secretary—an important official in a republic where the chief executive was likely to be illiterate. The members of the Council and the two chiefs were to be elected every four years by a majority of all male citizens who had reached the age of eighteen. There were also a national treasurer and a national interpreter chosen by the Council for four-year terms.

The nation was divided into six districts. Each had a judge elected by the Council, a prosecuting attorney appointed by the principal chief with the consent of the Council, and a lighthorse company of one captain and four privates elected by the voters. All district officers served for two-year terms. The district court tried all criminal cases and minor civil cases, and trial by jury was provided. There was a Supreme Court, of five justices chosen by the Council for four-year terms, to try all civil cases where the amount at issue exceeded one hundred dollars.

The criminal code was changed only slightly from that used before the war: for murder, there was the death penalty; for rape, fifty lashes for the first offense, death for the second; for theft, restitution to the aggrieved person, and for the first offense fifty lashes, for the second one hundred, for the third death; for women who took drugs to cause abortion, fifty lashes. The lighthorse were authorized to "search, find, and spill" intoxicants, and collect a fine of four dollars a gallon from the vendor. The old civil code was reënacted with little change; there were the same provisions regarding live stock, debts, wills and inheritance, the traders' tax, and the employment of white mechanics. Another law was apparently designed for the enrollment of freedmen who had returned too late to be listed by Dunn but within the twelve months specified by the treaty; and about 139 were adopted at some time during the year . An appropriation of six thousand dollars in addition to the amount specified in the treaty was made to rebuild the Tullahassee and Asbury schools.

Other laws passed the same day were in the nature of a schedule for the inauguration of the new government. The first Monday in November was set as the date of the first election; the principal chiefs were to appoint persons to preside in each town, "each voter shall select and call the name for whom he votes," the election officials were to report to the principal chiefs, and the chiefs were to call a council and present the returns. The National Council should convene the following December. The old council ground of Hitchitee Town on the north side of the Deep Fork was selected as the seat of government, and the principal chiefs were directed to appoint a committee to select a site for the erection of the council house. The compensation was fixed for the officers, jurors, etc. The six districts were named as follows: Coweta, northeast of the Arkansas River; Arkansas (changed in 1877 to Muskogee), from the Arkansas almost to the Deep Fork; North Fork (changed in 1877 to Eufaula), comprising the thickly settled valley near the junction of the North and the South Canadian; Wewoka, above the North Fork District on the main Canadian; Deep Fork, north of Wewoka District; and Muskogee (changed in 1877 to Okmulgee), north of Deep Fork.

All these acts were approved by Checote, Sands, Micco Hutke, and Pink Hawkins, a son of the Sam Hawkins who was killed with McIntosh. Micco Hutke and Hawkins apparently had in some manner been elected as second chiefs. George Washington Grayson, an educated mixed blood, served as secretary. So far as the action of this council was concerned everything seemed propitious for orderly governmental development under constitutional forms; but Sands' complaint two years later is a more accurate representation of the fullblood mind than the text of the enactments. "I wanted to make a law and told them to fix the old Indian law, but they made another, and when we found it out, it was the same as the white man's law."

The election was held in due form in November. Checote and Sands were, of course, the candidates for principal chief. Only the progressive party understood the new machinery. The full bloods paid no attention to the local elections, and when the council was called for canvassing the returns they innocently supposed that they would form in line behind their candidates and choose their chiefs. They were righteously indignant when they were given no opportunity to be "counted openly and fairly," and when through what they regarded as some white man's form of legerdemain Checote was proclaimed as principal chief by a majority of thirteen hundred. Micco Hutke, probably through an attempt at conciliation on the part of the progressives, was elected as second chief. Dunn, anxious to record the "advancement" of his charges, rejoiced over the successful installation of a new constitutional regime. The fact was that the change had been premature, and the cleavage that resulted was the greatest single hindrance to the progress of the Creeks during the difficult years that followed.[4]

Samuel Checote was admirably fitted to lead his people along the untried constitutional path they had chosen. His painfully acquired learning gave him an appreciation of the white man's culture and protected him against the white man's schemes; and no other Creek leader ever worked so vigilantly to guard the racial integrity of his people against white and negro immigration. At the same time his thoughts were those of a full blood; tolerant beyond the understanding of a white man, deeply and sincerely Christian without the acquisitiveness that usually marked the Christianized native, he conducted his administration with patience and forbearance. He was soon to need all his tact and steadfastness; for the conservatives, with the self-possessed stubbornness of their race, refused to recognize the constitution and quietly continued under their old organization.

The Council seems to have convened for a short session in December for the inauguration of the new government and the selection of the officers not chosen by popular vote. Timothy Barnett was elected as national treasurer. Later in the month the Creeks received the 1867 annuities—the first since the outbreak of the war. The Federal authorities had already expended a portion of the money for the supposed benefit of the tribe, but $53,786.05 was turned over to the new officials.

[4] United States Archives, Creek 1867/B77, 1868/W696, 1869/R382, 1869/S161, 1873/C278; Creek Tribal Records, Checote Manuscript, 36-38; Albert Pike McKellop, *Constitution and Laws of the Muskogee Nation*, 102 f.; Alice M. Robertson, Incidents of the Civil War; Five Tribes Files, No. 33, No. 63, 756 f., 926; O'Beirne and O'Beirne, *The Indian Territory*, 35.

A special session of the Council was called in January to take
over the financial administration. The camping place was near
Shieldsville, and apparently the deliberations were held in the open
air. The conservatives held aloof. Some of the disaffected towns
were entirely without representation; others were irregularly
represented by members who came on their own initiative. The
houses were organized according to Anglo-American practice, and
bills were introduced, debated, passed to first, second, and third
reading, etc. With their natural aptitude for conducting deliberative bodies and with some knowledge of the white man's forms the
members fell easily into a smooth parliamentary procedure. Ward
Coachman, Pink Hawkins, and a negro named Sugar George were
the most active, but some full bloods participated in the debates.

Checote advised that half the annuities be turned over to the
Sands party, according to some earlier arrangement between the
two factions; but the legislators refused to accept this departure
from constitutional forms. They tried to be fair, however, in dis-
charging the obligations left over from the old divided administration; appropriations were made for "Sand's lawmakers," for the
town chiefs, and for those who had served as head chiefs of the two
parties. Interest amounting to $4,438 had accumulated on the
$100,000 the United States had promised to pay the Loyal Creeks,
and this was turned over to Sands. Luce came to present his note,
and after a two days' speech he secured the passage of an act appropriating $9,396 in cash and the remainder in $15,000 notes, which
were subsequently paid from the annuities. Appropriations were
made for the officers of the new government, for the schools, and
for the erection of a council house. Sanford W. Perryman and G.
W. Stidham were appointed to attempt the revision of the Treaty
of 1866, apparently with the understanding that they would receive one-third of any money recovered. The Council then adjourned, after selecting the first Tuesday in October as the time for
the regular sessions.[5]

During the same month of January the courts were organized

---

[5] Creek Tribal Records, 34072, 39305, 39409, 39411; *ibid.*, Checote Manuscript, 46;
United States Archives, Creek 1868/B575, W696; Commissioner of Indian Affairs, *Annual
Report*, 1868, 283 f.; McKellop, *Constitution and Laws*, 95; Five Tribes Files, No. 2, 7-14.

in at least part of the districts. The trials were held at the judge's residence, a schoolhouse, a town square, or other convenient place. Most of the judges and district attorneys and nearly all the jurors were full bloods, except in the Arkansas (Muskogee) District, where the negroes were in the ascendant. There was an interesting struggle between the native sense of justice and the white man's rules of evidence; at first the trial consisted mainly in asking the accused if he were guilty, and the jurors based their verdict upon their personal knowledge of neighborhood happenings, but the courts gradually learned to introduce additional testimony. Most of the judges were illiterate, but they employed clerks who were able to keep the records in Creek or labored English and to make out the court scrip for the pay of witnesses and jurors and the board of prisoners when they were in the custody of the lighthorse awaiting trial. The scrip was simply a voucher made out on a scrap of paper. In a society so primitive and so destitute of financial resources as the Creek it was an important medium of exchange; the traders accepted it as currency and presented it for payment when the Council made its annual appropriations.

In electing the Supreme Court justices an attempt had been made to conciliate the conservatives by giving one of the places to Cotchoche; but he refused to serve, and the Council filled the vacancy at the January session. Coweta Micco, John G. Smith, Joseph Cornells, Walter Grayson, and G. W. Stidham were the members of this court. Its proceedings were informal, but the testimony shows a lively business activity on the part of the litigants, a sturdy sense of justice on the part of neighbors appearing as witnesses, and strong practical common sense on the part of the judges. A considerable portion of the population, however, denied the jurisdiction of the courts just as they ignored the authority of Checote and refused to participate in the Council.[6]

During the same winter of 1867-68 at least six teachers, most of them Creek girls, conducted neighborhood schools in the rude buildings provided by the communities. They received no salary until the Council met in January, but from that time on the Creeks had a steady income from the annuities. The blacksmiths—Creeks

[6] Creek Tribal Records, Courts; Five Tribes Files, No. 2, 6; No. 52.

and negroes—received their pay at the same time. The same Council elected young Pleasant Porter, of the Southern party—the son of a white man and a woman of the Perryman family—as superintendent of schools and shops. The Coweta boarding school was never rebuilt after the war, but Tullahassee and Asbury by this time had been partially repaired, and both opened before the winter was over.[7]

Soon after the January Council adjourned, Perryman and Stidham went to Washington to try to make a new treaty. The conservative party in some manner learned of their mission and suspected treachery. As they reasoned, the Treaty of 1866 had given them "their old law back," and they valued it accordingly; the progressives in "taking away their law" and setting up a strange government had violated its provisions, and now they had gone to Washington to have it changed to confirm their illegal actions. Sands as "Chief of the Creeks," Cotchoche, and Thlothlo (Fish) Yahola wrote at once to the Commissioner of Indian Affairs that their treaty suited them just as it stood except that they were still grieved over the land they had been forced to cede. But Harlan, Cooley, and Sells were now out of office, and the delegates managed to secure a treaty with the new Indian administration admitting the previous wrong so frankly that it makes strange reading as the voluntary expression of a powerful government.

It was signed September 2 by Commissioner Nathaniel G. Taylor and the two Creek delegates. The preamble contrasted the Creek and Choctaw treaties, stated the sharp practice of the Creek-Seminole land transaction, reviewed the inadequacy of the compensation to the Loyal Creeks, and virtually admitted that the threats of forfeiture had been invalid. It raised the compensation for the ceded land from thirty to fifty cents an acre, a grant of $650,112, and provided that one-half of this sum, rather than the $100,000 of the previous treaty, should be applied to the losses of the Loyal Creeks; it made restitution for several small claims such as the damage done to the Tullahassee property by Federal soldiers, sums wrongfully withheld from the annuities, etc.; and it provided that

---

[7] Creek Tribal Records, 36013-14, 36807, 37561; *ibid.,* Checote Manuscript, 46; Commissioner of Indian Affairs, *Annual Report,* 1867, 329 f.; 1869, 415 f.

no license should be granted to a trader except after approval by the Council.

The Council ratified this treaty in November, and the delegates returned to Washington to urge its acceptance by the United States Senate during the coming session of Congress; but the deluded Sands, Cotchoche, and Thlothlo Yahola, against the advice of Dunn, managed to reach the city as a rival delegation to oppose it. Probably there had never been a possibility of its approval by the Senate, although the Federal officials seemed hopeful of ratification, but the inopportune appearance of the full bloods was sufficient to destroy whatever chance it had. As it accumulated dust in the Indian Office, even the Creeks forgot that it had ever been nego-tiated.[8]

In the fall of 1868 the regular session of the Council convened in the new capitol. It was a substantial two-story building of hewn logs with a great fireplace at each end, and because it had an open porch in the center the Creeks usually referred to it as the "council houses." It stood just at the edge of the thick timber that fringed the Deep Fork. The matter of a name came up early in the session. Present-day Creeks recall that "Columbus," "New Town," and "High House" were suggested, and the legislative journals show that "Muskogee" was accepted by the House of Warriors, but a joint resolution adopted the name "Okmulgee." The modern town of that name, usually designated as Big Spring, was the town of the powerful Perryman family, and the Creeks had never forgotten the site on the Ocmulgee that was the legendary cradle of their Con-federacy. Even in Adair's time when they camped there they always heard "at the dawn of the morning, the usual noise of Indians sing-ing their joyful religious notes, and dancing, as if going down to the river to purify themselves, and then returning to the old town-house." The Creeks were no longer the proud and self-confident people that loved to relate in happy gatherings the legends of their origin; but the old traditions were still strong, and as they met here in this new capitol they hoped to rebuild a nation sturdy in its

[8] Commissioner of Indian Affairs, *Annual Report*, 1868, 275 f.; 1869, 413. United States Archives, Creek 1868/O51, S534, S557, S564, S686; 1869/S21. *Ibid.*, Treaty File, Treaty of 1868.

ancient union and wise with the dearly-bought wisdom of the white man.

The journals of this Council show that the members had a lively sense of needed legislation and real constructive statesmanship. They worked over their criminal code and adopted rules of procedure for their courts. They tried to control the great cattle drives, which had begun to cross their country on the trail from Texas to the northern markets; after considerable debate they finally imposed a tax—apparently of twenty-five cents a head—and stationed officials at the different river crossings to collect it. They passed an important law defining the position of intermarried whites. Such persons were to present proof of good moral character, and the principal chief was authorized to give them permits, conditioned upon continued good behavior, granting them the right of residence and all the economic privileges of citizens except to share in the annuities. The chief often revoked these marriage permits for cause, and they terminated automatically in case of the death or divorce of the wife.

The Fuller note was presented to the Creeks at this Council. After prolonged debating and resolutions to pay and not to pay, they finally acknowledged the obligation, but repudiated it two years later on the ground that no service had been rendered. The installments paid on the companion note made a serious drain on their income, but they managed to authorize a two-dollar-per-capita payment to be made the following spring. The Southern leaders had learned their lesson, and the negroes shared equally with the Creeks in this distribution.[9]

The payment was probably intended to conciliate the Sands faction. The disaffection of this group was due not so much to the division between "Cold Country People" and "Hot Country People," for some of the Loyal Creeks were leaders of the constitutional party; it arose mainly from the conservatism of the full bloods. Much of their dissatisfaction grew out of the appropriation of the tribal income for schools, govermental purposes, etc., by

[9] Adair, *History of the American Indians*, 36; Bartram, *Travels*, 52 f.; Creek Tribal Records, 29886, 35373 ff., 38896, 39305; Five Tribes Files, No. 2, 16-40; No. 40, 6 f.; No. 63, 581, 913. WPA Project S-149.

the constitutional authorities; and they tried constantly to persuade the Federal officials to turn half of it over to them to be used according to their old system of distribution.

The conservatives also had to blame somebody for the failure of the Loyal party to obtain indemnity for their losses in the war. For their military services they were, of course, entitled to the same pensions and compensations as other Union soldiers, but for a long time they received little money from this source because the government placed the matter in the hands of a notorious swindler. Worst of all, the United States delayed the payment of the $100,-000 set aside by the treaty for their property losses. The interest was regularly paid with the annuities, and the constitutional authorities continued scrupulously to turn it over to the Loyal party. But the money belonged to individual claimants, and the Loyal party and the Sands party were not identical; hence there was no system of accountability. Sands, it will be remembered received the 1867 payment, Coweta Micco and S. W. Perryman—both constitutional leaders—received it in 1868, and succeeding payments were turned over to still other Loyal Creeks. It seemed to be understood that Micco Hutke should assist in the financial administration, but the disputes growing out of such a system may be readily imagined.

Finally in July, 1869, Captain F. A. Field, who had just succeeded Dunn as agent, and another army officer were directed to pass upon the Loyal claims. The Indians brought carefully preserved lists of the property they had abandoned when they left their prosperous country and fled to the famine camps of Kansas. The totals amounted to more than five million dollars. The commissioners allowed $1,836,830.41, and in 1870 the $100,000 was prorated to the claimants. They were ready to reject the payment, but the special agent in charge convinced them that the remainder would be paid soon.

It was several years before the conviction penetrated to the full-blood mind that 5 per cent of the award constituted their full indemnity and that the money realized from the forced sale of their own land had been used to pay it. There is no doubt that at first exasperation over the delay and later dissatisfaction with the compensation increased the factional division within the tribe. The conservatives never understood that the constitutional authorities were constantly and vigilantly pushing this claim.

It was apparent by the spring of 1869 that this division was rapidly leading to a crisis. Lawless members of both parties began to commit depredations upon their opponents, relying upon their faction to protect them from punishment. In June, Checote called the Council to cope with the increasing disorder. There were protracted debates over proposals for conferences with the disaffected leaders, and apparently the district judges were empowered to summon citizens to assist in enforcing the law. In August, Sands sent his lighthorse to the North Fork settlement to arrest members of the other party, intending to punish them for alleged depredations, and he planned at the same time to seize the council house and take over the administration. Checote notified Field, and Field called on the garrison at Fort Gibson for military assistance. Captain Bayne with five men hurried to North Fork Town, and Field managed to communicate with Sands and persuade him to withdraw his forces.

When the Council convened in October, the two houses met in joint session and listened to addresses by Checote, Field, and Sands and his partisans. The progressives were ready to compromise by amending the constitution, but it was apparent that Sands and his followers would not participate in the government and seek their ends by constitutional means. They were, in fact, unable to understand or use the new machinery, and their only weapon was in the maintenance of an opposition government. Worst of all, their inexperience exposed them to the designs of white men seeking to further the interests of powerful political and financial combinations.

Field attributed the recent disorders to George A. Reynolds, who had served until August as Seminole agent, and had been employed immediately afterward—according to a statement he made in 1878 —by the railroad that stood to profit by the north-south grant across the Indian country. It is certain that in October as a "friend of the Creek people" he was forwarding the conservatives' complaints to the Indian Office with his private comment that the "rebels" had gained control of the government by election frauds and were squandering the annuities without the consent of a large majority of the tribe. His activities were apparent throughout the winter of 1869-70. At the same time Field wearied himself to no purpose by explaining "to this faction, time and time again, that the treaty of 1866 does not give them their old laws, which they are constantly calling for, but permits them to have just such laws as the majority of the people may choose to make."

In 1870 the disaffected party found another white friend in the person of Dr. J. B. G. Dixon, a British subject who took up a precarious residence in the Creek country. At a council held at Arbeka —Sands' town—in April he was adopted by this faction as a full citizen of the tribe, and from this time on he was often employed to conduct its correspondence and present its cause to the Federal officials. Although his motives are obscure, there is no doubt that this adventurer exerted a sinister influence in Creek affairs.[10]

But the conservatives were strangely quiet during the winter of 1870-71. Possibly they were put in a good humor by a per capita payment of $1.75, which was carried out under an act passed by the Council in October. The money was turned over to the town chiefs according to the old Indian custom for distribution to their people. Sands drew $297.50 for the 170 persons in Arbeka Town. All of the traders, native and white, drew large amounts for goods which they advanced on credit to individuals. The negroes again were not forgotten, and one enterprising trader drew 1,365 freedmen's shares at one time for goods he had sold in anticipation of the payment.

The main reason for their quiet, however, was their interest in the coming election. It was universally understood that a conservative victory would mean a return to the old system of government. The Federal authorities were anxious to prevent this retrogression. By this time Franklin S. Lyon was serving as the Creek agent. He was sincerely interested in the Indians, but like his predecessors he believed their only hope of progress lay in the white man's political institutions.

[10] United States Archives, Creek 1869/D67, F96, F107, O5, P73, R104, R342, S157, S160, S161; 1870/F245, F378; 1873/C278. Five Tribes Files, No. 2, 42-76; No. 63, 572. Creek Tribal Records, 35373 ff., 39410; Commissioner of Indian Affairs, *Annual Report,* 1869, 398 f., 413 f.; 1870, 298. 57 Cong., 1 sess., *Sen. Doc. No. 420;* 45 Cong., 3 sess., *Sen. Rep. No. 744,* 173.

The negro–full blood alliance was an important factor in Creek politics. At least as early as 1869 the freedmen had been organized in three towns—North Fork, Arkansas, and Canadian. These towns were entitled to participate in the government upon the same basis as the ancient Creek towns, and in spite of their disaffection enough Checote adherents had presented themselves to the Council to fill their representation. It was certain, however, that in the approaching election they would vote almost solidly for the Sands candidate.

Each party took precautions after its own fashion to insure a fair election. At its regular session the previous October the Council had enacted a strict election law. Each town should convene on the first Monday in September and cast its votes. The members of the Council were to act as judges, or in their absence the town chief might serve. At the close of the day a duplicate of the returns was to be retained by the town chief, and the original was to be sealed immediately and sent to the president of the House of Kings to be opened and canvassed at the Council. The new administration was to begin December 5.

The Sands followers were no less vigilant. They chose Cotchoche as their candidate for principal chief, and he decided to accept— after hesitating some time over an offer from the progressives to nominate him for second chief. He came in April to ask Lyon whether the Department would be willing for the Creeks to vote "standing upon their feet" and was informed that they would be expected to observe the election law. Later in the year the leaders of the two parties had a friendly conference and agreed upon a compromise.

On August 7 Cotchoche and Sands notified Lyon of the plan, charging that their opponents had counted the votes of twenty Seminoles in the previous election, and explaining that this compromise procedure would prevent such frauds. "The other party are intending to vote by taking the vote for their side on paper and then count the votes, but we of this party seeing so much underhanded voting done, and stealing of votes, do not intend anything of the kind shall be done by this party, as of the men being absent, and the name enrolled on a list, but that every man voting for this party must appear on the ground on election day and then and there Counted, and then justice in voting will be apt to be done. The two parties intend to Come together at Okmulgee the one party to vote on papers the other to be present in person on the Ground—This is what we wanted to inform you, and if it is done in this way we believe it is the only way in which it will be done satisfactorily— and right in the sight of God." In spite of the halting English it would be difficult to find a clearer statement of the grievances of the conservatives and the seriousness of the mistake made by the missionaries and agents in encouraging the progressive leaders to adopt the unfamiliar institutions of an alien people.

Lyon then notified both parties, in very friendly and conciliatory language, that the United States would not recognize officials chosen by this method. The Checote party accordingly observed the law. The conservatives quietly followed their own methods. They tried to prevent voting in the towns by prescribing a fifty dollar fine for any official who might be tempted to act as judge. On the first Monday in September they gathered at Okmulgee with their freedman allies and waited at the council ground for their opponents. At two o'clock in the afternoon, when the other party still had not arrived, "we formed ourselves in rank on the prairie west side of the Council House and the whole prairie was full. We elected our Chief by the majority." They chose Cotchoche as principal chief, Futchalike as second chief, Sands as "public Speaker," and Tustennuggee Chupco as treasurer. They wrote at once to inform Lyon of the result of their election and notified him that they would meet the first Monday in October at the council house. The specified date was, of course, the day before the Council would convene for its regular session and canvass the election re- turns. The probability of a clash was apparent.

The disaffected bands gathered quietly in the various neighbor- hoods and set out in the direction of the little village that had by this time grown up around the council house. By Sunday they were assembling there under arms. The constitutional adherents, called into the service of the nation by the district judges, also gathered near the capital and prepared to defend the government. Pleasant Porter, with the title of "General," was placed in command with

David Hodge as commissary. On Monday Sands and his followers quietly took possession of the council house and invited their opponents to join them in canvassing the election. When Checote's men remained in camp on the creek, they proceeded to organize the government with Cotchoche as principal chief. Porter then ordered the stores closed, sent the women and children from the village, and organized his men in three divisions for an attack. Sands' adherents were then ordered to vacate the council house, and they withdrew to their camp.

Lyon arrived that evening in response to urgent messages from both parties. He would have been glad of military support, but Fort Gibson had been abandoned again by the War Department. He found both parties in camp with their men armed, their horses saddled, and pickets set. Each side was anxious to avoid bloodshed, but determined not to surrender its claims. The conservatives were as aggrieved at his advice as though they had heard it for the first time. "He talked to our old men as though they had no treaty to govern them—and turned away different from what we expected ... They replied—you must not tell us that—When the United States made the treaty with us—they said—'This treaty will not interfere with your laws'—and we look to you to see that our laws are not interfered with.—The agent replied—'Your laws have no sence in them, but this constitution is the law for your Children and you must be governed by it—' " But the leaders of both parties readily agreed that neither would fire the first shot, and this promise was kept.

The next morning the stores were opened, and during the day the Council met and organized, with no interference from the Sands party. Lyon managed to bring both factions together for a series of conferences, and on Thursday he persuaded Sands and Checote to sign an agreement to abide by the constitution "and work together and be Brothers and friends." John Jumper and three other Seminoles were present when this concord was established. He was invited to make a speech, and then—to quote Checote—"he was called upon to ask of God a blessing upon them (their peace)—which he done before they parted." Both parties then gathered around the council house and Lyon exhorted them to live together in peace and friendship. Although, as one of the Sands followers expressed it, "I had never been used to making a chief with papers spread before me," they consented to make a record of their votes and present it to the Council for its decision. They appointed six men to be present while the votes were counted, and the armed forces of both parties disbanded and returned home.

On this same Thursday the Council created a committee of six members from each house to count the returns and invited the agent to meet with this committee. James McHenry was appointed as chairman, and Porter served as clerk. They first counted the votes cast in the towns according to law. Most of these, of course, had been cast for Checote. They then canvassed the irregular returns submitted by the Sands party. Apparently decisions were left largely to the judgment of the agent. When a list appeared to be padded, one-fifth the entire population of the town was placed in the Sands column. It was impossible under the circumstances to arrive at an accurate count, but the report of the committee has every appearance of fairness and integrity.

The three large colored towns voted unanimously for the Sands candidates, and so did the conservative stronghold of Nuyaka. The Tuckabatchees still remembered the feud that began on the frozen plains of Kansas; an estimated ninety-four refrained from voting, forty-four voted for Checote, and only twenty-two for Cotchoche. Probably similar influences swayed the Euchees, for about half the members of that most conservative of all towns refrained from voting, and the remainder voted for the progressive candidates. The final count gave 1129 votes to Checote and 862 to Cotchoche. The vote for second chief was divided: 1070 for Micco Hutke, 781 for Futchalike, 114 for Coweta Micco, and 17 —a conciliatory gesture on the part of a Checote town—for Sands himself.

The same Council appropriated a few thousand dollars for the pay of the militia that had been called out to defend the constitution, and for beef, flour, forage, and ammunition purchased by Hodge from traders and citizens. The recognition given the constitutional government by the United States and its resulting control of the finances was an important factor in maintaining its authority. The Sands officers were paid in "warrants"—probably scraps of paper written by hand—which were supposed to be redeemed when that party got in power. One disillusioned light-horseman admitted that he finally quit the service because his "warrant" for $125 would not buy a piece of tobacco.

As soon as the votes were counted and these appropriations made, the Council adjourned. Another session was then held from November 16 to December 4; here the real legislation was enacted and the judges and other officers elected or confirmed by the Council were chosen for the ensuing two-year or four-year terms. The elections were held in joint session by the old Creek method; to quote the journal of the House of Warriors, "The time appointed for electing officers having arrived the House retired out-doors for said purpose," and later "the members of the joint session retired to their respective Houses." A special session of the new Council was convened December 5 for the inauguration of the Chief and the organization of the houses. This cumbersome practice was followed during the rest of the tribal period: the "lame duck" Council met in October to count the votes and later in an adjourned session to pass laws and choose tribal and district officers; and the new Council was convened for three or four days in December to inaugurate the new administration. On other than election years it convened in October and transacted its business in one session.

The conservatives loyally observed their agreement to come under the constitution. Sands had taken ill soon after the near-war in October, and his enforced inaction may have contributed to the general harmony. Cotchoche called his adherents together as soon as he returned home and advised them to accept Checote as chief and take part in the new government; but he died almost immediately, and his town, Wewoka, was too deeply grieved and demoralized to hold its election. All the other disaffected towns chose their representatives to the Council. A large number of these new members entered upon their legislative duties in the November session, but in cases where the town was already represented they were, of course, not admitted until the new Council convened. Forty-six towns, including the three colored groups, were recognized at this time, and the number of members in the House of Warriors was fixed at eighty-three.[11]

Unfortunately for the Creeks a new element of discord entered their councils just as this apparent harmony was established. The Union Pacific, Southern Branch—soon to be known as the Missouri, Kansas and Texas—had become the beneficiary of the north-south railroad grant. The road reached the Kansas line in 1870, crossed the Cherokee Nation, and during 1871-72 it was constructed across the Creek domain following the old Texas Trail close to the eastern boundary. The construction crews were lawless and disorderly, and criminals of all kinds flocked to each temporary terminal. As the road advanced, most of these vicious characters departed, but they left behind a more dangerous class of intruders, enterprising adventurers who fastened themselves upon the Indian country and were determined to make it a white man's land.

In October, 1870—before the road reached the Creek country—the Council passed a law providing that only citizens might cut and sell timber and requiring them to obtain a permit from the district judge and pay a royalty to the nation. The officers of the railroad ignored this law and purchased construction material from white contractors operating without authority, and the Creeks were forced to see their fine timber cut down without receiving any compensation.

At the time of the election troubles the construction had halted on the north side of the Arkansas while a bridge was being built across that wide and sandy stream; and all the scum of the frontier had collected at the terminal, the vicious little tent town of Gibson Station. As soon as the election was settled, the Council spent most of its time deliberating on what the House of Warriors journal called "the formidable subject of railroads." George A. Reynolds and N. S. Gass were present with an offer from their company to purchase land along the right of way under the Treaty of 1866, apparently for the purpose of laying out townsites. The Creeks, unable under the treaty to refuse, "indefinitely postponed" their

[11] United States Archives, Creek 1871/L76, L377, L420, S162, S354; 1873/C278. Five Tribes Files, No. 2, 68, 87-101, 104-29, 320, 325-27; No. 29, 12 f. *Cherokee Advocate*, October 21, 1871; Creek Tribal Records, 34102-19, 35391-92.

decision, and their inaction on this and subsequent offers was sustained by the Indian Office. To the Creeks, railroad development was not a benefit bringing prosperity and convenience, but a menace to their way of life and their possession of the soil.

A large part of the Texas cattle drive had formerly passed to the west of the Creek country, but it was apparent that a portion would now be diverted to the terminus of the new road. The Indians had not had time to restock their range since the Civil War had swept away their herds; hence at a special session in March, 1871, the Council invited the drovers to herd their cattle in the Nation during the grazing season upon the payment of a tax of fifty cents a month on every head. The cattlemen tried to evade this payment by fictitious sales to Creek citizens, and the following fall the Council provided that only written bills of sale would be recognized. In 1873 the drovers were granted permission to cross the country tax free, provided that not more than twenty-five days were used in transit.

The same fall of 1871 the Council tried to deal with other economic complications that were heightened by the railroad development. Citizens were required to secure a permit from the chief before employing a non-citizen laborer, and persons living in the country under permit were forbidden to employ non-citizens. Improvements erected on Creek soil by intruders were declared to be the property of the nation. The Council tried to prevent the influx of mixed-blood and intermarried white Cherokees to the railroad stations by a declaration that the right of intertribal residence had never been recognized except with the consent of the tribe where the settlement was established. One Cherokee citizen was given a special permit to establish a trading house upon the payment of a license tax, but such concessions were denied to a number of other Cherokees whose names had been submitted by Chief Lewis Downing. The Creeks were greatly troubled at the increase of white traders along the railroad, but this matter was controlled by the Department.

At the beginning of 1872 the trains crossed the Arkansas and a new terminal was established south of the river at a station named Muskogee. This squalid little town of tents and shacks was the scene of the most feverish speculative excitement, and many traders sought to establish themselves there. As the construction progressed, the stations of Oktaha and Checotah were established and named in honor of Sands (Oktarharsars Harjo) and Checote and their recent peace; and Eufaula was laid out in the vicinity of North Fork and most of the native business men moved their stores to the new location. The first trains crossed the Canadian and entered the Choctaw country in the spring of 1872. By the middle of February, Lyon had already granted licenses to ten white traders to open stores at Muskogee and Eufaula, and more applications were coming in. He hesitated "to encourage this needless influx of those who manifestly wish thus to get a foothold in the Indian Territory, and who may coöperate with those outside, to hasten the overthrow of the Indian Nationalities," and Commissioner Walker instructed him to refuse licenses except where the need was plainly apparent. Permission was refused when a bank in a Kansas border town asked to establish a branch in the Creek country.[12]

The building of the railroad intensified the greed of every predatory interest that was watching the Indian Territory. The validation of the princely land grants, the gains to be made in townsite speculation, the thrill of turning over the rich sod—all these were worth promoting. Congress was flooded with "territorial bills" designed to break down the Indian governments, confirm the bribe to the railroads, and give the rest of the Indian land to settlers. The resistance of the Checote government to this kind of "progress" and the opposition of Lyon to those who were "trying to rob this people of their last home" stirred these schemers to bitter resentment. Against this background white men in the Creek country meddled increasingly in tribal affairs, and Senator S. C. Pomeroy, of Kansas, forwarded their complaints to the Indian Office. They managed to destroy the concord Lyon had established, and the constitutional disturbances broke out again during the winter of 1871-72.

[12] United States Archives, Creek 1871/L385, L368, L441; 1872/L490, L508, L522, M936. *Ibid.*, Correspondence Land Division, Letter Book 106, 84; Letter Book 118, 7 f. *Ibid.*, Correspondence Civilization Division, Letter Book 6, 187 f., 266, 297-99; Five Tribes Files, No. 2, 106-20, 320-47; No. 29, 7, 13-41, 54-66. Creek Tribal Records, 34741; Commissioner of Indian Affairs, *Annual Report*, 1871, 575-77; 1872, 77, 238 f., 320-49. J. H. Beadle, *The Undeveloped West*, 367-402.

One William Graham, of Chetopa, Kansas, was employed by Dr. Robertson in the fall of 1871 as the superintendent of Tullahassee. As soon as he arrived, he entered into violent disagreement with the Robertsons for their identification with native interests; and he soon began flooding the Indian Office with complaints against Checote and other Creek leaders "whose hands are stained with the blood of the rebellion." During the same winter Dixon and Charles Wheaton, of Kansas, worked among the negroes and communicated through them with Sands and other leaders in the fullblood settlements. A council was held in the spring, and it was decided to send Sands and Dixon to Washington to call for a new election; but Sands became ill and soon died, and Dixon went on alone. Lochar Harjo, of Nuyaka, who had long been one of Sands' trusted lieutenants, became the conservative leader. In a short time he was affixing his mark to documents as "Principal Chief," and again the Creek Nation had two rival governments.

Dixon and Graham finally persuaded the Commissioner to order an investigation of the election. Enoch Hoag, the Central Superintendent, accordingly came to the agency in July from his office at Lawrence, Kansas, to conduct the inquiry. Leaders of both parties testified, but Lyon was not permitted to question Dixon and Wheaton in an attempt to discover what influences lay behind the renewal of the disaffection. Hoag concluded superficially that Lyon had been "imprudent" in assisting to count the votes and adjured the Indians to await the decision of the Department.

By this time the demoralization caused by the war and the political disturbances had produced a class of young negro and Indian horse thieves, who joined the disaffected party to escape the jurisdiction of the courts. It is fairly clear that soon after the Hoag investigation Lyon advised the constitutional party to take drastic action to suppress the disaffection. A special session of the Council was called in August. The two "Houses retired to shade of trees" to listen in joint session to advice from Checote and Lyon. They then passed a "treason" law outlawing all meetings and secret movements designed to prevent the execution of the laws; forbidding any citizen to petition a "foreign power," to attend a meeting called by an alien for the purpose of subverting the constitution and laws, or to carry any subversive message; and imposing a penalty of from fifty to one hundred lashes for each offense. The chief was authorized to increase the lighthorse, and he was instructed to request Lyon to expel Dixon and Wheaton and other non-citizens.

Dixon and Wheaton left for a time, but Wheaton, at least, continued his intrigues from Kansas; and they soon returned and hid in the negro and fullblood settlements, where it was impossible for Lyon to find them. Lyon also attempted the removal of Graham, who was carrying on religious work among the negroes and writing letters for the disaffected party. Graham demanded to know "if the intercourse laws are such that a U. S. citizen can not have as much protection in his own country as he can in a foreign country," and Hoag directed Lyon to let him remain.

Checote could not touch these white men, but he attempted under his new authority to stamp out "sedition" and arrest the horse thieves. During the latter part of August and the first of September he called out about nine hundred assistant lighthorsemen. Part of them remained in their own districts as "home guards," but a large body was concentrated at Okmulgee. Lochar Harjo collected his forces in the vicinity of the agency. The constitutional party advanced to meet them and a battle seemed imminent. Lyon was temporarily absent, but a garrison had again been stationed at Fort Gibson, and Colonel B. H. Grierson managed to call the leaders of both parties together and arrange a truce. In the meantime he telegraphed to Hoag. Hoag held another conference with the leaders at the agency and again persuaded them to disband. A number of the young horse thieves were tried the following fall, but the court records show that they were given fair, if informal, trials, and several who confessed were pardoned by Checote. Lyon estimated, however, that the armed demonstration had cost the nation thirty thousand dollars.

A special agent sent by Hoag in October concluded that the Checote party was clearly in the majority, and that a new election would not affect the decision reached the previous year. He also listed every person who held office under the constitution, from the principal chief down to the lighthorse privates, and ascertained whether they had belonged to the Union or Confederate party during the Civil War. This examination showed that about two-thirds of the office holders were Southern men, but there was a large number of Loyal men in important positions—the second chief, several of the judges and district attorneys, more than one-third of the Council members, etc. The negroes also were represented, not only by the Council members from the colored towns, but in important district offices. This careful analysis should have disposed of the frequent charge of white politicians that the "rebels" had seized the Creek government and shut out the deserving Union men and their negro protégés.

Meanwhile the same influences that were fomenting the disturbance effected the displacement of Lyon, and E. R. Roberts was appointed as his successor. The Indians and their agent continued to request the long-awaited verdict of the Department, and the conservatives became increasingly restive. It was finally given in June, 1873. The Checote government was upheld, and emphatic notice was given that any attempt to overturn it would be put down by the United States. The Sands party accepted the result, and Roberts reported with the optimism of inexperience that the trouble was "forever" set "at rest." It had taken some soldiers and all the ponderous machinery of the Indian service to make exactly the same settlement that Lyon had made alone almost two years before. There is no doubt that Lyon had used a white man's decisiveness to strengthen the constitutional party and had discouraged Checote's natural disposition to compromise, but it was the policy pursued by every other Federal official.[13]

A few days after the government's decision, an event occurred that showed how actively the real Creek life went on behind the constitutional curtain. Timothy Barnett was the big man of Wewoka District. Prisoners awaiting trial were boarded at his house, witnesses and jurors traded out their credits at his store, and as court clerk he made out scrip to pay himself for his services. He built a stanch two-story house, and there he lived with one of his wives in feudal abundance, dispensing beef and hospitality to the

[13] United States Archives, Creek 1871/1277, I618; 1872/C80, G92, H230, H344, I1146, I1484, P274; 1873/C278, H300, I315, I533½, L192, L224, R118, S280. Creek Tribal Records, 28201-12, 31530 ff., 32283, 34123 ff.; Five Tribes Files, No. 2,342 f., 354-56; No. 31. Commissioner of Indian Affairs, *Annual Report*, 1872, 239 f.; 1873, 210.

whole countryside. But he had a second wife several miles away in the Greenleaf settlements, and he found it necessary to kill another Indian for paying her attentions. Judge Nocus (Bear) Yahola then called out twenty-one special lighthorse to arrest him. They went to Barnett's house, and after a considerable battle with his retainers they took him into custody with the promise of a fair trial, but as soon as he was away from the house they riddled him with bullets. The authorities never made any attempt to investigate the matter, but the lighthorse received the regular pay for their services.

The episode might be taken as an example of the crude justice dispensed by Creek enforcement officers, except that it was a secret society of full bloods known as the Pins that decreed his death. The origin of this society is unknown, but it exerted a strong hidden influence throughout the nation. Its political alignment at this time cannot be exactly determined, but it soon constituted the main strength of the Checote party.[14]

The following October the Council passed a law forbidding any citizen to carry a gun, bowie knife, dirk, or other weapon to a church, council, trading post, election, court, or any other place where people were assembled; but arms were permitted on the trails, in the wilderness, or at home. It was made the duty and privilege of the lighthorse to confiscate weapons carried in violation of this act and keep them as their personal property. This law apparently did not lessen the number of crimes of violence, but it brought many occasions of friction between turbulent citizens and covetous lighthorsemen.[15]

The prolonged disorder had been a serious strain on Creek finances, and in 1874 it became necessary to issue interest-bearing bonds for the funding of the national debt. The Checote administration was honest, if not frugal, in its financial policy. Court clerks made out scrip at will in the name of illiterate judges, trusted traders advanced goods on tribal paper and presented their accounts informally, and appropriation acts were often not recorded and the originals became lost or scattered, but no scandal resulted. The

[14] United States Archives, Creek 1873/R203; Creek Tribal Records, 28176 ff., 31552; WPA Project S-149.
[15] Five Tribes Files, No. 2, 388 f.

office of national auditor had been created by this time, but the chief and the Council exercised the main oversight of the financial administration.

Checote, less provident than his mixed-blood advisers, was impatient for the per capita distribution of the $400,000 accumulated under the Treaty of 1866, but the Council voted to retain it as a permanent investment. The nation, however, made payments to individuals for the purpose of relief. A serious drought and a plague of grasshoppers in 1874 brought a portion of the population to the verge of starvation, and two dollars' worth of supplies was furnished to each of 1,639 persons. The nation also adopted the custom of paying thirty dollars a year to crippled, blind, or aged persons who had no other means of support. Pensions were paid to 158 such dependents in 1873. This practice was continued throughout the remainder of the tribal period.[16]

The schools received increasing support. In 1871 the Council made a contract with Joseph M. Perryman to open another boarding school, under the auspices of the Southern Presbyterian Church. It was located at Prairie Grove, about ten miles west of Eufaula, and it accommodated about forty girls. Asbury and Tullahassee each cared for about eighty pupils. The mission boards appointed and paid the teachers, and the nation furnished the buildings and equipment and paid the living expenses of the children. Each school was under the special supervision of Creek trustees, usually mission school graduates, who took their responsibilities very seriously. They selected one boy and one girl from each town as pupils. A large number were full bloods. By 1871 the neighborhood schools had increased to thirty-one, of which six were allotted to the negroes.[17]

Christianity made steady progress. In 1873 the Baptists reported 29 churches with an estimated membership of 1,500 to 2,000, 23 native preachers, and 2 white missionaries. In 1877 the Methodists had 975 Indian, 16 colored, and 9 white members, and 32 local preachers. Checote was made a presiding elder in 1869, and he con-

[16] *Ibid.*, No. 31; No. 22, 4. Creek Tribal Records, 32509 ff., 35147 ff., 35570.

[17] Five Tribes Files, No. 2, 334 f.; No. 29, *passim*. Beadle, *The Undeveloped West*, 378-89; Commissioner of Indian Affairs, *Annual Reports*, 1869-75.

tinued to serve throughout his administration as chief. The Presbyterians still confined their work largely to training Creek leaders at Tullahassee, and their graduates showed a tendency in adult life to unite with the Baptist Church. But in spite of their religious interest the Creeks were vigilant to prevent land grants to missions under the Treaty of 1866, and they defeated an attempt of the Baptist board to erect a house for H. F. Buckner.[18]

In spite of their divided councils the Creeks retained their leadership in intertribal affairs. Before the constitution was adopted Sands sent his lighthorse and punished some wild raiders who were stealing Creek cattle, and as soon as Checote became principal chief he used his influence to restrain the Comanches from depredating upon the Chickasaws and the Texans. In 1870 Checote called a council of the Civilized Tribes to meet in June at Okmulgee to resist the "adventurous spirit of the white man." The self-contained Choctaws did not accept the invitation and only one Chickasaw delegate appeared, but the Creeks, Cherokees, Seminoles, and Osages met together in the new log capitol in the clearing to devise ways to hold their heritage. William P. Ross, a nephew of John Ross, was elected president. They adopted a resolution against the territorial bills and strengthened the Compact of 1843 by the provision that the principal chief of any member tribe might call an intertribal council.

The following fall the United States convened the first session of the council provided by the treaties made with the different tribes in 1866. It has been generally known from its place of meeting as the Okmulgee Council. Superintendent Hoag served as president, and Congress provided for the pay of the delegates. It was hoped, of course, that a territorial government would develop from this organization. The Choctaws and Chickasaws were brought to the meeting by a threat that as signatories to the treaties they would be bound by its actions, and from that time on they took a leading part in its deliberations. The other Civilized Tribes came voluntarily, as did the Osages and a few small tribes, but the

18 Minutes of the Indian Mission Conference; Commissioner of Indian Affairs, *Annual Report*, 1872, 240; Board of Indian Commissioners, *Annual Report* 1873, 242; United States Archives, Creek 1873/B1116, P528, R463, S821; Five Tribes Files, No. 29, 2.

wild Indians ignored the invitation to attend. Sands, who, it will be remembered, was at that time in a state of passive resistance to the constitutional government, served as a member of the Creek delegation. Cotchoche also had been appointed by Checote, but he became ill and sent a substitute. Most of the other Creek delegates were mixed bloods.

The council unanimously offered to mediate a peace with the plains Indians, who had been driven to desperate hostility against the United States by the encroachment of the settlements and the destruction of the buffalo herds. It adopted a report prepared by a committee, presenting statistical information about the natural resources and agricultural development of the Indian Territory and pointing out the importance of "homes and cultivated fields" to the preservation of the Indian race. It drew up a strong protest against any territorial plan forced on the Indians by Congress; and the main business of the session was the adoption of a constitution for a united "government of their *own choice*." There was nothing strange to Indian logic in the fact that Sands and G. W. Stidham served as the Creek members of the committee that drew up this constitution.

This document aimed to create a federal union similar to that of the United States. It provided for a governor elected by all the qualified voters, a General Assembly of a Senate and a House of Representatives elected from the various tribes to legislate upon intertribal matters, and a system of courts with judges appointed by the governor and the Senate. It was to go into effect when ratified by tribes representing two-thirds of the population of the Indian Territory. The Indians at no time had an untrammeled opportunity to act upon it; for upon the advice of the Secretary of the Interior, President Grant immediately transmitted it to Congress with the recommendation that it be amended so that Congress would have a veto over all legislation, and the executive and judicial officers and possibly some of the others would be appointed by the President.

Harlan, who was again in the Senate, hailed this opportunity to bring the Indians under the control of white men and introduced an amended version of the constitution as the basis of his territorial schemes. At the same time there was a general newspaper outcry against the "dangers" of the Indians' plan for self-government. There was a grave possibility that in drafting their constitution the Indians had furnished a pretext for the destruction of their nationality—the first essential step toward the seizure of their land.

The delegates, however, submitted the document in its original form to their tribes. The keen and cautious Cherokees refused, under the circumstances, to touch it, and the Seminoles followed their example. The small Chickasaw Nation rejected it because it was jealous of the representation given the large tribes in the Assembly. The Creeks ratified it at once; they feared the territorial scheme as much as the Cherokees, but they believed the Indians could oppose it more effectively through a union of their own. By the end of 1873 the Choctaws and several small tribes had taken favorable action, but the combined population of the ratifying tribes was still 12,243 short of the required two-thirds majority. In 1875 the Okmulgee Council prepared another constitution similar to the first; but only the Creeks were seriously interested.

In the meantime delegates appointed at the first session met their wild brethren in council on the Washita in April, 1871, and urged them to make peace with the United States. Several tribes promised to join the intertribal meeting, which was to convene that year in June, but Satanta, the leader of the fighting Kiowas, protested that "the time has not come yet." Within a month with one hundred of his fierce warriors he captured a wagon train carrying supplies to Fort Richardson, Texas, and killed and scalped the drivers. But the Cheyennes and Arapahoes and several small plains tribes came to join the council.

It was the strangest gathering that had yet assembled in the log council house. The plains warriors came in all the proud splendor of paint and feathers and buffalo robes and beaded buckskin, profoundly disturbed over the encircling menace of the white man's settlements, and seeking guidance to an untried way of life. Sands was selected by the council to give the official address of welcome. D. M. Hodge translated from Creek to English, and an interpreter with each delegation rendered it into the jarring gutturals and facile sign language of his tribe. Generals W. T. Sherman and

Randolph B. Marcy also addressed the meeting. Checote, as usual, had appointed a representative delegation, and Sands, Cotchoche, and other full bloods sat with Hodge and Porter and D. N. McIntosh.

The Creeks were deeply moved. They knew from their own dark history the dangers that were gathering about the prairie homes of their visitors, and they were convinced that only peace and agriculture would save them from extinction. The visitors were greatly impressed. The rude little cabins of the Creeks with their peach trees and cornfields, the growing herds of livestock, even the small cluster of buildings at the capital seemed to them not only desirable but attainable; they, too, would build "warm houses" and raise crops, send their children to school, and live in peace and security.

When the third session convened in June, 1872, Satanta had been captured and was serving a term in the Texas penitentiary for his raid on the wagon train, and the whole southwestern frontier was aflame with violence. The council therefore authorized President Hoag to appoint a peace commission to attempt another conference with the hostile tribes. Chilly McIntosh served as the chairman of this delegation. A meeting was held in July and August at a council ground near the Wichita Agency. The Kiowas were finally induced to come in, and they surrendered a number of white captives, but they refused to make peace unless Satanta was set free. The next year the Okmulgee Council devoted much of its time to the Indian wars and presented a formal request for the liberation of Satanta.

In 1874 Rev. John McIntosh, the son of Chilly, went as a Baptist missionary to the wild tribes of the Southwest. He found them very bitter against the white man and determined to continue fighting, but they welcomed him cordially as another Indian, invited him to eat in their tepees, and even listened to his warning about the white man's strength. He preached to a strange congregation gathered from a great spreading camp in the valley of the Washita. Painted warriors with scalps of white people hanging from their belts, blanketed women with crying babies fastened to their backs all sat on the short prairie grass crisped by the August

Menawa

Opothle Yahola

Oktarharsars Harjo (Sands)

Samuel Checote

Pleasant Porter

Okmulgee Council

Lochar Harjo

Ward Coachman

Creek Council House

Home of Samuel Checote

Joseph M. Perryman

Dwelling of Creek Full Blood

Legus C. Perryman

Square of Pukkon Tullahassee

Hotulke Emarthla (Edward Bullet)

Isparhecher

sun and listened to their first sermon. From that time to the present the Creeks have never ceased their missionary work among the southwestern tribes.

But the Creeks' influence upon their wild brethren was hindered by their own difficulties with the United States. In December, 1874, Clinton B. Fisk, the chairman, John D. Lang, Rush Roberts, and C. G. Hammond, of the Board of Indian Commissioners, visited Muskogee with the announced purpose of consulting the Indians concerning their real wishes in the matter of territorial legislation. By that time the Atlantic and Pacific Railroad had built from Missouri into the Cherokee Nation and therefore had a chance to gain more than three and one half million acres of Indian land under the east-west franchise. Fisk was the treasurer of this road, and several other members of the board were open to almost as serious suspicion of interested motives.

Delegates from all the Civilized Tribes except the Choctaw came to the squalid little negro settlement on the railroad to meet the Commissioners. Checote headed the Creek delegation, but it included all classes—Lochar Harjo, at least one negro, and several mixed-blood leaders. The delegates earnestly protested against any change in their treaty status, but the board reported that the Indian governments had failed and urged Congress to abolish them. Twelve territorial bills were introduced in Congress during that session.

Under these circumstances it is not strange that the government officials lost interest in the Okmulgee council. It had become a great unifying influence drawing the tribes together, a clearing house of information regarding agriculture, education, etc., and a school of diplomacy in the contest with the white man. The Civilized Tribes used it as a medium for memorials and protests, in faultless English, against railroad schemes and land grabs; and the bewildered nomads of the plains, fighting for their existence against odds they could not understand, came for sympathy and advice. In 1875 twenty-nine tribes were represented. Even the Kiowas and Comanches had come in by this time. The previous fall the white man's soldiers had converged from all directions upon their prairie fastness, and their fighting spirit was completely crushed. To the Texans they were painted fiends, who deserved only to be exterminated, but their brother Indians listened to their story of the wrongs they had suffered and drew up a memorial in their behalf.

By this time the Indian Office had fallen completely under the control of the land-grabbers. Commissioner Edward P. Smith reported that year that the Okmulgee Council had failed to create a territory, and he advised Congress to place the Indians under a government with a governor and judges appointed by the President and laws enacted by Congress. But the picturesque gatherings in the little capital on the edge of the prairie had attracted wide attention, and a tract was even published in France advising the Indians to adopt a union similar to the Swiss Confederation. This foreign author did not understand that the problem was not to assist the Indians but to restrain them. During the session of 1875-76 thirteen territorial bills were introduced in Congress, but the appropriation for the Council of the Indian Territory was discontinued and it never met again.

The last year of its existence the Creek delegates urged the council to establish a newspaper to defend the Indian cause, but the other delegates failed to approve and in October the Creek Council took it up as a tribal project. A charter was granted to a corporation to be known as the International Printing Company, composed of the chiefs of the Five Tribes. Dr. Myron P. Roberts, a white man from the North who apparently had suggested the plan, was employed as publisher, and William P. Ross served as editor. The first number was published at Muskogee in May, 1876, under the name of *The Indian Journal*. For several years it was subsidized by the Creek government.

The need of such a newspaper was apparent. In August, 1775, Elias C. Boudinot, a mixed-blood Cherokee commonly believed to be in the employ of the railroads, inspired a meeting of white agitators at Caddo, in the Choctaw Nation, to adopt a series of "booster" resolutions. Boudinot, George A. Reynolds, and Edgar Poe Harris, a white man who had come to the Cherokee country in a vain attempt to obtain recognition as an intermarried citizen, next hauled a building to Muskogee and attempted to establish a newspaper to be known as *The Indian Progress.* The prospectus stated that it would be "owned, edited, and printed by Indians," that it would carry columns in the various Indian languages, and that it would adopt as its creed the "Caddo Resolutions." Such an expression of "Indian" opinion was, of course, calculated to convince Congress that the tribes themselves were advocating territorial government.

When the Creek Council convened in October, it demanded the immediate removal of the building from Creek soil. Reynolds remained in the background, but Boudinot and Harris loudly complained to the Indian Office of this abridgment of a free press. The first issue of the paper was published October 22. It was surprisingly restrained in its tone, but the Creeks were not won. The light-horse moved against the plant and the owners hastily removed their press to the Cherokee Nation and resumed publication at Vinita. The Creeks were helpless to prevent this influence, but they had cleared their own soil of hostile propaganda.[19]

At the same time the Creeks were resisting the cession of some of their land to the Seminoles. In the fall of 1866 Reynolds had removed these much-shifted people from their refugee camps near Fort Gibson and attempted to establish them on the land ceded by the Creeks. Five years later the government surveyed the boundary and they discovered to their dismay that they had been located too far east and that their main settlement was on Creek soil. The Federal officials were determined not to shuttle the Seminoles about any further, and they tried to force the Creeks to sell

[19] United States Archives, Creek 1867/B77, 1868/D1037, 1870/F523, 1872/L581, 1875/I1482, 1876/W137; *ibid.,* Union 1878/U534; Creek Tribal Records, 31120, 34077; *ibid.,* Checote Manuscript, 43-47; Choctaw Tribal Records, 11712; Commissioner of Indian Affairs, *Annual Report,* 1868, 285; 1871, 587; 1872, 247 f., 466-68; 1873, 10 f.; 1875, 12-14. *Cherokee Advocate,* June 18, 1870; April 1, 1871; December 20, 1873; December 19, 1874; January 1, 1875; January 16, 1875. *Indian Journal,* April 5, 1877, and succeeding issues; *Indian Progress,* October 22, 1875 (United States Archives, Creek 1875/I1482); Five Tribes Files, No. 22, 52 f., 69; No. 29, 19-22. "Journal of the General Council of the Indian Territory" and "Okmulgee Constitution," *Chronicles of Oklahoma,* III (1925); *Journal of the Second Annual Session of the General Council of the Indian Territory; Journal of the Second Annual Session; Third Annual Session; Adjourned Session of the Sixth Annual General Council;* Fourth Annual Session; James D. Richardson, *Messages and Papers of the Presidents,* VII, 119; WPA Project S-149, article by G. Lee Phelps; Board of Indian Commissioners, *Annual Report,* 1874, 12-14; 1884, 11. Alice M. Robertson, Among the Indians: the Peace Conference at Muskogee; 43 Cong., 2 sess., *Sen. Misc. Doc. No. 71;* 45 Cong., 3 sess., *Sen. Rep. No. 744,* 173-88, 792-96; Grant Foreman, "The Five Tribes and the Prairie Indians," *Daily Oklahoman,* July 21, 1935.

the land where they were located. The Creeks were willing for the Seminoles to remain in their country, but they refused to cede any more of their greatly reduced domain. Judge Nocus Yahola, in whose district the Seminoles were living, prepared to exercise jurisdiction over them, but Secretary Delano ruled—in plain violation of the treaties—that they could not be brought under Creek law. The Creeks were too tolerant by nature to cause any real harm to another Indian tribe, and the Seminoles continued to live in the Creek country under their own government.

In 1867 the United States located the Sac and Fox tribe just north of the Seminoles. The same error was made, the Creeks made the same refusal to sell, and in this case the tribe was moved farther west. The Pawnees were located north of the Sac and Fox Indians on land ceded by the Creeks and Cherokees, the Pottawatomies were settled west of the Seminoles, the Iowas and Kickapoos were given reservations west of the Sac and Fox land, and the Cheyennes and Arapahoes received the extreme western part of the former Creek domain. Other wild tribes from the plains or dispossessed tribes from Kansas and other states were located on land ceded by the Cherokees, Choctaws and Chickasaws, and Seminoles at the close of the war. But an area in the middle of the tract ceded by the Creeks and Seminoles remained unoccupied; and in 1874 Commissioner Smith announced that not all the land secured in 1866 would "be required for Indian purposes," and he planned to concentrate the tribes in one portion and make a large amount available for whites.[20]

The Creeks, of course, favored the colonization of Indians within the Territory. In 1870 at the urging of their Alabama, Koasata, and Biloxi citizens they offered a home to their fellow tribesmen who were wandering in Texas, but the plan was eventually dropped because the United States failed to furnish the necessary coöperation.[21] At the same time the Creeks were the most exclusive of all the Civilized Tribes except the Seminoles in the admission

[20] United States Archives, Correspondence Land Division, Letter Book 152, 475 f.; Commissioner of Indian Affairs, *Annual Report,* 1867, 327-29; 1871, 586; 1872, 241; 1873, 146-52; 1874, 12 f.

[21] United States Archives, Creek 1870/F393, 1871/R237, 1873/R89; Five Tribes Files, No. 29, 10.

of white men to citizenship. F. B. Severs, who by this time had married a mixed-blood Creek girl, served as private secretary to Checote, and two or three white men who had been adopted before the war served the government in various capacities, but all subsequent requests for adoption were rejected.[22]

The Creeks usually trusted their agent and sought his advice in their constitutional difficulties. They were very eager for the establishment of the agency at Okmulgee, and they won numerous decisions from the Indian Office; but the agents were unwilling to remove to such a remote location and they always managed to delay the erection of the buildings. The agency therefore remained in temporary quarters in a purely negro settlement until the office was abolished in 1874. A Union agent was then appointed to the Five Tribes, and he rented a building at Muskogee.

Theoretically the Creeks should have communicated with the Federal government through their agent, but as an employee of the Indian Office he was often under instructions contrary to their interests. They found it necessary therefore to keep two or more delegates in Washington during the time Congress was in session. The Indian Office at first tried to prevent the tribe from maintaining these representatives, but eventually they received official recognition.[23]

When Checote's administration came to a close many problems still confronted the Creeks. Their prolonged constitutional struggle had been carried on with a restraint scarcely to be found among "civilized" people, but it had brought a serious disregard for law. The schemes of land-grabbers threatened the very existence of the tribe, and the abolition of the Okmulgee Council left them to stand alone in their resistance. The railroad had destroyed their isolation, and there was every indication that white immigration would continue to increase. But they had made a surprising economic recovery from the losses of the war, and their political problems seemed in process of solution when they held their first orderly election in 1875.

[22] Five Tribes Files, No. 2, *passim;* No. 31.
[23] United States Archives, Creek 1870/F245; 1872/C1040, C1112, L59; 1873/R451; 1874/I145. Beadle *The Undeveloped West,* 373 f.

CHAPTER 7

Further Complications

IN the election of 1875 the conservatives nominated Lochar Harjo for principal chief, but as second chief they supported Ward Coachman, who had served as a leading member of the Council during the whole constitutional period. The progressives nominated Checote and Pahose (a small clan related to the Deer) Yahola. The choice of each voter was recorded openly by a clerk, the candidates courteously voting for their opponents. Party lines were sharply drawn in voting for the chiefs, but in most of the towns personal and local considerations determined the selection of Council members. Lochar Harjo and Coachman received the unanimous support of the colored towns and of Arbeka and other conservative strongholds, and they were elected by a substantial majority. The political complexion of the Council could not be known until events should shape the policy of the members.

The old Council canvassed the votes at the beginning of the session. Checote delivered his annual message October 5. It was in the nature of a farewell address. He expressed gratification over the orderly conduct of the election—"the Campaign was not characterized by any ill feeling, nor illegitimate practices, but was dignified and honorable to all parties"; but he advised the legislators against using the change in administration as the occasion of "violent reforms" that might disturb "the onward advancement of our Government towards a more perfect system."[1]

This message had been written by William Harvison, a mixed blood who was then serving as private secretary to the Chief. Checote was not able to express himself in smooth and flowing English, but he directed the writing of his letters and state papers by means of brief notes to his secretary in labored English or more

[1] Creek Tribal Records, 29328 ff., 35570.

often in Creek; and it is clear that he and not the secretary was the real force in his administration. If Lochar Harjo had any political ability, it was purely of the primitive type, and in following the constitutional forms he was entirely dependent on white men. His administration began auspiciously, however. In his inaugural message to the Council, December 6, he gave some general good advice regarding education, agriculture, Christianity, and good government. It was expressed in the style of Israel G. Vore, who was then serving as clerk at the agency and was always a trusted friend of the Creek people.

In one significant respect the new chief—or his white adviser—recommended a change from the policy of his predecessor. In October, Checote had approved an act repealing the permit law and making it illegal to employ a United States citizen for any kind of labor. This act, of course, was unacceptable to the white men and it was unpopular with the enterprising mixed bloods, who were again establishing great farms and needed white labor to extend their holdings. Lochar Harjo recommended a return to the permit policy as "consistent with the advancement of our people." But the short session in December failed to act on his advice, and the Supreme Court then declared the repealing statute unconstitutional. The opinion was so labored and so manifestly forced that it is an unconscious parody upon the whole legal system of the white man. It began by quoting the preamble of the Creek constitution:

" 'In order to form a more perfect union, establish Justice, and secure to ourselves and our children the blessing of freedom and liberty, We the people of the Muskogee Nation do adopt this constitution.—'

"The first and second clauses of the preamble 'In order to form a more perfect union and establish justice,' asserts and proclaims civilization, and the privilege of exercising common right—giveing rights and Justice to whom they are due—They speak of Justice, and what is Justice but an instrument commanding, extending and protecting that which is right.

"And since it is a common right, created by devine authority for the benefit of man to say who shall cultivate his soil or perform any kind of labor, for a fair—compensation—You will be intruding upon this right, when you enact a law depriveing man of its privileges; Consequently trampling upon the second clause of your constitution which speaks justice, the very instrument that imparts us a privelege to exercise any right, so long as it does not injure others—

"The third clause of the preamble, Securing to ourselves and our children the blessings of freedom and liberty, plainly speaks the meaning, and too plain to receive any other construction than that which it speaks. Freedom is liberty granted us to perform any duty that is our personal interest and advantage if the performance of such duty does not interfere with the rights and interest of others, Hence to enjoy and exercise that liberty is to enjoy a common right.

"But your present law deprives us of the privilege of enjoying that right, by declaring it wrong for us to do so—and a right to not do so—thus commanding what is wrong and prohibiting what is right, which is contrary to the meaning of law. The law in a sense of Justice should command the enjoyment of that right or liberty, and prohibit all intrusion upon it. Unless that is done, the blessings of freedom and liberty as is proclaimed in the constitution will neither be enjoyed by us or our children, who may come after us, and as the liberties and freedom growing out of the constitution and due us are intruded upon, by laws enacted subsequent to the adoption of the constitution we deem it both constitutional and legal that remedy be applied to remove the intrusion. and restore us and our children the liberties due us, And for that purpose we render our decision removing such intrusion, and restoring to ourselves and our children the blessing of freedom and liberties.

.   .   .   .

"We the Supreme Judges of the Muskogee Nation in whom the law defining powing of this Nation is reposed by Constitutional authority do hereby declare, after careful examination of the law and constitution, that the law enacted and approved Oct—1875—depriving our citizens of the sacred liberty of employing citizens of the United States, is unconstitutional, null void and of no effect therefore cannot be enforced."[2]

Although the Council did not follow the Chief's advice in the permit matter, there was no evidence of discord in the December session. But within a month there were ominous indications that all was not well with the administration. After the conservative party had recognized the constitutional government in 1873, it had

---

[2] *Ibid.,* 31285, 35571; Five Tribes Files, No. 31, *passim.*

maintained its organization to work for the payment of the full property losses of the Loyal Creeks. Dixon had been employed as attorney, but the Department had refused to recognize him, and he had frequently found himself and his delegation of Creeks and negroes stranded in Washington without funds.

In the fall of 1875 the Council had appointed Chief-Elect Lochar Harjo and David M. Hodge as accredited agents in pushing this claim. As soon as Lochar Harjo became chief, he decided to ignore the Council and employ Dixon through the extra-legal organization of the Sands faction. On December 21 on behalf of sixteen of the Loyal towns he protested to the Commissioner against the recognition of Hodge. This letter was attested by Ward Coachman. Early in January, Dixon appeared in Washington as the "attorney and special Freind" of the Loyal Creeks. He presented credentials from Lochar Harjo, made out by one James Williams, private secretary. These letters stated that Dixon was an adopted Creek citizen, who had served the Union party seven years without compensation and had thereby incurred the dislike of the former administration and of all speculators and dishonest men, and that he would make known to the Indian Office the Chief's views on any matter that might arise.

The Creek delegates, D. N. McIntosh, Pleasant Porter, and David M. Hodge, immediately began to investigate his credentials. The answer to these inquiries was a series of letters to the Indian Office from Lochar Harjo, made out by William Harvison as private secretary, disavowing Dixon and stating that the credentials were forged. It is fairly certain that the Chief *had* appointed Dixon, and that he was trying to communicate with the Federal government secretly through a confidential agent rather than through the regularly appointed delegates. If Harvison's letters were authorized, the Chief was attempting to deceive his own secretary; if they were not authorized, Harvison, no doubt with the support of other mixed bloods, was attempting through his literacy to direct the administration without the knowledge of the Chief.[3]

A controversy soon arose between Lochar Harjo and the officials

[3] United States Archives, Creek 1873/L393; 1874/D99, H1711, I152, L67; 1875/D61, H1921; 1876/D167, H78, H213, L50, M47, U22.

of Muskogee (Okmulgee) District. The district judge was Samuel W. Brown, a wealthy descendant of the Barnard family, who was chief of Euchee Town; and Sunthlarpe, another prominent Euchee, was captain of the lighthorse. Apparently the Chief had removed a lighthorse private for drunkenness and failure to spill intoxicants. Brown protested respectfully against this interference with local affairs. His letter deserves to be quoted, for the lighthorseman's naïve defense, which seemed adequate to the judge, and for the judge's conception of the relationship between the Chief and the district officers.

"I have an honor to call on your attention again that one of the Light Horsement by the name of Edmond has made his complains before me to the statements I myself did not understand the law and the nature of the Law that I thought Christmas was free for ever body. on that day that was the reason I enjoy myself; but I was not to drunk to not know any thing and I was in proper mine duing the time and I again thought that I had to obey my captain to get his instruction to spill wiskey; I diden thought I had any right *to go before my captain* or *beyond his orders*—

"These is the Complains has made before me and I have Transfered the same to you for you to reconsidered this matter

"and I think it is proper channel for all seuch acts; that any citizen of any destrict bringing up charges against any person or light Horsement in the destrict. let it go before Destrict Judjes had Guriatiction in each Destrict before it can reach the executive department before it can act upon then it will be don officially and no other wise."[4]

But the controversy increased until the Chief suspended all the officers of the district from the judge down and ignored a petition of the citizens for their reinstatement. It is probable that the issue was purely partisan. Law enforcement was so lax that almost any district official was liable to removal for good and sufficient cause if his political opponents happened to be in control. Officers were subject to suspension by the chief during the recess of the Council, but as soon as the Council convened they were reinstated or removed through impeachment.

[4] Creek Tribal Records, 31561.

The court troubles were complicated by the activities of the Pins. In the summer certain papers—resolutions, bylaws, and names of members—supposed to belong to this secret organization were found in the possession of one Cumpsey, of Cusseta Town, by the judge of North Fork District. Lochar Harjo and Coachman called a mass meeting of officers and other leading citizens to decide what action to take. The presence of several educated mixed bloods at this meeting indicates that some of this class supported the administration, but leading negroes also were in attendance. Pink Hawkins was elected chairman, and John R. Moore, an educated mixed blood, was chosen as secretary. It was decided that the proper policy for the authorities to follow lay in a rigid enforcement of the criminal laws. The Chief was advised to furnish each district judge a true copy of the Pin papers, but it was the sense of the meeting that no man should be subject to indictment from the mere fact that his name was on the list. But the real Creek government still functioned obscurely outside the constitution. Another organization known as the Muskogee Society was in existence at this time and there is reason to believe that the opposition to the Pins was carried on through its secret channels.

It is not clear whether or not the Pins punished Cumpsey for the loss of the papers. They did sentence a member to death just at this time for betraying their secrets, but his identity seems impossible to discover. The appointed executioners found and killed their man, and three men were subsequently tried by the courts, convicted of the murder, and sentenced to death. Two were executed, but the third was pardoned by the Chief.[5]

With this formidable secret order working obscurely against his authority, with progressive leaders trying to hold him in the safe path of Checote, and with the deep-laid schemes of the adventurers he trusted, Lochar Harjo found his way beset with difficulties. The trouble broke out when his first regular Council convened in October.

A contest developed in the preparation of his annual message.

[5] *Ibid.*, 34166, 35576; United States Archives, Creek 1876/D167, H213, L50, M47, U22; Five Tribes Files, No. 31; *Indian Journal,* December 18, 1884, and December 25, 1884.

As one of his negro followers afterwards explained it, the progressives "had wrote a piece for him to make a speech for the national council of the muscogee nation. and the contains many sentance that say it is a good thing for Creek people to go under Louisiana & Taxes's governor and keep his laws. And they just begging him to make a speech by that, but Locher Harjo did not like it, So he make another speech." The chief and his illiterate followers may have believed that a constitutional government like that of "Louisiana and Taxes" was the issue, but the text of the message his real advisers prevailed upon him to deliver reveals more practical considerations. He began by paying the usual tribute to education and Christianity. He advocated equal school privileges for all; hence he advised the establishment of a boarding school for the negroes, and the location of a boarding school in the fullblood section and the suppression of the neighborhood schools in that region. He urged the Council to settle the status of all disputed citizenships. He asserted that no nation could prosper as long as it failed to meet its obligations, and he recommended that a certain sum of money should be set apart to be divided equally between the Sands and Checote parties to be used by them for the payment of debts due to officers, citizens, and merchants.

These educational recommendations were not unsound. The utility of the day schools in the fullblood settlements was seriously open to question, and the conservatives, although they had no real cause for complaint, always maintained that the existing boarding schools belonged to the Checote party. The negroes had long felt aggrieved over their exclusion from the boarding schools, and an equal provision for them was in keeping with the policy of the Sands party.

The settlement of the disputed citizenships had been undertaken by Checote. Some of the Creek freedmen had returned too late to be entitled to adoption, and many "state negroes" had come with them, attracted by the rich valley land and the careless freedom of the Creek country. The Checote administration had been vigilant to protect the tribal rolls against these immigrants, but the adopted freedmen constantly sought to include them in the membership of their towns. Just before Checote went out of office, he had approved an act notifying all persons whose citizenship was disputed to present their claims to the regular session of the Council in 1876.

The purpose of the financial recommendation is rather obvious; such a policy would have enabled the Sands faction to pay the officers of the rival government it had maintained, to pay certain merchants who had furnished supplies upon the gambler's chance of its ultimate success, and above all to reward Dixon and other white men who had attempted to shape its policy. The public finances were at that time in a rather hopeful state, but the assumption of the huge and unknown debt of the Sands faction would have thrown the nation into irremediable bankruptcy.

The Council did approve a contract with the Baptists for the establishment of a boarding school in the fullblood section. It also closed five of the neighborhood schools, but it appropriated the money thus saved to the education of eighteen young men, graduates of the boarding schools, to be chosen from the six districts and sent to higher institutions in the "states." It was willing to adopt a more liberal policy toward the colored citizens. A year before it had elected a substantial negro, Jesse Franklin, to the Supreme Court, and now it appropriated three thousand dollars to assist them to establish a boarding school. But it rejected the citizenship claims of about one hundred negroes, mostly McGillivray, Grayson, and Hawkins slaves and their descendants, and when the Chief vetoed the act it was passed by a two-thirds majority.

A more serious conflict developed regarding Dixon. The Council directed the Chief to report that wily favorite to the agent for removal. He vetoed the resolution, and when it passed over his veto he refused to carry it out. The Council also reinstated the officers of Muskogee District. The House of Warriors then impeached the Chief. He was charged with failure to execute the law for the removal of Dixon; with suspending the officers of Muskogee District "by the arbitrary and illegal act of the Executive, without neglect of duty by said officers"; and with affixing his name as chief to a promissory note for a large sum of money for private purposes, thus bringing "the nation into contempt by placing it in a false position, and betraying the innocent and well meaning lender of the amount so claimed into palpable loss by the unauthorized use of the national name by the Executive." On December 5 the House of Kings sustained the charges by a vote of twenty-eight to twelve. A large number of full bloods voted against the Chief along with James McHenry, Pleasant Porter, and two or three other mixed bloods. His supporters were full bloods and negroes.[6]

Ward Coachman served the remaining three years of the term as principal chief. Like most Indians he preferred to consider himself "almost a full blood," but he was more than half white; his mother was the daughter of Alexander McGillivray's sister, Sophia, and a white man named Lachlan Durant, and his father was half white and half Alabama. He had been rather sketchily educated in the state of Alabama before he came West to join the Creeks, and he spoke English, Creek, and Alabama with equal fluency. Harvison served most of the time as his private secretary, and Vore, his friend and confidential adviser, wrote his messages and other state papers, but he himself directed their content. He was an able administrator and devoted his attention especially to tightening the law enforcement machinery. He built up a political organization of his own, and several leading mixed bloods became members of his party. He won the negroes also to his support; in 1877 he advised the adoption of the unenrolled Creek freedmen, especially the McGillivray slaves, and the last year of his term he employed an educated "state" negro as his secretary. He was more liberal than Checote in his policy toward white immigration, but he too opposed white encroachment.

Coachman continued the custom followed at the time of the Pin crisis of calling the leaders of his party to Okmulgee to advise him on matters of policy. This extra-constitutional device was used by succeeding chiefs, and it became the most important influence in the Creek administration. Most of the Council members were illiterate and, whatever their native ability, were wholly unable to cope with the intricate problems of the new era; and this practice enabled the educated mixed bloods to direct the government. It was more than a party convention, for in times of crisis all leading

[6] United States Archives, Union 1877/P360; Creek Tribal Records, 32658, 35570, 35573, 39327; Five Tribes Files, No. 22, 17 f., 67, 88, 101 f.; No. 29, 11; No. 31.

citizens regardless of party affiliation were called to consult together and formulate a policy. The chief always followed their advice. He usually called a special session of the Council to act on their recommendations, and the Council seldom failed to adopt their program.[7]

It was soon apparent that Lochar Harjo would contest the impeachment proceedings. Sugar George and Thompson Perryman, the negro judge of Arkansas District, served at first as his "attorneys" and presented illiterate protests to the Indian Office; but by the following June one Daniel C. Finn, of Coffeyville, Kansas, had become his champion. The Kansas legislature had just passed a resolution expressing great interest in the welfare of the Indians and calling for beneficent legislation in the form of territorial government, allotment, and the opening of their country to white settlement; and Senator John J. Ingalls sponsored this legislation in Congress. The nature of the understanding between Finn and Ingalls may be inferred from a letter Finn wrote to the Senator from Coffeyville early in June; "I will return to Muskogee in a few Days and anything I can do for Your or the interest of Kansas will be performed."

Finn made out many petitions and letters purporting to come from the "Executive Office" at Okmulgee by Lochar Harjo, "Principal Chief"; and these papers were referred to the Indian Office by Ingalls. He claimed the impeachment proceedings were irregular and succeeded in getting the annuities withheld pending an investigation. He produced a permit from Lochar Harjo as chief giving him the right to reside in the nation. He brought up the old charge that a "rebel" minority had got control of the Creek government by fraud and was squandering the money, and that the delegates at Washington were members of this "corrupt ring." In Lochar Harjo's name he protested that the majority party had "entire confidence" that the President would "protect the Muskogee People against unfriendly Legislation," and desired to "dispence with Delegates hereafter unless called for by the Government of the United States."

[7] Creek Tribal Records, 32568, 35333, 35577-81; O'Beirne and O'Beirne, *The Indian Territory*, 341-43; Five Tribes Files, No. 63.

The significance of this protest is apparent, for the delegates at that time were fighting with consummate skill and the courage of desperation against the most formidable combination of railroad interests and land-grabbers that had yet been formed against their country. *They* knew how to evaluate the "protection" furnished by the President, for the very fall that Lochar Harjo was impeached, Commissioner J. Q. Smith published statistics to show that the Five Tribes owned more land than they would ever use, asked if "an extensive section of fertile country is to be allowed to remain for an indefinite period an uncultivated waste," and commended "a very general and growing opinion that observance of the strict letter of treaties with Indians is in many cases at variance both with their own best interests and with sound public policy."

Finn also prepared petitions with the names of full bloods and negroes asking for a division of the Creek money and land so that the "rebel" and Loyal parties could maintain separate governments. It is probable that these were genuine, for the conservatives were, of course, resentful over the impeachment of their leader and they were grateful when a white champion entered the lists in their behalf. But Finn hardly troubled to disguise the real authorship of the letters attributed to Lochar Harjo, and it is probable that the "Executive Office" most of the time was located at Coffeyville. Even Coachman does not seem to have suspected the complicated foreign intrigues that lay behind the opposition to his government.

By August, Lochar Harjo as principal chief was issuing proclamations calling a special session of the Council. The danger of another insurrection was imminent. Coachman called a convention of leading citizens at Okmulgee September 1. They advised him to warn Lochar Harjo and his adherents that their conduct might lay them liable to the penalty of treason. Union Agent S. W. Marston also sent a friendly letter to the deposed leader advising him not to create a division among his people.

It was fortunate for the Creeks that Carl Schurz by this time was Secretary of the Interior, for although he might make serious blunders in the unfamiliar field of Indian administration, the proposals for opening the Indian land to white settlement no longer emanated from the Department. It was even more fortunate for the progressive faction that Miss Alice M. Robertson was working as a clerk in the Indian Office, and that she was allowed to draft the report and recommendations that were adopted as the decision of the Secretary December 17. The permit issued to Finn in the name of Lochar Harjo was disapproved, the request for a division of the tribe was denied, the impeachment proceedings were sustained, and the annuities were turned over without further delay to the constitutional authorities. Marston used every expedient to remove Finn, but Finn protested to Senator Ingalls that he had as much right to remain as any "Rebell" and evaded all attempts to dislodge him. Finally in March, 1878, Schurz called on the War Department for troops, and Finn seems to have abandoned the Creek country. But the affair ended in a dark crime that was never solved.

Finn had put forth some sort of claim to Creek citizenship for his wife. The claim was apparently without foundation, for her parents lived at Coffeyville, but in January, 1878, he brought her and their two-months-old daughter to the home of Isparhecher, a close friend of Lochar Harjo. On the morning of March 21 she and the infant were murdered and their bodies were hidden along the creek. As soon as the crime was discovered, Isparhecher and other Indians of the Lochar Harjo party tried to trail the murderer, and the constitutional authorities offered a large reward for his apprehension, but his identity remained a mystery. Finn reported the tragedy to Ingalls as an example of the methods followed by the "rebel" leaders, and Marston conducted an investigation, but it was clear that Isparhecher and his friends did not connect their political opponents with the crime. There is no doubt that Finn had used his wife and daughter to further his claim to reside in the Creek country, but the leaders of both factions were completely ignorant of whatever dark forces had brought her to her death.[8]

The whole impeachment trouble shows how the Creeks' political development was complicated by external influences. Ever since the fatal spring of 1861 it had been the misfortune of the

[8] United States Archives, Union 1877/I436, I920, K115, P21, P311, P360, P513; 1878/I326, I334, I574, M797. Five Tribes Files, No. 63, 1; Creek Tribal Records, 34168, 35721; Alice M. Robertson, "The Creek Indian Council in Session," *Chronicles of Oklahoma*, XI (1933), No. 3; Commissioner of Indian Affairs, *Annual Report*, 1876, xi-xiii.

conservatives to give their confidence to the very white men who were plotting to despoil them. They had real cause for complaint when the government was taken out of their hands through a form of democracy that actually disqualified them from participation, but it was their white advisers that stirred their smoldering discontent. The progressive party unquestionably took unfair political advantages to gain control, but again it was the threat of these white men's schemes that furnished the motive and the justification.

The worst effect of the dissension was the factional control of law enforcement. Something had been gained when the conservatives came under the constitution, but on the other hand their participation in the government meant that every district was divided, and political opponents presented petitions and counterpetitions to the Chief for the suspension and reinstatement of judges, prosecuting attorneys, and lighthorsemen. But it is apparent through the broken English of this correspondence that the Creeks were gaining a real understanding of law. An incident in Wewoka District may be cited as typical.

The lighthorse captain had died and a few of the citizens petitioned the Chief to appoint one George Chupco (Long George) to fill the vacancy, at the same time that other citizens petitioned for a special election. It was the chief's duty to issue commissions to enforcement officers, and Coachman used this practice as his authority to make an appointment. He wrote to the party requesting the election, "Your request not complied with you will see enclosed copy. therefore you will try and beat them next jeneral elections[.] If you think the Law dont give the Chief power commission the Light horse that part of the Law must be interpreted by the suprime Judges." The petitioners indignantly replied:

"we dont want our rights to go but we want the law to take its course ... you put us off to the general election, where vacancies occasion, what branch so ever it would be fill, all the laws provided for it. we find in the constitution & laws Page 15 article 41, we see there laws the reason we request to you. There is a law for general election and a law Seperate for vacancies. we see that the laws dont coinsede, and you put us off till supreme Judges meet to explain the law. we did not say to you the law dont give right to commission light horse men we know you have power to commission the light horse men after they were elected according to law. The person gets the highest votes you have to commissioned. The law dont give you right to appoint Light horse men and commission them. ... You have not explain the law to us, we are on the points of law you don't listen at us when we ask on points of law. You dont give us a chance to get to gether to talk about on points of laws. we would like to know what law dont give us any right. We are Creeks and citizens of the Muskoke Nation & we live in this District. we made out request and we are still requesting. we will request till you all explain the points of law. when we know we will stop. what points of law we are alluding to we are willing to tell. according to our law we have no Captain & one light horseman. that what we think."

But Coachman's appointee served for a year until the general election, which he won by a majority of 164 to 131.

Log courthouses had been constructed under an appropriation made in 1870, but some of the trials were still conducted at the judge's residence. It had become common to employ attorneys. Nobody was allowed to practice law without a license, but these licenses were granted by the judges on payment of a fee, and no legal training was required. Some of these self-made attorneys acquired considerable familiarity with Creek law, and they were distrusted in consequence by conservatives, who felt that technicalities sometimes defeated the ends of justice. A bill was once introduced in the Council stating that the offices of district attorney and judge were usually filled by licensed attorneys "to the exclusion of capable and honest citizens," and providing that no licensed attorney should be eligible to serve in those positions.

The Creeks had no jails. Prisoners awaiting trial were chained and guarded by the lighthorse, but a good many escaped and others were killed. A man under arrest was likely at any time to express his feelings in a loud whoop and dash for the woods, and the guards were equally likely to take it into their heads to murder him without provocation; and the euphemism, "killed while attempting to escape," covered both contingencies. There were instances also when the guards connived at the escape of their prisoners through friendship or bribery.

The penalty of whipping was administered by the lighthorse immediately upon conviction. The culprit was prepared by fastening his feet down to a small log and stretching his arms above his head and tying them to the branches of a tree. The whips were long hickory withes drawn through a fire to make them flexible and used while hot. The punishment was always preceded by some good advice from the foreman of the jury or the judge, and a few young Indians really accepted this reproof and correction and settled down to orderly lives.

The death penalty was inflicted with equal gravity. The condemned always met his fate calmly and never failed to show a strong interest in the coffin purchased for him at public expense. A typical execution took place in Coweta District in 1879 when one Satanoke was shot for the murder of Foxtail. About two hundred and fifty persons had assembled. A religious service was conducted by Rev. James McHenry. Then Coweta Micco, the judge of the district, who was also a Methodist preacher, made a speech pointing out the seriousness of murder and advising all to take warning. The prisoner next addressed the crowd, and all came up and bade him good-by. His wife and baby were then brought up; he took the child in his arms, prayed for its welfare, kissed it, and returned it to its mother. He asked next to see the coffin and "said it was a good coffin." The speech-making and the informal reception following it lasted about two hours, and the condemned man apparently took a solemn pleasure in the whole affair. He was then told to prepare himself for execution. He seated himself, removed his boots, and arranged his clothes. He asked the lighthorse captain what guns would be used, and a change was made from shotguns to rifles to suit his convenience. He was then blindfolded, and a piece of red ribbon was pinned over his heart. The command "Fire" was given, the guns exploded simultaneously, and he fell lifeless. There were several executions during Coachman's term. Checote had shown a tendency to pardon almost everybody under sentence of death, but Coachman carefully examined the evidence and gave clemency only for cause.

The Creeks had discovered by this time that their graded system of punishment for theft was more logical on the statute books than in execution. More merciful than contemporary white men, who made short work of horse and cattle thieves, they were unwilling to take a man's life for an offense against property, and the third offense was for that reason almost invariably pardoned. But their habitual criminals, both negro and Indian, never stopped at the third offense. The question then arose as to the punishment for the fourth offense, and it had become a settled procedure to treat such persons as first offenders working up gradually to the second death penalty. The logic back of this practice was typically Indian; as Checote expressed it, "(death) would make him a *new man.*"[9]

The Creeks were subject to the criminal jurisdiction of Federal courts in cases involving United States citizens or violation of the Federal liquor laws. In 1834 their country had been placed under the Federal court at Little Rock, Arkansas, and in 1851 the Western District of Arkansas had been created with the court sitting at Fort Smith. Until 1875 this court was inefficient and part of the time it was corrupt, the jurors were usually prejudiced against Indians, and the government made no provision to pay an attorney to defend the helpless Creek who was dragged before this foreign tribunal. But Federal law enforcement was tightened in 1875 when Isaac C. Parker, of Missouri, received the appointment as judge. Parker had not been a friend of the Indians—he had served four years in the national House of Representatives, and he had been active in sponsoring territorial legislation—but after his appointment to the bench he came gradually to accept the Indians' point of view. He sentenced men to the gallows with a frequency and enthusiasm that made him a terror to the white criminals of the Indian Territory, and whatever mistakes he made were beyond correction for by a peculiar quirk of law there was no appeal from his decisions.

The Creeks eventually came to respect Parker for his firmness and integrity, but they always hated and feared the jurisdiction of his court. It paralyzed their action against white intruders. It also hindered their own law enforcement, for many mistakes of juris-

[9] Five Tribes Files, Court Records; *ibid.,* No. 2, 394 f.; Creek Tribal Records, Courts (especially 34029, 39305); *Indian Journal,* July 17, 1878; June 26, 1879. 45 Cong., 3 sess., *Sen. Rep.* 705 f.

diction occurred; Creeks were brought before the court and even sentenced in cases involving only Creek citizens when they had already been tried in the tribal courts, and Creek enforcement officers were sometimes punished for executing tribal law upon Creek criminals. The Council frequently appropriated money for the employment of attorneys in such cases, and there was an increasing tendency to pay for the defense of Creeks even when jurisdiction unquestionably belonged to the Fort Smith court.

It is doubtful that the court's jurisdiction over white criminals really benefited the Creeks. A few great deputy marshals of the unsleeping, fearless, western type eventually developed, but as a class they were interested mainly in the fees they received for arrests. They seldom disturbed the real liquor dealers, and some of them "planted" intoxicants in the wagons of innocent travelers in order to arrest them. As for the white outlaws that took refuge in the Indian Territory, they multiplied faster than even Parker could hang them. Moreover the drunkenness and lawlessness of that wicked border town of Fort Smith was extremely demoralizing to the Indians that were called there as witnesses. The hangings furnished an occasion for a Roman holiday; the railroads ran special excursion trains, and coarse, morbid crowds filled the jail yard, laughing, cursing, fighting for points of vantage, until it was hard to clear a path for the condemned to walk to the gallows.[10]

The back country Indian settlements were the most orderly in the Creek Nation, but even here the disorganization of their government was educating the Creeks in crime. The court dockets show that petty larceny had become frequent—killing a beef in the woods, taking a side of bacon from a smokehouse, stealing a coat, butchering a neighbor's hog, taking corn from the crib, stealing apples, etc. More ambitious criminals — especially Euchees — formed horse-stealing gangs, and a regular traffic developed with Coffeyville, where the thieves exchanged their horses for liquor to be taken back and sold in the fullblood settlements. Much more general lawlessness existed in the turbulent negro settlement on the Arkansas and Verdigris. In the fall of 1876 the *Indian Journal* gave

10 Five Tribes Files, No. 31; *Indian Journal,* August 2, 1877; August 21, 1878. Creek Tribal Records, 29227; S. W. Harman, *Hell on the Border.*

a friendly account of a camp meeting at the Fountain Baptist Church, the strongest negro church in the nation; about fifteen hundred worshippers were present, many sermons were preached, several converts were baptized, one minister was ordained, and "there was no disturbance, and everything passed off pleasantly."

But even the disorder of this negro community was surpassed in the settlements along the railroad, where a combination of non-citizen liquor dealers and Indian customers made life precarious for the bystander. Intoxicants were freely dispensed at Muskogee and Eufaula. Shipments came in on the railroad, druggists abused their permits to sell for medicinal purposes, and the sutler at Fort Gibson carried on an extensive traffic. One drink of whiskey was sufficient to change a quiet, orderly Creek into a whooping, galloping desperado, ready to shoot out the lights or ride his horse through the passages of the double log cabins. Murder was so frequent that it was one of the common causes of death, but even more deaths occurred from the stray bullets of the hilarious or the accidental discharge of the pistols that everybody carried. Life was so hazardous at Christmas time that prudent traders placed their wives and children on the train and sent them to Kansas to remain until the holiday season was over.

Muskogee presented the hardest problem. It had a population of about four hundred, of whom few, if any, were Creeks. Some were citizen negroes and their non-citizen relatives, others were white or nearly white Cherokee citizens or claimants to citizenship, and the remainder were United States citizens—traders, railway employees, and intruders. The presence of this vigorous foreign settlement on Creek soil created a serious problem of land tenure. Tribal law recognized the right of a citizen to his own improved farm, but no provision had ever been made for townsites, and non-citizens occupied Creek land only under a precarious right of residence. The Cherokees had platted their railroad towns and sold the lots to citizens only, and Coachman and several of his successors urged the Council to adopt the same plan, and to create a town government in which only citizens might participate. But the Creeks were suspicious of any action that might be construed as a surrender of their jurisdiction, and no provision for the growth of Muskogee was ever made. Citizens built pigpens at will in any convenient place, and the streets were an impassable morass of mud and filth. During the tenure of Secretary Schurz the Creeks might even have been able to clean up its lawlessness, but they regarded it as a foreign town and shrank from the responsibility of policing it.[11]

The alien spirit of this ambitious little settlement is illustrated by the progress of the so-called Indian International Fair. The project was approved by the Okmulgee Council in 1874, through the influence of Superintendent Hoag, as an encouragement to Indian agriculture. Enterprising business men of Muskogee and a few leading men of the Cherokee Nation subscribed for the stock. John A. Foreman, a white resident of Muskogee, who operated a mill, promoted railroad building, and raised sheep in defiance of Creek protests, was the president; and Joshua Ross, a substantial, almost-white Cherokee business man of the town, whose wife was a Granddaughter of Big Warrior, was the secretary. Annual fairs were held from the fall of 1874 through most of the tribal period. Prizes were offered for agricultural and homemaking exhibits, but horse races and baseball games furnished the principal attractions. Liquor dealers and gamblers and sharpers of all kinds flocked there, but they were held in check by special Creek and Cherokee police furnished by the coöperation of the two governments. The enterprise promoted the growth of the town and provided uplift material for the reports of the Union agent, but although fullblood Creeks and wild Indians from the plains enjoyed the gatherings, they attended mainly as spectators. Only once—in 1879—it held genuine meaning for the Indians. In 1881 the Creek Council provided that only Indians might serve as officers, but it remained largely a white man's project.[12]

Although the Creeks remained aloof from this white man's enterprise, they still practiced their all-inclusive hospitality to other Indians. In 1876 when the whole border was aflame with hatred against the Sioux for their recent defeat of Custer, the Commis-

11 United States Archives, Union 1877/U119, W319; 1878/M682, W797. Creek Tribal Records, 25424, 30433, 30445, 30808, 31687 ff., 32288 ff., 32610, 35572, 38914, 39115; Five Tribes Files No. 11, 92; *Indian Journal,* 1876-79.

12 *Indian Journal,* October 26, 1876; October 7, 1880. Creek Tribal Records, 29682; WPA Project S-149.

sioner of Indian Affairs tried to induce this formidable people to settle among the Creeks. It required considerable generosity and more courage to take in these wild strangers from the North who knew no way of life except the mobile tepee camps and the pursuit of the buffalo herds. The Kansans from a safe distance cried out in angry terror against the location of these bloody-handed "murderers" of Custer anywhere in the Indian Territory, but the Creeks, both educated and conservative, saw them only as dispossessed Indians and were ready to welcome them as fellow agriculturalists. Spotted Tail and a number of other prominent chiefs came late in 1876 and held a council with the Creek leaders near Okmulgee, but they decided to remain in their own country. Perhaps even the Creeks could not have tamed the Sioux, but their ability to fraternize with any wild tribe on the border was an eloquent commentary upon the bloody Indian wars of the white man.[13]

The Sioux incident reveals the diverse motives influencing the policy undertaken by the government in 1866 for the concentration of Indians in the Territory. To distant tribes, emigration meant the same catastrophe that had overwhelmed the Creeks and their neighbors when they were driven from their eastern homes; some, like the Sioux, refused to go, and others were almost annihilated by removal. But the main objection came from the land-grabbers, who wanted the Territory to be kept free for white people; the Kansans, for example, whose soil was now clear of Indians, had changed in ten years from the most ardent supporters to the most bitter opponents of the concentration policy. On the other hand the native hospitality and sympathy of the Creeks toward other tribes was reinforced by the knowledge that only the occupation of the Territory by Indians would prevent its seizure by white men.

Through the entire Lochar Harjo–Coachman administration the Creeks waged one continuous battle for their tribal existence. Holders of railroad bonds worked under cover at Washington, border newspapers brutally demanded the Indian land, and the "booster" press at Caddo and Vinita claimed to speak with the

<hr />

[13] *Indian Journal,* October 5, 1876; October 12, 1876; November 2, 1876; December 14, 1876.

voice of the Indians for "progress" and "civilization." Everyone felt that the exploitation of the Indian Territory was at hand. A railroad passenger temporarily delayed at Muskogee visited the newspaper office and expressed the universal sentiment. "I want to take the INDIAN JOURNAL. I am going north. I want to keep the run of things in this Territory. If the government is going to get possession of this land I want to know it. I want to get hold of some." The educated Creeks watched every session of Congress with fear and dread, and every adjournment was a reprieve that brought no hope. Through all the reports of the delegates there is a sense of impending doom. With the delegates of the other four tribes they formed a permanent organization, which met two or more times a week to examine the bills before Congress and agree upon concerted methods of fighting them.

When Rutherford B. Hayes became president in 1877, Coachman tried to interest the other tribes in calling a mass meeting at Eufaula to inform the incoming administration of the real sentiments of the Indians and offset the influence of the "booster" press. The meeting was not held, for both the Cherokee and Choctaw chiefs advised against the plan. They were in favor of reviving the Okmulgee Council and making official protests; but they were afraid the fatal reliance of the full bloods upon the honor of the United States would prevent an impressive demonstration. Coleman Cole, the statesmanlike but unwordly chief of the Choctaws, unconsciously revealed in his reply this same trait, with its tendency toward fatalism and passive resistance. "As for myself I dont believe no such doing in Washington. believing that the United States Government. Stands upon the fundamental principle of free Government which all Nations of the world have found thir. Government are founded. builded wholy upon the moral principle. as long as United States Government. have not lost that moral principle they Cannot violate the Solemn Treaty. Should the members of Congress would lose that moral principle. and violate the Solemn Treaties I am not the man that would help them to do it. when the United States Should become a gold piece. what is the use to Speak to them in regard to moral Virtue. No use in the world when we have no gold piece. we Cry for their help they will only laugh at our Calamities." But the Indians soon discovered that Schurz, the new Secretary of the Interior, in theory at least was on their side.

The *Indian Journal* rendered important service to all the tribes at this time. Ross was a graduate of Princeton and virtually a white man by blood; but he had served as chief of the Cherokees and editor of their tribal newspaper, and he presented the cause of all Indians with the white man's words and none of the white man's racial blindness. The paper, however, never became truly Creek; its arguments were mainly Cherokee, and its local news was confined almost entirely to the white society of Muskogee or the near-white society of Eufaula. Attempts were made from time to time to establish a department in the Creek language, but they were soon abandoned. Roberts succeeded Ross as editor, and the ownership of the paper eventually passed into private hands. It led a precarious financial existence, and it moved back and forth several times between Muskogee and Eufaula. In 1878 plans were made to establish a "booster" newspaper at Muskogee, but the attempt was quickly suppressed by an order from Coachman.

Believing as they did that the railroads and their bondholders were responsible for most of the agitation in Congress, the Creeks and their neighbors sought through the *Indian Journal* and their delegates for a repeal of the land grants. This may have been a trap set by their opponents, for such a measure probably would not have stood in the courts and it would have furnished a safe cover for destructive legislation. At this time, however, the Indians believed that repeal would remove most of the incentive to destroy their tenure. They persuaded one of their friends in the Senate to propose an investigation of the investments that had been made upon the basis of the grants; but the resolution was amended to include an inquiry into the possibility of territorial government without the validation of the grants, the extent to which the Indians were using their school funds for the support of delegations at Washington, and the means by which such misuse of tribal money could be prevented. A subcommittee of the Senate Committee on Territories, with John J. Patterson, Reconstruction Senator from North Carolina, as chairman was charged with the investigation.

The committee held most of its hearings in Washington during the spring of 1878. No attempt was made to discover the ramifications of the railroad investments, but a few superficial facts were recorded. The Missouri, Kansas and Texas had issued bonds to the extent of about fourteen million dollars to finance the building of the road, and the bonds were secured by a mortgage on the entire railroad property and the contingent land grant. Most of them were held by foreign capitalists, but bonds in the amount of about five and one-half million dollars were held in New York. They were then worth about forty-two or forty-three cents on the dollar, and the bondholders had employed agents to defend their interests. The Atlantic and Pacific had built only to Vinita, about thirty-three miles into the Cherokee Nation; but upon this short stretch it had issued bonds amounting to half a million dollars predicated upon the grant and over a million on the road. The bonds were worth about five cents on the dollar, and the company was suing the United States in the court of claims to compel the validation of the grant so that it could finance the construction. It would have been interesting, and no doubt revealing, if the committee had attempted to trace the ownership of the bonds and the influence of the investors upon Indian policy.

Much testimony was taken regarding conditions in the Indian Territory and the need for changing the tribal government. The tribal delegates were present and alert, but white men of the "booster" class were the main witnesses. Although Boudinot was not even a resident of the Indian Territory, he was present throughout the hearings and was allowed to take an active part in the questioning. When the governor of the Chickasaws challenged his right to conduct the investigation, he said only, "My authority is that I am a citizen of the Cherokee Nation." The Indians resented the ex parte nature of the inquiry, but they hoped their own people could present a good case when the committee would visit the Territory during the recess of Congress.

There was the closest possible coöperation between the Creek delegates and the Chief and the leading men of the nation, whom he called in council at Okmulgee. Coachman also corresponded freely with the executives of the other tribes. To Charles Thompson, Chief of the Cherokees, he confessed that he had a serious problem; Lochar Harjo's party was planning to present its grievances to the committee, and he feared that the Creek division might furnish a pretext for hostile action in Congress. Thompson volunteered his good offices, and five Cherokees accordingly came to Okmulgee while the National Council was in session and apparently they managed to bring the leaders of the two parties together in conference.

A settlement must have been made, for a few days later the Council passed a resolution removing the political disabilities Lochar Harjo had incurred as the penalty of his impeachment, and expressing a desire to conciliate not only "our brothers of our own race" but the freedmen. Sixty-eight Creek negroes, including the Graysons, who had returned too late to establish their citizenship, were adopted at this time, and the McGillivrays and others were promised similar recognition as soon as they would furnish the necessary proof. Possibly the negroes used this opportunity to drive a further bargain, for the colored members of the Council pointed out a discrepancy in the educational provision, and the promised boarding school was opened that fall under a contract with the Baptist Home Mission Society. A substantial building the United States had constructed for the Union agency on the hill west of Muskogee and had temporarily abandoned was used for the school plant. The negroes knew by this time that they held the balance of power in Creek politics.

Porter, Hodge, and Stidham were appointed to represent the tribe before the visiting senators and to serve as delegates at Washington during the coming session of Congress. The long-expected visitors arrived in November. Only one member—L. F. Grover, of Oregon—was present besides the chairman. They held hearings at Vinita, Muskogee, and Eufaula, and Patterson bestowed a brief glance upon the Choctaws and Chickasaws. Boudinot still attached himself to the committee, cross-questioning the witnesses, and presenting an elaborate argument to show that the Indians desired territorial government.

Not a discordant note marred the effectiveness of the Creek

presentation. Coachman and his aides had planned their work well. His messages had gone out to every remote settlement, and mixed bloods, full bloods, and negroes all came to uphold the tribal cause. Over and over people of all classes reiterated their adherence to the treaties, their growing prosperity and progress, and their desperate hope that they might possess their land in peace. No coaching could have been so perfect; however they might differ in matters of procedure, the Creeks were one in their fundamental convictions. The senators questioned the negroes very closely with regard to their treatment. As a Supreme Court justice, several members of the Council, a lighthorseman, etc., who had once been slaves, testified to their full participation in the government, their growing herds of live stock, and their unrestricted use of all the rich land they wanted, even a Reconstruction senator could find no cause of complaint against the "rebel Indians." It was plainly apparent that the negroes had opportunities here for untrammeled development existing in no other part of the United States.

The Creeks easily refuted the charge that they were misappropriating their school funds for the support of expensive delegations in Washington. Their educational annuities for the preceding five years had totaled $65,000, but during that period they had spent $170,165.03 for education, making up the difference from their general annuities. The amount they had spent on their delegations averaged slightly more than three thousand dollars a year. In comparison with some of the other tribes the Creeks were a "backward" people, but their financial administration at this time was free from scandal and excessive fees to delegates and attorneys.

The fear of allotment ran all through the hearing. The Creeks based their opposition upon their own memory of their losses in Alabama. No Grant Foreman had yet written this sordid chapter of American history, but these full bloods described in simple, vivid language the whole process by which they had been cheated out of their homes through the forms of law. Only H. F. Buckner said that he personally believed individual land tenure would be a benefit if the Creeks would accept it voluntarily; but he said that they were universally opposed to the policy and that it would be very wrong for the government to force it upon them. Robertson testified that the Creeks discussed allotment a great deal "as one of the great subjects that disturbs and troubles them." He considered the agitation to change their tenure as "the greatest evil the Creeks are subjected to. It has a decided influence in retarding their progress toward civilization. This continued agitation makes their whole future uncertain and keeps them in an unsettled condition of life."

The Creeks were the only Indians that succeeded in presenting their cause. In the other tribes the non-citizen element crowded the hearings, and Indians who had come long distances to testify had no chance to be heard. Former Agent Marston, who stated that he was living in the Indian Territory as an "intruder," gave especially damaging testimony. The Indians, he said, were incapable of advancement, and all their progress was due to the efforts of whites, mixed bloods, and negroes. He described the rich resources of their country and argued that if it were thrown open to white settlement all branches of moral and religious work and industry would be benefited.

At the very time the committee was taking this hasty glance at the Indians through the eyes of their enemies, the Missouri, Kansas and Texas stock suddenly advanced 75 per cent and the bonds 25 and 37 per cent, although the earnings of the road declined during the same period. To the Indians this was an ominous indication that the end of their regime was in sight. When the committee report came, it was not reassuring. It stated that none of the tribes except possibly the Cherokee was using its school money for the support of delegations, and that it was possible to allot the land without confirming the railway grants. It recommended, however, that the grants be repealed and that the Indians should be made United States citizens, that the Indian Territory should be organized under the Treaties of 1866, and that a Federal court should be established there. The Creeks feared the last proposal most, for while other tribes had been granted jurisdiction over their own citizens, the Creek treaty of 1866 imposed no limit upon the extension of Federal law. The Creeks, therefore, seldom opposed the court bills; for weak as their treaty was, it was their only defense and they were afraid to protest against any of its provisions.[14]

Although Lochar Harjo's partisans had been successfully kept in the background during the senatorial visit, they did present their grievances during the succeeding session of Congress. Early in December they wrote to Patterson and to the Indian Office making the old complaint of a "rebel ring," and asking for a division of the tribe. They planned to send Lochar Harjo as a delegate to Washington, but he became ill and died in February at his home in Nuyaka. Isparhecher succeeded him and continued as "Acting Principal Chief" to present the claims of his party.[15] But this time the opponents of the Indians did not make capital out of their disaffection, and the Commissioner's report for 1878 pointed out the connection between the territorial bills and the land grants, and protested against the proposed spoliation. This statement and the arguments of the delegates had some effect. No hostile legislation was enacted during the greatly dreaded session of 1878-79, and from that time on the territorial schemes were somewhat discredited. But early in 1879 a new menace appeared, and the Indians believed this movement was instigated by the railroads.

In February, Boudinot published an article in a Chicago newspaper stating that the land ceded by the Creeks and Seminoles in 1866 and never assigned to other Indians was subject to homestead entry. The news of this "discovery" swept the country. Colonies of "Boomers" hastily gathered on the Kansas border and prepared to set out for the unassigned lands. On April 26 President Hayes issued a proclamation warning them that the lands were not open to settlement; but the border newspapers loudly urged them to defy the President, published wild stories of gold discoveries in the Indian Territory, and gloated over the recent seizure of the Black Hills from the Sioux. A few Boomers attempted the invasion in April and May, but they were promptly removed by Federal troops.

[14] *Ibid.*, 1876-79; Five Tribes Files, No. 11, 26-61; No. 63, 84-93, 108-16, 130-75. Creek Tribal Records, 25908, 29743-66, 30436-43, 30619-21, 30804-807, 35582, 38465, 38468; William P. Ross, *Indian Territory; Testimony Taken Before the Sub-Committee of the Committee on Territories of the Senate of the United States;* 46 Cong., 2 sess., *Sen. Doc. No. 124;* 45 Cong., 3 sess., *Sen. Rep. No. 744.*

[15] United States Archives, Union 1878/H1981, 1879/L296; Five Tribes Files, No. 63, 206.

From that time on, this small area of level prairie and blackjack jungle in the heart of the Indian country became an enchanted land, offering opportunity to the ambitious, sudden wealth to the speculator, and to the shiftless or unfortunate, the never-ending American magic of a fresh start. Many home-seekers addressed inquiries to Boudinot and to T. C. Sears, an official of the Missouri, Kansas and Texas; and they received circulars and maps and directions to assist them in reaching the "Oklahoma Lands."

The Indians were more deeply alarmed than they had ever been before at this new threat to their existence. Chief Thompson took the initiative and called an intertribal council, which met at Eufaula in May. Delegates of the Five Tribes and the Sac and Fox were present. Coachman served as chairman. Strong resolutions were adopted thanking the Federal administration for the removal of the Boomers, and asking Congress to prescribe effective penalties against such invasion of the Indian country. A second meeting at Eufaula in July advised the formation of a permanent organization with annual meetings; and the Creek Council accordingly elected two regular delegates to serve for a four-year term. By this time the Indians felt that the prompt action of the government had given them a breathing spell, but they watched events with unceasing vigilance. Stidham wrote to the Chief from Washington in June, "tell the people that while their minds are at rest and the Government shows a protecting hand, to keep their children in school regularly, so as to prepare them whenever the worse comes. that is the only salvation for our race. we must advance to that point so as to be able to compete with the pale faces. they are bound finally to force upon us their own laws in the end."[16]

It was the strengthening of intertribal unity by the Boomer menace that made the Muskogee fair that fall a real Indian gathering. Secretary Schurz was present, the leaders of the Civilized Tribes were deeply interested, and plains delegates were in attendance. The wild visitors brought beautiful specimens of their handiwork and sold them at a good price to Indians who had forgotten

[16] Creek Tribal Records, 29733, 29799, 30952, 35584; Five Tribes Files, No. 11, 91 f.; *Indian Journal*, 1876, *passim*; May 8, 1879; May 15, 1879; June 5, 1879; July 17, 1879.

their native crafts. Most of the time was taken up with meetings and councils in the large barn-like pavilion erected for the exhibits by the Fair Association. Even the Chippewas of the North sent a pipe and a message of friendship. The Osages came to ask the Secretary for self-government like that of the Five Tribes and the right to send their own delegates to Washington. Asahabbee, a Comanche, once a great warrior on the plains, described the influence of the peace commissions sent out by the Okmulgee Council— "When I was on the plain fighting fifteen years I saw nothing good, but Col. Adair, our Cherokee brother, came out to see us at Fort Cobb and gave us a good talk and we did not fling it away on the ground but kept it. He told us to stop on a piece of ground and work corn and raise pig and cow and build house. White man had told us to do this before, but we would not listen to him, but when our Cherokee brother told us we tried his advice, and have found it true and good. . . . God knows that my heart is true in these words. Long time when I lay down to sleep I think of all you my brothers, and want to see you, and when I wake up I want to see you, and to-day I am glad I see you."

A Sunday School convention of the Five Tribes was also held in the pavilion during the fair, and the wild visitors attended this meeting and listened to sermons by Indian preachers and heard Christian hymns sung in the native tongues by fullblood choirs. The only jarring note during the whole gathering was some advice from the Secretary to the Indians to take their lands in severalty.[17]

The Creeks continued to resist white immigration, but it was apparent by this time that their country was gradually filling up with these unwelcome settlers. The Department was willing to co-operate in the removal of intruders, but the process was rather involved. The district officers furnished the Chief with the names of unauthorized residents; the Chief then reported them to the agent; the agent investigated and reported to the Indian Office, and the Indian Office relayed the matter to the Secretary of the Interior; the Secretary requested the War Department to act, and the Secretary of War relayed the order through several army officers to the commander at Fort Gibson; a detachment of soldiers then

[17] *Indian Journal,* October 9, 1879; October 30, 1879; March 25, 1880.

reported to the agent and if the agent was still in the same mind they conveyed the intruder to the border and dropped him on Kansas or Texas soil. That was supposed to end the matter, but the intruders simply turned around and came back again and the whole process had to be repeated. There was no penalty for intrusion except a fine, and the shiftless, penniless class who made up the majority of the intruders cared very little about such a punishment. Enforcement was further complicated by the inability of the Creeks to make the kind of reports required by the Department. In 1877 Marston asked the tribal authorities for a complete list of the intruders and a description of their status. Judge Coweta Micco prefaced the report from his district as follows: "Dear Sir and the white man and zitizen. of the Muskoke Nation. and he didnd have know. permit: Some white. peoble difficulty Somay Indians. and going on. I am informing you. these we got the drouble So many times and Some of and gainst our. Law." His list followed— ten men, some of them with families. No doubt the list was a correct one, for Coweta Micco was reliable and intelligent, but it did not conform to Indian Office standards.

A more serious intrusion was the tendency of non-citizens lawfully residing in the Creek Nation as railway employees, traders, mail carriers, etc., to deal in rental property in Muskogee and establish farms and ranches. The Indian Office supported the Creek contention that such use of tribal land was illegal, but very little was ever done to prevent it. The Creeks could have stopped the practice by seizure of the property, but in 1876 Judge Parker ruled against the Cherokees for attempting by that method to enforce a graziers' tax. "The mere fact of a man being in the Indian country without a permit is no excuse for seizing his property. Neither the Indian Sheriff nor any other officers of the Indian country can seize or remove him or his property." The proper remedy for the Indians, said the judge, was by the enforcement of the Intercourse Laws by the Federal government. In practice this meant that the Indians were without remedy.[18]

The Creeks also began at this time to have trouble with white men who cut and shipped the fine walnut timber that grew along

[18] *Ibid.*, April 5, 1877; Creek Tribal Records, Intruders; United States Archives, Union.

the rivers. They tried to regulate lumbering operations by levy-
ing royalty upon all timber shipped from the nation, but very little
royalty was ever paid. Judge Parker ruled in a Cherokee case in
1879 that there was no law against stealing timber from Indian
land, but in spite of the urging of the Indian Office, Congress did
not correct the omission until 1888. The Creek enforcement officers
sometimes seized the stolen timber, but as one white man said,
"They seam afraid. Fort Smith is such a terror to all Indians from
the lowest to the Higest." They hesitated therefore to dispose of it,
although in this case Parker apparently would have sustained
them.[19]

At this time there were about 235 white men settled in the Creek
country: about 75 under Federal permits and licenses, about 50
under laborers' permits, about 60 intermarried whites with and
without permits, and about 50 intruders. The majority of these men,
of course, had white families. In addition the negro population,
citizen and non-citizen, had increased to an estimated 2,500. From
the white men the Creeks collected $1127.18 in taxes during 1878.
Of this amount $506.33 was paid by Creeks who employed non-
citizen laborers under permit; at this time the tax stood at one
dollar a month for each laborer, and 25 per cent was deducted to
pay the treasurer for collecting it. The next year the collection from
this source rose to $767.[20]

Coachman was disappointed at the failure of the Creeks to realize any appreciable income from the timber royalties, for public
finances went from bad to worse during his administration. The
annuities at this time were $69,978.90, an income too small to run
the schools, the blacksmith shops, the government, and the courts;
to subsidize the *Indian Journal;* and to finance delegations to Washington and intertribal councils. The government was not notice-
ably corrupt and not seriously extravagant, but it appropriated
money lightly without considering the revenue available. Some of
the mixed bloods would have economized by abolishing the town
system of representation and thus reducing the size of the Council.

[19] Creek Tribal Records, Intruders; United States Archives, Union; Five Tribes Files,
No. 11, 42-45; *ibid.*, No. 31.

[20] Creek Tribal Records; United States Archives, Union, 1877/U276.

G. W. Grayson expressed their impatience with fullblood legislators, who "are good enough men otherwise, but have no more
ideas of government than the Bedouins of the plains of Arabia."
But several attempts to amend the constitution were unsuccessful.
It was fortunate that such proposals failed; considering the damage
the Creeks had already suffered from too much "progress," it would
have been a crowning act of unwisdom to effect financial reform
by depriving the full bloods of their participation in the government.[21]

The only extraordinary expenditure during this administration
was the construction of a new council house. A plain, sturdy building of native stone, beautiful with the simplicity of honest work-
manship, it was the pride of the Creeks throughout the rest of their
national life, and it still stands as an impressive memorial of a
vanished era. It was erected by William G. Fryer, a white contrac-
tor, at a cost of $12,750. The white man's Masonic ceremonies were
observed at the laying of the cornerstone, and a copy of the *Indian
Journal,* a due bill of F. B. Severs' store, a roll of the school children
of Okmulgee, etc., were deposited there. The white and near-white
participants in the ceremonies did not know that the watching full
bloods believed, and still believe, that "medicine" was being placed
in the cornerstone to insure the site forever against tornadoes. The
new building was ready for use when the Council convened in
the fall of 1878. It was placed in the care of a janitor, who was
almost a public functionary, and a committee of three local citizens
was responsible for its use. It was opened for religious services, political meetings, and other community gatherings; the teachers of
the neighborhood schools met there regularly every summer for
their institutes; and it was used as a schoolhouse by the people of
Okmulgee.[22]

The year after the capitol was built, the Creeks held their election.
The factions and secret societies had taken the semblance of political parties, and the campaign was conducted outwardly at least
after the white man's manner. The impeachment of Lochar Harjo

[21] Five Tribes Files, No. 11, 33; No. 31; No. 63, 105-109. *Indian Journal,* August 7,
1879.
[22] Five Tribes Files, No. 11, 72-75; *Indian Journal,* May 1, 1878; WPA Project S-149.

had brought a new division, and three parties met in convention and nominated candidates and drew up platforms. The supporters of Coachman, or the Muskogee Party, met at Okmulgee in July. From four to ten delegates were present from each district. Most of them were full bloods, but negroes took a prominent part. Coachman and Micco Emarthla were nominated. The National Constitutional Party, or "Pins," also met at Okmulgee in July and unanimously nominated Checote and Taylor Postoak, who was also known as P. O. Taylor or Nocus Yahola. The disaffected Indians, who called themselves the Loyal Creeks, held their convention in the Deep Fork District in August. Most of the delegates were full bloods, and all the districts but Okmulgee were represented. They nominated Isparhecher, who was also known as Cochar (Tiger) Emarthla, and Silas Jefferson.

Silas Jefferson (known also as Tucker or Ducker), of Tuskegee, had been one of the most dependable men in the conservative party throughout its turbulent history and had served a number of times as its interpreter and as one of its irregular delegates to Washington. Isparhecher (pronounced and frequently spelled Spi-e-che), of Cusseta, had come only gradually to the leadership of this faction. He had served in the Confederate army but had changed his allegiance and enlisted with the Union forces at Fort Gibson in the spring of 1863. He had entered the House of Warriors at the adoption of the new constitution and had served the full four-year term. He had then been elected by the Council as judge of Muskogee (Okmulgee) District, and in 1872 he had called out his lighthorse under Checote's orders to put down the "sedition" of Sands. But in 1873 while still serving as judge he had entered actively into the councils of the conservative party in pushing the claims of the Loyal Creeks. During this or a second term he had been removed from office, apparently because he had killed a man in his zeal for law enforcement; and when Mrs. Finn was staying at his house in 1878 he was recognized as an adherent of Lochar Harjo. From the time of Lochar Harjo's death he was the unquestioned leader of the conservatives throughout the rest of the tribal period. He was a full blood of great native ability and force of leadership, wise in medicine and tribal tradition, and at the same time a devout Methodist; and his memory is still revered by old-time Creeks.

The three platforms were mainly platitudes—adherence to the treaties, friendship with other tribes, honesty in government, etc. All three bid for negro support by a pledge of equal justice to all regardless of color. The Muskogee Party made a concession to white immigration by promising "a wise and liberal policy towards labor," and the National Constitutionalists used the opportunity to deplore the bad government and extravagance of the party in power.

As the campaign progressed, local conventions were held in different parts of the nation. The people assembled at the home of some prominent leader and listened to general good advice about agriculture and education and morality while the politicians quietly held their caucuses and made up their "slates" for the district offices. It is not clear what happened to the Loyal candidates; apparently they withdrew from the contest and refused again to participate in the government. The two other parties entered into the struggle with deadly seriousness, and the election was marred by some frauds and irregularities. The vote was so close that the result could be determined only by the decision of the Council in contested cases.

The Council appointed a committee composed of leaders of both parties to draw up rules to govern the canvassing of the returns. It was decided to reject votes cast by proxy or by Creeks living outside the nation and votes recorded at other than the place appointed for the election, but honest returns were not to be discarded because of informality. A committee of six from each house was then appointed to count the votes, and the members of the Council testified from their own knowledge regarding the citizenship, residence, age, etc., of challenged voters. In towns where the returns were closed and sealed on election day the committee removed the names of ineligible voters and counted the remainder; but where the roll was kept open after the election for the purpose of adding votes from time to time, the entire list was thrown out. Two of the colored towns suffered from this procedure. They explained afterwards that they had neglected to seal the returns "from the fact that there was no envelope in the place." The majority of the committee decided that Checote had been elected by a vote of 836 to 821 and Postoak by 835 to 817, but a minority report gave the victory to the other candidates. After several weeks of wrangling, the House of Kings adopted the majority report by a majority of one, and the House of Warriors accepted the other count by a majority of eight. After this, the procedure is not clear, but in some way Checote became chief. He delivered his annual message December 6.

A few days later Checote approved a measure enrolling sixty-one McGillivray negroes according to the pledge made by the previous administration, but he vetoed a bill authorizing a blanket adoption of all Creek freedmen who had failed to establish their rights under the treaty. In January the negro citizens prepared a petition to the Indian Office literally yards long protesting against the exclusion of the election returns from the colored towns, and many full bloods affixed their marks to petitions expressing their sympathy and asking an investigation. The Commissioner, however, declined to intervene. Coachman soon accepted an appointment as delegate to Washington, and he continued to serve the government in various capacities; but he always asserted that he had been cheated out of the election by an unfair count. More ominous was the sullen disaffection of the Isparhecher faction. But constitutional forms had been satisfied, and Checote undertook to guide the Creek Nation through four more turbulent years.[23]

[23] United States Archives, Union 1880/T620, T853; *ibid.*, Correspondence Land Division, Letter Book 158, 236 f.; Five Tribes Files, No. 11, 75-80; Creek Tribal Records, 29374, 29375, 29377, 31339, 32396, 35585; *Indian Journal*, 1879.

CHAPTER 8

The Green Peach War

THE administration started off smoothly. Checote even had hopes of paying the national debt. The bonds voted in 1874 had not been retired, but the interest had been paid annually; and in the fall of 1880 the Council took them up and issued non–interest-bearing warrants to the holders. At that time the warrants issued upon the school funds stood at par, but the general warrants were worth only sixty cents on the dollar.[1]

The nation suffered a serious financial loss when the Tullahassee school was destroyed by fire in December, 1880. The Indian Office, urged by Miss Robertson, generously provided for the accommodation of twenty-five of the students at Carlisle, and Congress made a gratuity appropriation of five thousand dollars to assist in rebuilding the school. The Chief called a convention, and it was decided to locate the new building in an Indian neighborhood and turn what remained of the old plant over to the freedmen, who had lost their boarding school when the United States reoccupied the agency in 1879. Three substantial colored citizens—Henry C. Reed, the judge of Muskogee District; Snow Sells, the chief of Arkansas Town; and Sugar George—were appointed as trustees of the negro school, the Council made generous appropriations for buildings and furniture, and it was opened in the fall of 1883 under a contract with the Baptist Home Mission Board. It continued the name of Tullahassee, but the great school that had done so much to shape the course of Creek history had passed out of existence.

The new school was located south of the Arkansas at a site known as Wealaka ("coming water" or intermittent spring), and it was built and equipped at a total cost of about twenty-five thousand dollars. The faithful Robertson had died soon after the de-

[1] Five Tribes Files, No. 11, *passim*; No. 63, 655. Creek Tribal Records, 35590.

struction of his school, and Loughridge was recalled from Texas to take charge. It had a capacity for one hundred children. The school at Prairie Grove had been closed in 1877, mainly because J. M. Perryman, its superintendent, had entered the Baptist ministry; but the Baptist boarding school authorized during the preceding administration was opened in the fall of 1881 with fifty boys and fifty girls. The latter school was located in Wewoka District at the old home of Ward Coachman at a place called Wetumka ("sounding water"). Israel G. Vore was appointed as superintendent. Unfortunately, the month it was opened the Asbury plant burned down and the educational expansion was halted until this school could be reopened.

The Creeks continued to send older students to the "states" for training equivalent to that of the modern high school or junior college. The number was gradually increased from eighteen to twenty-six, and the annual allowance for each student was two hundred and fifty dollars. Most of the students were Indian boys, but a few Indian girls were sometimes selected, and from 1881 on three or four colored students were included in the number. The quota from each district was selected by the district judge upon the basis of educational attainments, and mixed bloods naturally were the most likely to qualify. Some of these young people felt a strong obligation to their race. One boy wrote from a school in Arkansas in 1881, "Although I am a school boy yet I feel a great interest in the welfare of my people, and some future day, if I live, I expect to take the pen and fight for my country."[2]

Although this growing educational program was essential to the welfare of the Creeks, it was beyond their financial capacity. A solution was sought in the settlement of the vexing Seminole land question. It was certain that the United States would never restore this land to the Creeks. The conservatives were unalterably opposed to any cession, but the educated leaders realized that they had the alternatives of losing the land without compensation or selling it upon the best possible terms. They reluctantly concluded to sell.

[2] Creek Tribal Records, Schools; *Indian Journal,* August 19, 1880; August 26, 1880; January 20, 1881; February 10, 1881.

The matter had hung fire all through the preceding administration, as Coachman vacillated between his own conviction that a forced sale was inevitable and his dread of conservative opposition. The Seminoles continued to exercise jurisdiction over this portion of Creek territory, and when Creeks or Seminoles who had committed crimes there fled to the Creek Nation, Coachman honored the requisitions of the Seminole chief. But in 1879 when the leaders of the National Constitutional Party held their convention, they petitioned the Chief to refuse such requisitions, and in their platform adopted the same day they put his recognition of Seminole jurisdiction in their list of things to deplore. The Chief as usual called a council of his leading men, and apparently they too advised him to resist the Seminole claims. He accordingly protested to the Seminole chief concerning the punishment of some Creek thieves, who had been turned over to the Seminole authorities and punished without a jury trial in the direct Seminole way after a decision of the Council. Checote followed the same policy and carried on an acrimonious correspondence with John F. Brown, a mixed blood who was the influence behind the Seminole administration. At the same time Judge Thomas Canard, of Wewoka District, wanted to know whether to collect taxes from a licensed trader and a mill operator among the Seminoles on the Creek side of the line.

The Council finally instructed the delegates to sell the tract if they could secure no other redress. An agreement was accordingly made with the Department officials, February 14, 1881, for the cession of 175,000 acres for one dollar an acre. But Congress struck the item from the appropriation bill, and the two tribes spent another year wrangling over Creek thieves whipped by Seminole light-horsemen.

The ensuing summer was one of terrible drought, and before the next crop matured there was a serious food shortage. The suffering became so severe that Checote called a special session of the Council early in April. He advised the legislators to obtain money for per capita distribution from the $400,000 accumulated under the Treaty of 1866 and to replace it from the Seminole settlement. The Council authorized the transaction and fixed the amount at $50,000; and the

Chief accordingly issued the warrants for a four-dollar payment. But the prospect of getting the money from the United States seemed remote. Commissioner Price even said that no funds had accumulated to the Creeks under the treaty. The delegates then reported that they had found an attorney willing to push the appropriation for a contingent fee. Checote at first rejected the offer, but he called a convention of leading men and they advised him to make such an arrangement provided it was subject to ratification by the Council. Congress then appropriated the whole $175,000 due from the Seminole cession, and in the fall the Council approved the payment of $8,750 as a 5 per cent attorney's fee. Besides the redemption of the per capita warrants, fifty thousand dollars was applied to the payment of the public debt. The remainder of the money was turned over to the action of the Council.

The Creeks were discovering the sinister fact that something was needed besides logic and justice in presenting their claims. It was certainly unwise for them to eat up their capital in "bread money," but that was not the reason the government ignored its financial obligations to them. Although their delegates were able and alert, and a whole army of officials at the Indian Office were paid to represent their interests, it always seemed necessary to employ attorneys before they could get any action by Congress. In most cases the attorneys' fees were nothing less than blackmail used to purchase influence in the right quarters. The practice was corrupting to their delegates, and it had a disturbing effect upon their internal politics. The Creeks did not yield to this demoralizing influence as much as some other tribes, but they received less consideration in the allowance of their claims.

The Seminoles were now the undisputed owners of the land where they were settled, and requisitions of criminals, etc., continued as smoothly as before the dispute. There was always considerable exchange of population between the two kindred peoples, but they tried to keep their citizenship rolls and per capita payments separate. Seminoles living in the Creek Nation were sometimes permitted to vote in Creek elections, but the Seminole government tried to prevent the practice, and in 1894 the Creek

Supreme Court decided that the rights guaranteed them under the Treaty of 1856 did not include the right of suffrage.[3]

A more serious difficulty arose with the Cherokees over intertribal law enforcement. In the Coweta District a few miles north of Muskogee the negro settlement of Marshalltown lay in the "Point" between the Arkansas and the Verdigris. It was a thoroughly vicious community, and horse and cattle thieves plied their vocation unmolested, protected by the close-knit racial consciousness of the Creek negroes. Several well-to-do mixed-blood Cherokees lived just across the boundary and their cattle drifted over into the Creek country, where they were speedily converted into beef by the Marshalltown negroes. These proud and autocratic and not too law-abiding cattlemen were impatient of the delays and impotence of the Creek courts and inclined to take their redress into their own hands. The mixed-blood Cherokee aristocrats were contemptuous of all negroes, and some of their imperious young men liked to ride over to Muskogee and swagger about the streets armed to the teeth shooting at Creek freedmen upon the slightest provocation. These young firebrands hotly resented the attempts of the Creek lighthorse, who in Muskogee District were usually negroes, to disarm them.

Serious trouble broke out in Muskogee on Christmas Day, 1878, when the negro lighthorse disarmed John and Dick Vann, two young Cherokees of prominent family connections, who were passing through the town. A lawless Texan, who also was passing through, undertook to reduce the negro officers to their proper place in the universe, and placed himself at the head of the Cherokees. In the ensuing battle one of the lighthorsemen was killed and three others were wounded. The following August another fight took place in Muskogee between the Cherokees and the negroes. This time John Vann was killed, several negroes including the lighthorse captain were wounded, and a white man working in a store was killed by a stray bullet. Railroad promoters of Mus-

[3] Five Tribes Files, No. 11, 71-94, 158-76, 217-44; No. 63, 358, 854-88, 951 f. Creek Tribal Records, 26021-22, 28299, 29722-871, 30598-736, 35393-586, 39131; United States Archives, Union 1875/J1635, 1880/C820, S734, S1136; *ibid.*, Correspondence Land Division Letter Book 152, 475 f.; *Indian Journal*, July 13, 1879; May 19, 1881; June 9, 1881; August 25, 1881; June 1, 1882.

kogee immediately carried the news to the Cherokees hoping to start a disturbance that would lead to the liquidation of the two tribes, but Vore, who was in charge of the agency, persuaded the Cherokees to await the orderly processes of Creek law. The white residents of Muskogee, tired of dodgings bullets, held an indignation meeting in one of the churches, but they too decided not to intervene.

Coachman immediately called a meeting of leading Creeks and asked their advice about placing an Indian lighthorseman on guard at Muskogee. Apparently they approved, for he ordered Richard Berryhill, the reliable and efficient captain of Eufaula District, to undertake the work. But Berryhill protested that the assignment "Seems to me to Be a Savere one. If the Town of Muscogee was really an Indian Town I would not weight a moment, but as it is there are but few Indians There. I am more than willing to serve my Peopple but the way things are I dont see how I am to Risk my life for non zitizens."

Muskogee was left for the time to its negro defenders, but a force of Indian police was soon established for the Five Tribes under a recent act of Congress. These Indians in the United States service worked under the orders of the Union agent in the enforcement of the Intercourse Laws. They spilled intoxicants, removed intruders, and arrested white criminals and turned them over to Judge Parker's court. They soon made Muskogee a law-abiding place where it was comparatively safe to live in a house, work in a store, or walk on the street.

Meanwhile Coachman, and later Checote, entered into correspondence with Chief Dennis W. Bushyhead of the Cherokees regarding the trial of the negroes who had shot Vann. They offered to admit three leading citizens of each tribe to the courtroom to see that the trial was conducted fairly, and it was finally decided that John Drew, a prominent Cherokee, should conduct the prosecution. But when the trial began, the Cherokee witnesses became alarmed for fear they would be held as participants in the affray, and they hurriedly left the vicinity. Judge Reed also delayed the trial on various pretexts and the case was finally dropped; but the Creek Council eventually paid the negro lighthorse captain two hundred dollars to compensate him for the injuries he had received in the fight.

During the same time the Cherokees made several raids on the Marshalltown settlement, shooting into the houses, and killing several of the negroes. On the night of July 26, 1880, a mob took two men supposed to be horse thieves from their houses, conveyed them to the Cherokee side of the line, and hanged them. The Cherokee government did not make any real attempt to discover the identity of the perpetrators, although it was well known that they were mixed-blood Cherokees. The next morning two parties of negroes from the settlement rode over into the Cherokee country in search of the bodies. One party under Dick Glass met seventeen-year-old William Cobb and young Alexander Cowan, both members of prominent Cherokee families. A running fight ensued that took them back and forth across the Creek-Cherokee line. The Cherokee boys and several of the negroes were wounded, and Cobb died as soon as he reached the house. The mixed-blood Cherokees were thoroughly aroused, and more than one hundred started from Fort Gibson to destroy the settlement, but Bushyhead managed to dissuade them.

The two chiefs exerted all their influence to keep peace, and they promised a fair and speedy trial as soon as the question of jurisdiction could be settled. A mixed commission examined the ground, but they failed to agree. The matter was then referred to John Q. Tufts, the Union agent, and he decided in favor of the Cherokees. The Cherokees then indicted ten negroes, the members of both parties that had crossed the line the morning of the fight, and asked Checote to deliver them for trial. Checote according to Creek custom called on Judge R. C. Childers, of Coweta District, to make the arrest, but Childers refused to comply. The Council then directed the judge to hold an examination and turn over only those who had actually participated in the affray; it was in fact fairly evident that five of the accused had not even been present when the shooting occurred. But Childers still failed to act, and Checote suspended him and appointed James McHenry in his place. McHenry and the negro prosecuting attorney went to work energetically to clean up the Point, and a number of negroes were convicted of stealing cattle from Cherokees. Several were whipped, and two of the number under Cherokee indictment were apparently subject to the death penalty. But the evidence against one of the latter was not entirely convincing, and in the case of the other— one Douglas Murrell—the court records were too fragmentary to indicate whether he was a hardened third offender liable to death or an innocent fourth offender subject to fifty lashes. The too merciful Checote took the easiest course; he pardoned the first upon the ground that he was probably not guilty and advised the judge to treat Murrell as a first offender.

McHenry, like his predecessor, hesitated to turn the accused negroes over to the Cherokees. In the fall of 1881 the Council elected Coweta Micco for the succeding term. Checote repeated the familiar request to this third judge, but he made no real move to comply. The Cherokee officers then told Coweta Micco that Checote had authorized them to make the arrest, and they went to the negro settlement, kidnaped one Daniel Lucky, and killed another of the accused.

Lucky's trial was held in April. All the safeguards provided by the enlightened Cherokee law were disregarded. The prominent mixed-blood judge who presided found it unnecessary to state that he was the uncle of the dead boy, and not one of Lucky's witnesses was present. It was fairly clear from the testimony of Cowan and a statement made by Cobb before he died that Lucky had been in the fight, and he received a sentence of death for first degree murder. Checote called the attention of the Cherokee Chief to the irregular procedure of the court, and Bushyhead granted a reprieve pending investigation. In the meantime Dick Glass, Douglas Murrell, and another of the accused negroes named Ben Doaker were discovered near Okmulgee with a herd of stolen horses. The Creek lighthorse attacked, killing Doaker and badly wounding Glass. By this time Bushyhead had a reward out for Glass and apparently for the rest of the indicted negroes. The negroes on their part raised a large defense fund and employed excellent Cherokee attorneys to work for a pardon for Lucky.

In some manner the Cherokees soon got possession of Murrell and placed him on trial. Apparently his witnesses were not even subpœnaed, and although it is fairly certain that he had not been present at the fight he also received a death sentence. The two men remained in the Cherokee prison at Tahlequah while Checote continued to protest and Bushyhead continued to grant reprieves. Finally in 1884 Murrell received an unconditional pardon. Lucky's fate is not clear, but it is probable that he too was set free. Dick Glass was never apprehended, but he engaged in more ambitious lawbreaking and became the leader of a gang that hid in the Seminole Nation and dealt in stolen Creek horses and Texas whiskey. He was killed in the Chickasaw Nation by Federal deputy marshals in 1885, but before that time he was to figure prominently in the internal history of the Creeks. Another of the indicted negroes killed a Creek officer in 1892 and fled to the state of Washington. It is probable that none of them ever settled down to an honest life, but no further trouble arose with the Cherokees because of their depredations.[4]

Throughout the whole trouble the chiefs of the two tribes conducted their intercourse with mutual courtesy and good will. Both men had cause for embarrassment—Checote over the impotence of Creek law enforcement, Bushyhead over the farcical nature of the Cherokee trials. Both conditions encouraged the growth of crime, the one by failure to control the criminals, the other by placing the whole negro community on the defensive. It is only fair, however, to point out that if the trouble had occurred in one of the neighboring states the negroes would not have received greater justice and the affair would probably have ended in a destructive race riot.

During the time the dispute was pending the Cherokee and Creek governments were coöperating actively against the Boomers. A persistent agitator named David L. Payne had assumed the leadership of the invaders. A society was formed with branches in the border towns, with officers and membership dues and enthusiastic meetings; and home-seekers went out in organized parties, staked out claims on the fresh prairies, and began building colonies. The

[4] *Indian Journal*, 1879-80, 1884-85; *Cherokee Advocate*, 1880-84; *Indian Chieftain*, 1883; Five Tribes Files, No. 5, 205 f.; No. 11, 157, 204-206; No. 63, *passim*. Creek Tribal Records, 25807, 30449-35589.

soldiers removed one body of these trespassers after another, a procedure that inconvenienced but did not deter them. In the summer of 1880 they turned Payne over to Judge Parker's court for prosecution under the Intercourse Acts.

The Indians were deeply concerned lest a court decision in Payne's favor would "legalize the overwhelming of our entire territory" by a Boomer population. At Bushyhead's suggestion the five chiefs or their representatives met at Eufaula and appointed a member of each tribe to attend the trial and employ an attorney to assist the Department of Justice in the prosecution. G. W. Grayson served as the Creek member of this committee. It decided not to employ outside counsel but to entrust the Indian cause to D. W. C. Duncan, the Cherokee member. Parker gave his decision in May, 1881. He ruled that Oklahoma was not public land subject to homestead entry; it had been taken by the United States for the settlement of Indians, and whether or not Indians had been located upon it, it was still Indian country. Payne was fined one thousand dollars for trespass, a punishment that was purely a matter of form since he would never possess one thousand dollars.

The conduct of this case offers a pleasing contrast to the usual murkiness of Indian litigation. The Council had appropriated five hundred dollars to compensate Grayson, and the Creeks had expected to pay $1040 as their share of an estimated five thousand dollars to an attorney. Grayson thriftily returned $320.70 of his allowance to the treasury, and reported that no attorney's fee was due except a voluntary payment to Duncan. The Council therefore voted to pay the able Cherokee four hundred dollars. The Creeks had paid and were yet to pay excessive fees to attorneys for rendering no service and equally excessive fees for services that should have been freely rendered by the Federal government, but for $579.30 they won the most important victory in the history of their relations with the United States.

While this case was pending, J. Milton Turner, a negro of St. Louis, sent circulars to negroes throughout the United States informing them upon the authority of Boudinot that the Oklahoma land had been ceded for Indians *and negroes,* and promising a quarter section to all who would join his organization. But the Commissioner of the General Land Office ruled—erroneously, as it happened—that the freedmen referred to in the treaties of cession were the freedmen of the Indian tribes. These victories reassured the Indians, and although Checote urged the formation of a permanent intertribal organization similar to the Okmulgee council, only the Creeks and Cherokees were seriously interested. But the Boomers continued their invasions, and the Creeks still believed that the whole agitation was promoted and financed by the railroads.[5]

In 1881 the Creeks became deeply aroused at an attempt to build a branch of the Missouri, Kansas and Texas from Muskogee to Fort Smith without the consent of Congress, the Indians, or the Department of the Interior. In April John A. Foreman, M. P. Roberts, and other enterprising non-citizens of Muskogee held a meeting to promote the project, and Roberts seems to have been delegated to enlist the support of Jay Gould, A. A. Talmage, and other officers of the road. G. W. Stidham informed Checote of this meeting, the Chief protested to Tufts, and the non-citizens hastened to explain that they had meant nothing in particular. But Foreman examined routes for the projected road, and when the Council convened that fall Talmage courteously asked permission to build it.

The legislators decided to favor the new road if it could obtain recognition as the east-west road of the treaty; this action, of course, was designed to block the Atlantic and Pacific and its land grant. The same day, however, the Council requested the removal of Foreman and Roberts as intruders. Tufts delayed action on various pretexts, and when Roberts died that fall he hastened to grant a license to the deceased man's sons to continue the newspaper. Checote immediately requested the removal of the younger men, but Tufts was unable to comply because of the license. The Indian Journal was really a benefit to the Creeks; under the new management it ceased to champion the Indians, but its influence was educational and it never joined in the demands of the "booster" press.

[5] Five Tribes Files, No. 11, 155, 176, 225, 239; No. 63, 430-93, 635 f. *Indian Journal,* 1880; *Cherokee Advocate,* 1881; Commissioner of Indian Affairs, *Annual Reports,* 1880-83; 47 Cong., 1 sess., *Sen. Ex. Doc. No. 111;* 47 Cong., 2 sess., *House Misc. Doc. No. 18;* United States, Office of Indian Affairs, 1882/8336, 1883/2392, 4471; Board of Indian Commissioners, *Annual Report,* 1882, 9, 28-36; Creek Tribal Records, 30818-36.

There is little doubt that Checote's main objection to the Roberts brothers was due to the desire of Albert Pike McKellop, an able young descendant of the Perrymans, to establish a newspaper at Okmulgee. It was natural that Checote should favor a Creek project, for the *Indian Journal* at its best was a foreign publication. It may also have been natural, but it certainly was not reassuring, that young McKellop asked and received a recommendation from the Chief to assist him in the enterprise and that the recommendation was addressed to A. A. Talmage. For this one short period in their history it is possible that the Creeks themselves were becoming entangled in railroad matters.

But the Department never recognized the proposed Muskogee–Fort Smith extension, and the Atlantic and Pacific resumed its construction under a ruling made by the Secretary in the spring of 1882. During the summer it entered the Creek country and established a station in the valley of the Arkansas, which received the old Creek name of Tulsa. Several members of the Perryman family and other prominent Creeks lived in the vicinity, but most of the business was conducted by non-citizens. As the terminus of the road, it was an important shipping point for cattle. A typical western "cow town" with celebrating cowboys and occasional outlaw visitors, it formed still another type of foreign settlement within the Creek domain.[6]

The Creek Nation had all at once become a ranch country. It was a cattleman's paradise. The bluestem grass grew with a luxuriance incredible to those who have never seen the richness of virgin prairie. "Old-timers" remember that "it grew as high as a man's head," "it came to the saddle horn," "we could see only the tops of the mover's wagons," and in the valleys "it was as tall as a man's head on horseback." A traveler who drove from Muskogee to Okmulgee in the fall of 1879 said that from the edge of the trail to the horizon the prairie stretched away, covered with grass averaging "as high as the horses' backs, brown, untouched, waving and dimpling in the wind." Part of these descriptions might be only the

[6] *Indian Journal,* 1881; *Cherokee Advocate,* 1881; Commissioner of Indian Affairs, *Annual Report,* 1881, xxviii; 1882, xxvi. Five Tribes Files, No.11, 191-222; No. 63, 809 f., 893, 920 f., 961-63, 991. Creek Tribal Records, 29832-35728, 39150.

haunting memory of a lovely, unspoiled land, but in 1880 Mrs. Robertson arranged a bundle of wild grasses as an exhibit at the Indian Fair and many of these tasseled stems measured from seven to nine feet high.[7]

A portion of the great northern cattle drive from Texas moved across the Creek country. Thousands of head from Texas and Arkansas were also driven through in the spring to graze on the Cherokee Outlet, which bordered the Creek country on the north; and in the fall other thousands crossed the Creek land to shipping points on the railroads. The main northern trail from Texas traversed the west-central part of the nation and crossed the Arkansas close to the mouth of the Cimarron. Other herds entered by way of the old Texas Trail and struck to the northwest soon after crossing the North Fork, or they were shipped by rail to Muskogee and driven across the Creek country to the western and northwestern ranches. Another important trail led from the terminus of the Atlantic and Pacific to the Sac and Fox Reservation.

Some of the drovers willfully or carelessly added Creek cattle to their herds, but the main difficulty was with the so-called Texas, or Spanish fever. The nature of the disease was not understood at the time, but many of the Indians' cattle became infected and died when these southern herds passed through. The Creeks consulted the Department officials, and upon their advice passed a quarantine law just at the close of Coachman's administration. Importation and driving of cattle from Texas and southern Arkansas were forbidden from April 15 to October 31, and the lighthorse were charged with the duty of guarding the frontiers.

This first year the agent assisted the Creek officers with the Indian police, and some of the herds were turned back. But so many entered at unguarded points that Checote advised the Council to tax and regulate the drives under the Federal Intercourse Acts. This statute provided that "every person who drives or otherwise conveys any stock of horses, mules, or cattle, to range and feed on any land belonging to any Indian or Indian tribes, without the consent of such tribe, is liable to a penalty of one dollar for each animal of such stock." Checote reasoned that the "consent" of the

[7] WPA Project S-149; *Indian Journal*, October 7, 1880.

Creeks might be conditioned upon the payment of a tax that would compensate them for their losses and enable them to control the drives. In the fall of 1881 the Council therefore placed a tax of ten cents a head upon all horses and cattle crossing the Creek country and provided that eight collectors should be stationed at various points on the rivers where the trails crossed. But the drovers refused to pay the tax, and Tufts decided that the Creeks had no right to levy it. Delegate Porter then obtained a favorable ruling from the Commissioner, but Judge Parker soon decided against a similar law of the Cherokees upon the ground that only Congress had the power to regulate interstate commerce. Under this decision the Indian Office abandoned all responsibility for the cattle drives.

More troublesome than the trail drives were the great herds that were kept by non-citizens in the Creek country. The Creeks still did not own enough cattle to stock their range, and the combination of Indian tenure and rich grass going to waste was too much for the morality of any white cattleman. Instead of confining their use of the Creek country to the ten days or so that were required to cross it, many of the drovers followed a zigzag course and grazed their herds there throughout the season, and the number of horses and cattle illegally kept by traders, railway employees, farm laborers, and plain intruders grew into immense figures. The Chief reported these cases to the agent, but although the Indian Office theoretically upheld the Creeks, the white men somehow managed to escape the lumbering machinery of removal.

In the fall of 1882 the Council created the office of stock superintendent in each district and authorized these officials to employ deputies and collect intruding cattle and keep them in close herd for thirty days. During that time the owner might reclaim them by paying a fine of one dollar a head and promising to remove them from the Creek domain. All unclaimed cattle were to be sold at public auction. The stock superintendent was to retain for his compensation and the payment of his deputies one-half of the money collected.

This law also proved ineffectual, and the danger of clashes between armed bands of Indians under the orders of the stock superintendent and armed bands of cowboys trying to protect their herds was unpleasantly apparent. In Coweta District there was also considerable trouble with three or four wealthy white ranchmen married to Cherokee women, who had brought thousands of cattle from Texas and apparently had turned them loose purposely on the Creek range. They "mix up all the cattle in this District," said Coweta Micco. But when the Creeks began to round up these herds Bushyhead protested to Checote; he admitted that the Cherokees had no right to use the Creek range in preference to their own, but he asked for mutual tolerance where the cattle drifted across the border, and he insisted that white Cherokee citizens were entitled to the same privileges as Indians by blood. The Creeks had never admitted the residence right of intermarried Cherokees, but Tufts found it easier to assume that it existed, and he ordered Mutto Locko, the stock superintendent, to surrender several thousand head he had seized. Bushyhead used all his influence to prevent his people from trespassing upon the Creeks, but in practice Coweta District was largely overrun by cattle owned by white Cherokees or claimants to citizenship or even white men from the "states" who held their herds on the border changing their allegiance from Creek to Cherokee when the officers of either tribe came in sight. Strangely enough no trouble developed between these intruders and the Marshalltown negroes.

The foreign cattlemen did not defy Creek authority so much as they ignored it. They seemed unconscious of its existence. The *Indian Journal* was filled with ranching news, and legal and illegal activities were reported together in the encouraging, friendly tone of the country newspaper. "George Perryman shipped five carloads of beef cattle from Tulsa last Saturday" might appear in the personal column; but of equal news value was the fact that a licensed trader of Muskogee "went to Texas Tuesday to buy cattle," that a Texas cattleman "unloaded two thousand cattle at our yards this week" to graze them in the Creek Nation, or that a notorious intruder whom the Creeks had been fighting for years "reports that he did well with his last shipment of cattle." Another news paragraph might show that "Texas fever prevails to an alarming extent around Tulsee." Apparently Tufts did not read the local newspaper, for he reported to the Indian Office in June, 1884, that he knew of no cattle on Creek land except the trail herds, which were by Judge Parker's decision outside the Indian Intercourse Acts. It should be stated, however, in justice to the agent that if he had tried to protect the Creeks he would have been reduced to impotence by the dilatory tactics and facile excuses of the intruding cattlemen, and by the endless relaying system of the government offices.[8]

White immigration of all kinds was increasing at this period. Checote did not relax his opposition, but the Creek laws were always badly drafted, and they were repealed and reënacted with bewildering instability. The mixed bloods were still unwilling to forego the employment of non-citizen laborers. Most of these "laborers" were really agricultural lessees, who were engaged to improve an unoccupied portion of the public domain for their employers; and the feel of the plow in the rich valley sod was enough to make any pioneer American forget his humble status and begin talking about "my claim." Checote persuaded the Council to repeal the permit law except for the employment of "clerks," but the well-to-do Creeks then employed "clerks" to work their farms, and the next Council disregarded his advice and restored the permit policy. The Chief also protested to the Indian Office against the multiplication of traders, and the Commissioner adopted the custom of consulting the delegates before granting a license. The change really had little effect, for the Creeks found it hard to refuse any applicant of good character. They did amend their tax law upon the Chief's recommendation. Many non-citizens in Muskogee and Eufaula had been running hotels, livery stables, harness shops, etc., and buying pecans and furs without paying a tax of any kind. In the fall of 1881 the Council raised the tax on merchandise dealers to two hundred dollars a year and placed a tax of from fifteen to two hundred dollars on other businesses; and the enforcement was soon placed in the hands of an officer known as the national tax collector. This law was the most easily enforced of all the Creek statutes governing the activities of non-citizens.

The Creeks apparently tried to tax intermarried white Cherokees

[8] *Indian Journal,* 1882-83; *Cherokee Advocate,* July 11, 1884; Five Tribes Files, No. 11, *passim;* No. 63, 520 f., 633-827. Creek Tribal Records, 30478-84, 34744-807, 35589-90; Indian Office, 1883/11903, 1884/13481.

as licensed traders, but the law was so badly drafted that it could not stand against Tufts' unwillingness to enforce it and Bushyhead's courteous reasoning. In 1881 the Council in a moment of aberration voted to grant citizenship to their own intermarried whites, but the bill was vetoed by Checote. The Chief thought that even the residence permit was too liberal, and the next year he persuaded the Council to repeal this law, but in practice intermarried white men continued to reside in the Creek country and exercise the economic privileges of citizenship without the former requirement of good behavior.

The Checote administration had to contend with an intruder evil of new and menacing proportions. It was apparent after 1881 that the Indian Office was no longer seriously concerned with the enforcement of the treaty pledges against unauthorized white residence. One has only to trace the recurrence of certain names in intruder lists to realize the futility of the Creeks' constant appeal for protection. Several such families remained in the Coweta District from the beginning of Checote's term to the end of the tribal period, farming on a large scale, cutting and shipping walnut timber, and resisting the Creeks' repeated attempts to dislodge them.[9]

If the Indians had needed an illustration of the weary process of government redress, it was furnished them at this time by the payment of a claim that had been pending for fifty years. The Federal officials had reserved the land set aside for Creek orphans by the Treaty of 1832, had sold it for $108,713.82 and invested the money, and had counted 573 orphans; but nobody had remembered to use this fund for their benefit. The interest had been reinvested until in 1840 when Commissioner Crawford happened to notice it, the amount had increased to $126,000; and he advised that since some of the original beneficiaries were grown and others were dead, the income should be used thereafter for the benefit of any orphan children of the tribe. The Department accordingly followed this policy for a while, but it soon made the matter worse by using the income for the support of the Creek schools. Some of

[9] Creek Tribal Records, 29819-39170; Five Tribes Files, No. 11, 113-227; No. 63, 624-956. Indian Office, 1881/15521.

the Creek leaders by this time had gained enough legal knowledge to understand that money belonging to some of their citizens was being used for the benefit of others. In the Treaty of 1856 they tried vainly to obtain the distribution of the money to the proper beneficiaries, and from that time on the delegates regularly presented this claim. Agent Garrett and Superintendent Rector both urged the settlement, and a census of the original orphans had actually been made and Congress was apparently ready to authorize the payment when the Civil War stopped all action in the matter.

The Creeks were able to secure such provision in their treaty with the Confederate States, but this stipulation of course was never carried out. In the meantime the United States used $106,-799.68 of the money for the benefit of refugees of various tribes, but the orphans still had about $200,000, which was continually increasing by the accumulated interest. This money had been invested in stocks and bonds, some of which were the greatly depreciated bonds of the southern states. In the treaty negotiated with the helpless Loyal delegates at the close of the war this fund was diverted to established a boarding school and the protests of McIntosh and Smith were disregarded, but the United States Senate struck out the article as a violation of the vested rights of the orphans. It is possible that the two Southern delegates at that time had individual contracts with the orphans under an arrangement made in 1859; it is certain that they presented such contracts to the Council in January, 1868, and that with Timothy Barnett they went to Washington to represent the orphans the following summer. Here they managed to effect the sale of all the par and premium stocks for $142,890, and the following fall this sum was paid out by Dunn. The middle-aged "orphans" and their heirs thus received the first benefit from the provision that had been made for their upbringing thirty-six years before. The following Council considered a bill to use a portion of the permanent school fund to purchase the depreciated bonds and protect them against further loss. It was apparent that the claim was exerting too much influence in Creek affairs.

In 1870 the aging orphans received another payment of $31,-

012.75. From this time on, the government seems to have made them an annual payment of $4,182.68 as interest on the depreciated bonds. In 1872 the Attorney General decided that the United States was liable for the expenditure of the money for unauthorized purposes and for the investment in state bonds, and the Indian Office began to urge Congress to settle the claim. Just at the close of Coachman's administration an attorney was employed by the Creek government, whose delegates also worked diligently for the recovery of the money. Finally in 1882 Congress made an appropriation of $338,904.39: $70,800 as par value of the depreciated bonds, $106,799.68 to restore the amount misappropriated for refugees, $69,956.29 to return the amount misapplied to general tribal purposes, and $91,348.42 as interest on the last two sums since the Attorney General's decision in 1872. It was provided, however, that the amount used for general tribal purposes should be charged against the Creeks and gradually deducted from their annuities. Even with this offset it would obviously have been cheaper for the United States, as well as more advantageous to the orphans, to have observed the terms of the treaty in the first place.

Apparently 10 per cent was deducted for attorneys' fees, leaving $532.32 as the share of each original claimant. Creek mortality had been high during the fifty years that the claim had run, and only about twenty-five gray-haired orphans remained to participate in the payment. Some of the inherited claims had been divided into as many as forty-eight parts. Other heirs were enriched by several entire claims. The lists were certified by the town chiefs, and the decisions of the Creek courts were followed in settling questions of heirship. The court records are full of such testimony as the following:

"Tim-me-se-be use to Keep the orphan he or they were Tum me se be's daughter's childern one of the orphans was Mer-yie-che—the other Chee-kil-ler. The orphans grand mother's sisters children and grand children are claiming the claim. Tup-ars-so-lar. har-jo was a brother of Tim-me-se-be and also Pu-ho-ke was a brother of Tum-me-se-be. Also Yo-har-le was a daughter of Tim-me-se-he's sister. Nittar-ko-me was a Nephue of Tim-me-se-he. They were kin by the pedigree of pole cats or pole cat's clan. Ful-le-chus' mother was a sister of Nottar-ho-me. To-thler-tar-ke is a claimant, Sarwe is another."[10]

At the time this belated restitution was made to those who had been children at the time of the Removal, the Creek Nation was convulsed by the most serious political disturbance of its history. Fundamentally it was a part of the old protest against the constitutional government, but it was aggravated by the negro-Cherokee "war," the Seminole cession, and the activities of non-citizens. Following the familiar pattern the disaffected party supported a rival government, using as the nucleus the organization made to push the Loyal claims against the United States.

Just as the estranged party had never been exclusively Loyal, it was not now identical with the Sands following, but always there was the organization ready to be used by successive groups of malcontents. The fullblood settlement in the tangled blackjack hills west of Okmulgee was the center of the disaffection, and Nuyaka Square became the capital of the insurrection. The alienation of this party had been apparent during the election of 1879, and it had been increased by the methods used to seat Checote. By the fall of 1880 there were indications that the prolonged councils in Nuyaka Square and the hurrying to and fro on secret missions had some portentous significance. It is doubtful that any definite plans were made, but friendly relations were established with the negroes, with a portion of the Seminoles, and with the Creeks of the Greenleaf settlement in the wooded Cherokee hills southeast of Fort Gibson.

As usual the administration of justice was the main source of friction. In September Isparhecher and Jefferson notified Checote that one of their party had been killed and demanded punishment of the murderer. The following March when Judge McHenry was rounding up the criminal negroes at the Point they wrote again to the Chief demanding the release of the arrested men and warn-

[10] Creek Tribal Records, Orphan Payment, Courts (especially 29219); Commissioner of Indian Affairs, *Annual Reports,* 1840-83; Kappler, *Laws and Treaties,* II, 934; Document No. 14, Oklahoma State Historical Society Library; United States Archives, Creek 1866/M245, 1868/B636; Indian Office, Special Case 36; Five Tribes Files, No. 2,13, 40; No. 63, 334 f., 363-66. Robertson, The Peace Conference at Muskogee; *Indian Journal,* January 25, 1883; 42 Cong., 2 sess., *House Ex. Doc. No. 246.*

ing him "to examine carefully and not step too quick." The leaders of the Isparhecher party were men of character and self-restraint, but Dick Glass and other negro outlaws seized the opportunity to join them, and their fastness in the Deep Fork District became a rendezvous for horse thieves. On the other hand it is clear that the administration sought to use the courts to punish political opponents under the pretext of law enforcement.

Typical of these disturbances was a case in Wewoka District, where one Heneha Chupco, a well-known horse thief, was on trial. He was convicted and sentenced, but it was afterwards charged that the jury's verdict had not been unanimous; and Checote accordingly suspended Thomas Canard, the judge. A petition then came requesting Canard's reinstatement, and the Chief called the judge, the jurors, and other witnesses to the capital and himself presided over the hearing .The dissenting juror testified that "it was reported that the jury had agreed—but *I did not* agree for conviction—I said that I would have to give up—but did [not] say that I agreed with the bal of the jury . . . I told them that I would stop—but did not agree for conviction." Micco Emarthla, the foreman, testified that three or four at first had been in favor of acquittal, "but all turned over except this man (Henethloccochee) who said he would stop and I asked if all had agreed & all said yes—& I told them that they would have to set a price for value of stock stolen & they set price $35.00 & I told the judge of this and we adjourned." Other evidence showed that the juror had outwardly conformed, but the judge remained suspended until the Council convened and reinstated him.

The next year Checote suspended Canard again on similar charges and for "violation of treason law," although Grayson, Stidham, and other leading mixed bloods of Eufaula District tried to convince him that the complaints had no foundation "outside of party difference." In this case the Chief was apparently trying to be fair to both parties, but he had not heard the last of Heneha Chupco.

Conditions in Okmulgee District also were typical of the confusion throughout the nation, and here again the actions of the government were to have important repercussions. Sunthlarpe, who had been judge in 1879, was succeeded by David Anderson, the father-in-law of F. B. Severs. Anderson resigned in December, 1880, disgusted at the political wrangling. He was succeeded by John Freeman, but Checote soon removed Freeman in response to a petition from the leading men of the district and apparently appointed Sunthlarpe to take his place. When the Council convened in October, Sunthlarpe was formally elected to finish the term. Within two months—December 1, 1881—Sunthlarpe informed Checote that he had "a very important Case against Ispihecher and am ready to try it at this term of court."

This charge against Isparhecher shows the ominous nature of the court disturbances. It was said that he had lived with his cousin as his wife during the preceding summer and had thereby run afoul of a statute passed in 1874 forbidding marriage between relatives by blood and prescribing a penalty of fifty lashes "for each and every such offense." The Creeks were becoming self-conscious at this time regarding their marriage customs, but it is fairly certain that this charge was pressed purely to destroy a dangerous opponent. In February Checote or his secretary gloated unpleasingly to delegates Coachman and Porter over the approaching trial and announced righteously a few days later that the court was functioning smoothly with "all looking to law for justice." The fourteen years of dissension had not been good for the fair minded and patient Chief.

Checote and Sunthlarpe should have known that they could not bring Isparhecher to trial for incest. A month later the Chief was writing a worried letter to Tufts stating that the disaffected party was holding councils every few days and electing lighthorsemen and other officers to uphold the authority of the rival government. Tufts did talk to some of the leading malcontents in his office, but without convincing them. They had a new grievance now in the Seminole cession.

The conservatives could not understand that their progressive brethren had reluctantly yielded to the inevitable. As far back as 1878 when Lochar Harjo's followers were protesting against their leader's impeachment, they cited a sale resolution then before the Council as proof of the perfidy and corruption of their opponents. When the special session of the Council in April, 1882, authorized the four dollar per capita distribution, they immediately held a meeting at Nuyaka Square and protested against the cession. When the rolls were made by the members of the Council for the distribution of the "bread money," they held another indignation meeting and informed Checote through a negro secretary that "the members of the Okmulgee house, have taken a great many Names of the Loyal people without their consent, and that is not right, and those men who call themselves members of the house, we do not recognize them as our business men because we did not place them there to do any business for us, Therefore we wants them to let our names alone for we do not want any headright, but those men that are members of the house must leave us alone, but go and get the names of those people that have place them there, because they are stealing by takeing our names unknown to us that is nothing else but rogueing." In spite of the famine that prevailed in the Creek country that year, a large number of this party refused to touch their "bread money" and thus acknowledge the sale. Even to the present day, Creeks who were adherents of Isparhecher seldom fail to give distorted accounts of this payment as the main cause of the disturbance.

The clash came in July. Isparhecher's men were holding a council. They afterwards said they had been preparing a petition to send to Washington protesting against the payment for the Seminole cession. As usual they were armed. For some time their "lighthorse" had carried weapons everywhere with the assurance of regular enforcement officers. Sam Scott, the lighthorse captain of the district, and a deputy named Joe Barnett came upon them at this meeting, disarmed them, and arrested Heneha Chupco, who had been especially defiant, for "resisting an officer." About thirty of the opposition "lighthorse" went in pursuit, killed the two officers, and released the prisoner. Warrants were then issued for their arrest, and Checote, realizing the gravity of the situation, asked for the assistance of Tufts' Indian police in taking them. It is probable that if the agent had acted, the trouble would have ended at once, for the Creeks were too peaceable even in their "wars" to resist Federal authority, but Tufts with pardonable reluctance declined to intervene. The officers of Wewoka District then attempted to make the arrests, three hundred armed Isparhecher men prepared to resist, and the conflict started.

Checote called out the militia, and William Robison, a mixed-blood Creek who had been a colonel in the Confederate army, was placed in command. An "army" of 1,150 men served eight days during the last of July and the first of August, and several independent volunteer companies were in the field. The insurgents, decked in war paint and identifying corn-shuck badges, gathered in armed groups to defend themselves. A few "battles" were fought with much medicine and few casualties, and when the hungry constitutional "soldiers" helped themselves to the orchards in the negro settlement on Pecan Creek, Indian humor bestowed upon the conflict the name of Green Peach War. At the same time the Chief had authorized each district judge to call out fifty assistant lighthorsemen to disarm the insurgents, arrest those guilty of sedition, and restore order in his district; and he had suspended the law that forbade private citizens to carry weapons to public gatherings.

By the middle of August the insurrection was broken, the leaders had fled to the Seminole and Cherokee nations, and dozens of prisoners were on trial for violation of the "treason laws." The "army" had been demobilized the first week in August, but the assistant lighthorse remained under arms for thirty or even forty and sixty days.

In Coweta District it proved impossible to secure convictions, for the negro community was too strongly knit together since its recent private war with the Cherokees to testify against its members. Moreover Daniel ("Goob") Childers, a violent mixed blood who had long lived with the Creeks and had been adopted as a citizen in 1875, was one of Isparhecher's lieutenants. But before the end of August most of the other districts had convicted ten or fifteen men of treason and sentenced each to one hundred lashes. Most of them were pardoned by the ever merciful Checote, but twelve negroes in Muskogee District who had aggravated their offense by trying to escape received their punishment. The majority of the men arrested were released without prosecution upon taking an oath of allegiance to the constitutional government.

Isparhecher himself took refuge among the Cherokees. S. B. Callahan, who was his trusted friend, wrote to him on August 19, "I am truly sorry that you have got into this trouble. There is but one honorable way to get out. And that is to come home and stand your trial. You will find plenty of friends to see you out. . . . Submit to the laws of your country, and fight your battles in the halls of your Council house. If you are right you can never accomplish your purpose in the way you are trying. . . . I advise you as a friend to come home and stand trial for I believe you will come out all right. Jas McHenry says for me to tell you that he and all his friends on his side of the River would sign a petition for your reprieve should you be convicted and I believe he will do what he says." By this time the constitutional authorities remembered that Isparhecher had killed a man back in 1873 when he was too zealously and crudely administering the law, and they sought to try him for this crime also.

The Cherokees declined to deliver him and he remained in the Creek settlement in their country. But eleven members of the party that had attacked Scott and Barnett were apprehended, tried in Wewoka District, and sentenced to death for murder. Petitions with hundreds of names of prominent mixed bloods, full bloods, and leading negroes were presented to Checote asking for their pardon, but he delayed action until he could ask the advice of the Council. In the meantime the Seminole chief complained that the officers of Wewoka District had followed the insurgents into his country "disarming one man and shooting around generally," but he promised to deliver criminals upon requisition. Many terrified women and children had fled from the country, and Checote tried to induce them to return and attend to the gathering of their crops.

When the Council convened, Checote reported that "the late excitement" had "happily terminated," and that Creek affairs were in a more hopeful condition "than has been known since the civil war." The Council recommended executive clemency for the men convicted of the murder of the two officers, and the Chief therefore pardoned all but three who were considered the leaders. Two were accordingly shot. The third seems to have escaped death because the wound inflicted by the executioners was not fatal and they hesitated to fire a second time. The Council also passed a resolution granting amnesty to all political offenders who would take the oath of allegiance, and Checote wrote personally to Isparhecher and other leaders inviting them to return under these provisions. The Chief was also authorized to restore the operation of the law against carrying firearms; and he notified the district judges that the suspension would cease October 28 and directed them to turn the arms furnished the assistant lighthorse over to the executive office. A law was enacted, which remained in force during the rest of the tribal period, providing that convicted criminals might have their political disabilities removed after five years of good conduct upon petitions approved by the district judge and accepted by the chief. An appropriation of nineteen thousand dollars was made to pay the militia and assistant lighthorsemen, and other appropriations were made for ammunition and supplies. It was fortunate for Creek finances that seventy-five thousand dollars of the amount received from the Seminole cession came into the hands of the Council at this time.

Still the insurgents did not return. Isparhecher and most of his negro followers remained in the Greenleaf settlement in the Cherokee Nation. Sleeping Rabbit, the leader of these Creeks who were Cherokee citizens, was his close friend, and there was no doubt that Sleeping Rabbit was in constant communication with Greenleaf Town in the Creek Nation and with other full bloods who had remained at home. The other party of insurgents under the leadership of Tuckabatchee Harjo, a nephew of Opothle Yahola, was distributed among the Seminoles and the tribes farther west. There were indications that Isparhecher aspired to be another Tecumseh to unite the Creek conservatives and the western tribes, invade the Creek country and seize the government, and build an Indian league upon the basis of the ancient customs.

During December there were constant rumors that the two bands would unite in the vicinity of Nuyaka and renew the war. The district judges were nervous and vigilant. Reed told Checote that among the negroes "on the Sugar Creek and Pecan Creek the old womans Seems to be in a great deal of Secret Excitement of another trouble going to be very soon." Finally Checote sent runners to the different settlements with a call for volunteers, and by December 16 they were assembling at Okmulgee. He also called on Tufts for troops, but as late as December 21 Tufts refused to be alarmed. Within three days the Creek country was invaded from both directions.

On December 22 the Checote forces went to a house on Pecan Creek and attempted to capture three thieving negroes who were believed to be stirring up trouble. In the ensuing melee one of the negroes was killed. Dick Glass hastened to Isparhecher's camp and reported the occurrence, and fifty men set out at once to avenge the death. In full war paint they passed through Muskogee on the morning of December 24 and went on west to the negro settlement, but failing to find any of Checote's men they returned the same evening to the Cherokee Nation. It was probably at this time that Sleeping Rabbit also invaded the Creek country with his armed Creek Cherokees.

Tufts at last discovered that something was happening. He immediately called on the commander at Fort Gibson, and fifteen soldiers were sent to report to him at Muskogee. He did not yet know that a battle was being fought that same day about twenty miles southwest of Okmulgee. Tuckabatchee Harjo, with his insurgent Creeks and a number of Seminole volunteers, had entered the nation from the west and was traveling in the direction of Nuyaka. Not far from the North Fork he met Jim Larney, the lighthorse captain, and Tulwa Fixico (Joseph Dunston or Dunsey), the judge of Wewoka District, who were on their way with the men from their district to join the mobilization at Okmulgee. In the ensuing battle the insurgents were victorious and seven of the constitutional party were killed; but Tuckabatchee Harjo withdrew again to the west.

A runner came to Muskogee and notified Tufts of the battle. The whole Creek country was in a state of wild excitement: Okmulgee was filled with constitutional soldiers; the insurgents were believed to be gathering at Nuyaka; women and children from the upper North Fork streamed down the valley and found refuge at the Wetumka boarding school; the men at Eufaula, anticipating an insurgent attack, placed their families on the train and sent them to Muskogee or to the Choctaw Nation. On Christmas Day Tufts left for Okmulgee with fifty Federal soldiers, ten were left to guard Muskogee, and seven were dispatched to Eufaula. Chief John Jumper and John F. Brown made a circuitous journey to Okmulgee by way of Eufaula and Muskogee to express their regret for the participation of their citizens in the battle.

The presence of the Federal soldiers brought immediate quiet. Tufts submitted a proposition for an arbitration tribunal to be chosen by a committee of five from each side, both parties in the meantime to declare an armistice from which the Glass Gang was specifically excluded. Checote consulted a convention of leading men and accepted the plan and appointed his committee January 1. By January 3 the constitutional forces had been disbanded and the Federal soldiers were all back in Fort Gibson. Tufts returned to Muskogee and Isparhecher with twenty-five armed men came over from the Greenleaf settlement to visit him there. He accepted the peace plan January 6 and started at once for Nuyaka with the avowed intention of calling his adherents together in convention for the election of his committee. But this opportunity to establish an armed camp in the heart of his own hills proved too great a temptation to the unyielding old full blood. His followers began to commit depredations upon their opponents in the Okmulgee District, and he found pretexts to delay the proposed mediation.

Meanwhile the money for the orphan payment came by express to Muskogee January 23 and was hauled the next day to the capital. Even with affairs in this disturbed state only eight soldiers from Fort Gibson were required to guard the funds. Some of the orphans' heirs were, of course, in Isparhecher's camp, but Tufts persuaded them to come in and receive their shares. The Creeks as usual were ready to postpone their war for more important business, and the payment passed off quietly. A large shipment of whiskey intended for that promising market was spilled by the Indian police. Checote and Isparhecher had an interview during the payment, but Isparhecher delayed and finally refused to appoint his committee.

Checote notified Tufts February 3 that he would wait no longer for Federal mediation. The agent agreed; he thought that the Creek government should be allowed a free hand to crush the insurrection within the nation, and that Federal soldiers should arrest the insurgents that might seek refuge elsewhere and turn them over to the tribal authorities. Checote at once raised an "army" of seven hundred men and placed "General" Porter in command. Isparhecher's followers began to desert, but Porter with characteristic vigor and energy organized his men by towns, placed guards at strategic points, and set out February 11 for Nuyaka. Isparhecher loaded his women and children and his provisions in wagons and started for the Sac and Fox country. When Porter arrived, the fires were still smoldering at the abandoned camp. He started in pursuit and found the insurgents just across the Sac and Fox boundary. Dick Glass dashed out to attack but was driven back, and Porter surrounded the enemy camp. But the Sac and Fox Indians protested against a battle on their soil, and their agent ordered Porter to withdraw. Leaving some of his men to guard the border Porter then returned to Okmulgee capturing a number of stragglers on the way. From there he hastened to Muskogee to confer with Tufts and Inspector Pollock, who had just been sent out from Washington.

While Porter was at Muskogee, Daniel Childers came in on the train from Washington, where he had gone to present Isparhecher's cause to the Department; and Sleeping Rabbit, Heneha Chupco, and about forty other Isparhecher men came over from the Cherokee Nation apparently to consult the agent and the inspector. Porter summoned a detachment of his soldiers, dashed into the town, and captured all but one or two of the surprised and unresisting insurgents. Childers was released almost immediately. According to the story told by the guards Heneha Chupco put his horse at full speed and broke for freedom, and the guards killed him as he fled; whatever the circumstances, the man who started the war now paid with his life for his mistake. The other prisoners were conveyed to Okmulgee and confined in the council house. Sleeping Rabbit was allowed to step out of the building under guard and was shot "while attempting to escape." It is probable that the old man was deliberately murdered. The Cherokees were deeply incensed; although he was an ignorant conservative he was greatly loved and respected, and he had apparently come to Muskogee that day on a mission of peace. But the Creeks had reason for their bitterness against the interference of these Creek Cherokees in their internal affairs; it was admitted that at least once

Sleeping Rabbit had led an armed band into the Creek Nation, and the Cherokee government was not blameless in permitting the invasion. The other prisoners took the oath of allegiance and were set free. Others rounded up in the districts were released by the judges after taking the oath.

The dreaded shuck was no longer seen in the nation, but the insurgents from outside were stirring up internal disorder and threatening another invasion. People were afraid to plant their crops, and the rural schools were closed because of failing attendance. Checote asked the Cherokees and Seminoles to deliver the fugitives in their country, but both chiefs courteously declined. The constitutional leaders were sure that some of the white traders were fomenting the disturbance, and they asked repeatedly for the removal of John A. Foreman. About the middle of March, Porter decided to disregard intertribal boundaries and capture Isparhecher. He raised another army of seven hundred men and started for the Sac and Fox country, but before he reached the line he was notified that the War Department was ready to act. He led his men back to Okmulgee and discharged them, saying that they might now go home and plant their crops in safety.

Major J. C. Bates accordingly set out from Fort Gibson, but Isparhecher by this time had taken refuge among the Comanches. He now had about two hundred men with two or three hundred women and children. They had forty-two wagons and were still purchasing supplies with their orphan money. Asahabbee had become their friend, and it seems that he had promised to join them in an invasion of the Creek country as soon as the grass should be grown enough to fatten the ponies.

Bates followed the insurgents to the southwest. He received reinforcements from Fort Sill and now had four troops of cavalry, enough to take Isparhecher and intimidate any wild Indians that might join him. On the morning of April 23 he found the Creeks encamped nine miles east of the Wichita agency. The warriors had taken a strong position on a hill and apparently intended to resist. Bates sent a messenger promising protection if they would return home with the troops. They gave an evasive answer, and the troops were deployed for the attack. The Creeks then retreated, and when the soldiers without firing a shot tried to surround and capture them, they broke and ran. Isparhecher and Tuckabatchee Harjo were taken and within the next few days all the fugitives were rounded up. Still in war paint and arms they were conducted to the Sac and Fox Agency and across the Creek country to Fort Gibson, where they were subsisted by the military at Creek expense.

In June the constitutional party suffered a severe loss in the murder of Benjamin E. Porter, the brother of Pleasant Porter. He was a young man of brilliant promise, and he had served since Checote's last inauguration as his secretary. Apparently the killing was not directly due to the political disorder, for the murderer was not a member of Isparhecher's party. There was no attempt at violence on the part of Porter's friends, and the murderer was subsequently tried and sentenced to death.

But peace with the insurgents seemed as far away as ever. Checote insisted upon their return to their own country, promising to punish only the criminals among them; but they requested military protection until the nation could be divided by a boundary that would leave each party independent, and it was the opinion of a special army officer sent out by General Sheridan that they would be exposed to assassination unless they were guarded by troops. They were accordingly disarmed by the soldiers, and on July 15 they were taken through Muskogee on the way to Wealaka. They were kept for a time in camp, and John A. Foreman had the contract for subsisting them. They gradually dispersed to their homes, where they were guarded by five small detachments of Federal soldiers. Any crimes they committed were supposed to be reported to Bates at Fort Gibson and punished by martial law. The only armed force maintained by the Creek Nation at this time consisted of five lighthorsemen in each district.

Chairman Fisk and Secretary E. Whittlesey, of the Board of Indian Commissioners, finally came to Muskogee and held a conference August 9-10 with the leaders of both parties. Checote and Postoak headed the constitutional delegation, and the steady and dependable Silas Jefferson, who had never joined the insurrection, was included because of his influence with the insurgents. Among the other members were Coweta Micco, G. W. Stidham, Legus C.

and J. M. Perryman, Samuel W. Brown, H. C. Reed, Pleasant Porter, G. W. Grayson, and James Larney. With Isparhecher were Tuckabatchee Harjo, who was now recognized as second chief, Efa Emarthla, who had been his commissary, the negro William McIntosh, Daniel Childers, and others.

The white mediators forgot about railroads and land grabs and entered into their work with active good will. They refused to divide the nation and advised the Creeks not to "talk so much about how loyal a man was to the United States Government twenty years ago but how loyal each man can be to the Creek Government[,] to his own nation." They opened the meeting with prayer, and the susceptible Creeks and negroes began in a spirit of religious earnestness to compose their differences. The final agreement was signed at an open session before a deeply moved and attentive audience that packed the little Methodist church at Muskogee. Checote said in his difficult English, "We have come together here and signed these papers, we have adopted this agreement and promised to be united just like a man taking an oath in the name of God," and Isparhecher affixed his mark and gave his assent in guttural Creek.

Both parties recognized the constitution but promised to amend it by reducing the representation in order to cut the cost ^f government. Amnesty was granted for all offenses growing out of the insurrection, and the Council was to appoint a commission of men from both parties to audit the claims of those whose property had been destroyed during the disturbance. The constitutional authorities promised to dismiss all lighthorsemen who had been oppressive and replace them with "good men who will firmly but cautiously exercise their authority." Both parties were to participate in the approaching election and abide by the result.

The Creeks' long constitutional struggle was at last ended. They had fought their war after their own fashion. They had shown none of the disciplined courage and little of the ruthlessness of a "civilized" people; the almost pacific character of their fighting and the conciliatory spirit of their peace are in sharp contrast, for example, with the white man's own internal conflict during 1861-65 and the bitterness of Reconstruction. But the disturbance had caused more suffering than would be inferred from their bloodless battles. The disorder had encouraged assassinations, and both sides had been guilty of wanton pillage. Frightened refugees had collected their possessions and fled in all directions when either "army" passed through.

The conservatives had lost their fight. It was their misfortune that criminals had joined their ranks, for their cause was not ignoble. In 1885 Porter explained to a senatorial committee that "under their primitive institutions there was no question as to the ends through which justice was to be reached or difficulties settled. Everybody understood that. At that time each town governed its own citizens. Now it is general, and everything goes before the courts; and they have lawyers before the courts who, instead of furthering the ends of justice, render it less effective. . . . The older class of citizens . . . still look back to the time when there was less difficulty in governing themselves. They felt a reluctance in giving up their old system, and that same feeling exists to-day, and they will die in the same opinion." If the Creeks were to survive, it was necessary for them to learn from the white man; but there is little doubt that if they had confined their "progress" to essentials they would have been a happier and a more truly progressive people.[11]

It was unfortunate that 1883 was an election year. All three parties held their conventions shortly after the peace agreement was signed at Muskogee. The Loyal Party nominated Isparhecher and James Fife; the Muskogee Party chose Joseph M. Perryman and Ward Coachman, but Coachman declined and Samuel W. Brown was selected; and the Pins nominated Checote and Coweta Micco. The three platforms contained the usual platitudes, but in addition the Loyal Party promised to grant citizenship to all intermarried persons "irrespective of race or color." This proposal was of course intended for the hundreds of "state" negroes married to Creek freedmen, but it would have applied also to intermarried whites.

11 WPA Project S-149; Creek Tribal Records, Courts (especially 28065-69, 29227), 29294, 29857-62, 30481, 30677-93, 31041-42, 31859 ff., 32399, 32409, 32700 ff., 34170-304; Five Tribes Files No. 11, 239 ff.; No. 63, *passim. Muskogee Phœnix,* September 12, 1895; *Cherokee Advocate,* 1882-83; *Indian Journal,* 1882-83; United States Archives, Union 1878/H1981; Indian Office, 1882/1671, 2783, 3517, 3581, 10058; 1883/1630, 4424, 7521, 7872, 9120, 9522, 13982, 14605, 15217. 49 Cong., 1 sess., *Sen. Rep. No. 1278,* 208; C. W. Turner, "Events Among the Muskogees During Sixty Years," *Chronicles of Oklahoma,* X (1932), 29 f.

Checote called the election on the first Monday in September according to the act passed in 1870. The Creeks with their usual love of juggling their statutes had passed a law in October, 1879, changing the date to Tuesday; but it had been copied in a blank book and forgotten, and a code printed in 1880 and approved by the Council had carried the old date.

No disturbance marked the voting except in the Arkansas colored town, which embraced most of the Marshalltown population. Here only fifteen votes had been cast when a fight broke out and Snow Sells, the chief, stopped the election. Fights were not unusual in that riotous community, but it seems probable that Sells and a negro lighthorseman used this method to keep a Isparhecher town from recording its vote. Sells' own account is interesting, though probably not altogether truthful—"it seem the spihicher party did not come perpoly for the Election But it seem that they came for a fuss & further more they were men seen with shuck on they Hats & . . . they were hooping & throughing great insinavation to each other & treechers [three cheers] hooping and speaking saying huraw for spihica But still was going on with the Election until the Disturbance commence we was compell to adjoin the meeting." When Checote was notified of the occurrence, he ordered a special election according to law to fill the vacancies in the Council. There was no legal method of calling a second election for chief even if he had desired to do so; but Tufts directed the negroes to record their choice in order to present their case in a possible Federal inquiry.

Two small Indian towns also lost their votes—one through a political trick by its chief, the other through a technical irregularity —and these also held a second election. The Council threw out all three returns and counted 641 votes for Perryman, 608 for Checote, and 486 for Isparhecher. In the contest for second chief Coweta Micco had received 765 votes to 440 for Brown and 539 for Fife. None of the candidates had the majority required by the English version of the constitution, but the words "plurality" and "majority" were synonomous in the Creek language. The Council accordingly declared Perryman and Coweta Micco elected.

Isparhecher immediately protested to the Department, but Checote conceded the victory to Perryman. But during the recess of the

Council the Checote and Isparhecher leaders held a secret convention at Okmulgee and united their forces. When the Council reconvened, Checote tried in every way to have provision made for a "legal" election, and Coweta Micco declined to accept the office of second chief. Just before the session ended, an attempt to conciliate Isparhecher by electing him to the Supreme Court failed by a narrow margin, but Isparhecher, Checote, Hodge, and Grayson were elected as delegates to Washington. This Council expired December 4, and the new members took their seats the following day. About two-thirds of this new body belonged to Isparhecher's party.

On December 5 Perryman took the oath of office and delivered his inaugural message to the Council. In spite of his English education and his experience first as a Presbyterian, and later as a Baptist, preacher, he had chosen to rely upon Callahan, his secretary, for the expression of the appropriate sentiments. The new Council soon decided upon a recount of the votes, admitted the returns from the three towns, and on December 17 proclaimed Isparhecher elected by a vote of 682 to 645 for Perryman and 611 for Checote. Coweta Micco was still in the lead, and he assumed office as second chief. Isparhecher was immediately inducted into office, and Callahan as *his* secretary composed another inaugural message expressing the same sentiments in slightly different language. It is to be hoped that nobody smiled when the new Chief was made to say that he would have preferred to remain at home in modest retirement, "yet these private preferences will not be urged by me in opposition to my sense of patriotic duty."

From December 18 on, Isparhecher actually served as chief, approving acts of the Council and issuing executive orders. He and Perryman both employed white attorneys and presented their claims to the Department, but the entire dispute was conducted amicably. On November 1 the commander at Fort Gibson had returned the guns taken from the insurgents, and one of Isparhecher's first official acts was the approval of a bill for the sale of the arms and ammunition belonging to the government. The new chief gratified his partisan supporters by granting a pardon to the murderer of Benjamin Porter, but in general only routine business was transacted during the dispute. Just before the Departmental decision was announced, he discovered he had lost, and he suggested to Perryman that both waive their claims and return home and hold a new election.

The decision was announced February 27. The Secretary ruled that the word *majority* in the Creek language meant simply "to come out ahead"; that the election date, whether right or wrong, had been accepted by the voters; and that according to Creek law only the outgoing Council had the power to canvass the returns. The delegates returned home and read this decision to a large assembly that had gathered at Okmulgee from all parts of the nation. The general sentiment of the meeting was that it was best to go home, plant crops, educate the children, and live in peace; and Perryman quietly took charge of the administration. With characteristic magnanimity he appointed Callahan to assist Isparhecher in carrying out his duties as delegate. The legality of Isparhecher's acts as chief was never questioned, and the next Council made an appropriation to pay his salary for the two and one-third months of his term. The defects of their constitution remained to trouble the Creeks in subsequent elections, but from this time on in disputed cases the Council uniformly recognized the plurality choice.

Checote did not serve his people long as delegate. He became ill of Bright's disease while at Washington, and after his return his health continued to decline. In August his friends attempted to raise two hundred and fifty dollars to send him to Hot Springs, Arkansas, but he died early in September at his humble farm home near Okmulgee. He left a widow and six children, and his property consisted of the modest possessions of the old-time Indian— a few horses and cattle, some improved farm land, five apple trees and a garden, a watch and chain worth eighty-five dollars, and a small store building and stock of merchandise which he had purchased mainly on credit. Except for the Lochar Harjo–Coachman term his public service had covered the entire period of constitutional adjustment. Now it was left for other leaders to carry on the government he had worked so faithfully to establish.[12]

[12] Five Tribes Files, No. 11, 77; No. 32, 54-65, 136 f.; No. 47, 12-22. *Indian Journal,* 1883-84; *Indian Chieftain,* December 14, 1883, and December 28, 1883; Indian Office, 1883/13982, 16920, 19304; Creek Tribal Records, 25452, 28842, 29382-85, 29426-33, 29906-34, 32753-814, 34619, 35593-96.

CHAPTER 9

The Creek People at Peace

THE administration of Joseph M. Perryman was the brightest period in the post-war history of the Creeks. At last they were one people living under one law. There were ominous signs of financial ineptitude, and the ring of white enemies was surely closing in, but these were the problems of the future. The new chief was a man of kindly and retiring disposition and personal integrity, with no special ability as an administrator; content to serve as a constitutional executive, he relaxed the control of the courts usually exercised by the Creek chief, and law enforcement almost ceased. But although the nation drifted on without leadership, the drifting was a pleasant experience after the years of stress and turmoil. The Chief was greatly respected by the wealthy whites and mixed bloods, especially at his home town of Eufaula, and through his family connections and his natural habits of thought he was in sympathy with this class of the population.

Most of these people lived in the eastern portion of the country, especially in the northern part of the Coweta District and in the vicinity of Eufaula. They lived in great ranch houses or comfortable town residences, which they built in Eufaula, and later to an increasing extent in Tulsa and Muskogee. They were proud of their Indian blood and sympathetic toward the real Indians, and they formed a closely-knit but kindly aristocracy. They owned trading houses in the towns, and they operated great farms with non-citizen labor, raising corn and feeding hundreds of hogs in the valley of the Arkansas, and growing cotton on a large scale along the Canadian. Most of all they joined in the great recent development of the ranching industry.

A number of the Creek ranchmen handled from one to twenty thousand cattle yearly, buying them in Texas, shipping them in on the railroad in June, and fattening them on the abundant grass. F. B. Severs operated the largest ranch. He enclosed extensive rail pastures, bought Durham bulls, and graded up his own cattle; raised from three hundred to five hundred horses for his own use and for sale as polo ponies; and bought from fifteen to twenty thousand Texas cattle yearly to run on the open range. He had a large ranch house and extensive orchards at his headquarters northeast of Okmulgee; but he lived first at Okmulgee, where he owned most of the town, and later he started a store at Muskogee and established his home there in 1884.

Bluford Miller, an able mixed-blood Creek; H. B. Spaulding, a white man who had married a daughter of S. B. Callahan; Turner and Porter, who established a partnership in 1884 when Clarence W. Turner, a white trader, married a Creek woman; N. P. (Nip) Blackstone, a mixed-blood Cherokee who lived in Muskogee; and about thirty others of their class operated ranches almost as extensive. In the fall of 1884 they established the Muskogee and Seminole Live Stock Association, of which Pleasant Porter was president. They divided the country into eleven roundup districts and appointed a captain for each, placed inspectors at the railroads to watch the brands of the cattle and hides offered for shipment, and obtained the coöperation of the butchers and the hide dealers in the recording of brands. In 1885 Blackstone, Severs, Porter, and Turner attended the first National Cattle Growers' Convention at St. Louis as delegates of this association; and Porter defeated a resolution introduced by the Montana delegation favoring the reduction of Indian reservations in the West.[1]

The great values represented by the cattle trade stimulated the building of railroads. The St. Louis and San Francisco, which had purchased the Atlantic and Pacific, crossed the Arkansas and established a station at Red Fork. This town for a time became the most important shipping point in the Territory. In the spring of 1886 the road advanced further into the cattle country and built the station of Sapulpa. Meanwhile Congress had begun to grant charters to railroads other than the two authorized by the treaties. The

[1] WPA Project S-149; *Indian Journal;* Ella B. Wilson, *Parsons' Memorial and Historical Library Magazine*, 290-318.

Cherokees fought these franchises, but in 1888 Judge Parker, and in 1890 the United States Supreme Court, decided that the United States had the right of eminent domain across the Indian country.

In 1886 the Kansas and Arkansas Valley was granted the right of way across the Cherokee and Creek nations from Fort Smith to Coffeyville. The charter contained none of the obnoxious provisions of the earlier grants; the company was required to pay the tribes fifty dollars a mile for the right of way and fifteen dollars a mile as an annual tax, and no bribe was offered for the destruction of the Indian title. The road was constructed during 1887. It ran only about twenty miles in the Creek country, crossing the northeastern corner. Several white men and mixed bloods and the right of way agent of the road entered into an ambitious townsite speculation at the point where it crossed the Missouri, Kansas, and Texas tracks; but Perryman, for once, took decisive action and the scheme was exposed and defeated. The town of Wagoner grew up at this junction and became a center of land speculations and "booster" propaganda.[2]

Wagoner with its white man's plots, Muskogee with its boundless ambition and its growing refinement, Red Fork and Tulsa with the endless streams of longhorns passing through, Eufaula with its cultured society of mixed-blood Creeks, and the smaller stations consisting mainly of stockyards and loading chutes—all of these railroad towns were foreign to fullblood life. The quiet, orderly village of Okmulgee with its capitol dominating the square, its few trading houses, and its camping legislators and visitors was the real Creek metropolis. Other trading centers existed in remote places—a store kept possibly by a white man, possibly by a full blood, and a family hotel or a cottage camp. But the most important trading houses for Indians were in Okmulgee, Muskogee, Tulsa, and Eufaula.

Some of these traders had lived among the Creeks since the Civil War or even earlier, and they had become an integral part of the economic life of the tribe. They paid their taxes without question,

[2] *Indian Journal,* June 5, 1884; June 19, 1884; July 17, 1884; March 18, 1886; May 12, 1887; May 19, 1887; May 26, 1887; June 9, 1887; March 1, 1888. *United States Reports,* CXXXV, 641-61; Commissioner of Indian Affairs, *Annual Report,* 1884, xxx-xxxii; 1886, 266-69; 1887, 119. Indian Office, 1897/F39192.

cashed court scrip and tribal warrants, and issued credit upon the expectation of per capita payments. They were the only bankers in the community. If an Indian received a large windfall from a Civil War pension or an orphan payment, he carried the money to a trusted trader and left it in his safe, probably for several months, until he was ready to invest it, or perhaps he even loaned it to the trader and received interest. If an Indian wanted to borrow money on his crop or his live stock, the trader would extend credit, issuing due bills for the amount of the loan. Some traders simply wrote out the due bill on a scrap of paper. Severs once issued long strips of paper in five and ten dollar denominations with a succession of long and short marks for dollars and quarter dollars; and the salesman cut off marks as the Indian made his purchases. H. B. Spaulding, who owned a store in Muskogee, adopted printed scrip resembling United States currency. These different kinds of traders' scrip passed freely from hand to hand and were even accepted by other dealers. The merchants who depended upon Indian trade were scrupulously honest in their accounts, but they protected themselves against the uncertainties of depreciated tribal paper and Federal caprice by a ruthless rate of discount.

The traders had large, roomy, frame or stone buildings with spreading wings, and they carried immense stocks of all kinds of merchandise—dry goods, groceries, furniture, lumber, farm implements, saddles, etc. In addition they usually operated cotton gins and grist mills. The Creeks sometimes traveled fifty miles to these trading establishments. They packed their produce on ponies, or the men of the settlement joined together and loaded five or six or even a dozen wagons with venison hams, dressed hogs, wild turkeys, pecans, peltries, beautifully dressed buckskin, and possibly a little cotton. The wagons were usually drawn by oxen. Numerous children rode their ponies alongside, and dogs trailed the caravan. Once at the trading post they camped in the wagon yard behind the store and brought supplies for the whole settlement—flour, coffee, sugar, tobacco, clothing, and household conveniences. The traders also sent agents through the country to buy the hogs and cattle that the Indians desired to exchange for commodities.

A few men purchased peltries and other Indian produce for cash without operating a trading house. The most important of these dealers was a German Jew named Joseph Sondheimer. He established his headquarters at the agency in 1867 and began to travel all over the country on horseback buying pelts and shipping them down the Arkansas. When the railroad came through, he moved to Muskogee and built a great warehouse there and a branch house at Okmulgee; and he sold directly to dealers in Chicago, St. Louis, and Leipzig and other German cities. He also shipped pecans, and sometimes prairie chicken and quail. The number of pelts he and other dealers purchased and shipped from Muskogee within fifteen days during the winter of 1881 may be taken as typical: 4,595 raccoon, 2,947 skunk, 1,936 opossum, 394 gray fox, 293 beaver, 221 wildcat, 134 wolf, 78 pole cat, 42 otter, and about 3,000 pounds of deer skins. During the year 1883 seven carloads of pelts and five carloads of pecans were shipped from Muskogee. Part of these purchases, of course, were from the Cherokee Nation, but a large proportion came from the Creek country.[3]

Most of the freight was shipped by rail, but steamboats still came up the Arkansas to the Muskogee landing. Stage lines connected Muskogee and Okmulgee with Fort Smith, the Sac and Fox agency and other places. For a short time the pony express carried mail across the country from Vinita to the Sac and Fox agency and on to New Mexico. The roads were only trails winding in and out between the haphazard enclosures of the Indians, but it was forbidden to fence a recognized highway "without first cutting out and establishing a good road as near as practicable to the original road." Each judge was responsible for the condition of the roads in his district, and all men were supposed to spend four days each year in road work under the direction of foremen.

The many wide rivers were crossed by ferries established by citizens under an exclusive franchise from the Council, and lawsuits frequently arose over conflicting titles to valuable ferryboat landings. The Council also granted citizens the right to build toll bridges over the smaller streams, with the provision that only non-citizens should be required to pay toll. One of these franchises with delightful native logic set the charge at fifteen cents for ve-

[3] *Indian Journal;* WPA Project S-149; Turner, "Events Among the Muskogees."

hicles drawn by one or more animals and twenty-five cents for those
drawn by two or more. Goods were hauled by wagon over these
roads to the inland trading houses. Some of the traders owned their
own freighting outfits, but there were white men at Muskogee and
other towns who paid a license and engaged exclusively in freighting for hire; and some Indians and whites carried on freighting in
addition to their farm work.[4]

In the eastern part of the country the smaller business enterprises
—ferries, inland trading houses and hotels, the building of rental
property in the railroad towns—were often conducted by thrifty
negroes. The colored citizens now constituted more than one-fourth
of the population, and "state raised" negroes passed rapidly from
intruder to citizen status by the friendly connivance of their town
chiefs. Aristocrats like the Graysons, the Stidhams, and the McIntoshes watched this growing power with apprehension, but they
had failed in their attempts to enforce racial segregation. A few full
bloods lived among the negroes, mingling with them socially and
intermarrying freely with them; but most of the full bloods had
withdrawn to the back country where they might live their own
life apart. Intermarriage between the races was checked somewhat
by this separation of cultural and neighborhood interests, but it was
not disapproved, and many "full bloods" who were members of
Creek towns and spoke only Creek showed negroid characteristics
as a heritage from some former proximity. Moreover the ablest and
most prominent mixed-blood family in the nation had received a
noticeable strain of negro blood in its early history. The members of
this family ignored this admixture without attempting to deny it and
associated themselves with the white-and-Indian Creeks; and so
great was the respect felt for their character and ability that they
were freely accepted even by this proud and aristocratic group.
But except for this one numerous family the negro-Indian admixture was confined to the "full bloods."[5]

Back from the feverish activity of the railroad towns and the

[4] Creek Tribal Records, 30416 ff., 32811, 35885-90; Five Tribes Files, No. 50; McKellop, *Constitution and Laws*, 97, 122-26; 49 Cong., 1 sess., *Sen. Rep. No. 1278*, 237 f.;
Indian Journal; WPA Project S-149.

[5] Five Tribes Files, No. 32, 120 f.; No. 34. O'Beirne and O'Beirne, *The Indian Territory*, illustrations.

riotous exuberance of the negro communities, the remote streams were dotted with the settlements of the full bloods. With these people the town was still the most important unit of collective life. Although it was barely mentioned in the constitution, it was the most vital part of the tribal government; voting, distribution of relief, enumeration of citizens, etc.—all was done by towns. Some of its members might be distributed throughout the nation, but in general they still showed a tendency to settle in the same section. With the dispersion of population, intermarriage between members of different towns was, of course, very common. An intermarried man was given numerous courtesies in his wife's town; he was allowed to participate in the ceremonials, and he might even represent the town in ball games. It was the general custom to enroll the children in the mother's town, but the opposite practice was sometimes followed. Ward Coachman, for example, was always considered a member of his father's town of Alabama.

It was not impossible for a man, even to change his town. In 1883 the chief of Tookparfka informed Checote that one Wiley Hawkins had "lived a very long while in our town and was considered as one of us. The Oyokofkeys however claimed him and elected him to the Council four years ago where he has served up to the present time. In the recent election our town understood that he was going to withdraw from the Oyokofkey and identify himself with the Tookparfka town as he formerly did." They accordingly elected him to the Council, but "he did not withdraw himself from his town," and it was necessary to hold a special election to fill the resulting vacancy. But no matter where he lived, no Creek ever forgot his town membership; and in their personal intercourse and their political decisions, the men were still guided by the relations of their towns in the dim legends of their prehistoric life.

Each town still had its chief and other officers, chosen according to its own custom from the membership of certain clans, usually holding office for life. There was a feeling that the town should elect its chief to the House of Kings, but the custom was not universal; and there was a growing tendency for the member of the House of Kings, if different from the chief, to assume responsibility in matters pertaining to the central government. In the general elections each town voted after its own manner at a place designated by its chief. The voters stood in line to be counted or they voted in a meeting by a show of hands or each gave his name separately to the literate citizen who served as clerk; and the clerk recorded the name and choice of each voter on a return sheet sent out from the office of the principal chief.

The Creek settlements laid out ceremonial grounds according to their own convenience, but after the adoption of the constitution the Council regularly decided what constituted a legal town entitled to representation. During the insurrections the white disturbers often charged the "rebel ring" with gerrymandering, but such assertions were stupid as well as false; the towns were too fundamental to Creek life to be juggled about for political advantages. Changes took place from time to time with the shifting of settlement and the wishes of the people, and new towns petitioned to the Council for recognitition or related towns asked for the privilege of uniting. It never occurred to the Creek town officials to obtain political importance or greater per capita shares by padding the rolls.

The ceremonial meeting place of the town followed the old plan in a greatly degenerated form. At least two towns—Thlopthlocco and Pukkon Tullahassee—built chokofas after the Civil War. William Fields, a present-day Creek, says that the one at Thlopthlocco was made of logs; it "was oval centered and had a cone shaped top. There was one room built on opposite sides, and in the oval room was held the dances when the weather was unfavorable." Both these structures were destroyed by fire, and they were never rebuilt. But even after the chokofa disappeared from the Creek country, some of the towns marked a circular area in the proper place near the square and lighted a fire there on ceremonial occasions. The chunkey game had long been abandoned, but a form of the chunkey yard survived; some towns constructed banks of earth in the old fashion around a space used for dancing and the ball game between men and women. The square was the most important; it was a cleared space partially enclosed by three or four simple brush arbors, and possibly there was a log hut in the background for the storing of the sacred utensils. Logs were laid lengthwise of the arbors as seats. In spite of the simplicity of the arrangements, distinctions of clan and rank were rigidly observed in the seating; but women and children were now permitted by most towns to occupy one of the arbors.

The town meeting place was no longer the center of a populous village, but on ceremonial occasions the people assembled from their distant farm homes and camped in the surrounding woods. The green-corn festival was still the chief celebration of the year. The chief summoned his people as of old by bundles of sticks, and the town enforcement officers collected a fine from all who failed to attend. During the celebration the men and little boys in at least part of the towns submitted to a scratching ceremony, which was supposed to preserve the health and insure long life; pins or thorns were used, and the flesh was torn rather deeply in four scratches on the arm or leg or breast. Women participated freely in the dances, and there was a growing custom to admit them to the drinking of the emetic. The dances were accompanied by the beating of a drum made by stretching rawhide over an iron pot or the end of a hollow log, the shaking of gourd rattles, and the clattering of dried terrapin shells filled with pebbles, which were worn on the legs of the women. Songs were used describing or expressing appreciation for the subject honored by the dance. The words were repetitious and the tunes somewhat unmelodious, but even to an educated ear the unison of voices was not unpleasing, and the music had a certain wild beauty of rhythm as it swelled through the silent woods. Each town renewed its continuity with the past by the use of sacred objects. The Thlopthloccos had the same drum that had beat time for the dances in their happy eastern home and had been carried with them through all the vicissitudes of their later wanderings. The Tuckabatchees brought out their plates and polished them with fearful reverence, and even today they keep them in a secret cache away from the prying eyes of the white man.

Although the Creeks no longer had occasion for conferring war honors, they still bestowed the old titles upon their young men at the busks. Every man therefore had his "square name," which he might use almost exclusively as did Lochar Harjo, occasionally as Isparhecher used his title of Cochar Emarthla, or only during the ceremonials as was the custom of men like Pleasant Porter. The few native personal names in use had distinctive meanings; Isparhecher, for example, said that his name meant "whooping while taking off the scalp." Names like "Chupco" were nicknames given because of personal peculiarities. There was an increasing tendency for every Creek to have an English name, which was usually known as a "Christian name" because of the habit of bestowing such designations in church or school. Some of these were given arbitrarily for no particularly reason, many like Deer, Tiger, Bear, etc., were translations of clan names, and others were inherited from a white father. These English names became surnames and were carried by the whole family after the white man's custom, and some of the native titles like Harjo and Fixico also developed into surnames through the white man's insistence.

Secretaries and court clerks often produced rather fantastic variations of Creek names in their attempt to conform to "civilized" customs; thus Tulwa Fixico became T. W. Fixico, Hotulke Emarthla was changed into Hotulk E. Marthla, and even Isparhecher when he was serving as judge was transformed by a zealous clerk into I. S. Sparhecher. There was an increasing tendency to name the women Jane, Peggy, Betty, etc., and with the adoption of surnames for the men they followed the custom of their white sisters and became known as Mrs. Tiger or Mrs. Fixico.

Active church members might join in the fasting and medicine of the busks, but as Baptists or Methodists they thought it was "wrong to dance." Because of this fact and other disintegrating influences the busk itself declined in importance, and with this decline it tended to lose its religious significance and degenerate into a drunken sexual orgy. The Creeks had always gratified their robust sense of humor by a few obscene songs and dances, but it is perhaps significant that among the most licentious were the chicken dance, the mule dance, the drunken dance, etc., which, as their names indicate, developed after the coming of the white man. It is the opinion of a modern Creek preacher that "there is nothing religious about the whole thing any more . . . it is a very poor imitation of something that once was good." By the end of the century the interest in the busk was falling off until a large number of towns discontinued the observance.

The Creeks also produced music for their private enjoyment and their informal social intercourse. Violins made of gourds with raccoon or squirrel skin strings were very common. A native instrument similar to the flute, made of a reed or piece of hollowed hardwood with holes at intervals, was used especially by the young men in courting. It produced a plaintive sound very affecting to the player, and it was supposed to arouse tender emotions in the heart of any girl who listened.[6]

During the green corn festivals and at other gatherings the Creeks amused themselves with the two kinds of ball games. The game between the men and women was purely recreational, and the contestants were equalized by rules favoring the women. Red and White towns still played as opponents in the men's game. The entire population of both towns assembled at these contests, sometimes traveling two or three days to reach the rendezvous. There was much excited betting, prolonged and serious dancing, and urgent medicine making as each side brought all of its resources, both material and supernatural, to bear upon the event. The players were stripped naked except for a breechclout and the tail of an animal or the feathers of a bird, their bodies were decorated with paint, and often their arms and legs were bloody from scratching. In the huddles, as one white spectator said, they looked like "a knotted bundle of angle worms." If all went well, the game went on to its finish with a few players killed or disabled; if things went badly, as they often did, it broke up in a fight in which women and all joined until one party was driven from the field.[7]

The town farm had entirely disappeared, but some towns owned common herds in addition to the live stock belonging individually to their citizens. A few of the branding irons used to mark the

[6] WPA Project S-149; Swanton, "Creek Social Organization"; Swanton, "Creek Religion and Medicine"; Frank Gouldsmith Speck, "Ceremonial Songs of the Creek and Yuchi Indians," *Anthropological Publications of the University Museum*, Vol. I, No. 2 (1911); Speck, "The Creek Indians of Taskigi Town"; Speck, "Ethnology of the Yuchi Indians"; *Extra Census Bulletin, The Five Civilized Tribes in Indian Territory*, 66; Creek Tribal Records, 32754; Five Tribes Files, No. 29, 17 f.; No. 30, 76, 120.

[7] Many accounts of Creek ball games are given in WPA Project S-149; see also *Indian Journal*, July 12, 1877.

town cattle are still in the possession of the old leaders. For their own live stock the more independent Creeks used individual brands, but in the conservative settlements it was common to use the town brand, each citizen placing it in a different position to distinguish his property from that of his neighbors. Members of the town acted together under the direction of the chief in keeping all their stock upon a fairly well defined range, and some closely related towns worked together in roundups and the collection of strays.[8]

The native church formed another expression of the Creeks' community life. During the first hard years after the war the buildings were windowless log huts daubed with clay, with stick fireplaces, earthen floors, and clapboard roofs; but in time frame buildings like those of the white man were erected. In 1878 the Tuskegee congregation near Eufaula, with a technique learned in the old communal fields, planted and tended eight acres of cotton and applied the proceeds to the building fund. On the church grounds were numerous camp houses for the storing of cooking utensils or the use of individual families, and in the summer several large brush arbors were commonly erected for holding the meetings and serving the meals; and there was a tendency to arrange these structures in the familiar form of the town square with the church building forming one side.

There was probably some conformity to denominational requirements, but in practice each congregation selected one of its own members to serve as pastor as long as he lived. Some of the Creeks formed the pleasant habit of rotating their services among four neighboring towns, each town entertaining the other three in its own church once a month. Such services usually lasted for three or four days, and during the summer there were frequent camp meetings lasting for a week or longer and bringing people together from a large area. Careful preparations were made for these meetings, and the members of the local congregation worked together in cutting the weeds, cleaning the grounds, repairing the camp houses and arbors, and sometimes painting the church. The men hunted

[8] See Creek Tribal Records, 34809, for brands of Hutche Chuppa and Alabama in 1885; WPA Project S-149 gives additional information about town control of cattle.

game and killed beeves and hogs, and the women cooked great pots of food to be distributed among the various camps. The services were almost continuous throughout the day and often during the whole night, and the conduct of the worshippers was reverent and devout. They used the Creek version of the Bible; their sermons were preached in Creek, but sometimes translated into English as a courtesy to visitors; and they sang Creek translations of English hymns and, as one Creek woman expresses it, "other songs about nature; that is, the flowers, etc., that they made up."

The Creeks had found in Christianity a means of expressing the strong community ties, the moral aspiration, the mystic communion with nature, the deep sense of reverence that had once been expressed by the native ceremonials. Even its forms were native: the arrangement and care of the church grounds, the feasting, the camping, the community labors, the continuous day and night services. It was of course more suited to the growing intellectual development of the Indians, and it imposed a higher moral standard upon its adherents; but on the other hand it never exerted the same social compulsion upon the wayward members of the tribe.

In their religious development the Creeks were still influenced to a certain extent by white people. All three of the denominations modified religious thought through their boarding schools. H. F. Buckner was very active at Baptist camp meetings and conventions although he never learned to speak the Creek language. The Methodist Church maintained a certain control over its native preachers through its denominational organization. The white people settled in the railroad towns also set up churches of various kinds, but although the Creeks gave a grudging consent to the erection of the buildings on their soil they were influenced only slightly by these alien congregations.[9]

The Creeks did not put away their native superstitions with the adoption of Christianity. Their country was still inhabited by mysterious beings. At a camp meeting on the North Canadian in 1885 a white missionary inadvertently chose a pool infested with tie snakes for the immersion of two Tuckabatchees; and when his con-

[9] WPA Project S-149; *Indian Journal*; 45 Cong., 3 sess., *Sen. Rep. No. 744*; 59 Cong., 2 sess., *Sen. Rep. No. 5013*, I, 690 f.. 696.

verts failed to appear he learned that no Tuckabatchee would run
the risk of being tied and carried to the subaqueous town of these
strange reptiles. The horned snakes also were as much at home in
the Indian Territory rivers as they had been in the old streams in
Alabama, and medicine men sometimes lured them to the surface
and took their horns. There was a vague, formless creature known
as the *ehosa* which came to frighten men and animals, but was
itself in mortal terror of the sound of a gun. A "tall person" (*este
chupco*) lived in the hills near the Canadian; nobody had ever seen
him, but he could be heard passing through the upland and "slap-
ping the trees." More common were the Little People, who lived in
the trees and used raccoons for dogs. Large objects were small to
them, and small objects large, and in the same reverse order they
found tasks easy that appeared difficult to men. They were fond of
pranks but were not malicious, and although they laughed heartily
at the Creeks for their awkwardness in climbing large trees, they
were grateful for assistance in crossing small streams.

The Creeks still treated rattlesnakes with respectful friendliness,
and if one of these reptiles crawled into a camp during a ball game
he was sure to bring success to that side. Wolves also were capable
of doing good to the Creeks, but were likely to punish the irrev-
erent. "The fathers and mothers gave warning to their little children not to speak bad or unkindly of the wolf. If any reference was
to be made to the wolf only the best words were to be used." They
seldom referred to the animal by its name of *yaha* but by the more
respectful "great-grandfather" or "night wanderer." Children also
were forbidden to play with corn cobs; they were told, "The corn
is an old lady and all old ladies are easily provoked and are cranky.
If you do not care for the corn you will lose it." Widely divergent
legends were told of the manner in which the old woman who was
the corn gave her flesh to a young man she had reared and through
him to the tribe.

All the Creek ceremonials were accompanied by endless bathing
—washing in medicine or taking a dip in the creek. In the fall, to
obtain immunity from cold they used "the water turning a dark
color from the leaves maturing in it. Upon the steady falling of the
leaves they would remark, 'Our medicine is being prepared.' " For

four mornings in succession they drank the "leaf flavored water" in four sips facing east and then dipped in it four times. Mist, they said, was pure water; therefore the women used it for hair tonic. They also went out in the woods, cut the wild grapevine, and spread their hair under the dripping sap so that it would grow long and luxuriant like the vine. Leaves in the unconscious poetry of their language were known as "tree hair."

All the small details of life were regulated by quaint superstitions or formulas based on analogies. Monie Coker, an aged Creek woman of the present day, gives the following list: Pointing with the finger at a rainbow will make the finger crooked. If a person does not spit four times on seeing a shooting star, he will go blind or all his teeth will fall out. When a hunter kills a squirrel, if he will pull some of the hair from the right foot and bury it under the tree, he will kill more squirrels. If small pups are given young wasps [larvae?] to eat for four mornings, they will be turned into ferocious watch dogs. Earache may be cured by blowing through a pipestem three times into the sound ear, and the fourth time into the aching ear. If a small infant is fed the tongue of a mocking bird, he will grow up to be a mimic; if his feet are scratched with the toes of a quail, he will become fast and nimble, or if the toes of a lizard are used, he will become a good climber; if he is given liquid from an old bell, he will be a good singer.

Besides these simple home remedies and formulas there was the professional conjuring of the medicine man. He usually served as the official priest of the town, and some of his services were paid by the group; as one Indian says, "A bunch would gather and cut him a lot of wood, plant his corn, make a fence or any work he needed to have done." He also had his private practice—treating disease, supplying charms to the lovelorn, and, it might be, even causing harm to enemies. When he treated sickness, he expected a fee from the patient, and the court records show that he sometimes went to law to collect.

In cases of illness he diagnosed the trouble by occult means, prepared an appropriate brew, and treated the disease by blowing into this concoction through a hollow reed and chanting a magic formula over it. According to Creek belief most diseases were caused by animals, and there was usually an analogy between the animal and the symptoms: the hog, which was a notorious glutton, caused indigestion; the raccoon, which roamed about at night, caused sleeplessness; diarrhea was attributed to birds because of the nature of their excrement; boils, which resembled ant hills, were caused by ants. The brew for diarrhea was made of birds' nests, and the song formula, ending in the call of the bluejay, ran as follows:

> *"They chatter.*
> *They chatter and flutter about.*
> *They chatter.*
> *Their settlement is here.*
> *Gathering together they make a fluttering noise.*
> *Martin, martin.*
> *They chatter, they chatter."*[10]

The Creeks believed implicitly in these cures, and this faith was shared by the ignorant frontier whites that lived among them. But the modern Creek's wistful belief that in his youth all people were "healthy" because they took the emetics at the busks and employed skilled medicine men is not supported by the census statistics. The population never recovered from the losses of the Civil War and even diminished during the generation of peace and prosperity that followed it. It is of course impossible to determine with accuracy the causes of this decline. Although the Creeks no longer died in such appalling numbers from malaria, they were constantly subject to its debilitating effects. Infant mortality was probably high, and apparently the whole population suffered from improper diet. Every winter pneumonia caused many deaths, the result, as Dr. M. P. Roberts thought, of poor housing and inadequate clothing. Enough able-bodied men were killed in shooting affairs, etc., to cause an appreciable loss in population. As serious as the mortality was the prevalence of blindness. "Sore eyes" was frequently and casually mentioned in school reports and personal letters, and every town had from one to half a dozen indigent blind supported by an

---

[10] Methvin, "Legend of the Tie Snakes"; *Indian Journal,* July 3, 1878; November 2, 1882. WPA Project S-149; Speck, "The Creek Indians of Taskigi Town"; Speck, "Ceremonial Songs of the Creek and Yuchi Indians"; Swanton, "Notes on the Creek Indians," 154-57; Creek Tribal Records, 28031, 28855.

appropriation of the Council. Although the condition was unnoticed by white physicians, it seems fairly certain that the whole tribe was infected with trachoma.

Several white physicians lived in the railroad towns, operating drugstores or other forms of business under traders' licenses, or practicing their profession under special permit from the chief. In 1890 they finally prevailed upon the Creeks to establish an examining board to restrain the activities of non-citizen quacks. In general the Creeks had no contact with white physicians, but they had learned to trust in vaccination, and they used the white man's medical science to stamp out a serious smallpox epidemic in the summer of 1882.[11]

Some of the older Indians still buried their dead under the floor. It had become more general to bury in a family cemetery close to the dwelling, and the Christians were beginning to carry their dead to the churchyard; there a small house was erected over the grave. The funeral rites lasted four days, for the spirit was supposed to linger for this length of time in the vicinity. If the observances were pagan, the neighbors remained at the house, watching and carrying out various formulas for the welfare of the dead and the protection of the living; if the services were Christian, the body was carried to the church, and the community gathered there to watch and join in songs and prayers. Tobacco, food, clothing, and cherished possessions of the deceased were buried with the body or placed in the house over the grave. The bodies of stillborn, or very young, infants were commonly put into hollow trees, and the opening was closed without ceremony.[12]

In their funerals and other neighborly relations the Creeks showed a community helpfulness reminiscent of the old town life. If one was prosperous, his friends combined to eat him out of house and home. If one wanted to build a dwelling or a fence or plow a field, they turned out in a body to assist him. If a young couple married, everybody helped to build their cabin and set them up in household furnishings and live stock.

[11] Creek Tribal Records, Doctors, also 35198 ff., 38510; Five Tribes Files, No. 30, 80 f.; *Indian Journal*.

[12] Burial customs are described in detail in WPA Project S-149; see also Speck, "The Creek Indians of Taskigi Town."

A few of the houses were still made of upright posts, but more were windowless cabins of unhewn logs, with puncheon or earthen floors; in the fall they were chinked with clay or plastered with clay and straw, and in the spring the chinking was knocked out to admit air and light. A few were of hewn logs, substantially built; and the more progressive citizens adopted the double log cabin so familiar to southern whites. When a Creek wanted to enlarge his dwelling, he constructed an additional cabin; one was used for cooking and eating, one or more for bedrooms, one for the monthly retreats of the women, etc. The family ate and slept out of doors during the summer, and a brush arbor was usually erected in the yard for that purpose. Even the barns were in small separate units, and additional cabins were made for smokehouse, corn crib, henhouse, etc.; hence a well-improved Creek homestead looked almost like a small village. The yard was always kept swept and neat. Close by was a garden plot, and almost every family had an extensive orchard of apple and peach trees and a few cherries.[13]

The women carded and spun their cotton, wove their cloth, knit their stockings and mittens, pieced their quilts, and made their soap as the pioneer white women did; and the men made bedsteads, tables, chairs, benches, and cupboards of rough lumber. The women bought dishes and cooking utensils, but they still made pottery and ornamental figures of clay, wove baskets and sieves, and fashioned bark containers. They washed their clothes in the creek by beating them with paddles or switches.

Both sexes wore their hair long. The women wore dresses cut like those of the pioneer whites, but they were fond of beads and fluttering ribbons; and the men slowly adopted the boots, trousers, shirt, knotted handkerchief, and even the broad-brimmed hat of the western whites. The boys wore only one garment, known as a "sweep"; it was a long shirt, reaching almost to the heels, sometimes belted at the waist. For ceremonial purposes the men painted their faces and sometimes their ponies with pulverized stone, pokeberries, or dyes made from bark.

Creek cooking was a highly specialized native art. Corn was the

[13] WPA Project S-149; Beadle, *The Undeveloped West*, 386 f.; Creek Tribal Records, Courts; Speck, "The Creek Indians of Taskigi Town."

staple article of diet. In every yard stood a mortar (*kecho*), made by hollowing a log with fire, and a heavy-topped wooden pestle (*kechupe*); and the corn was cooked with lye or mixed with ashes to remove the hulls and beaten to form hominy grits or meal. *Sofkey* was the most important food; the beaten corn was cooked with lye and water to form a gruel thin enough to drink, and it was left for two or three days to sour. A bowl of this food was set near the door of every Creek dwelling, and the visitor was invited to help himself upon entering. "Blue dumplings" were made of the beaten corn and the burned shells of the field pea. The *apuske,* or "cold flour," was a food drink made by stirring a meal made of parched corn into a glass of water and sweetening to taste. Besides their corn the Indians raised beans and some rice for winter use, and they dried sweet potatoes, pumpkins, peaches, and apples. They smoked and preserved their pork the way the white people did, and they cut beef, venison, and buffalo meat into strips and dried it in the sun. They obtained most of their salt for household purposes from a spring in the northwestern part of the country near the Euchee settlements or from a deposit on a creek near Wetumka. Community kettles were kept at these places, and the people came from long distances to boil down the water and carry home a supply of salt.[14]

The Creeks still depended partly upon hunting for their meat supply. Their country abounded with deer, squirrels, turkeys, prairie chickens, and other game, and the men made regular trips to the West for buffalo until the herds disappeared in the early 1880's, and to the Choctaw country for bears. Bows and arrows were preferred for buffalo hunting, and were used extensively for small game. A certain amount of medicine still attended the use of arrows; one kind known as the rattlesnake arrow because of its diamond-shaped markings was "a dangerous arrow to make ... because after you make one you are supposed to shoot something of real life with the very first shot or a snake will bite you."

Besides the native game the Creek country was filled with hogs that had strayed away and gone completely wild. The men hunted them on horseback, butchered them in the timber, and carried

[14] The most interesting and complete description of household manufacturing, foods, etc., may be found in WPA Project S-149.

home the meat. Hundreds of wild horses also lived in the rugged hills of the West and ventured out to graze on the prairies, sometimes enticing the domestic ponies away. The Indians built a brush corral with a wide mouthed chute as the entrance, and by working their own horses in relays they sometimes drove whole herds into this trap and captured them. In other cases the herds were chased until completely tired out and then lassoed.

Fishing also was important. In the summer when the water was low, it was customary for a whole settlement to camp on a convenient stream for a fish fry. A deep pool was selected and cut off from the river by a rude dam or a fence of closely driven stakes. The young men were sent to gather roots of the devil's shoestring (*Tephrosia virginiana Pers*) or sometimes of the buckeye, and they brought them in bundles to the appointed place. The medicine man then solemnly painted the faces of the men who were to participate and made incantations over their bows and arrows. Any man whose wife was pregnant was obliged to remain in the background, for the fish would not rise if he looked into the water. When all was ready, the roots were pounded to a juicy pulp and thrown in. When the drugged fish began to rise, the men entered into an excited contest of marksmanship with their bows and arrows, and immense quantities of fish were taken and flung on the bank. The women prepared pots of sofkey and fried the fish, and the whole community joined in the feast.[15]

But in spite of their hunting and fishing, the Creeks' main dependence was on agriculture and stock-raising. The average humble full blood cultivated from six to twenty acres of improved land, which was enclosed by a rail fence. He raised mainly corn, for which he had no market because of the prohibitive freight rates; a little cotton, which he carried on horseback to Eufaula or Muskogee; and possibly some wheat, which he had ground into flour at the mill. Some of his farm implements were still homemade. "The hoe was made in this way," says a Creek woman. "The men would go out and look for a tree that had a straight branch as long as a hoe handle and they would cut the tree down and cut off about ten or twelve inches long where the limb was and split the log and

[15] *Ibid.; Indian Journal.*

hew it as thin as a hoe. They held it over the fireplace to dry, and then it was ready to be used." A plow was *"made out of wood* that had *a big fork in it."* They made rude, two-wheeled carts with a wooden axle and wooden wheels held in place with wooden pins, and saddles were sometimes made of wood and covered with hides. But the average Creek farmer owned a wagon, a plow or two, possibly some other farm machinery, a saddle, some harness, one or two augers, a frow, a hoe, two or three axes, etc., of the white man's manufacture. He used oxen or horses to plow his field. The family owned from six to twenty horses, mostly ponies; from six or eight to fifty cattle, running on the range, but branded and known; ten to twenty hogs, running almost wild, but ear-marked and irregularly penned and fed; a few chickens about the yard; and possibly ten or fifteen turkeys that had been domesticated by placing the eggs of the wild fowls under barnyard hens. A few of the more thrifty full bloods owned hundreds of cattle, horses, and hogs, and considerable farm machinery, employed two or three white farmers, and lived in rude and open-handed abundance sharing their prosperity with the whole settlement.

Under their communal land system the Creeks recognized a residence right and ownership of improvements that was rapidly developing into an individual tenure. Houses and improved fields were conveyed by sale, gift, devise, inheritance, etc., and bills of sale, which were deeds in all but name, were frequently employed by the mixed bloods. A form of mortgage was also used. In 1880, for example, a negro woman "pawned" a house in Muskogee to Jesse Franklin for one hundred dollars. She paid no interest but Franklin leased the property and collected the rents until she recovered it nine years later through the courts. The real Indians never engaged in such transactions, but when a full blood plowed and fenced a field and built a house upon any portion of the public domain he controlled it as fully as though he had held it under a fee simple title.

There was still a feeling that the house a man built for his wife when he married her was her individual property. As late as 1894 an Indian testified before the Supreme Court, "Jno Burk A poor citizen married Sarah Bittle and he built a place for her— and the woman quite Jno Burk and went off toward Coffeeville — and Mahala Burk was living Cross the river and Jno B. took her over. and put her in Sarah Bittl's house. . . . The place . . . was made for Sarah Bittle and I thought it belong to her and if Jno Burk got married again he ought to make a place—for her." Aside from the woman's claim to the house, husbands and wives were completely equal and independent. As each acquired property through inheritance, trading, the investment of orphan claims, etc., the wife was as likely as the husband to own improved fields, rail fences, live stock, farm machinery, fruit trees, and corn cribs, while the husband might possess houses and dishes and furniture. Apparently the Creek family had too strong a sense of solidarity to dispute over the joint use of these separate possessions, but the traders learned to sell a cow's worth of goods to one and three hogs' worth to the other in completely independent transactions. Every Creek child owned live stock and other property in his own right, and although his parent or guardian took care of these possessions, tribal law recognized his absolute ownership.

When a man or woman died, the estate, no matter how small, was partitioned by the courts. The judge and two disinterested neighbors rounded up the live stock, counted the fruit trees, listed the fields, houses, and fence rails, enumerated the debts and the amounts due from creditors, and made an inventory of every "sarcer," "pilar slip," hammer, hoe, "coffee poiler," etc.; and they evaluated everything carefully and divided it, article by article, among the heirs. Soon after the adoption of the constitution the old custom of disinheriting the husband or wife was changed. If there were children, the widow or widower received the same share as one child; if there were no children, he or she received one-half, and the blood relatives of the deceased inherited the remainder. But the Creeks very often directed the disposition of their property by informal oral or written wills.[16]

At first if a man left two or more widows, all shared equally in

16 The general references for Creek economic development are the *Indian Journal,* the court records in the Five Tribes Files, and the Creek Tribal Records. See especially Creek Tribal Records, 28883, 28890, 28901, 29063, 29072, 32811, 35049, 38928; Five Tribes Files No. 50, 110-12; No. 2, 373. 49 Cong., 1 sess., *Sen. Rep. No. 1278,* 254; William A. Sapulpa, "Sapulpa," *Chronicles of Oklahoma,* IV (1926), 329-32.

the division of his estate, but the Council attempted gradually to bring marriage into conformity with civilized customs. The law of 1874 prohibiting marriage between relatives had neglected characteristically to state the degree of relationship. The first comprehensive marriage law was passed October 22, 1881, under the influence of the religious Checote; it legalized existing unions, forbade in future all plural marriages and marriages between closer relatives than third cousins, provided for a written contract before a minister or a district judge in the presence of witnesses, and authorized the district judges to grant divorces upon the grounds of adultery, desertion, or cruelty. This law had little effect so far as the marriage customs were concerned, but after its passage the courts recognized only the first or "lawful" wife in the division of property. Apparently no distinction was made in the legitimacy of the children.

Among the more stable Creeks a girl's marriage was arranged by her uncles, her parents, or even the church, and good advice was given to the young people in some public manner by a "clan uncle" or the pastor; but the written record was often omitted. The more thoughtless entered into the so-called "blanket marriages" without ceremony of any kind; if they disagreed, they separated and found other partners in the same informal manner, but they often lived happily together for a lifetime without benefit of Council, church, or clan. Only the more sophisticated went to the court for their divorces. The ones who did usually made their own arrangements; they simply drew up a petition stating that they wished to separate "for causes best known to ourselves," and the judge granted it as a matter of routine. Only the negroes habitually entered into recriminations and quarrels over the division of the property.

More fundamental than any law on the statute books were the old unwritten customs. Marriage within the clan was repugnant to the feelings of even the most undisciplined and was prohibited by the community almost as rigidly as of old. Clan relationships also influenced the Creeks in their personal friendships, their political alignments, their business intercourse, and their determination of heirships. Most of the women still observed their menstrual retreats, not strictly, but as a matter of good taste and in order to keep their husbands "clean and healthy"; and the old customs and taboos were carefully followed at the birth of a child. A widow still performed the mourning rites in the home of her husband's relatives, but the time was generally shortened to four months or even less.[17]

The Euchees were more rigid in these observances than any other Creeks, mainly because their language cut them off from outside influences. They had to communicate with the rest of the nation through interpreters who had learned the Muskogee language, and even their children in the boarding schools commonly learned Muskogee from their fellows and then painfully acquired a little English. The Shawnees who lived among them shared their isolation. The Alabamas and Koasatas, the Hitchitees, and the few Natchez families and other fragments of tribes had nearly all learned through intermarriage and political and social intercourse to speak the regular Muskogee dialect. This growing uniformity of language was a great help in promoting literacy and an informed public opinion.

Loughridge and Mrs. Robertson with their Creek assistants continued their language studies. One New Testament book after another was slowly added to the growing Creek library until the work was finally completed by Mrs. Robertson in 1892. Loughridge and David M. Hodge published a dictionary and grammar of the language in 1890. Before the burning of Tullahassee the Council had purchased a small printing press for the use of the school and had made occasional small appropriations for the printing and public distribution of the Creek First Reader. A little monthly news periodical in English and Creek was issued by the Robertsons from this press during 1873-75. Although there were no schools for teaching the native language, the alphabet was as nearly phonetic as the missionaries could make it, and the people enjoyed spelling out these publications. Very few could read Creek at the close of the Civil War, but Miss Alice Robertson estimated in 1906 that 90 per cent of the full bloods were able to read their own language.

Probably it would have been wiser to conduct the day schools in Creek, for they were almost a complete failure in teaching Eng-

[17] WPA Project S-149; Five Tribes Files, No. 11, 210 f.; Creek Tribal Records, 25866A, 25908, 31265.

lish. The a-b-c method in vogue at the time was bad enough for English-speaking children, but it was worse for the young Creeks. They learned to pronounce nonsense syllables like parrots, and to read rapidly in the First and Second Readers before they dropped out of school in disgust without knowing the meaning of a single word. Some of the teachers tried to work out a technique of their own by the use of objects, but they were under such strong pressure to show results in the glib reading of meaningless sentences that few were able to resist it. To make matters worse, none of the white teachers and few of the mixed-blood Creeks were able to speak the native language.

White girls from the railroad towns and Creek girls from the boarding schools showed great hardihood in teaching in the full-blood settlements. They lived in Creek families where they did not hear a word of English, submitted to the conglomerate sleeping arrangements of a fullblood home, ate sofkey and blue dumplings, walked two or three miles to their work, cut the wood to warm the mud-daubed cabin, and taught twenty-five or thirty shy young Indians from six to twenty years old, with whom it was impossible to exchange one word. But they always found kindliness and hospitality, and a genuine, if uncritical, interest in their school.

The rural schools were under the administration of a superintendent, who was assisted after 1875 by a board of education. The superintendent located the schools, employed and assigned the teachers, appointed three local trustees in each community, and with the help of the board conducted teachers' examinations and institutes. He also had charge of the public blacksmith shops until they were discontinued in the 1880's. He received a salary of six hundred dollars a year, but the other school officials usually served without pay. The schools were in session for ten months a year, and the usual salary was forty dollars a month.

The Creeks established Nuyaka Mission in the fullblood section through the efforts of Miss Alice Robertson, who traveled throughout the East securing contributions from Presbyterian women. It was completed in the fall of 1884. Augusta Robertson Moore, a daughter of the Robertsons who had married a prominent mixed blood named Napoleon B. Moore, became the superintendent.

Nearly all the pupils were full bloods, and very few were able to speak English at the time of their admission. The unfamiliar routine of manual labor and English studies proved difficult for the untamed little Creeks. The school records for 1888-89 show that thirty-six of the forty or fifty boys ran away from one to four times during the term.

The approximate enrollment and the amount spent by the tribe in maintaining the schools were reported for the year 1886-87 as follows:

	ENROLL- MENT	COST
Boarding Schools		
Wetumka	100	$7,000
Wealaka	100	7,000
Asbury	80	5,600
Nuyaka	80	5,600
Tullahassee (colored)	50	3,500
Neighborhood Schools		
22 Creek	550	8,800
6 Colored	150	2,400
Youths in the "States"	24	6,500
	——	——
Totals	1,134	46,400

In a few places white children were allowed to attend the day schools upon the payment of tuition, and a few voluntary subscription schools were established by white people in the railroad towns. A Methodist school known as the Harrell International Institute was opened at Muskogee with the permission of the Council, and a few Creeks were enrolled among its pupils. In 1879 the Baptists decided to establish an Indian university for the young people of the various tribes. It was opened at Tahlequah, but with the reluctant permission of the Creek Council it was moved to Muskogee in 1885. A "magnificent" building known as Rockefeller Hall was erected at a cost of twenty-four thousand dollars. It became known as Bacone University from the name of its first president. It was the pride of the Indian Territory, and it still holds a unique place in Indian education, but the Creeks were slow to use its facilities. The Council, however, did make a few small appropriations to pay the tuition of students there.

Muskogee had still another school for Indians—a girls' boarding school, of which Miss Alice Robertson took charge in 1885. Tuition was paid by the parents or by the Presbyterian Church, and a number of Creek girls were trained there. It soon lost its special character as an Indian school and developed into a coeducational college. It remained at Muskogee throughout the tribal period, but it moved eventually to Tulsa, and became the University of Tulsa. It never exerted a vital influence upon Creek life.[18]

Whatever its imperfections the Creek educational system was now reaching all classes of citizens. The negroes obviously were not receiving their share of the boarding school appropriations, but the discrimination was due principally to the fact that they had no language handicap. The non-English-speaking Creek children still constituted the main problem, but it was hoped that the new boarding schools would bring the solution. Some of the returned students from the "states" showed great promise, and they were rapidly assuming political and economic responsibilities among the mixed-blood group. The cleavage between progressives and conservatives was not so sharp as formerly. The greatest single gain was the political unity. The Creeks were not yet culturally homogeneous, but they had at last learned to express even their differences through a common government.

The principal chief, with the advice of his unofficial convention of leading men, was the real power in the government. The Council usually carried out his recommendations; and for the untutored majority in that body his messages were an important source of

18 WPA Project S-149; *Indian Journal;* Beadle, *The Undeveloped West,* 382 f.; Creek Tribal Records, Schools; R. M. Loughridge and David M. Hodge, *English and Muskokee Dictionary;* Alice M. Robertson Collection; 45 Cong., 3 ses., *Sen. Rep. No. 744,* 672-76, 731; 49 Cong., 1 sess., *Sen. Rep. No. 1278,* 201, 217, 225-30, 355, 361-66; 59 Cong., 2 sess., *Sen. Rep. No. 5013,* 690 f.; Commissioner of Indian Affairs, *Annual Report,* 1886, 153; 1887, 108 f.

information about the outside world and furnished a real training in statecraft. He managed the tribal finances, for he issued all warrants, often upon his own responsibility, trusting the Council to validate his actions by an appropriation. He controlled the district courts through his orders and directions to district officials, his practice of suspending officers and making temporary appointments, and most of all through the dependence of illiterate judges and prosecuting attorneys upon his legal advice. He was not required to reside at the capital; hence his secretary conducted most of the routine duties of his administration. The secretary even read some of the chief's important messages to the Council—a heritage from the ancient custom of depending upon a "speaker" for the expression of official sentiments—but Perryman, unlike his predecessors, wrote many of his letters in his own hand from his home at Eufaula. The second chief commonly served as the chief's assistant, advising him on matters of policy and assuming his duties during his absence or illness. The salaries were moderate—one thousand dollars for the principal chief, seven hundred for the second chief, and three hundred for the secretary.

The delegates exerted an important influence upon the administrative policy and the shaping of public opinion. No matter what party was in power men like Porter, Stidham, Grayson, or one of the Perrymans served in this capacity. These delegates were always leading members of the Council, often the presiding officers of the houses. They went to Washington freshly instructed by the Council and remained on guard throughout the session of Congress. They were in constant communication with the chief, and in important crises they returned home to report to a convention of leading men and to assist in formulating a policy to meet the emergency. They always reported to a joint session of the Council, and the most conservative legislators thereby gained a certain understanding of Creek-Federal relations. In general they were men of integrity and great diplomatic ability. The Council had begun to appoint defeated candidates for principal chief or fullblood leaders as additional delegates, but except in the promotion of tribal harmony their influence was nominal.

The Council itself was composed largely of full bloods. Most of its work was done through joint committees, upon which an educated Creek or even a white man served as clerk. An interpreter was employed by each house, and the debates were conducted in either Creek or English. Each house also employed a clerk, and one of its members acted as chaplain. The houses in joint session still cast their votes occasionally by forming lines in front of the council house. The deliberations were always conducted with smoothness and dignity. The length of the regular sessions was limited by law, usually to fifteen and thirty days on alternate years. The usual salary of members, clerks, and interpreters was three dollars a day. An attempt was made to carry out the peace settlement of 1883 by substituting artificial units of representation in place of the towns, but it was not successful.

The Creeks never knew what laws were in effect. Comprehensive codes were published in Creek and English by authority of the Council by L. C. Perryman in 1880 and by A. P. McKellop in 1893, but both compilers found it impossible to obtain complete files of legislative enactments. In 1885 the Council created the office of national translator and made it the duty of this official to prepare the Creek version and have the laws of each session printed and distributed among the judges. Apparently the most capable linguists were not always appointed to this position. The incumbent reported to the Council in 1887, "Your servant, To whom you have trusted with the office of National Translator, has endeavor to do its duty, but have been delayed by reasons that can not be reminded by him." The original statutes were often so badly drafted as to be unintelligible to anyone except a Creek; but the Creeks showed considerable skill in interpreting their laws according to what they had in mind when they passed them.[19]

In spite of their struggles with the unfamiliar disciplines of a written law, the Creeks had a real genius for government. They achieved a democratic conduct of public affairs seldom, if ever, attained by the white man. The Council members consulted their towns, the chief asked advice of the Council and the citizens' convention, the delegates kept in constant touch with their people.

[19] Creek Tribal Records, 25456; Legus C. Perryman, *Constitution and Laws of the Muskogee Nation;* McKellop, *Constitution and Laws.*

Partly because of native tolerance and partly because of the ancient custom of grave deliberation, it was the purpose of the Creek leaders not to dictate and dominate but to confer with others and carry out a collective policy.[20]

Unfortunately their financial ability was not equal to their political capacity. Fiscal matters were very simple to the followers of Isparhecher, who controlled the Council during Perryman's administration. Their opponents had been in control for sixteen years "squandering" all the money; now the treasure was in their own hands, and they expected to make the most of it. The Green Peach War had left an enormous debt for the pay of militia and the purchase of supplies, and this was increased by the obligation assumed in the settlement to pay all property losses of the conflict. In the fall of 1884 the Council created a commission to audit claims and report to the following session. Chief Perryman, mindful of the public finances, counseled moderation. It was the last time that anybody ever thought of the public finances.

Probably most of the claims allowed in 1885 were genuine, once the principle of compensation for all losses was accepted, but the total value of broken crockery, butchered hogs, scattered featherbeds, lost tools, felled peach trees, and plundered corn cribs ran into appalling figures. Isparhecher himself received an appropriation of $1,227.25 for his personal property losses, and Efa Emarthla was allowed a claim for $795.50. The war debts of the insurgents were casually presented and allowed as a matter of routine; Isparhecher, for example, requested that a certain man be paid twenty dollars for flour furnished Efa Emarthla "for the payment of which we pledged the good faith of the Muskogee Nation." Awards were made for personal hardships also. One Tilda, of Thlewarle, testified that the lighthorse came and fired revolvers in her yard, and "I was excited, & I was cause to lef home & run off into the woods, and there I walk for Two days without eating any thing, and during that time I could not find any house at all, & my feet got frost bit, and I was compell to Stop as I could not go any further, and there I would have died, but Lucinda, Beggy, & Dina found me &

[20] For Creek governmental procedure, see Five Tribes Files and Creek Tribal Records.

They carrie me to the house by puting me on horse back as I could not walk. I was away from home Seven days or more." She thought her sufferings were worth one thousand dollars, but the committee scaled the amount to two hundred and fifty and the appropriation went through.

After his initial caution Perryman approved every appropriation without comment, and no real attempt was made even to guess the amount of the national debt. The work went joyously on during the 1886 session, although Pleasant Porter, Samuel Grayson, Taylor Postoak, James Fife, and other substantial citizens who had supported the constitution issued a solemn warning to the Council that the end would be "national bankruptcy and consequent collapse of the Muskogee Government." There was some slackening in 1887, but the raids on the treasury were renewed during succeding administrations. Year after year new items were remembered or invented, and the allowance of padded and fantastic claims through the bribery of Council members became the most corrupting influence in Creek politics.[21]

If Creek finances had not been past help they might have been restored by a special appropriation from the United States. As early as 1878 the delegates had discovered that the boundary under the Treaty of 1866 had been run too far east and that they had unwittingly ceded 151,870.48 acres more than the amount contemplated. They employed an attorney for a 10 per cent contingent fee to push this claim; and in 1884 Congress appropriated $45,561.14 to pay for the extra land at the treaty price of thirty cents an acre, and the next year they received $41,004.90 as interest during the period they had been deprived of their income from the sale of the land. Several licensed traders who held large amounts of Creek paper persuaded Samuel W. Brown, the treasurer, to turn most of the first payment over to them before the Council convened. The Creeks no longer tried to pay their debts in order. The current income was used for the schools and the running expenses of the

[21] *Indian Journal,* October 15, 1885; October 28, 1886; October 13, 1887. Creek Tribal Records, 32855, 33027, 33051, 34317 ff.; Five Tribes Files, No. 28, 48-59, 85 ff.; No. 32, 66 ff., 130 ff.

government—including, of course, the salaries of Council members—and the holders of old warrants and lost property warrants remained unpaid. In 1885 non-citizen outlaws robbed Treasurer Brown and obtained about six thousand dollars in Creek funds, but this loss scarcely made matters worse.[22]

The only relief in sight lay in capitalizing the partial title to the Oklahoma land. The Boomers continued their invasions and the troops continued the empty farce of removing them. They had won enough public support so that the colonization of the land by Indian tribes or its return to the Creeks and Seminoles was completely out of the question, and during the 1884-85 session a bill was introduced in Congress to throw it open to homesteaders. By this time it was occupied by cattlemen, who built corrals and dugouts and divided the range as systematically as though their tenure had been legal. The Creeks were forbidden to use it or even to lease it to the cattlemen, but they believed if it were opened to settlers the opening of their own country would eventually follow. But on February 4, 1885, the Creek delegates, Efa Emarthla and L. C. Perryman, the chief's cousin, made an unauthorized contract with Samuel J. Crawford, of Kansas, who had represented the tribe in the excess acreage matter, instructing him for a 10 per cent commission to negotiate an absolute cession to the United States.

On March 3 Congress passed a law authorizing the purchase of this land from the Creeks and Seminoles and the Outlet from the Cherokees. The Cherokees were deriving a large revenue from the lease of the Outlet to cattlemen. In alarm they called a council at Eufaula and delegates of the Five Tribes passed a strong resolution against any change in the status of the land. This policy was approved the following fall by the Creek Council. The news of the Crawford contract soon leaked out, and the Chief after consulting a convention of leading men, formally notified the Department that it was not recognized by the tribe. Matters thus stood at a deadlock, and nobody benefited but the cattlemen, who by this

[22] Creek Tribal Records, 29832, 29917-18; Five Tribes Files, No. 22, 240; No. 28, 106 f.; No. 32, 5f., 151 f. Indian Office, Special Case 36; *Indian Journal,* November 6, 1884; June 4, 1885; May 27, 1886.

time no doubt were working covertly against the Boomers and their allies.[23]

The Creeks were not disturbed over the use of Oklahoma by white cattlemen, but they continued with increasing desperation to fight the occupation of their own domain. Just as they had previously been enjoined from taxing the drives that crossed their country, they were now forbidden to enforce the law of 1882 imposing a fine upon the herds that ranged there. The test came when the Saginaw Cattle Company brought the stock superintendent of Muskogee District before Judge Parker's court upon a charge of larceny. Parker decided against the Creeks, January 4, 1888, and they were left with only the non-existent protection of the Intercourse Acts. To make matters worse three owners of trail herds filed claims with the Department totaling $25,912.50 for alleged depredations by the Creeks. It appears from the evidence that the claims were fraudulent, that the losses had been caused by Texas fever and swollen rivers, but the possibility of recovery was an ominous warning to the Indians.

They tried also to limit the operations of their own wealthy cattlemen. The smaller ranchmen and the full bloods with their growing herds objected to the danger of Texas fever from imported cattle, the increasing monopoly of the range, and the tendency since the invention of barbed wire to build large enclosures. This class controlled the Council, but the Chief was in sympathy with the cattle barons. First he vetoed a bill requiring all persons to reduce their pastures to one hundred acres. The Council next passed a bill forbidding citizens to introduce cattle between June 1 and September 1 of each year and imposing a tax of three dollars a head upon those introduced at other seasons. The Chief disapproved this measure also, but it was repassed by a majority of 83 to 3 in the House of Warriors and 37 to 6 in the House of Kings.[24]

[23] Commissioner of Indian Affairs, *Annual Report*, 1884, xl-xliii; 1885, lviii-lx; 1886, xlvi, 158-60. Indian Office, Special Cases 36, 111, 134; *ibid.*, 1884/L15917; 49 Cong., 1 sess., *Sen. Rep. No. 1278*, 445-49; Five Tribes Files, No. 28, 72 f.; Creek Tribal Records, 29942, 30493; *Proceedings of the International Territorial Convention* (Phillips Collection, University of Oklahoma).

[24] *Indian Journal*, January 12, 1888; Creek Tribal Records, 29927-28, 34797-808, 35143; Indian Office, 1885/16842, 18819, 19011; 1886/16349, 19017; 1887/8165. United States Archives, Correspondence Land Division, Letter Book 139, 70 f., 313-16; Letter Book 140, 101 f.

The Council made two attempts to repeal the permit law, once imposing a fine of five hundred dollars upon any member who should attempt to revive it, but Perryman vetoed one bill and the other was declared unconstitutional by the old decision of the Supreme Court. A movement supported by the native merchants for the expulsion of all licensed traders received the support of the Chief, but the policy of the Indian Office from this time on became increasingly liberal toward the granting of licenses. In 1885 Treasurer Brown reported collections of $3,259.43 from the permit tax, and $5,158.06 from traders' licenses and other taxes and fines.[25]

The Creeks had become so disgusted at the failure of the Federal government to remove intruders that just at the close of Checote's term they had passed a law creating the office of inspector general and directing that official to examine the status of all non-citizens, report intruders to the agent and the Indian Office, and sell to citizens at public auction the improvements of all who failed to remove. A full blood named Itchas (Beaver) Harjo, or James Harlan, received the appointment. He employed deputies and made out a long list of intruders, many of whom the nation had been trying for years to dislodge; and when his representations to the Federal officials brought no result he began to sell their town property and farms. The intruders were alarmed and a few actually left the country, but the ones whose property had been sold refused to give possession and appealed to Tufts for protection. They all managed to establish some sort of claim to hold the property, and the Council refunded the purchase price to the buyers and abolished Harlan's office as soon as his two-year term expired. The Creeks had again been balked in their attempt to defend their homes.[26]

Several of those whose property had been condemned were self-styled Cherokees. The same year another such "Cherokee" who had openly brought his cattle into the Coweta District ran afoul of the stock superintendent there. Most of these people were not rec-

[25] Creek Tribal Records, Traders, also 31058 ff.; Five Tribes Files, No. 32, 184; No. 34. Indian Office 1885/C21207; *Indian Journal,* October 23, 1884; October 30, 1884; October 29, 1885; November 5, 1885; December 24, 1885.

[26] Creek Tribal Records, 31054, 31062, 31141, 32855, 32882, 38920; *Indian Journal,* January 17—February 28, 1884; May 22, 1884; September 11, 1884; March 19, 1885; April 19, 1885.

ognized as citizens by the Cherokees, but a few were intermarried white men, whose residence right in the Creek Nation was upheld by the Cherokees and denied by the Creeks. Both tribes were anxious to avoid any Departmental ruling that would take citizenship matters out of their hands. Commissioners of the two tribes met at Muskogee in October, 1884; they advised the construction of a fence along the entire Coweta-Cherokee boundary, and they drew up an agreement enlarging the Compact of 1843, suspending the seizure laws until the following August, and authorizing the Council of each nation to define the right of intertribal residence. The Creek Council ratified the agreement, but in view of its inability to obtain the removal of white intruders it took no steps to carry it into effect. The controversy, however, increased the movement for intertribal unity. The impulse was strengthened further by the threats of the Federal government.

Fortunately for the Five Tribes the schemes of their adversaries had become discredited in Congress and several objectionable bills were easily defeated. In 1885 Chairman Henry L. Dawes, of Massachusetts, and four other members of the Senate Committee on Indian Affairs visited their country. They gave the Indians a chance to be heard, and although Dawes himself believed in the dissolution of all Indian tribes, he assured them that Congress would not change their treaty status without their consent. But although the integrity of the Five Tribes was not so directly and brutally assailed as formerly, their position was slowly undermined by the policy of the government toward their weaker neighbors. J. D. C. Atkins, who became Commissioner of Indian Affairs in 1885, was one of the most savage enemies of the Indians that ever occupied that office; he used all the prestige of his position to destroy their land titles, and he vented his rage especially against the Five Tribes because they were the only ones capable of exposing his designs. This new attack aroused the strongest desire for intertribal organization that had yet developed.

Important councils of the Five Tribes and their wild neighbors were held at Eufaula in 1885, 1886, and 1887. Called at first to protest against the sale of Oklahoma and the Cherokee Outlet, the sessions of 1885 and 1886 extended the Compact of 1843 and the recent Creek-Cherokee agreement to other tribes, provided for the compulsory arbitration of all intertribal disputes, and made a serious attempt to draw up a constitution for an Indian confederation. The meeting in 1887 was dominated by the plight of the wild tribes.

During the winter of 1886-87 Atkins had visited the more backward tribes of the Territory trying to persuade them to accept allotments and open the rest of their land to homesteaders. According to Ne-ka-ke-pa-hah, principal chief of the Osages, he argued "if I would do that I would have an everlasting home for myself and children and my people and their children and that each one of our people could control at least 700 head of cattle and other stock accordingly that we would bee the Happist people in Gods Kingdom." It was Ne-ka-ke-pa-hah's opinion, however, that "as to letting white settlement with our people would soon Disfranchise the poore Indians and as to the stock we only look out to the state of Kansas we see the whites who live on alotments they have two ropes one to lead there cow and one to stake out the calve." In his perplexity and fear he turned as usual to the Creeks. He wanted all the Indians to meet "and have a good understanding with each other and to read our old treaties to each other and pass our old anciant Pipe renew our national love and respects to each other," and he asked the Creeks to "take it in hand and see the other civilize tribes and Pick the ground and time and notifie all."

Atkins went on from the Osages to the southwestern tribes, where he met the same determined opposition. In February, Chief Jake, of the Caddoes, and Lone Wolf, of the Kiowas, started out for Washington to protest. Their agent tried to arrest them for leaving their reservation, but they managed to reach Eufaula, where Perryman and other Creeks indignantly intervened, and they were allowed to buy their railroad tickets and proceed on their journey. The wild Indians probably did not know that a general allotment bill was then before Congress. Although it exempted the Five Civilized Tribes, their delegates worked earnestly to defeat its passage; but it became a law—the so-called Dawes Act—on February 8. The government's policy therefore was already fixed when the two chiefs reached the capital, but they insisted upon seeing Atkins,

and—as Chief Jake later described it through an interpreter—
"I told the Commissioner that in former times and up [to] the
present time he and all his people had advised us and all the Indians
to labor and gain education, etc., and now when my people are just
now beginning to realize and accept the benefits of knowledge how
to work you are attempting to change our customs and entail ruin
on my people."

After they returned, a council of all the southwestern tribes was
convened at Anadarko by Lone Wolf. They drew up earnest protests to the Commissioner against allotment and sent a copy of these
"talks" to the Creeks. No government official ever paid any attention to such inarticulate protests of full bloods, but this time they
found a champion. A disastrous fire had swept Muskogee that
spring and destroyed the plant of the *Indian Journal*. A Creek stock
company, of which G. W. Grayson was president, then purchased
the paper and moved it again to Eufaula. Dr. Leo E. Bennett, a
young white man who had recently married Stidham's daughter,
became its editor and it began an ardent defense of the Indian
cause. It was inevitable that the wild tribes would turn to the
intertribal council, and Bennett gave this gathering much advance
publicity and printed a full report of its proceedings.

The council was in session during June 6-10. Fifty-seven delegates from nineteen tribes were in attendance; the Five Tribes
sent their ablest leaders, and many of the great war chiefs of the
Southwest were among the members. It is plain that the Five
Tribes had expected to dominate the meeting, and their cattle and
railroad troubles had been placed on the agenda; but as soon as
the council began, Chief Jake and Lone Wolf described their recent
futile trip to Washington and several other wild chiefs joined in
an appeal to their "elder brothers" against allotment. Towaconie
Jim, of the Wichitas, told them, "It is now thirty-two years since
you five tribes advised the Wichitas to be peaceable and to obey
the will of the great government at Washington. And for thirty-
two years we have followed your advice, and have sent our children to school, and have made us some farms, and built houses,
and raise stock. You also invited us to adopt the Christian religion
and we have done so. We have always thought our lands would

remain ours, and never be divided in severalty, and *it can never be done with our consent*. The government treats us as if we had no rights, but we have always lived at our present place, and that is our home."

Their insistence changed the whole course of the meeting. Although the educated Indians were deeply stirred they realized that the law had already been passed and that resistance was hopeless; but the wild delegates were so desperately persistent that the committee on resolutions drew up a memorial to the President entreating him to stay the execution of the law "upon powerless and protesting people" until they were at least given the opportunity to test their rights in court. The memorial was carefully translated into all the diverse languages of the assembly, and it was unanimously adopted. A resolution sponsored by the Cherokees protesting against the granting of railroad charters not provided by treaty was also adopted. The council then adjourned to meet the next year at Fort Gibson.

Commissioner Atkins was furious when he learned of this action. In the *Washington Post* he gave a distorted account of the meeting, which he said was attended only by the Sac and Fox and the Five Tribes, who were specifically exempted from the operation of the Dawes Act. As for the tribes to which it applied, "I know that many of them have expressed approval of the policy and sought to have the law passed." In his published annual report he fulminated against the Five Tribes for "their insubordinate and unpardonable meddling" and their attempts "to manufacture a hostile sentiment against this solemn act of Congress." If the *Indian Journal* had not published the full proceedings of the convention, it would never have been known that the harassed tribesmen had come of their own initiative to the only people they knew that would give them a sympathetic hearing.[27]

Perryman's administration closed with the Creeks still guarding their heritage—the mixed bloods with skill and diplomatic adroit-

[27] Five Tribes Files, No. 28, 102-106; No. 32, 105-107, 118, 144, 174. *Indian Journal*, 1884-87; Creek Tribal Records, 30487-97, 30841-44, 31054-32882, 34800-804; *Proceedings of the International Territorial Convention;* Commissioner of Indian Affairs, *Annual Report*, 1885, viii-xiii; 1886, v-xiv, 134; 1887, x-xiv, 111-13. 49 Cong., 1 sess., Sen. Rep. No. 1278.

ness, the full bloods with instinctive stubbornness and fear. They had not made a complete success of their "civilized" government; but in spite of widespread lawlessness and chaotic finances and some official corruption, their tribal affairs were not hopeless. They had lost much of their ancient strength, but there was every indication that they would be able to make the adjustments necessary for survival in a white man's world. Their leaders believed that only time was needed. Time, however, was not given. During the next administration the long dreaded blow fell, and the end of their separate life as a people was in sight.

CHAPTER 10

Crumbling Defenses

THE election of 1887 was conducted in an orderly manner under the constitution, and all parties accepted the results. The Creeks had at last learned to express themselves through the elective franchise, and they entered into their campaigns with the deadly seriousness that had once characterized their primitive councils. The Pin and Muskogee factions still divided the voters in district and town elections, but these parties broke up into other groupings in the election of the tribal executive. The Creeks began to form numerous, rapidly shifting parties according to bargains and alliances made by the leaders; but these temporary political alignments were closely drawn and they learned to build "machines" and handle patronage with all the skill and precision of white politics at its worst. In spite of these new divisions it was still good tactics to place a mixed blood and a full blood together as candidates for principal and second chief.

In the fall of 1886 a group of educated and public spirited young men met to protest against the ruinous allowance of war claims and the laxity of tribal law enforcement. They held a number of meetings during the winter and spring trying to arouse the citizens to the need of reform, but only a few of the political leaders joined the movement. In June they held a convention at Okmulgee and organized the Independent Party. In their platform they called on the voters to ignore distinctions based on Civil War divisions or the quantum of white blood, and to join "in an earnest effort to save our country from impending ruin." They were opposed to relinquishing the tribal interest in Oklahoma, and they were in favor of reducing the size of the Council and the number of lighthorsemen. They nominated John R. Moore and James Fife as their candidates.

The Union Party, which had been formed by the coalition of the Checote and Isparhecher supporters four years before, also met at Okmulgee. Isparhecher served as chairman. This party advocated a law regulating the size of pastures, and in view of an increasing tendency of citizens to form corporations, it favored legislation governing the granting of charters. The rest of the platform had no meaning: economy in government, the removal of intruders, and, with regard to Oklahoma, the observance of the Treaty of 1866 by the United States. Legus C. Perryman, who was then serving in the House of Warriors, was nominated for principal chief, and the venerable Hotulke (Wind) Emarthla, of Okchiye Town, for second chief. It proved impossible for Isparhecher to let any election pass without running for office; he and his adherents accordingly withdrew from the party and formed a separate organization to support his candidacy. Tulwa Fixico, the judge of Wewoka District, received the nomination for second chief. The Muskogee Party also held its convention at Okmulgee. It adopted a platform composed entirely of platitudes, even to a promise to pay the national debt, and nominated Joseph M. Perryman for reëlection. Coweta Micco had died in office, and Hotulke Fixico, a Supreme Court justice, was nominated for second chief. The negroes this time supported the Union Party, and L. C. Perryman and Hotulke Emarthla were elected. Isparhecher received a consolatory appointment to the Supreme Court.[1]

L. C. Perryman and Hotulke Emarthla were reëlected in 1891 over Isparhecher and Tulwa Fixico, John Reed and James Colbert, and Wesley Smith and National Auditor W. A. Palmer. The power of the negro towns was strikingly shown in this election. Out of a total of 2,332 votes they cast 534, of which Perryman received 448 and Hotulke Emarthla 419; but Perryman was elected by a plurality of only 323 votes over Reed, his nearest opponent, and Hotulke Emarthla by a plurality of 250 over Palmer. The Council again elected Isparhecher to the Supreme Court, and Palmer was chosen for another term as national auditor.[2]

[1] *Indian Journal,* December 22, 1886; June–July, 1887. Creek Tribal Records, 31974, 31989, 32009.

[2] Creek Tribal Records, 29491 ff., 32995, 35600; Five Tribes Files, No. 30, 230.

L. C. Perryman proved to be a much more able executive than his cousin. He had energy, decisiveness, and a keen and logical mind; and he wrote his own letters and directed his own administration without undue dependence upon secretary or adviser. But the eight years covered by his two terms was not a happy period in Creek history. The tribe waged a losing battle with cattlemen, intruders, increasing crime, and, most of all, with the United States. Tribal politics became grossly corrupt, and the conduct of the Chief himself was not above suspicion.

Much of the difficulty arose from the disorganized condition of Federal law. The Creeks' experience with the Fort Smith court had served mainly to show them how inadequate was the legal system that was supposed to protect them. The white people in the nation were sadly in need of more Federal courts—they had no civil remedy of any kind, and the Fort Smith court was too distant to protect them against criminals—but to the Creeks the increase of Federal law meant greater harassment of their tribal officers and more confusing decisions.

Congress created the long-dreaded Indian Territory court at Muskogee in 1889. It had jurisdiction over civil and minor criminal cases involving United States citizens and cases between citizens of different tribes, but the self-government of the tribes was expressly recognized. The next year three divisions of this court were created, and it was given concurrent jurisdiction with the Fort Smith court in liquor and larceny cases. The same law gave Indians the right to accept United States citizenship by applying to the court, but very few Creeks availed themselves of this provision. An act passed in 1895 divided the Indian Territory into three judicial districts, placing the Creek, Cherokee, and Seminole nations in the Northern District; created a territorial court of appeals, composed of the three judges, sitting at South McAlester in the Choctaw Nation; and abolished the criminal jurisdiction of the Fort Smith court over the Indian Territory after September 1, 1896. These laws provided for appeals from the Territory courts to the United States Circuit Court of Appeals for the Eighth Circuit. In the absence of any legislative authority, sections of the Arkansas statutes were placed in effect.

In the ordinary administration of Anglo-American civil and criminal law these courts extended greatly needed protection to white residents in the Creek Nation, but they brought absolute chaos into the undefined field of Indian administration. The judges were short tenure patronage appointees, usually from distant states, and all of them were entirely unfamiliar with the complex system of treaties and the crazy patchwork of intercourse laws that regulated the Indians' relations with the government. Their decisions formed a jumble of conflicting rulings and reversals and sheer guesswork. If the Creeks themselves had possessed legal ability, and if they had sought to use instead of to avoid the courts, they might have presented their case more effectively and thereby aided in developing a workable system of justice. If more time had been given, the courts might eventually have created an orderly body of precedents, but the tribal regime was brought to an end before any system had been established.

An example of this confusion may be found in the interpretation of the Federal laws against the sale of intoxicants in the Indian country. The Creeks themselves were lukewarm in their support of this policy, but in 1882 under the influence of Checote they had enacted a strict "prohibition" law, and except during one demoralized Council session in 1894 their lighthorse generally managed to spill intoxicants and maintain a reasonable amount of sobriety in the vicinity of Okmulgee and other places of public gathering. But beer saloons were operated openly under traders' licenses in the railroad towns throughout the 1890's, while Congress legislated to no purpose and courts with concurrent jurisdiction differed as to whether beer was an intoxicant, whether laws against "introduction" also forbade the sale, or whether Departmental regulations governing the licenses had the effect of law.[3]

The agent continued to carry out Department orders with his Indian police, but the Department, of course, was bound by Federal court decisions. Because of the legal uncertainty these orders were given with extreme caution, for the police were always liable to be

[3] *Indian Journal*, July 14, 1892; *Muskogee Phœnix*, June 7, 1894; December 1, 1894; February 23, 1895; January 9, 1896; April 7, 1898; October 6, 1898. Creek Tribal Records, 32300, 32311.

brought before the Federal courts in any conflict involving United States citizens. If a member of the force was killed by an Indian, the trial took place in the tribal courts until Congress in 1888 gave them the protection of Federal law.

Organized crime increased in the Creek Nation during this period. Regular outlaw gangs of whites, negroes, and Indians terrorized the country. In 1887 a white man came to the negro settlement and made an arrangement with the thieves to purchase all the stolen horses they would deliver at Red Fork. Such an epidemic of horse-stealing broke out over the nation that Chief J. M. Perryman authorized each of the district judges to commission five assistant lighthorsemen to make arrests. Several of the criminals were caught and whipped, but organized horse-stealing continued. A well-defined "rogues' path" led from the Muskogee District across the nation to the mouth of Little River and on to the Seminole country; and a chain of negroes and full bloods transported stolen horses in relays along this underground railroad.

In 1888 a number of young Creeks banded together under one Wesley Barnett and engaged in liquor-dealing, robbery, and murder. They became so bold that they broke up a religious service in the council house and held the building for a time. United States marshals, Indian police, and Creek lighthorsemen all set out to capture them, and after several fights the gang was broken up and its members killed or sent to the Federal penitentiary.

During 1894 the Cook gang of white outlaws and renegade mixed-blood Indians engaged in daring train robberies and store robberies in the Creek and Cherokee nations. White business men lived in constant fear of their raids and every train that crossed the Territory was heavily guarded. The situation was so serious that the Federal district attorney sent the following call to Chief Perryman: "Notify your People that any Citizen of the Nation has the right to arrest any member of the Cook Gang or any other person who has Committed a felony[,] without a writ, whether he be whiteman or Indian ... If in the arrest of a Robber —he resist—The citizen has the same right to kill as an officer, if necessary to effect the capture." Perryman, with the consent of the Council, then directed each of the judges to select ten good men and send them anywhere in the Territory to make the arrests, and the nation subsequently paid for their services. The gang was completely exterminated by Creek, Cherokee, and Federal officers during the winter and spring of 1894-95.

The following summer five Creeks and negroes formed the Buck gang under the leardership of Rufus Buck, the son of a prominent Euchee politician. They operated in the northwestern part of the Creek country, committing fiendish crimes from sheer bravado and wantonness. They flourished only a few weeks until the whole country rose up against them. They were surrounded and captured by Creek lighthorse, United States marshals, and a large body of outraged citizens and conveyed to Fort Smith, where all five were hanged together by Judge Parker for the rape of a white woman. The act of 1895 increasing the number of Indian Territory courts was passed just at this time, and it seems to have had some effect in reducing the amount of crime.[4]

The court at Muskogee handled an immense amount of litigation; lawyers flocked to the town, and all kinds of businesses were greatly stimulated. The first bank in the Indian Territory was established there in 1890. The Creeks with the approval of the agent extended their definition of trader to include all business and professional men. Merchandise dealers paid an ad valorem tax of one-half per cent on all goods introduced during the year; other business men paid fixed amounts varying from twenty to two hundred dollars annually; there were such special taxes as fifteen dollars a day on a circus and one dollar a month on a pedestrian peddler; and doctors, dentists, and lawyers were charged twenty-five dollars a year. Under this broad definition about two hundred traders were reported in 1895: Muskogee had about seventy, Wagoner forty-four, Tulsa thirty-eight, Eufaula fifteen, Sapulpa ten, and Okmulgee three; and about twenty operated country stores in remote places.[5]

In their permit policy the Creeks still vacillated between the in-

[4] Harman, *Hell on the Border, passim;* Commissioner of Indian Affairs, *Annual Report,* 1889, 209 f.; Creek Tribal Records, 26442, 27022, 28115, 31998 ff., 32932.

[5] Creek Tribal Records, 39260 ff.; Indian Office, 1891/L3316, 1893/L33761, 38957; United States Archives, Correspondence Land Division, Letter Book 265, 265-77; Letter Book 267, 228 f.

sistence of their wealthy mixed bloods and the conservatism of the genuine Indians. They changed the amount of the tax several times, abolished it entirely in 1892 upon the advice of the Chief, and restored it in 1894. From 1887 on it was collected by district inspectors, and the nation paid 50 per cent of the cost of collection. The first year after it was restored about $4,500 was collected from about eight hundred employees of licensed traders and Creek farmers and ranchmen. The practice of leasing raw land for a term of years to a non-citizen who would improve it was forbidden in 1893 under penalty of a one-hundred-dollar fine and forfeiture of the land; and the Supreme Court subsequently decided that under this law no lease to a non-citizen was legal for a longer period than one year. In 1894 the Council passed a bill forbidding any lease to a non-citizen, but it was vetoed by the Chief.[6]

The full bloods watched the increasing white immigration with bewilderment and fear. Wilson Clark, a Euchee, describes his impressions as follows:

"Must be time of 1889 or 1890, I see white men coming into my country. Some men would be walking and carry a stick on shoulder with a little bundle tied to it. We don't know where the men are going or where they come from.

"There's no road but white man goes on anyhow through the grass and tall weeds. Maybe we sometimes follow him and we often find white men resting under the trees. Sometimes we see him making fire and cooking, then again he stay all night but he goes on again next morning.

"Sometimes there are three or four men and at other times there is a big bunch of them in wagons with women and children. They stop at a good place where there is plenty good drinking water, near the woods and near a good stream for fishing.

"They try to claim the land where they stop by sticking up a pole or short stick and tying a red cloth to the end of it. If they stayed, a lot of them stole our hogs and cattle.

"We chase them out of our country for doing this. I use to help my Indians by watching the white men and see that they don't cut down

[6] Creek Tribal Records, 31456 ff., 35049; Five Tribes Files, No. 28, 130 f.; No. 30, 274. *Indian Journal*, October 12, 1894; *Acts and Resolutions of the Creek National Council, 1895*, 16.

the trees—at least not so much of them. We could chase out white men and they be right back the next day. Sometimes there are more white people back than we had chased out."[7]

The creation of the Indian Territory courts made it even more difficult for the Creeks to protect themselves from intruders. After the abolition of the Inspector General's office the tribal district attorneys occasionally went through the form of selling their improvements and in a very few instances managed to secure their expulsion by the agent. In these few cases the purchaser entered into possession of their property. But in 1890 a dispossessed intruder sued the Indian policemen who carried out the agent's orders to evict him and the purchaser who assisted; and he received a judgment of one hundred dollars and costs. This suit cost the nation $518.25 to reimburse its citizens and pay their attorneys' fees. The Indian Territory courts ruled as Parker had previously decided that the only remedy lay with the Department under the Intercourse Acts. In practice this meant the dreary writing of reports to lie in forgotten files at Washington. Because of his own impotence the agent hesitated except in the most extreme cases to serve notice on intruders; in 1894 Agent Dew M. Wisdom complained of "the awkward dilemma of issuing an order, which I cannot enforce, & thereby bringing the Agency into contempt." The Creeks in despair passed one futile law after another; but distressing as these conditions were, the tribe had been more successful than any of its more advanced neighbors in resisting white immigration.[8]

The Creeks finally declared their independence of the Cherokee citizenship claimants who put forth such vociferous demands for recognition as fellow Indians. In a case referred to him in 1889 Commissioner T. J. Morgan ruled that a Cherokee citizen had no rights in the Creek Nation except under Creek law. In 1892 the Council directed the Chief to take steps to effect the peaceable removal of all non-citizen Indians. No attempt was ever made to carry out this

[7] WPA Project S-149.

[8] Creek Tribal Records, 26107, 27568, 33055; Indian Office, 1894/L8719; United States Archives, Correspondence Land Division, Letter Book 210, 162 f.; Letter Book, 237, 295-304; Letter Book 278, 61 f. *Muskogee Phœnix,* October 3, 1894; June 1, 1895. *Acts and Resolutions of the National Council of the Muskogee Nation 1893–99 inc. [lusive],* 12-14.

measure, but intruders claiming Cherokee citizenship no longer occupied a privileged position in Departmental rulings. In any policy regarding non-citizen Indians the Creeks excepted the Seminoles because of their special status under the Treaty of 1856.[9]

The Creeks admitted to their citizenship a few persons of recognized Creek descent who had remained in Alabama or settled in Texas at the time of the Removal. The district courts passed upon their claims until that power was conferred upon the Council in 1883. They were required to renounce their United States citizenship and take an oath of allegiance to the Creek Nation. The largest number recognized in this way was 129, who came during 1888-90. Most of them were white people in all but name, who had been attracted to the Creek country because of its economic opportunities, and few ever became truly identified with the tribe. In 1889 the Council declared that except for those whose applications were still pending, all who had lived outside the nation for twenty-one years were thereby debarred from admission.[10]

Some interesting population statistics were obtained when the first Federal census of the Creek country was taken in 1890. The Indians shrank in fear from the enumeration as a new scheme of the white man to drive them again into exile, but Perryman finally persuaded them to coöperate. Negroes and Indians were employed as enumerators, and considering the isolation of the fullblood homes their work was surprisingly accurate. They found 9,999 Indians, of which 9,291 were Creeks and 708 citizens of other tribes, mostly Cherokees (462) and Seminoles (172); 4,621 negroes, citizen and non-citizen; and 3,289 whites and 3 Chinese. Of the total population of 17,912 the Indians thus formed 55.82 per cent. The main towns were Muskogee, with a population of 1,200, Eufaula with 500, and Okmulgee with 136. There were six post offices in the nation.[11]

In 1891 the Council made a complete census of citizens. It is apparent that the members from the colored towns placed nearly all

[9] Creek Tribal Records, 30848, 39281; Indian Office, 1889/L20031, 1890/L5293; United States Archives, Correspondence Land Division, Letter Book 187, 428-31; Letter Book 196, 144.

[10] McKellop, *Constitution and Laws*, 58, 103-105; Five Tribes Files, No. 29, 16 f.; No. 30, 58, 93 f., 180; No. 32, 135. Indian Office, 1892/A13724.

[11] *Extra Census Bulletin*, 3-7, 10, 62.

the negroes in the nation upon their rolls, but this enumeration received the official sanction of the tribe. The figures are as follows:[12]

Alabama	171	Kialigee	246
Arbeka—Deep Fork	141	Locker Poker	194
Arbeka—North Fork	132	Nuyaka	237
Arbekoche	73	Okfuskee—Canadian	136
Artussee	150	Okfuskee—Deep Fork	98
Big Spring (Wekiwa Thlocco)	180	Okchiye	212
		Osochee	87
Broken Arrow (Thlikach-ka)	431	Pukkon Tullahassee	102
		Quassarty (Koasata) No. 1	79
Chiaha	154	Quassarty No. 2	48
Concharty	194	Talledaga	159
Coweta	593	Thlewarle	196
Cusseta	434	Thlopthlocco	334
Euchee	580	Tookparfka	92
Eufaula—Canadian	236	Tuckabatchee	785
Eufaula—Deep Fork	133	Tullahassochee	59
Fish Pond (Thlothlagalga)	160	Tulmochussee	86
Greenleaf	109	Tulsa—Canadian	140
Hickory Ground (Ochia-pofa)	331	Tulsa—Little River	360
Hillabee	109	Tuskegee	401
Hitchitee	182	Tulwa Thlocco	171
Hutche Chuppa	196	Wakokiyee	50
Kechopatarky	391	Wewogufke	185
		Wewoka	102

TOTAL INDIANS	9,639
Arkansas Colored	1,970
Canadian Colored	1,444
North Fork Colored	789
TOTAL NEGROES	4,203
TOTAL CITIZENS	13,842

Except for the negroes the Creeks had little trouble with citizenship claimants, but after the creation of the Federal courts white

[12] Indian Office, 1892/A1282.

men began to acquire a lien upon the landed wealth of the tribe. The courts showed an increasing tendency to assume jurisdiction in probate cases involving the property of intermarried non-citizens and to recognize their right to inherit Creek land. The right of all non-citizens who were legal residents to buy and sell the possessory title to Creek real estate was also legalized by the Federal courts; and in such cases the residence right of Cherokee citizens was accepted without question. By 1893 traffic in occupancy titles had developed to such an extent in Muskogee District that Leo Bennett carried on a real estate business in Muskogee, advertising farms and town property for sale or rent.[13]

Better conservationists than the white man, the Creeks tried also to guard their timber as a part of the public property of the tribe. They had repealed their royalty laws and imposed a fine of from one thousand to five thousand dollars upon any citizen who should cut or sell timber for exportation, and in 1893 they prescribed a penalty of fifty lashes for any person unable to pay the fine. But during the 1890's the Creek country was stripped of the walnut that grew along the Arkansas and branches of the Canadian and the cedar from the Cimarron. Much of the walnut found its way to eastern furniture factories, but Louis Norburg (or Lewis Norberg), the most extensive dealer in Creek timber, made gunstocks and sold them in immense quantities to the American and foreign governments.

The timber was cut by night or citizens were paid a small bribe to claim the down timber until it could be spirited out of the country. The Indian Office was completely indifferent, and some of the tribal district attorneys were not incorruptible; and although the Creeks now had a remedy in the Federal courts they hesitated to undertake the unknown perils of litigation. The Chief wrote a number of urgent letters in his own hand to district attorneys and judges calling attention to the violation of the law. In 1892 he reported Norburg's activities to Bennett, who was then Union agent; but Bennett declined to act unless the nation would show its good

[13] *Muskogee Phœnix*, October 5, 1893; January 18, 1894; April 12, 1894; September 13, 1894; September 19, 1895. Creek Tribal Records, 27570; Five Tribes Files, No. 30, 278; No. 34. McKellop, *Constitution and Laws*, 106.

faith by punishing its own citizens "who act as go betweens." But at least two citizens of Wewoka District were arrested, placed in irons and guarded by lighthorse, tried, convicted, and fined one thousand dollars each at the very time Bennett was writing this letter. Several other arrests followed in different parts of the nation, and some logs cut by non-citizens were seized and sold for the benefit of the tribe.

Early in 1895 the Chief issued special commissions to the prosecuting attorneys to sell all down timber in their districts. Robert W. Stewart, the prosecuting attorney of Wewoka District, then— according to his own statement—entered into a contract with the Chief's secretary and a white timber-dealer to sell the timber to them without offering it at public auction; and apparently Hotul-koche, the illiterate fullblood attorney of Deep Fork District, was tricked into giving a similar instrument.

Whatever the form of sale, the timber by a rapid series of transactions passed into the possession of Norburg, and it does not appear that the nation realized any benefit. Thomas Yahola, the judge of Wewoka District, tried to prevent Norburg from securing the timber and the court broke up in a near riot. Pompey Manley, the attorney of Eufaula District, then tried to attach the gunstocks when they were brought to Eufaula for shipment, but his notice was torn down and a large shipment went out. He did succeed, however, in seizing 1,542 gunstocks, which he sold for the benefit of the nation. Judge Yahola then appealed to Agent Wisdom. Wisdom examined the bills of sale given by Stewart and decided that "the blame, if any" rested with the Creek authorities; he assured Norburg's foreman that "any interference with your property by Indian officers is unwarranted and is hereby prohibited," and he warned the judge that Norburg as a United States citizen was outside Creek jurisdiction, "and I certainly would interfere to prevent an[y] sale of his property by you." But the case became important in tribal politics, and Stewart was removed from office. His successor employed white attorneys upon his own responsibility and applied to the Federal court for an injunction against Norburg. The case came up for trial in December. The Creeks won and secured possession of forty-six thousand feet of down timber. But the tribal officials did not work consistently to protect their timber, and this temporary inconvenience to Norburg hardly checked the wholesale lumbering operations.[14]

The Creeks were more deeply concerned over the occupation of their country by cattlemen, but again their defense was weakened by the irresolution of their officers and the corrupting and intimidating power of great financial interests. All these influences were brought into play during the passage and administration of the so-called contract pasture laws.

The first law was passed in the fall of 1889 under the active leadership of Perryman. The Chief, like his cousin, was inclined to favor the wealthy citizen cattlemen, and he objected to the taxation of imported cattle. At the same time he sympathized with the full bloods in their opposition to enclosures. All classes of Creeks were disgusted at the occupation of the border by intruding cattle; Coweta District in particular was almost entirely lost, and the nation derived no revenue from its use.

A law that would permit the wealthy cattlemen to build enclosures and import Texas cattle free of tax, protect the humble citizens against land monopoly, guard the borders, and at the same time bring a substantial revenue to the nation seemed a perfect solution of all cattle problems. Ostensibly it was designed purely to prevent land monopoly by citizens and intrusion by white men. It limited enclosures in the interior of the country to one square mile for a citizen head of a family and provided that all larger pastures already in existence should be taken down by the following May. But it provided that citizens might protect themselves from "the influx of stock from adjoining Nations" by erecting pastures of unlimited extent along the border. Any number of citizens might petition the district judge stating their need of "protection"; the judge would call an election, and if a majority of the voters "of the neighborhood thus to be protected" gave their approval the judge would grant a contract for the construction of the pasture. The contract was to run three years, and the holder was obligated to construct a fence of four or more wires, and to pay the nation

[14] WPA Project S-149; Creek Tribal Records, 26131, 35626, 35967 ff.; Five Tribes Files, No. 53, 76 ff.; *Indian Journal*, July 3, 1890; May 24, 1895.

an annual rental of five cents an acre to be collected by the judge. The law said nothing about the use of these contract pastures, but it was certainly the intention of its sponsors to lease them to Texas cattlemen; and the Chief always assumed that the law prohibiting the introduction of cattle by non-citizens and requiring citizens to pay an import duty was inoperative so far as the contract pastures were concerned.

As soon as the law was passed, enterprising mixed bloods began to lay out pastures along the eastern border, especially in the Muskogee District, but several of their petitions were defeated by the voters. It soon became customary for the applicant to enter into separate contracts with the citizens of the neighborhood to secure their consent, usually by an agreement to pay twenty-five dollars a year to everyone living within the proposed enclosure. Several pasture contracts were in effect by the spring of 1890, and by the following fall complicated suits had been instituted in the tribal courts between rival claimants to desirable tracts. A few of these contests were eventually carried to the Federal courts by intermarried white men or recent mixed-blood immigrants who were "Creeks" only in economic pretensions.

Along the western border, where the full bloods lived, the Indians themselves formed pasture companies upon their own initiative or under the leadership of white men. It was customary to form the organization at a community gathering and sign the petition to the judge at the same time. The members then cut and set the posts, and a white man made the necessary business arrangements.

C. W. Turner—apparently with the assistance of N. P. Blackstone—planned to enclose most of the Deep Fork District by building a great pasture on the Sac and Fox border. As he was not a citizen, he organized a company of one hundred Creeks, most of whom lived within the proposed enclosure. He was to take all the financial risks and realize all the profits, and he agreed to pay each member of the company one hundred dollars a year. There was strong feeling in the district against the pasture, and a similar proposition by another company had been voted down; but the agents of Turner's company persuaded Judge Jacob Knight to call another election. The opponents of the pasture then went to Ok-mulgee to request Knight's suspension, but the Chief decided that the judge was within the law. Some of them, however, received the impression that the election order had been canceled; hence they were not present at the meeting, and the proposition carried by a vote of 59 to 30. This election was held October 11, 1890, and the judge made the contract the same day. Just a week later the Chief approved an act of the Council prohibiting the granting of any more contract pastures.

The tract secured by the company embraced about two hundred and fifty thousand acres. It lay between the Deep Fork and the North Fork and was twenty-five miles in extent from east to west—a border pasture only in the sense that it touched the border at one edge. Turner leased it to Waggoner and Son, of Texas, for an annual rental of $27,500, of which $10,000 was paid in advance. The wire was purchased through Turner's hardware store at Muskogee, and Waggoner's ranch hands were sent to cut posts and build the fence. They measured the land by tying a white rag on a buggy wheel and counting the revolutions as they drove. By June they had construc-ted about sixty miles of fence, and several thousand cattle had already been brought in. Each of the Creek members of the com-pany had received $22.50 of his first payment.

Patriotic Creeks watched this work with apprehension. Napoleon B. Moore, the national treasurer, and Isparhecher, who was then on the Supreme Court, became their leaders. Isparhecher sent out no-tices to trusted lieutenants, telling them that the cattle were on the way and that it was time to act. Quietly they held a meeting and laid their plans. The cowboys building the fence had heard a few ominous mutterings, and they tried to be on their guard; but sud-denly—as one of them remembers it—"the prairie was black with Indians" working in orderly sequence cutting the posts. "We esti-mated four or five hundred Indians took posts on all four sides of the pasture. They were on ponies, armed with rifles or pistols, knives and axes. . . . We had to sit steady and watch the fence go down. We were in camp when they came by on that part of the fence, sitting there watching them and hoping they wouldn't scalp us. As they passed one big buck Indian came riding up to us, stopped and said, 'Um, too much big pasture,' and rode off. We decided maybe it was too much big; anyway, we had to abandon it." Waggoner spent several weeks trying without success to come to an agreement with the Indians. Then he moved his cattle to the Osage country.

Turner tried repeatedly to obtain compensation for the destruction of his fence and the loss of his lease. In 1893 a claim for $10,078.16 was allowed by the Council, but it was vetoed by Perryman. In 1896 the company obtained a decision from the Supreme Court that the contract was legal and presented a bill to the Council for $17,558.64 in damages, but it was not paid. In 1908 Congress passed an act under which Turner brought suit against the Creek Nation in the Federal court of claims for $115,698.03, but he lost his case here, and in the Supreme Court, where the litigation finally ended in 1919.

Most of the pastures were constructed without violence, but it was apparent during the grazing season of 1890 that the contract pasture law had not brought the expected peace. The Creek cattlemen were divided into two hostile groups: those who wished to protect the range for native herds, and those who dealt mainly in foreign cattle and leases to non-citizens. Although the Chief upheld the leasing of the contract pastures—his brother, George B. Perryman, in fact, held a border pasture of sixty thousand acres in Coweta District and leased it that year to Texas cattlemen—he repeatedly and vainly urged Judge E. H. Lerblance to destroy several unlawful interior pastures in Muskogee District.

Agent Bennett, himself the president of the Muskogee and Seminole Live Stock Association, bitterly denounced the Chief for his "twisted construction" of the contract pasture law, but he was unable to obtain any Departmental instructions on the subject. W. F. Crabtree, the national tax-collector, classed the lessees of border pastures as intruders. He applied to the Federal courts for redress under the Intercourse Acts, but he was required to file an indemnifying bond for a million and a half dollars. He complained to the Department, and the Federal officials expressed some fierce intentions to clear all foreign cattle from the Creek country; their determination, however, was smothered in the dust that accumulated on

Bennett's reports. Finally the Department of Justice feebly undertook the prosecution, but that effort also faded out in uncertainty. While the tribal and Federal governments alike were paralyzed by clashing interests and conflicting policies, one hundred thousand longhorns grazed undisturbed over the Creek prairies.

When the Council convened, it defined the law in a manner satisfactory in the main to the holders of contract pastures. Further contracts were forbidden, but existing contracts were to stand until the expiration of the three-year period; the introduction of foreign cattle to stock the contract pastures was expressly legalized between November 30 and May 15; other citizens were required to pay a tax of two dollars a head for importation, the period of introduction was shortened to January, February, and March, and a penalty of three dollars a head was imposed for violation; the joining of mile-square pastures was prohibited; and citizens were forbidden to hold cattle belonging to non-citizens upon the open range.

This clarification of the pasture laws scarcely helped the enforcement. Holders of contract pastures forgot to pay the rental to the nation; few of the large interior pastures were taken down, and several new ones were constructed; citizens introduced foreign cattle to graze on the open range without paying the tax; non-citizens brought their cattle into the Creek country in defiance of tribal and Federal law, or they covered their ownership by false sales to citizens, protecting themselves by a mortgage for the full value of the stock. Nothing in particular was done during 1891, but the Council asked the United States to prosecute "Barbecue" Campbell and other great western cattle barons for holding their cattle on the Creek range.

The Chief never showed much concern over the collection of rentals from the contract pastures, but in 1892 he made a determined effort to enforce the rest of the law. He prodded the officials of Muskogee District until in June Prosecuting Attorney R. C. Hawkins instituted proceedings against N. P. Blackstone, M. L. Minter, T. F. Meagher, and George Shannon and Company for introducing Texas cattle without paying the tax. Minter and Meagher were intermarried white men. Shannon also was a white man; his wife, a granddaughter of William McIntosh, had died a few years before, but he was associated in business with her brother, J. D. Willison, who was, of course, a Creek citizen.

Lerblance was so unwilling to act in the cattle cases that he finally resigned, and the Chief appointed Temaye Cornells, an elderly mixed blood of the old conservative type, in his place. Hawkins, who was accused of harboring some of the cattle in his own pasture, was so lukewarm in the prosecution that Perryman suspended him and appointed David Lee, a well-known colored citizen of the district. Neither Cornells nor Lee was fitted to resist the ruthless, driving power of determined white men, but the Chief kept up their morale by insistent letters, and a mass meeting of Creeks from nearly every town in the nation drew up declarations against the violation of the cattle laws. Lee then brought charges against H. B. Spaulding, F. B. Severs, and Benton Callahan, the son of S. B. Callahan.

Apparently the charges against Severs were dropped; he had been accused of introducing only two hundred cattle, and he paid the required four hundred dollars in taxes. The other cases were tried before Judge Cornells in August. Six convictions were secured and fines totaling fifty thousand dollars were imposed. Meagher made a payment of three hundred dollars, either as a fine or as a voluntary payment of the tax. The largest judgment was against Shannon and Company for thirty thousand dollars for the introduction of ten thousand cattle. The lighthorse seized the cattle to satisfy the judgment, and United States citizens from whom Shannon and Company had obtained the cattle produced a mortgage and appealed to the Federal court for an injunction against the Creek officers. Other United States citizens intervened to prevent the execution of the judgment against the 2,110 cattle held by Callahan and produced a mortgage for $36,120 given by Callahan to "Barbecue" Campbell. Minter and Spaulding appealed to the Federal court on the ground that they were United States citizens. Blackstone also applied for an injunction, but the final disposition of his case is not clear.

Special lighthorsemen were employed to hold the cattle until the owners furnished bonds covering the amount of the judgment. The

Chief employed S. S. Fears, a white attorney, to defend the nation
in the Federal court. The docket was so crowded that only the
Shannon and Company case was tried during 1893. The court
ruled that not only Willison, a citizen, but Shannon, who held
his rights through intermarriage, was under Creek law, but it
decided that the holders of the mortgage were beyond tribal jurisdiction. Fears appealed to the United States Circuit Court of Appeals, and in 1894 he won a complete victory. It is not altogether
clear in the general financial confusion of the time whether the other
cases were carried to a final settlement or whether the nation ever
benefited from the judgments, but for the first time since the
foundation of Georgia it was demonstrated that the Creeks had a
judicial remedy against the intrusions of white cattlemen.

The Council that met in the fall of 1892 after the institution of
the cattle suits was completely dominated by cattle legislation.
There was a special Committee on Pastures, and bills were introduced limiting all pastures to 320 acres, prescribing fine and whipping for all introduction of foreign cattle, creating a pasture two
miles wide along the border to be built and maintained by the tribe,
etc. The law finally enacted was an extension of the contract policy,
but this time the administration was in the hands of the Chief.
The width of the border pastures was limited to ten miles; the citizens of the neighborhood were again given a referendum; the contracts were to run for six years; and the nation was to employ surveyors to measure the land. Two-thirds of the revenue was to go
to the schools, and the remainder to the general fund.

The Chief gave at least one contract on the day the law was
approved. Nearly all the leading citizens obtained pastures, which
they leased to Texas cattlemen, keeping their own cattle on the
open range in the interior of the country. The usual size of a
pasture was thirty-two thousand acres, but a few were much larger.
The law was not strictly enforced, but it was much more effective
than the one enacted three years before. Because of the general
financial depression in 1893 a number of those who had secured
contracts were unable to stock their pastures. The Chief therefore
decided not to enforce the payment of the rentals in such cases,
and the survey, which under the law should have been paid from

the rentals, became a charge on the treasury. Samuel Grayson, the treasurer, reported that he collected $7,340.44 and expended $9,601.80 for surveys. In 1894 he collected $16,000, and in 1895 he received $18,633.52. It is apparent from his reports that substantial citizens like George B. Perryman and Pleasant Porter paid in full, but that many evaded payment. About thirty thousand head were unlawfully introduced during the grazing season of 1894. But in spite of their difficulties the Creeks seemed to be reaching a solution of their cattle problem when their efforts were paralyzed by the approaching dissolution of their government.[15]

The Dawes Severalty Act was the beginning of the end. The Creeks sympathized deeply with the Indians that came under its provisions, but very little could be done and the other Civilized Tribes were inclined to drop the matter. When the intertribal council convened at Fort Gibson in June, 1888, delegates of twenty-two tribes were in attendance, and two or three thousand people were present as spectators. S. H. Benge, a Cherokee, served as president. Once again the wild tribes took the lead. They had come for help in their desperate opposition to allotment, and feeling their own tribal life breaking up, they had resolved to unite "and live as one family under one Indian government." They forced the idea of unification upon the council. Pleasant Porter from the committee on resolutions recommended favorable action, and when President Benge, mindful of the practical difficulties, tried to temporize, he answered, "This is an important question—one of life and death."

The resolution was unanimously adopted. It provided for the appointment of a committee to draft a constitution for an "Indian Territorial Government" and submit it to the next council. The President was memorialized to defer allotment under the Dawes Act until after an investigation of the manner in which the work

[15] Creek Tribal Records, 26106, 27149 ff., 32071 ff., 34822 ff., 35716, 38652; Five Tribes Files, No. 1, 22-24; No. 30, 133, 193-202. WPA Project S-149; *Muskogee Phœnix*, October 12, 1893; November 2, 1893; September 13, 1894; July 25, 1895; January 19, 1919. Indian Office, 1890/L17229, L20699, L24702, L26549, L36074; United States Archives, Correspondence Land Division, Letter Book 198, 142 f.; Letter Book 202, 269. *Indian Journal*, July 14, 1892; April 26, 1894. *Indian Territory Reports*, I, 199-215; *ibid.*, II, 365-71; *Federal Reporter*, LXIII, 305-307; *United States Reports*, CCXLVIII, 354-59; Turner, "Events Among the Muskogees," 31 f.

was being done by the special agents in charge. Purcell, in the Chickasaw Nation, was chosen as the next place of meeting.[16]

White Man, an Apache delegate, had advocated the recovery of the Oklahoma land and warned the council against its settlement by the whites. But in spite of the platform upon which Perryman had been elected, his personal record indicated that he was ready to surrender to the United States. In the fall of 1888 he persuaded the Creek Council to authorize an absolute cession, and the delegates—Porter, Hodge, and Isparhecher—then entered into negotiations with the Department officials. They argued that they had ceded their land for thirty cents an acre only because they expected it to be used for other Indians, and if it was to be opened to white settlement the purchase price should be increased to the usual $1.25, not only for Oklahoma but for all surplus land remaining after the allotment of the tribes that had been located upon the ceded tract. The agreement was signed in Washington on January 19, and ratified by the Council on January 31. The Creeks received an additional compensation of $2,280,857.10 for this cession.

The Seminoles made a similar agreement to surrender their claim to the ceded land. Congress ratified these articles, and the President issued a proclamation throwing the Oklahoma land open to white settlement April 22. Vast crowds of home-seekers gathered on the borders, and when that wild day was over the lonely wilderness had become a settled land of tented cities with soaring ambitions, and staked claims ready for the plow. Only the Cherokees and Creeks troubled to attend the intertribal council at Purcell, for with the formation of this alien settlement in the heart of the Indian country the Indian statehood project, which had been urged for more than a century, was lost forever. Congress soon formed a territorial government for the Oklahoma settlers, and they began with characteristic energy and enthusiasm to create the institutions of a white man's land.

The western tribes still brought their allotment troubles to the Creeks. The Iowas came for advice in 1890. "We want to know if you know anything about it tell us all about it Well we dont dake

16 *Indian Journal*, June 28, 1888; Commissioner of Indian Affairs, *Annual Report*, 1888, 124-27.

lotment they told they going get soldier to move us Some Where Bad place. Well I am think of great god will help." But the Iowas and their neighbors were given allotments in spite of their protests, their surplus land was thrown open to homesteaders, and their country was added to the growing Territory of Oklahoma. When the Sac and Fox Reservation was opened in accordance with this policy in 1891, the new white frontier touched the Creek country. Those who failed to secure homesteads pushed over the boundary and established an unbroken line of settlement on the Creek side, and all the land along the border was quickly stripped of every tree that could be used for fuel or fence posts. The Sac and Fox Indians, completely submerged in this alien society, came to Okmulgee in 1893 to negotiate for a tract of land where they might settle in the Creek country. The Creeks expressed their sympathy, but for once they refused to share with a dispossessed tribe. The same year the Cherokees were forced to sell the Outlet, and the Pawnee surplus was proclaimed ready for white occupancy. The greatest of all land openings followed, and the Creeks were confronted by another white settlement on their northern and western boundaries.

It was apparent that the Five Tribes were next on the list. Successive Commissioners of Indian Affairs condemned the "degrading communism" of their land system and urged Congress to abolish the tribal regime by force. Agent Bennett recommended individual land tenure as the only protection against intruders. Even the officials in charge of the Federal census argued the need of change, and to show the dangerous and subversive character of Indian nationalism they quoted the old "treason" law passed at the time of the constitutional difficulties. The *Indian Journal* under successive white editors and the *Muskogee Phœnix,* which Bennett had founded in 1888, did not join the "booster" press, but they cautiously opposed the tribal policy. During the winter of 1892-93 it became apparent to the ever watchful delegates of the Five Tribes that the blow could no longer be averted. In February they sent out printed circulars warning their people that Congress was determined to abrogate the treaties and liquidate the Indian republics— if possible by negotiation, but if necessary by force. On March 3 Congress authorized the appointment of a commission to negotiate. President Cleveland came into office the next day. Although he was determined to break down the tribal status, he was well disposed toward the Indians and was willing to be very patient in giving them time for voluntary surrender.[17]

Cleveland appointed Henry L. Dawes as the chairman of this commission; hence it was commonly known as the Dawes Commission. Before it reached the Territory, the Creek Council convened for its regular session and adopted strong resolutions declining to surrender the tribal status and expressing confidence that the United States would "prove true to her many pledges and keep perfect faith with our people." The Commissioners arrived soon after and established headquarters at Muskogee. In February an intertribal council was called at Checotah. The Creeks sent their ablest statesmen—men like G. W. Grayson and Pleasant Porter, the aged D. N. McIntosh, and such fullblood leaders as Hotulke Emarthla and Isparhecher. The meeting was dominated by a profound sense of impending disaster. Members of the Commission addressed the delegates without being able to shake their unalterable determination, and a solemn memorial was adopted once more calling on the United States to observe its plighted faith.

The Chief then sent notices to the district judges calling all citizens to Okmulgee on April 3. Two or three thousand men, mostly full bloods, crowded the capitol square, and the Commissioners addressed them from the veranda. The speakers stated that the United States was determined to divide the communal property, abolish the tribal governments, and create a territory; if the Indians would negotiate they might modify the procedure, but if not, Congress would liquidate their institutions without consulting them. The Chief then spoke briefly to the assembly:

"Muskogees, you have heard the talk of the representatives of the United States. ... It has been said by men in high places in the states and at Washington that the full blood Indians are willing to embrace just such propositions as have to-day been made to you, but that they were prevented by the half-breeds and educated fullbloods who were getting the lion's share of the benefits of the country. For this reason

[17] Creek Tribal Records, 30760-63, 30847, 38877; *Indian Journal*, October 27, 1882; July 3, 1890. Commissioner of Indian Affairs, *Annual Reports*, 1887-92.

you will excuse me if on this occasion I shall offer you no advice on the propositions made by the commissioners. ... But before we adjourn this meeting I desire that you, without my advice or that of any of your leading men, to take a vote in their presence upon the propositions as they have been explained to you. This will be necessary to guide your council, which I shall call in extraordinary session tomorrow, in formulating an answer to the honored commissioners."

He then asked all in favor of acceptance to occupy the left of the yard, and all who opposed to step to the right. In the most intense seriousness the entire body moved as one man to the right. The next day the council convened. It adopted a resolution refuting the charges made against the Indians in the interest of territorial and allotment projects, pointing to their educational and economic progress, and expressing again the faith that "the great American people ... will keep their treaties, respect our weakness, render encouragement and strengthen our hand in this supreme effort we are making for the survival of our race."

During the same month a senatorial committee came to the Territory to investigate conditions. They paid no attention to the Indians, but they addressed enthusiastic audiences of white people, commiserating them as "wards of the Indians," and assuring them that "the United States has not forgotten you." Their report to the Senate contained not only distortions of truth but positive misstatements of plain fact. The Dawes Commission also reported to Congress on this and succeeding years and presented a terrible indictment of the Indian regime. The United States had finally determined to break down the autonomy of the Five Tribes and erect a white man's state upon the ruins of the Indian governments; and the Commissioners were the official spokesmen of this policy. It was not enough for them to point out the undoubted fact that a few Indians were occupying a large area of valuable land that would support a greater population of white men, but they felt it necessary to malign the governments they were about to destroy. They enlarged upon the many imperfections of the Indian republics, even throwing in falsehoods for good measure; and they described the full bloods as groaning for deliverance from the economic oppression and political tyranny of the tribal leaders. Their statements naturally were welcomed at the time, but unfortunately they have been accepted uncritically ever since by historians who should have recognized the ex parte character of their presentation.

In the fall of 1894 the Creek Council again declined the propositions of the Dawes Commission. A. P. McKellop and G. W. Grayson represented the tribe at Washington that winter. With the other delegates they formed an organization with a Cherokee as president and McKellop as secretary, held daily meetings, and mapped out every morning the duties of each member. The law enlarging the Indian Territory courts was enacted that winter, and they were not able to defeat a measure providing for a survey of their land. Otherwise they were able to report to the next Council that "this Nation is to-day in the same condition as when a year ago her life was entrusted to our hands." Another council of the Five Tribes held at Eufaula in 1895 reaffirmed the action taken at Checotah and drew up an able defense of the Indian cause.[18]

At the very time the Creeks were engaged in this life and death struggle, their government was more venal than it had ever been before in their history. This condition hardly affected the result, for the policy of the United States was motivated by the desires of the white man rather than the failures of the Indians. It did not even weaken the Creeks' resistence, for their devotion to their own way of life was too deeply fixed to be dependent upon political expediency. It did, however, provide their adversaries with a convenient argument.

The presentation of the war claims had shown the humble citizens the ease of raiding the public treasury, the financial power of the cattlemen had corrupted their officials, but the sale of the Oklahoma land demoralized all classes of the population. As soon as they undertook the negotiation, Porter, Hodge, and Isparhecher found it expedient to revive the unauthorized contract that L. C. Perryman and Efa Emarthla had made with Crawford in 1885. They also entered into an agreement to pay the note given to Perry Fuller for his supposed legal services in 1866. Although the tribe

---

[18] Creek Tribal Records, 29991 ff., 30852-56; *Muskogee Phœnix*, 1893-95; *Indian Journal*, 1893-95; *Acts and Resolutions of the National Council*, 1893-99, 14, 29 f.; Commission to the Five Civilized Tribes, *Annual Reports*, 1894-1904; 53 Cong., 2 sess., *Sen. Rep. No. 377*.

had repudiated this debt, the note had passed into the possession of persons who exerted a strong political influence at Washington and the delegates decided that it was necessary to purchase their favor. The holders were willing to receipt in full for $42,198, one-half the face value of the note. When the Council convened in January to ratify the cession, the delegates made a complete report and the Council formally accepted these obligations. Considering the usual procedure in the allowance of Indian claims at Washington it is probable that the transactions were necessary, but there is little doubt that the consent of the Council was obtained by the bribery of some of the members.

The articles of cession had provided that two million dollars of the purchase price should be retained by the United States to draw 5 per cent interest for the Creeks, and only $280,857.10 in cash was turned over to the delegates. Obviously after Crawford received his 10 per cent fee of $228,085.71 and the holders of the note their forty-odd thousand, only about ten thousand dollars remained to the tribe. The Creeks never parted with an acre of land except through coercion, but when they *were* forced to sell they wanted to spend the money as soon as possible. When they realized that none of it would reach their hands, they began to hold meetings and pass angry resolutions against their officials. The size of the attorney's fee also aroused unfavorable comment in Washington.

Charges were soon circulated to the effect that Crawford had divided his fee with the delegates and other Creek leaders. D. N. McIntosh and other Creeks employed an attorney and attempted to recover the money under a law of Congress requiring Departmental approval of attorneys' contracts. The Chief then attempted to make peace by calling the Council on June 19 to petition the United States for a per capita distribution of the $400,-000 accumulated under the Treaty of 1866. After a violent three days' debate, the House of Warriors censured the delegates for paying the Crawford fee, but the resolution was lost in the House of Kings. A motion to impeach the Chief also failed to carry. The Council then adopted the resolution calling for the per capita distribution and adjourned.

A special investigator was then sent out by the Department, but he made little attempt to find out what had become of the fee. Porter, who had actually handled the money, admitted that he had not paid it to Crawford, "but as per verbal agreement, he directed and authorized me to pay it to others, which I did." He stated that none of the delegates had shared in the distribution, but he declined to name the recipients. Other testimony indicated that several members of the Council had received small bribes, but nothing was actually proved. McIntosh and his associates then instituted proceedings in Judge Parker's court against Crawford, C. W. Turner, and the three delegates. The court found that Secretary of the Interior W. F. Villas had informed Congress of the unapproved contract and had recommended that the matter of compensation be left entirely to the Creeks; and that therefore the act of Congress giving the Creeks full control over the money was in effect a repeal of the usual requirement of Departmental approval of attorneys' contracts. An attempt was made at the regular session of the Council to investigate *"the loss of money arising from the sale of Oklahoma and to recover the same,"* but this measure also failed. It is fairly certain, however, that if the matter had ever been fully investigated it would have brought greater discredit to the Federal government than the Creek.[19]

In 1890 Congress authorized the requested per capita distribution. The traders immediately advanced credit for about half the amount at a profitable discount. The Creeks prepared their census rolls, not without some grumbling at the inflated population of the negro towns. Each share was twenty-nine dollars. The payment was made by special Department agents at Okmulgee from January 22 to March 4, 1891. The quiet village became a humming center of business activity—street stores, patent medicine venders, boarding houses, and tent theaters. The traders who had extended credit were in assiduous attendance. Distant St. Louis felt the wave of prosperity as the traders paid their debts to wholesale houses. Only the Creeks failed to benefit; they neglected their farms and live stock and imperiled their health camping at Okmulgee in the win-

---

[19] Creek Tribal Records, 29968 ff., 32971; Five Tribes Files, No. 30, 1-10; Commissioner of Indian Affairs, *Annual Report*, 1889, 209; *Federal Reporter*, XLVII, 561-71; Indian Office, 1889/4980, 14788, 19376, 21797; United States Archives, Correspondence Land Division, Letter Book 185, 357; Letter Book 188, 326 f.

ter weather, while—to quote Bennett—the money "went through their hands like water through a sieve."[20]

The year before the sale of Oklahoma the Creeks had received $74,678.40 in annuities. The sale added $100,000 to their national income, but their improvident request for this per capita payment cut the amount $20,000. They still had $154,678.40, which should have been adequate for all tribal purposes; and although all their local revenue measures were disappointing, they collected about $6,000 in taxes and $18,000 in pasture rentals during 1895. The Creeks, however, made no attempt to live within their income. The bars had been let down by the Green Peach War claims. Now a negro remembered that he had cared for a Creek refugee family during the Civil War, a full blood had been sent to visit the plains Indians during the 1850's, an Indian woman was destitute because her house had caught fire and burned down. Every imaginable claim was allowed—for a consideration. Tribal warrants rose from twenty-five cents on the dollar to eighty cents in 1889, but from no cause at all except financial mismanagement they declined again to fifty cents in 1895. The Creeks did keep their school income separate and when they wasted it, they wasted it on schools; hence the educational warrants usually sold for seventy-five cents. In 1895 the Supreme Court decided that the practice of issuing preferred warrants was unconstitutional; however, the Council continued to specify that certain appropriations, especially for the running expenses of the government, should take precedence over other obligations. Guesses concerning the amount of the public debt varied from seventy thousand to two hundred thousand dollars.[21]

The articles of cession had provided that fifty thousand dollars of the income from the sale of Oklahoma should be used for education. The Creeks therefore increased the number of day schools to fifty, maintained fifty young people in the "states," and established additional boarding schools. When the building program

[20] Creek Tribal Records, 35411 ff.; Five Tribes Files, No. 30, 217 f.; Indian Office, 1889/L21797, 1890/L32557, 1891/A3804, 1891/A11356, 1892/A1282; Commissioner of Indian Affairs, *Annual Report*, 1890, 101, 251; *Indian Journal*, January 29, 1891; October 27, 1892.
[21] Creek Tribal Records, 33193 ff.

was completed, the nation had seven boarding schools for Indians and three for negroes. For the Indians, Nuyaka, Wetumka, and Wealaka were still in operation; a new school known as Coweta was established in the Coweta District; an orphanage was erected near Okmulgee; a school was built at Eufaula to take the place of Asbury, which had burned down in 1888; and a boarding school for the Euchees was located at Sapulpa. The negroes still had Tullahassee; another small boarding school known as the Pecan Creek Mission was located west of Muskogee; and as the Union agent had rented an office in Muskogee, the nation purchased the stone building on the hill from the United States and used it for a colored orphan asylum.

The new boarding schools were all controlled by the nation, and as soon as arrangements could be made with the mission boards, all the older schools except Nuyaka—which was under a long-term contract with the Presbyterians — passed under tribal management. The superintendents were political appointees, nominated by the Chief and confirmed by the Council; the teachers were selected by the superintendents. The tribal politicians imitated their white contemporaries in their sordid use of patronage, and their schools suffered to a degrading extent. A few superintendents were men of probity and education, but most of them were incompetent. Many were corrupt in their financial administration, and some were guilty of gross immorality. Even at the best their tenure was uncertain. Creek patronage at its worst was found in the colored schools, where corrupt and illiterate superintendents were appointed and removed in bewildering succession at the behest of negro politicians, and one after another was accused of using the school plant as the base of stealing operations or the scene of drunken orgies.[22]

All the officials appointed by the chief or elected by the Council had become patronage appointees; this list included the judges, district attorneys, tax collectors, and all executive officers except the two chiefs. When appointments were to be made, the party in power held a caucus, made out a "slate," and handed it to the chief with

22 *Ibid.*, Schools; Five Tribes Files, No. 30, 85-91, 110, 251.

a courteous request amounting to a command that he "favor them with the Nominations of their choice."[23]

The Creeks were always inclined to substitute for real reform the easy remedy of passing a new law. In addition to the old dissatisfaction with the ambiguous wording of their constitution and the expensive size of their Council, they now decided that their government would be less corrupt if all their officials were made elective. In 1893 in spite of the impending dissolution of the tribe, the Council made provision for a constitutional convention. An election was held in December, and two delegates from each town met at Okmulgee in January and drew up a constitution. It clearly provided for election by plurality and cut the size of the Council from 166 to 94 by reducing the representation in the House of Warriors to one member from each town, but only two additional offices—national auditor and national treasurer—were made elective. The disturbance over the Dawes Commission was reflected in a provision that no treaty to sell or divide the tribal land "shall ever be made," and in the declaration that the Council might "prescribe such regulations for the individual use thereof as it shall deem wise and proper; provided always, that no law or laws shall be enacted individualizing the fee in the soil." The people voted on this document at a special election in June. The Indians favored it by a substantial majority, but it was defeated by the almost unanimous vote of the negroes, who would have lost their influence in the Council by the change in representation. As it was impossible to elect a chief under the strict letter of the old constitution, the Council again declared that a plurality election should stand.[24]

If the proposed constitution had been adopted, it would not have cured the Creeks' financial ills. In 1892 the voters of Wewoka District met in convention and requested the distribution of one million dollars of the Oklahoma money. A bill to that effect was introduced in the Council, but with rare moderation the amount was cut to $600,000. In that time of general financial depression Congress refused to make the appropriation. W. B. Hord, of New York, and C. W. Turner then came forward with a plan to sell this in-

---

[23] See for example Creek Tribal Records, 32992.
[24] *Ibid.*, 25465 ff., 29538 ff., 33115.

terest-bearing debt against the United States to a New York firm
for cash. The Chief called a special session of the Council in January, 1895, at which time the Council authorized the transaction
and provided that Turner and Hord should be paid 3 per cent, or
$18,000, for their services as financial agents. But Congress refused
to recognize the transfer and appropriated $200,000 in cash. With-
out specific authority Samuel Grayson, the national treasurer, then
drew out $6,000 to pay the financial agents, and an additional
$7,300, which he afterwards said was used only to assist some Mus-
kogee traders in making exchange with St. Louis firms. The Chief
called the Council in May to provide for the distribution. As soon
as the bill passed Congress, brisk trading on "head rights" began
in all the stores throughout the nation, and soon $150,000 in credit
stood on the books.[25]

While the Creeks were lightly planning to dissipate their capital,
other persons had laid their plans to secure it. In 1891 Congress gave
the court of claims jurisdiction over all claims for depredations
committed upon United States citizens by Indians, waived the
statute of limitations, and provided that all judgments should be
charged against the tribe. Citizens of Alabama then brought 1,003
claims totaling one and one-half million dollars for damages
alleged to have been done by the Creeks during the Removal difficulties in 1836; and the three owners of trail herds mentioned in
the preceding chapter also seized this opportunity to present their
claims.

The jurisdictional act had provided that the Attorney General of
the United States should defend the Indians, but General Leonard
W. Colby came out from Washington in 1893 and persuaded the
alarmed Creeks to employ him for three years at an annual salary of
four thousand dollars. None of the claims was allowed except one
thousand dollars for a trail herd supposed to have been stampeded
in 1873. When the Creeks realized that they were safe, they began
to regret the employment of Colby. In 1894 after the first year's
salary had been paid they repealed the law creating the contract.
The Chief at Colby's request referred this act to the Supreme Court,
which declared that the Council had no power to revoke this

[25] *Ibid.*, 35448 ff.; *Indian Journal*, February 1, 1895; March 15, 1895.

obligation. Perryman then issued the warrant to pay Colby's salary under the original agreement. He explained his action when he called the Council in January to devise means of securing the per capita payment, but the Council threatened to impeach him and passed a resolution again repudiating the contract, forbidding the payment of Colby's salary, and notifying the Department officials that Colby's employment was not recognized. Perryman signed this resolution, but Treasurer Grayson made a payment on the warrant in February.[26]

The smoldering financial dissatisfaction burst into flame when the Council convened in May. Reports of the payment to Turner and Hord began to circulate, and the people were ready to believe that the entire $200,000 had been lost through embezzlement. Armed bands from different parts of the nation began to collect at Okmulgee, and on the afternoon of May 24 a delegation of the malcontents seized Chief Perryman and Treasurer Grayson, seated them in a drugstore on the square, and addressed accusing speeches to them. The frightened officials promised to return the six thousand dollars and entreated their accusers to present their grievances to the Council, but a crowd quickly assembled and began to abuse them. The House of Kings had not adjourned for the day. A member was sent to quiet the mob. He mounted the fence that enclosed the capitol and began to speak. The crowd gradually turned to listen, and the imperiled officers went to their hotel without molestation. A guard was placed around the building during the night, but all was quiet. The next day Perryman reported his humiliating experience to the Council and asked for protection against its recurrence, but a resolution to create a special police force failed to pass. Perryman then went to his home near Tulsa and remained there during the rest of the session.

Hotulke Emarthla or Edward Bullet, as he came to be called, followed the informal Creek custom of acting as chief during Perryman's absence. He was a sturdy Indian of the old type, who had guided the people of Okchiye Town over the long trail of the

26 United States, *Statutes at Large,* XXVI, 851-54; 25 Cong., 2 sess., *Ex. Doc. No. 127;* Creek Tribal Records, 29030 ff., 29227, 33171, 35607; *Muskogee Phœnix,* November 2, 1893; United States, Court of Claims Records, 716, 1752, 3141, 3584; United States Archives, Depredation Claims, 3373, 3978, 4008, 7079.

Removal, located them in their new home, settled their disputes with wise and simple justice, served them as lawmaker under the old government, and represented them in the House of Kings continuously from the adoption of the constitution of 1867 to his election as second chief. His grave, wrinkled face and his treasured old pipe-tomahawk were familiar throughout the nation, and everywhere he was loved and respected. In native intelligence and integrity he was a greater statesman than some of his educated contemporaries, but he spoke no English and read neither English nor Creek.

Within the next few days the House of Warriors impeached Perryman, and the Council suspended him from office and formally installed Bullet in his place. The charges against Perryman were the issuance of the warrant to Colby, the issuance of the $9,601.80 in warrants for the pasture surveys that should have been paid from rentals, the issuance of $500 in duplicate warrants in favor of Nuyaka Mission, and the issuance of the special commissions to the district attorneys to dispose of the down timber. Grayson also was impeached upon the grounds that he had withdrawn $13,300 from the per capita money, that in 1893 he had exceeded the school appropriations by $13,896.28, and that he had cashed the warrants for the pasture surveys; and Bullet was instructed to warn the Federal officials against honoring his requisitions for tribal funds. The Council also created a special committee, of which E. H. Lerblanche was chairman, to call in and examine all outstanding warrants; and it forbade the cashing of any tribal paper not approved by this committee. The House of Kings then decided to postpone the impeachment trials until the regular session, and the Council adjourned. Bullet immediately suspended Grayson and appointed Napoleon B. Moore as treasurer.

Perryman and Grayson declined to surrender their offices, Bullet asked the Supreme Court for an opinion, and the court ruled that an officer under impeachment might be suspended—the chief by the Council, and other officers by the chief. After this decision was published in the newspapers, Chief Justice W. F. McIntosh prevailed upon the court to rule that the suspension was illegal, but J. H. Land, the court clerk, refused to change the record, and except for the word of the chief justice the first decision stood. There is no doubt that the traders hoped to retain Grayson as treasurer. It was generally understood that he planned to pay the per capita money directly to those who had extended credit to the Indians, and that Moore would pay it to the citizens, allowing each to settle his own obligations. Agent Wisdom was determined to uphold the suspended officials; he sent a copy of the second Supreme Court ruling to the Department and recommended that the money be paid to Grayson, and he warned Bullet that any seizure of Grayson's books might be interpreted as "domestic strife" calling for Federal intervention.

In this crisis Bullet convened the Council for further instructions. Turner—who was hardly a disinterested spectator—then sent an urgent telegram to the Department: "Please have Grayson sustained. His bond is good all merchants want him to make payment. This fuss is groundless politics answer." Thomas W. Perryman, the Chief's brother, was president of the House of Kings, and Ellis B. Childers, a strong Perryman supporter, was speaker of the House of Warriors. Neither recognized Bullet's call, but enough members of the Council responded to constitute a quorum. Quoting the only Supreme Court decision on the record, they reaffirmed the suspension of Perryman and requested the United States to recognize the new officers.

Wisdom then called Perryman and Bullet to his office for a conference. Bullet declined the invitation, but Perryman and his advisers came and arranged matters to their complete satisfaction. Wisdom informed the Department that Bullet, "an old Ignorant full-blood Indian," was in "rebellion to the constituted authorities of his own Nation" and again urged that the money be turned over to Grayson without delay. But the Federal treasury officials remained unmoved, and the traders soon capitulated. They were convinced of Moore's personal integrity, they never found it too difficult to collect from individual Indians, and they had already waited too long for their money.

Early in September Grayson was induced to resign, Perryman was persuaded to appoint Moore to fill the vacancy, and Grayson agreed to produce the $13,300 in time for the distribution. The

Federal treasury then released the money, and Moore began the payment at Okmulgee the same month. The May Council had taken special precautions in preparing the rolls. A committee of eighteen had gone over the list from each town and removed a few names found to be fraudulent; and a citizenship commission had been created "to sit as a high court" with power to summon witnesses, take testimony, and make final decisions in disputed cases. But the new roll was not materially different from that used four years before except that it contained the names of two hundred more negroes.

Perryman and Bullet still exercised their rival authority as chief. Each attempted to control the courts, and in some districts law enforcement ceased entirely. Bullet had possession of the tribal seal and the executive office and archives, but Perryman from his home at Tulsa continued to issue warrants duplicating those issued by his rival. When the regular Council convened, Bullet transmitted messages, approved bills, made nominations, etc., as the constitutional executive.

The Council began a systematic house-cleaning. It undertook to purge the Supreme Court for its equivocal action in the chieftainship controversy. McIntosh and another justice hastily resigned and a third was suspended; their places were filled by Bullet supporters. In a preliminary report Lerblance stated that his committee had approved warrants amounting to $180,527 issued before Perryman's suspension, had discovered fifteen hundred warrants for which no appropriation existed, and had found $3,577 and $700 respectively drawn against the 1894 appropriations for the modest salaries of Perryman and his secretary. It was his opinion that many fraudulent warrants were in circulation that had not been presented to the committee. Grayson was convicted by the House of Kings on October 16, and Moore was formally elected to serve for the remainder of the term. National Auditor Palmer had also been impeached and suspended from office at some time during the proceedings, but the disposition of his case is uncertain. Perryman was convicted by the House of Kings November 25, and Bullet served the remaining nine days of his term with no possible question concerning his constitutional authority.

There is no doubt that Perryman and Grayson were "guilty as charged," but whether they were actually corrupt is more difficult to discover. Grayson's use of the $13,300 was irregular, but not necessarily dishonest, and he had no difficulty in recovering it upon the request of the nation. His other offenses consisted in carrying out the Chief's orders. As for the Chief, it was not proved that he had benefited from the manipulated timber sales or had known that duplicate warrants had been issued in his name, and his other acts were in keeping with the informal character of the Creek administration. It is certain, however, that he had taken no aggressive steps to check the vast corruption that went on during his term.

The Creeks' financial troubles went deeper than the possible misconduct of one or two officials. They had reached an unfortunate stage in their educational development. Few of their officials were able to add a column of figures, and accurate bookkeeping was beyond their capacity; and it was still a common practice for clerks and secretaries to affix the names of the illiterate to important documents without the formality of consulting them. In earlier times they had managed the tribal finances with a careless approximation to correct accounting and possibly a few innocent favors to an inner circle, and the general public had not even understood how to take advantage of their incapacity. Now the whole population had become literate enough to tamper with the tribal paper, but not literate enough to correct abuses. Perryman, however, was well educated and able, and his failure to undertake thoroughgoing financial reform is as serious a blot upon his administration as the suspicion that he may have participated in the general corruption.

The events culminating in the impeachment of the officials had aroused the Creeks against official peculation but had not cured them of the demoralizing practices that invited it. During the same fall the Council upon the advice of Bullet voted to ask the United States for $400,000, of which $100,000 should be applied to the public debt and the remainder distributed per capita; but the regular delegates were authorized to act as financial agents without additional compensation. The last day of Bullet's term an appropriation of $2,300 was made to compensate Mrs. Timothy Barnett for damages done to the house and orchard when her husband was killed in 1873. This act was a fitting close to the waste and mismanagement of the Perryman era. There was no prospect that the incoming administration would be characterized by more intelligent financial discipline.[27]

27 *Acts and Resolutions of the Creek National Council, 1895,* 3-19; Creek Tribal Records, 33175 ff., 33290, 33382, 35474 ff., 39352 ff.; Five Tribes Files, No. 30, 178; No. 34. Indian Office, 1895/L22264, F24541, L28873, F29767, F31671, F32247, F33219, L41384, L41631; *Muskogee Phœnix,* 1895; *Indian Journal,* 1895.

CHAPTER 11

The End of the Tribe

THE political campaign of 1895 was conducted during the stirring events that attended Perryman's impeachment. Six tickets were in the field. The Union Party was disrupted by the impeachment controversy. Its official nominees were Ellis B. Childers and David Anderson, but Thomas W. Perryman and John R. Goat, a full blood of Wewoka District, received the support of a considerable faction. Pleasant Porter and Oche Harjo were the candidates of a third party that drew much of its strength from the old Union following. Isparhecher, as always, was the candidate of the full bloods, and Roley McIntosh, an able but uneducated conservative probably unrelated to the famous McIntosh family, was nominated for second chief. The other candidates were not important.

In spite of the political disturbance the campaign was conducted amicably. The colored towns supported Childers and Anderson, but for once their influence was negligible. Every one of the parties opposed any surrender to the Dawes Commission, but the Indians felt instinctively that Isparhecher and McIntosh would be the most uncompromising in their resistance. Even with six parties in the field these candidates received 1,043 and 1,047 votes out of a total 2,454—almost twice as many as Childers and Anderson, their nearest opponents. Their platform pledged them to oppose allotment, remove the pastures so far as it could be done lawfully, prevent the introduction of cattle, resist land monopoly, repeal the permit law and request the removal of all non-citizens, and encourage education and economic development.[1]

Isparhecher possessed native statesmanship of a high order, and so far as he could he directed his own administration. But the problems of his office were too complex for an illiterate full blood who

[1] Creek Tribal Records, 29586 ff.; *Muskogee Phœnix*, 1895; *Indian Journal*, 1895.

spoke only the Creek language; he had to depend upon other men for many details, and some of his official acts were performed without his knowledge. His old friend, S. B. Callahan, served part of the time as his secretary, but Daniel C. Watson also held that office. He suffered a paralytic stroke and was ill during most of 1896, and McIntosh, with the secretarial assistance of his gifted daughter, Mildred, was the real head of the government; but Isparhecher returned to his duties as soon as he was able. His relationship with his advisers is illustrated by a letter written by G. W. Grayson to Watson in 1898. Grayson enclosed a copy of a communication he had sent in the Chief's name to the Commissioner of Indian Affairs, "which is about all the old man can well say on the subject"; and he submitted the draft of an important letter to the executives of the other four tribes, directing Watson to "interpret it to him very fully and let him see if it suits him."[2]

The patronage evil continued unabated during Isparhecher's term of office. As soon as the Council convened in October at the close of Bullet's administration, separate conventions of "the political friend[s] of Esparhechee" and "the friends of Ellis B. Childers" met on successive evenings in the hall of the House of Warriors. After some friendly jockeying they voted to meet as one group, "each faction agreeing to support the other" in dispensing patronage. They made out a "slate," and their nominations went through the Council with oiled smoothness. One result of this alliance was the appointment of Childers, the most ardent of all Perryman's supporters, to succeed Moore as national treasurer.[3]

The new administration tried to carry out its pledge to rid the country of white men. Isparhecher called a special session of the Council immediately after the brief inaugural meeting and a number of laws were passed in accordance with this policy. Congress, however, gradually undermined the tribal authority; the Federal courts were uncertain; and it was evident by this time that the Indian Office not only tolerated but encouraged white immigration in order to reinforce the arguments of the Dawes Commission. The Council raised the ad valorem tax on traders to one per cent

2 Creek Tribal Records, 30099.
3 *Ibid.*, 33240 ff.; *Muskogee Phœnix*, October 10, 1895.

and imposed an additional tax of fifty dollars a year. The fixed charge was designed to discourage persons who secured traders' licenses with no intention of introducing goods, in order to deal in Muskogee real estate, raise live stock, cut hay, etc.; but Wisdom with the approval of the Indian Office vetoed this portion of the law. Early in 1896 Isparhecher employed a white attorney to prosecute two notorious white intruders in the Federal courts, and when one attempted to secure a traders' license Wisdom refused to grant it. There were three trials, two before the United States Commissioner at Eufaula and one before the court at Muskogee. There was no possible doubt of their guilt, and both the commissioner and the judge instructed the juries very clearly; but the first trial resulted in a hung jury, the second brought a conviction and a fine of only fifty dollars, and when the intruders appealed to the court at Muskogee there was another hung jury. The Creeks then paid their attorney and abandoned the attempt to seek redress in the courts. The bias of the white men who served as jurors was only too apparent.

The same Council directed the district inspectors to make a list of intruders, appropriating three thousand dollars to be expended by the Chief in securing their removal. The Indian Office had long protested that it had no funds to pay the expenses of the Indian police in expelling them, and the Creeks hoped by paying the expense themselves to obviate this difficulty. Isparhecher submitted the list and the money to Wisdom, but the agent in view of the policy of his superiors hesitated to act. Isparhecher then made a trip to Washington and later sent the second chief in an attempt to persuade the Commissioner to use the money, but after several months of deliberation the Federal officials decided that the intruders were probably citizenship claimants who should not be disturbed. The discouraged Chief reported to the next Council that he had used $880 of the appropriation without effecting the expulsion of a single intruder.

The Council of 1896 then repealed the permit law and provided that any Creek employing a non-citizen laborer after December 31 should be subject to fine or whipping. For once the "progressive" citizens were alarmed, for it was known that Isparhecher had every intention of carrying the law into effect. They had a meeting at Eufaula and decided to obstruct its operation. In December, according to newspaper accounts, they obtained a Supreme Court decision setting it aside. The Council itself with characteristic oversight had elected inspectors for all the districts that same fall, and they continued to collect the tax. But the most serious opposition came from the Indian Office. Acting Commissioner Thomas P. Smith directed Wisdom to inform the Creeks that the law was regarded as "an improvident piece of legislation," and although he evaded a direct question it was apparent that he intended to block its enforcement.[4]

A severe blow was given to Creek jurisdiction at this time by the creation of foreign municipal governments within the nation. All classes of non-citizens in the ambitious little towns on the railroads welcomed the opportunity to incorporate. Some of them wanted waterworks and lighting systems, all of them needed schools, and they were eager to fill up the hog wallows and remove the dead animals from their principal streets. Their transactions in occupancy titles are evidence of a vigorous, illegal growth impossible to confine. Long before the creation of the Dawes Commission it was apparent that speculators were purchasing town lots in order to establish a claim that might be validated in case of allotment; and legal residents who really needed a place to live and conduct their business would have been glad for a less precarious title to Creek real estate.

In the fall of 1895 Judge William M. Springer, of the Northern District, ruled that Indian Territory towns had a right to establish municipal governments under sections of the Arkansas statutes placed in effect by the court act of 1890. The vociferous colony of "boosters" that made up the population of Wagoner took immediate action. On January 4 they presented to Judge Springer a petition signed by 229 persons, of which two were Creek citizens, 46 were licensed as traders, and most of the remainder were white and Cherokee intruders. Isparhecher in alarm called a mass meeting of leading citizens. They drew up a petition to the court quoting

[4] Creek Tribal Records, 25810-13, 26114, 29171, 31077-79, 31481-83, 33353, 39263-75; Indian Office, 1895/L7024, 1896/30161; United States Archives, Correspondence Land Division, Letter Book 337, 439; *Muskogee Phœnix,* December 19, 1895; March 5, 1896; October 8, 1896; December 10, 1896; February 4, 1897.

portions of the treaties and the Intercourse Laws, and showing that Congress had expressly limited the application of the Arkansas statutes to matters not inconsistent with these provisions; and they advised the Chief to employ an attorney and carry their case if necessary to the United States Supreme Court. Isparhecher did employ an attorney, but Springer overruled his objections and granted the charter.

The people of Wagoner held their election and established their government in April. The Creeks then appealed to the territorial court of appeals, but the contract with their attorney expired and the case was dismissed upon the motion of the attorney for the town. They tried to revive it again in 1897, but apparently they dropped the contest. By that time the end of their government was in sight, and a victory in the courts would have had only a temporary effect.

Speculators flocked to Wagoner with the announced intention of making it the capital of a new state to be created by white men upon the ruins of the Indian governments. They tried to purchase the townsite from the Creeks, but their offer was not even considered. W. J. Watts, the most persistent of all Cherokee citizenship claimants, then "bought" forty acres of raw land within the incorporated limits from a trading firm, which of course had no right to own Creek land, and thirty-five acres from an intermarried white man, whose claim was equally fraudulent; and he proceeded to lay out an addition and sell town lots. William Robison, exercising his rights as a Creek citizen, then put a fence around the tract and began to improve it as a "farm"; but the mayor upon the request of Watts had Robison's fence removed. Robison then appealed to Wisdom.

The Federal officials were indifferent toward gradual white penetration, but apparently they feared the scandal that might result from townsite speculations. Wisdom reported that Watts was an intruder and that he and his surveyor were liable to a fine of one thousand dollars for trespass upon Creek land; and the Commissioner directed Wisdom to remove him immediately and to request the United States district attorney to proceed against him under the Intercourse Acts. Watts was genuinely alarmed, but he managed to persuade the Commissioner to delay action until his dispute with

Robison could be settled by the court. In 1898 Judge Springer ruled against him, and one of the chief objects of incorporation was thereby defeated .

Meanwhile another townsite scheme had developed on a new railroad built from the Choctaw Nation to Oklahoma across the southwestern corner of the Creek country. In 1896 at the station of Holdenville a white promoter secured a power of attorney from several Creek citizens, induced them to lay out claims on the townsite, and sold lots in their names. The St. Louis and San Francisco next started building beyond Sapulpa to Oklahoma, and an intermarried white man laid out a townsite at one of the stations. Indignant citizens notified Isparhecher of these speculations in Creek land, but the discouraged old Chief apparently took no action. The purchasers of the lots, of course, expected to realize fantastic profits when the country should be opened to the white man's enterprise. In 1896 a recently organized Board of Trade in Muskogee tried to purchase that townsite from the Creeks, but there was no possibility of inducing them to sell, and the old system of occupancy titles continued. The town was incorporated under the doubtful authority of the Arkansas statute in 1898. It began immediately to assess taxes on personal property for civic purposes, and the following fall its first public school opened with 253 pupils. The substantial white residents of the railroad towns had indeed suffered many inconveniences, but it was impossible to separate legitimate development from feverish speculation in Creek land.[5]

A parallel procedure was the acquisition of Creek agricultural land through illegal, long-term leases. The practice became serious in 1895 during the disorganization of the courts at the time of the chieftainship controversy, and within a few months it had reached alarming proportions. Unlike previous white infiltrations this invasion reached the fullblood section, for it came mainly from the west across the Oklahoma boundary. In the fall of 1895 Ben McIntosh, the permit inspector of Okmulgee District, estimated that in this

[5] Creek Tribal Records, Townsites, also 39262; Indian Office, 1893/L4933, L9749; 1897/40455. United States Archives, Correspondence Land Division, Letter Book 361, 483-85; Letter Book 364, 68-72; *Muskogee Phœnix,* November 3, 1894; October 3, 1895; February 27, 1896; April 30, 1896; September 30, 1897; March 31, 1898; June 2, 1898; September 29, 1898.

one district there were five hundred of these so-called "labor contracts" running from three to twenty years and involving tracts of land from forty to one thousand acres in extent. White farmers, he said, were in complete possession of a strip three or four miles wide on the Creek side of the Oklahoma boundary, and it was reported that one white man, formerly intermarried, had given twenty-seven of these land leases along the Cimarron.

The Creeks took action against their own citizens who gave the leases, and a number of convictions were obtained in the tribal courts. The lessees then tried to hold the land through Federal court action, but in 1897 the territorial court of appeals ruled that a lease made in violation of tribal law was void, and that the Indian lessor could recover the farm at the expiration of the one-year legal period. The Creeks then made a careful census in 1897 and 1898 listing thousands of white people living on farms under such contracts; however, their own officers were forbidden to touch the improvements, and the Federal officials used every possible excuse to delay action until they finally decided that with the approaching allotment the problem would magically disappear. But like the town-lot speculators the holders of "labor contracts" looked forward with confidence to the destruction of the Indian title and the recognition of their "claims" by a sympathetic government.[6]

Other undeveloped tribal resources offered an increasing attraction to white men. The Creeks had long known that they possessed valuable coal deposits. Ward Coachman had been the first to recommend the development of the mines as a revenue measure, and under his influence a law was passed in 1878 requiring citizens to pay royalty on all coal offered for sale. In 1881 provision was made for the admission of non-citizen capitalists in the formation of mining corporations. The most important mining laws were passed in 1885 and 1887 through the influence of J. M. Perryman; and under these acts, leases covering most of the Creek country were given to corporations of wealthy Creeks and outside capitalists. But the development of the actual mining was disappointingly slow, and the revenue from royalty never became important.

[6] Creek Tribal Records, 28574 ff., 31083 ff., 31477, 33541, 38877; Indian Office, 1897/L29737, 1898/L24583, L44756; *Muskogee Phœnix*, January 28, 1897.

In 1894 the mining laws were extended to include petroleum production, and several Chicago capitalists became deeply interested. They secured leases and began to drill in Muskogee and Eufaula in 1896. A showing of oil was reported, but no profitable development occurred during the tribal period. It was perhaps as well for the Creeks that nobody discovered that they owned one of the great potential oil fields of the world. They were still unable to protect their timber, and the lumbering operations continued unchecked throughout Isparhecher's administration.[7]

Isparhecher was equally unsuccessful in restraining the cattlemen. He was supported by overwhelming fullblood sentiment and by the substantial mixed-blood leaders, but his efforts were powerless against the adroit evasions of negro citizens and a small group of mixed bloods who were not truly identified with the tribe. When his lighthorse cut illegal fences, they were haled before the Federal courts and indicted for "malicious mischief." When he appealed to the Indian Office, he was requested to compile statistics pending an "investigation" that invariably lasted through the grazing season. In spite of all his efforts, it was generally estimated that the importation of cattle in 1898 was the greatest in Creek history. By this time the tribal authority had been broken down by act of Congress, but the doughty old Chief borrowed money on his personal note, employed a firm of white attorneys, and instituted suits upon his own responsibility in the Federal court against a large number of foreign cattlemen. He won the first of these suits, and a fine of $1,500 was imposed against one of these intruders for the introduction of 1,500 cattle. The cattleman appealed, but Isparhecher won again in the fall of 1901. The old man died the next year, and it is probable that the remaining cases were never carried to a final decision. By this time the tribal estate was in process of liquidation, and the whole matter came under Federal control.[8]

One after another the tribal defenses were undermined by act of Congress. The land was surveyed under the law of 1895. The

[7] Creek Tribal Records, 29078, 32318 ff., 35069, 35667, 35994 ff., 36001; Five Tribes Files, No. 11, 42-45, 198; No. 28, 119-26, 238. Indian Office, 1890/L25836, 1897/L32569; *Indian Journal,* December 13, 1883; *Muskogee Phœnix,* 1895-97.

[8] Creek Tribal Records, 35058 ff., 39276; Indian Office, 1898/L10136, 1899/L17514, L19334-35, L19802, L54579; *Muskogee Phœnix,* 1895-98; August 23, 1900. *Federal Reporter,* CXV, 1019.

Creeks watched the work with fear and dread; no white man ever fathomed their mystical love of the soil that made them regard its division into metes and bounds with a horror of dismemberment. In 1896 Congress directed the Dawes Commission to make rolls of the tribes, and gave rejected applicants for citizenship the right of appeal to the Federal courts. Drastic bills were introduced during that session, and only the knowledge that the Choctaw resistance was breaking saved the tribes from annihilation. Pleasant Porter came at this time to believe that the battle was lost, and he began to advise his people to treat with the Dawes Commission. Isparhecher called an intertribal council, which met at Eufaula in July, and for the first time recommended negotiation. The next month he called the Creek Council in special session. The delegates explained the narrow margin of their escape during the preceding session of Congress and advised the Council to make the best possible terms before it should be too late. The Council did create a delegation of five to meet the Dawes Commission, but instructed them to refuse all proposals.

The Dawes Commission had already notified Isparhecher of its new duty to prepare a roll of the tribe. The Chief now advised the Council to take a systematic census. The old method of preparing rolls by towns, he said, had worked well except with the negro towns, and he advised the creation of a special commission to take a census of the colored citizens. The next day the Supreme Court decided in response to an inquiry by the Chief that the Council had a right to *recognize* any person entitled to citizenship by Creek blood or adoption under the treaty, but that it had no power to *grant* citizenship to other persons. This ruling would have struck nearly three thousand names from the rolls—the names of all negroes adopted at various times by the Council or included by the connivance of the colored-town chiefs.

The Creeks were not strong enough for a contest with three thousand people, who would have had all the tenacity and resources of other intruders and the almost certain support of the Federal government. The Council took no action except to increase the authority of the citizenship court created at the time of Perryman's impeachment. This court struck a few names from the rolls, but it confined its work mainly to passing upon applicants. It admitted 79 negroes and 156 persons of Indian descent, and rejected 202 colored, and 99 Indian, claimants.

As soon as Congress had authorized the Dawes Commission to make the rolls, people from distant states had flocked to the Territory hoping to share in the impending division of the tribal property. The Creeks employed an attorney to contest their claims, and of 1,356 applicants (210 negroes, 10 intermarried whites, and 1,136 persons claiming Indian blood) only 255 were enrolled by the Commission. The unsuccessful claimants then appealed to the court, and seventy more were admitted by Judge Springer. While these aliens were clamoring for admission, the real Indians used obstructive tactics to protect their names from the white man's inquisitiveness , and in 1898 the Dawes Commission was forced to resort to a court order to obtain possession of the tribal rolls.

The final list of citizens compiled by the Commission was even more generous to the negroes than the tribal policy. It cannot be cited as a census, for it contains several overlapping rolls of newborn infants, but it shows that the negroes comprised 37 per cent of the citizenship. One has only to talk with a few present-day "Creek freedmen" to discover that many were admitted whose ancestors had never lived in the Creek country. The Creeks, of course, had invited this result by the laxity of their own policy. Characteristically they had offered an asylum to a deeply wronged people, and only a few of their Southern leaders had foreseen the oblique but constant aggressiveness of this humble and pliant race. The full bloods discovered their mistake in the 1890's, when it was too late to correct it. The negro influence within their tribe had been second only to the encroachments of the white man in the destruction of their nationality.

In the fall of 1896 the Council, after careful and solemn consideration, created a commission to negotiate with the Dawes Commission. Porter served as chairman and both mixed bloods and full bloods were among the members. In November upon the invitation of Green McCurtain, chief of the Choctaws, they attended a meeting of the Five Tribes at South McAlester and assisted in formulating a policy of financial indemnity and limitations upon future statehood to be accepted by the United States as the basis of negotiations.

In December they made overtures to the Dawes Commission in accordance with this policy, but the Commissioners, regarding their demands as excessive, curtly refused to treat and threatened them with the power of Congress. The same month the compliant Choctaws reached the first agreement made by any tribe with the Dawes Commission. Through an interpreter a *Phœnix* reporter questioned Isparhecher about his intentions. " 'The Savior of Mankind,' said the Chief, 'brought peace and good will to the people on earth and set up the golden rule and the Creeks, though often oppressed and banished in the years past, were still hopeful and believed that eternal right would at last prevail. On these lines they (the Creeks) expect to continue the fight.' " But that year Congress placed them under the jurisdiction of the Federal courts and provided that all tribal legislation except resolutions for adjournment and acts relating to negotiations with the Dawes Commission should be subject to presidential approval. These measures were to go into effect January 1, 1898.

The Creeks felt their defenses falling. The mixed bloods were divided: some were in favor of continuing the negotiations, while others believed that they should resist the acts of Congress and thus test the validity of their treaties in the United States Supreme Court. The full bloods, like the old Chief, were inclined to refuse everything and put their trust in abstractions. But the Chief and the special commission held a number of informal conferences with the Dawes Commission and reported their work freely to a mass meeting at Okmulgee.

The Chief then issued a call for a special session of the Council to meet August 24, and he requested the members to convene their respective towns and "take a vote by name" to determine the sentiment of the people in the impending crisis. At this informal election the voters, both Indian and negro, expressed themselves almost unanimously against further negotiations. By this time the Chief in conference with his mixed-blood advisers had decided upon a vigorous policy of resistance. When the legislators assembled with their fresh popular mandate, he advised them to abolish the authority of the special commission and employ competent counsel to fight for the integrity of their treaties in the Federal courts. But the Council voted to continue the negotiations, and when the Chief vetoed the act it was passed over his veto.

The next month the commission drew up an agreement with the Dawes Commission. It was true to the tragic history of the Creeks, for it was the worst agreement negotiated with any of the tribes; the townsites were to be sold for the benefit of the lot speculators, the tribal government was shorn of every possible power of defense, and the land was to be divided without protection of any kind for the allottees. The Chief submitted it to the regular session of the Council and advised rejection. The Creeks had tried allotment in Alabama and Georgia, he said, and had found it disastrous. The whole agitation for change was due to the "yelping" of the "boomers," and if the tribe would accept allotment "these will be the people that will first throng this country to scheme us out of our homes." He still urged the Council to challenge the power of Congress to abrogate the treaties, and he favored a plan for the tribes to forestall statehood by a voluntary union.

Meanwhile a delegation of fullblood Cherokees came to Okmulgee and with much smoking and oratory entered into a council with the fullblood Creeks. A member of the Dawes Commission addressed a tactful and conciliatory speech to this gathering, but he was unable to make any impression. Strengthened by this influence, the Creek Council rejected the proposed agreement by an almost unanimous vote. It declined, however, to take action upon the two proposals urged by the Chief. He called another session in November and pointed out that only thirty-nine days of tribal independence remained, but his advice was again rejected. The conservatives feared to invoke the unknown power of the United States Supreme Court and they shrank from the unpredictable results of voluntary statehood; they read their treaties and found them good, and decided that they were safe under the old guarantees.

In January the Council was finally persuaded to appropriate twenty thousand dollars to test the constitutionality of the act abolishing the jurisdiction of their courts, and President McKinley immediately vetoed the bill. From this time on, their hands were tied.

But this condition hardly affected the result; the Supreme Court would no doubt have upheld the legal right of Congress to repeal their treaties, and the Chief's Indian statehood project would never have received the necessary Federal sanction. The long dreaded blow fell that year, when Congress passed the so-called Curtis Act. This law provided for the allotment of their land and the sale of their townsites, and placed their financial administration, and incidentally their schools, under the control of the Secretary of the Interior. Their tribal affairs were liquidated by the Dawes Commission partly under these provisions and partly under special agreements subsequently made with the tribe. Every citizen received one hundred and sixty acres as his share of the tribal land, and these allotments were protected to a limited extent against alienation. The contingent grants to the railroads were never validated, the intruders who had fastened themselves upon the agricultural land received no legal acknowledgment, and the mineral leases were canceled, but in the main the speculators in town lots obtained recognitition of their claims.[9]

The tribal finances were close to chaos when the Federal government took charge. The Council with the approval of the chiefs—both Isparhecher and McIntosh—had continued its efforts to obtain and dissipate four hundred thousand dollars of the nation's invested funds. No attempt was made to keep expenditures within the tribal income. As the Council continued to allow claims for a cow killed in the Isparhecher War or to compensate a negro thief who had received one hundred lashes for the second offense when he was entitled to only fifty for the fourth, the national debt mounted to unknown figures. The taxes brought in very little revenue; Treasurer Childers reported in 1896 that only $13,130.05 had been collected from the pasture tax, $726.64 from permits, $1,962.30 from licensed traders, and $782.58 in coal royalties. He had been able to pay only twelve cents on the general warrants and forty-six cents on the school warrants presented at the time he received the regular remittance from the United States. Traders customarily doubled

[9] Creek Tribal Records, 29607 ff., 30028 ff., 33432, 35632; *Muskogee Phœnix*, 1895-98; Commission to the Five Civilized Tribes, *Annual Reports;* Commissioner of Indian Affairs, *Annual Report*, 1919, II, 342; WPA Project S-149.

the price of school supplies and other materials furnished the nation to protect themselves against probable loss.

It was known that fraudulent warrants not presented to the auditing committee in 1895 were in circulation, and that court scrip had been raised in amount or forged outright. The Council therefore, upon the advice of Acting Chief McIntosh, created a warrant committee to call in all warrants, stamp the fraudulent ones as void, and report the valid ones for reissuance in convenient large denominations on a better quality of paper. Three mixed bloods, Charles Gibson, James H. Crabtree, and G. W. Stidham, son of the elder G. W. Stidham, served as members of this committee. They carried on their work at Eufaula during 1897. It was reported at the time that they could be persuaded to approve warrants for a consideration, but the tribal authorities made no serious attempt to investigate. That spring Congress made the long requested appropriation of Creek money; it was provided that $333,-000 should be drawn out, not for a per capita distribution, but to be paid out under the direction of the Secretary of the Interior to defray the public debt. In the meantime the Superintendent of Public Instruction had been forced to shut down all the boarding schools but the orphan asylums because of the shortage of funds.

By September warrants amounting to $352,246.16 had been approved by the committee and reissued by Isparhecher through Secretary Callahan, and a tabulated list had been furnished to Agent Wisdom. A number of prominent Creeks, including George B. Perryman and David M. Hodge, then notified the Department that some of these warrants were believed to be fraudulent and asked that the payment be delayed until the meeting of the Council. The Indian Office accordingly sent inspectors to make an investigation. Upon information furnished by these special agents Isparhecher then removed Childers from office, charging a shortage of $23,637.73 in his current accounts and irregularities in the reissuance of the warrants; and he appointed the ever dependable Napoleon B. Moore to take his place. When he reported this action to the Council, the House of Warriors sustained Childers and impeached *him* instead, but through some inadvertence the House of Kings adjourned without acting upon a resolution to suspend him.

The inspectors had already rejected warrants passed by the committee to the amount of $92,000 and prepared to present their findings to a Federal grand jury to show that Childers, the members of the committee, and several holders of tribal paper had conspired to defraud the Creek Nation. Apparently the Council abandoned its championship of Childers at the special session in January, for Moore served from that time on as treasurer. During the next two months Wisdom cashed the $260,000 in warrants pronounced genuine by the inspectors.

The conspiracy trials began at Wagoner the following November. Crabtree had died, and the government dismissed its case against Stidham in order to use him as a witness. The defendants demanded separate trials and chose Gibson first. The government then dismissed the case against Gibson. Childers was chosen next. After a trial that aroused great excitement throughout the nation, he was convicted and sentenced to serve two years in the penitentiary. Three white defendants then confessed; two received five-year sentences, and the other was sentenced to one day in jail and a fine of five hundred dollars. Two more white men who had handled the fraudulent warrants were tried, but the government failed to prove that they had guilty knowledge of the transactions. Callahan pleaded guilty to a technical violation of the law in signing the warrants reissued according to the findings of the committee, but the district attorney exonerated him of criminal intent. This was the end of the famous warrant cases. It was a climax to the sordid financial history of the Creeks during these latter years that their tribal life ended in scandal and that they were extricated from their difficulties by the unfriendly hand of the United States.[10]

The Creeks secured one concession from the Federal government for the surrender of their tribal institutions. The Loyal Creeks had never abandoned the hope of obtaining the award made by the Federal commission under the Treaty of 1866. For a number of years Hodge had been their official agent, but all the delegates were instructed to push their claim. They finally secured authority

[10] Creek Tribal Records, 30024 ff., 33371 ff., 36955, 38703, 39380, 39421 ff.; Five Tribes Files, No. 12, 147; *Acts and Resolutions of the National Council, 1893-99*, 61 ff.; Indian Office, 1897/F39429; *Muskogee Phœnix*, 1896-98; November 16, 1899; June 7, 1900; September 27, 1900; September 19, 1901.

to carry it to the court of claims, but they lost their case in 1884. Now they obtained a provision in one of their agreements with the Dawes Commission to refer it to the United States Senate for arbitration. The Senate awarded them $1,200,000, but the House of Representatives cut the appropriation to $600,000 and it passed Congress in that form. An Arkansas attorney received 10 per cent and Hodge was paid 5 per cent according to the provisions of the appropriation act; and the remainder was prorated to the claimants and their heirs.[11]

In 1899 Pleasant Porter was elected to succeed Isparhecher upon a platform of compromise with the Dawes Commission; and he was reëlected to a second term in 1903. Able in the white man's law and diplomacy but with an appreciation of the Indian spirit that no white man ever possessed, he was the greatest chief of the constitutional period. With the tribal government shorn of most of its powers, it became his duty to obtain the best possible terms for his people and to guide them into the untried path of individual land-holding and United States citizenship. Most of the transition took place during his administration, and he died just before the Creeks with their white and Indian neighbors became citizens of the new state of Oklahoma.

It was a sad and disillusioning experience, for as the white people rushed in to build the towns and develop the oil pools and purchase the farms, the fullblood Creeks were wholly unable to adjust themselves to the new order. Under a great native statesman named Chitto (Snake) Harjo, of Hickory Ground, they quietly withdrew from the hated complications of the Curtis Act, the Dawes Commission, deeds and land titles, and mixed-blood leadership and attempted to set up a separate government based upon their ancient treaties, with their own lighthorse carrying out their decrees against unwelcome white men and apostate Creeks; and they interfered so seriously with the functioning of Federal law that it was necessary to arrest their leaders and bring them to trial and place them under suspended sentences to Federal prisons.

Porter knew the limitations of his people too well to hope that

[11] Creek Tribal Records, 35677; *Indian Journal*, August 7, 1884; *United States Court of Claims Reports*, LXXVIII, 502 f.

they would soon become contented members of the white man's society. He told a Senate committee in 1906, "It is not so much a question of capacity as it is of time. ... You are the evolution of thousands of years, and we the evolution of thousands of years, perhaps ... Who can say but that we would finally have reached a stage of civilization, toward which we were progressing slowly, but none the less surely, which would have suited our life better than the civilization which has been so violently and suddenly thrust upon us." But in his more philosophic moments he tried to look beyond the darkness and despair of crumbling institutions to the place of his people upon the scroll of history. One of his messages to the Council may be taken as the valedictory of a people strong and confident in its native environment, steadfast and unchanging in misfortune, but unable to acquire the skills of the counting house or the will to push and crowd.

"The vitality of our race still persists. We have not lived for naught. We are the original discoverers of this continent, and the conquerors of it from the animal kingdom, and on it first taught the arts of peace and war, and first planted the institutions of virtue, truth and liberty. The European Nations found us here and were made aware that it was possible for men to exist and subsist here. We have given to the European people on this continent our thought forces—the best blood of our ancestors having intermingled with [that of] their best statesmen and leading citizens. We have made ourselves an indestructible element in their national history. We have shown that what they believed were arid and desert places were habitable and capable of sustaining millions of people. We have led the vanguard of civilization in our conflicts with them for tribal existence from ocean to ocean. The race that has rendered this service to the other nations of mankind cannot utterly perish."[12]

[12] Creek Tribal Records, 35664; 59 Cong., 2 sess., *Sen. Rep. No. 5013.* I, 627 f. For the history of the Creeks after the dissolution of the tribe see Angie Debo, *And Still the Waters Run.*

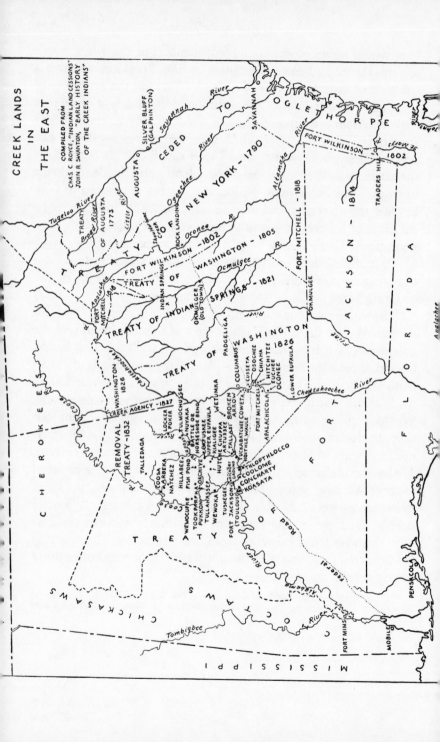

CREEK LANDS
IN
THE EAST

COMPILED FROM
CHAS. C. ROYCE, "INDIAN LAND CESSIONS"
JOHN R. SWANTON, "EARLY HISTORY
OF THE CREEK INDIANS"

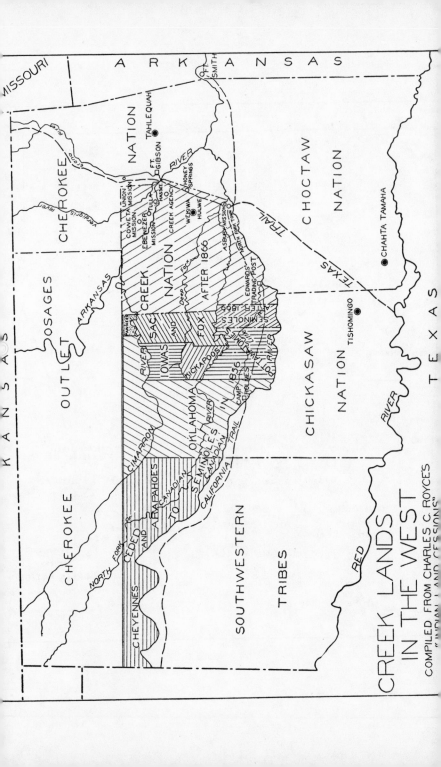

CREEK LANDS
IN THE WEST

COMPILED FROM CHARLES C. ROYCE'S
"INDIAN LAND CESSIONS"

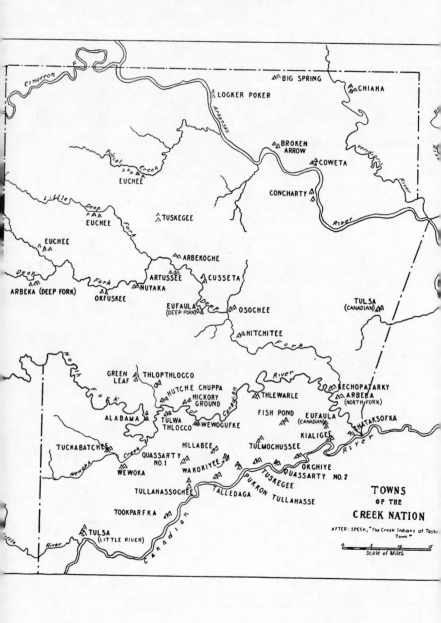

Cimarron

BIG SPRING

LOGKER POKER

ACHIAHA

Arkansas

BROKEN
ARROW

COWETA

Cedar Creek

EUCHEE

CONCHARTY

Verdigris River

Little

River

Deep
Fork

EUCHEE

TUSKEGEE

EUCHEE

Deep

Fork

ARBEKOGHE

ARTUSSEE

CUSSETA

ARBEKA (DEEP FORK)

NUYAKA

TULSA
(CANADIAN)

OKFUSKEE

EUFAULA
(DEEP FORK)

OSOCHEE

HITCHITEE

Fork

North

Fork

GREEN
LEAF

THLOPTHLOCCO

River

AECHOPATARKY

HUTCHE CHUPPA

ARBEKA
(NORTH FORK)

HICKORY
GROUND

THLEWARLE

Canadian

ALABAMA

FISH POND

EUFAULA
(CANADIAN)

THATAKSOFKA

TULWA
THLOCCO

WEWOGUFKE

KIALIGEE

River

TUCKABATCHEE

Wewoka Creek

HILLABEE

TULMOCHUSSEE

QUASSARTY
NO.1

WEWOKA

WAKOKIYEE

OKGHIYE

TUSKEGEE

QUASSARTY NO.2

TULLAHASSOCHEE

PUKKON TULLAHASSE

TALLEDAGA

TOOKPARFKA

TULSA
(LITTLE RIVER)

Canadian

River

TOWNS
OF THE
CREEK NATION

AFTER: SPECK, "The Creek Indians of Taski
Town"

0   5   10   15
Scale of Miles

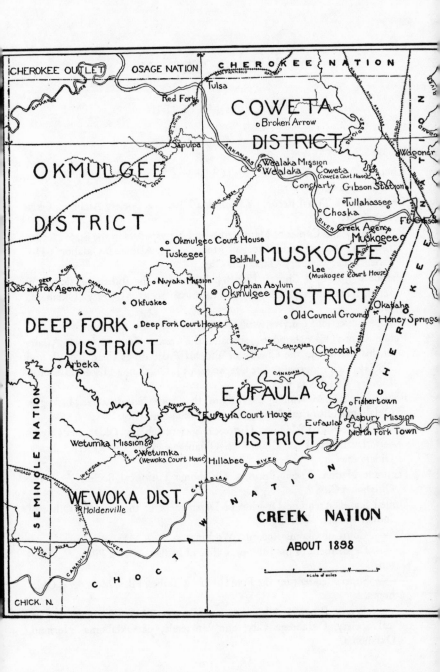

CHEROKEE OUTLET   OSAGE NATION   C H E R O K E E   N A T I O N

CIMARRON RIVER

SAN FRANCISCO RAILROAD

Tulsa

Red Fork

COWETA

o Broken Arrow

DISTRICT

Sapulpa

OKMULGEE

ARKANSAS RIVER

POLECAT CREEK

DEEP FORK

Wagoner

Wealaka Mission
Wealaka
Concharty

Coweta
(Coweta Court House)

Gibson Station

DISTRICT

DUCK CREEK

Tullahassee

Choska

Creek Agency

Muskogee

o Okmulgee Court House

Tuskegee

Baldhill

MUSKOGEE

Lee
(Muskogee Court House)

Sac and Fox Agency

CANADIAN

Nuyaka Mission

o Okfuskee

Orphan Asylum
Okmulgee

DISTRICT

Old Council Grounds

Okatahe

Honey Springs

DEEP FORK

o Deep Fork Court House

DISTRICT

NORTH FORK OF CANADIAN

Checotah

Arbeka

NORTH FORK

CANADIAN

EUFAULA

Fishertown

SEMINOLE NATION

Eufaula Court House

Asbury Mission

Eufaula

Wetumka Mission

Wetumka
(Wewoka Court House)

DISTRICT

North Fork Town

CHICAGO ROCK ISLAND PACIFIC RR

UFEWOKA

Hillabee

RIVER

CANADIAN

N A T I O N

WEWOKA DIST.

Holdenville

CREEK   NATION

ABOUT 1898

CHOCTAW

CANADIAN RIVER

scale of miles

CHICK. N.

Bibliography

SOURCE MATERIAL

I. Manuscript Material

Choctaw Nation. Tribal Records. Oklahoma Historical Society Archives. Oklahoma City.

Creek Nation. Tribal Records. Oklahoma Historical Society Archives. Oklahoma City.

Foreman, Grant. Copies of Manuscripts and Newspapers in the State Department of Archives and History of Montgomery, Alabama. Oklahoma Historical Society Library. Oklahoma City.

Methodist Episcopal Church [South]. Minutes of the Indian Mission Conference [photostat]. Oklahoma Historical Society Library. Oklahoma City.

Phillips Collection. University of Oklahoma. Norman, Oklahoma.

Public Record Office, London. Journal of the Commissioner of Indian Affairs on his journey to the Cherokees and his Proceedings there [copy], and Tobias Fitch's journal to the Creeks [copy]. Oklahoma Historical Society Library. Oklahoma City.

Robertson, Alice M. Among the Indians: the Peace Conference at Muskogee. Oklahoma Historical Society Library. Oklahoma City.

———. Collection. Oklahoma Historical Society Library. Oklahoma City.

———. Incidents of the Civil War. Oklahoma Historical Society Library. Oklahoma City.

Seminole Nation. Tribal Records. Oklahoma Historical Society Archives. Oklahoma City.

United States. Archives, Division of Department of the Interior, Office of Indian Affairs. Washington.

———. Court of Claims Records. Washington.

———. Department of the Interior, Office of Indian Affairs, Files. Washington.

———. Superintendent for the Five Civilized Tribes, Files. Muskogee, Oklahoma.

———. Works Progress Administration, Project S-149. Oklahoma Historical Society, Oklahoma City, and University of Oklahoma, Norman, Oklahoma.

II. Official Documents

1. United States Documents

American State Papers, Foreign Relations, I. Washington, 1832.
———, *Indian Affairs,* I. Washington, 1832.
Board of Indian Commissioners. *Annual Reports,* 1873, 1874, 1882, 1884.
Commission to the Five Civilized Tribes. *Annual Reports,* 1894-1904.
Commissioner of Indian Affairs (variously published in War Department, Department of the Interior, Secretary of the Interior, Commissioner of Indian Affairs, *Annual Reports*). *Annual Reports,* 1829-1900, 1919.
Executive Document, 25 Cong., 2 sess., *No. 127.*
Extra Census Bulletin, The Five Civilized Tribes in Indian Territory. Washington, 1894.
House Ex. Docs., 19 Cong., 2 sess., *No. 76;* 20 Cong., 1 sess., *No. 248;* 20 Cong., 2 sess., *No. 91;* 33 Cong., 2 sess., *No. 15;* 42 Cong., 2 sess., *No. 377.*
House Misc. Docs., 32 Cong., 2 sess., *No. 10;* 47 Cong., 2 sess., *No. 18.*
Kappler, Charles J. *Indian Affairs, Laws and Treaties* (57 Cong., 1 sess., *Sen. Doc. No. 452*), II. Washington, 1904.
Laws of the Colonial and State Governments Relating to Indians and Indian Affairs from 1633 to 1831, inclusive. Washington, 1832.
Malloy, William M. *Treaties, Conventions, International Acts, Protocols, and Agreements Between the United States of America and Other Powers,* II. Washington, 1910.
Senate Committee on Territories. *Testimony Taken Before the Sub-Committee of the Committee on Territories of the Senate of the United States.* Washington, 1878.
Senate Docs., 46 Cong., 2 sess., *No. 124;* 57 Cong., 1 sess., *No. 420.*
Senate Ex. Docs., 47 Cong., 1 sess., *No. 111;* 50 Cong., 1 sess., *No. 198.*
Senate Misc. Docs., 30 Cong., 1 sess., *No. 147;* 43 Cong., 2 sess., *No. 71.*
Senate Reports, 45 Cong., 3 sess., *No. 744;* 49 Cong., 1 sess., *No. 1278;* 53 Cong., 2 sess., *No. 377;* 59 Cong., 2 sess., *No. 5013.*
Statutes at Large of the United States of America, V, XII, XIV, XXVI. Boston, Washington, 1850-68.
War of the Rebellion, Compilation of the Official Records of the Union and Confederate Armies, First Series, Vol. XII, Part 2; Vol. XXXIV, Part 2; Vol. XLI, Parts 2 and 4; Vol. XLVIII, Part 2; Vol. LIII. Washington, 1888-98.

2. Creek Documents

Acts and Resolutions of the Creek National Council, 1895. Muskogee, Creek Nation, 1896.

Acts and Resolutions of the National Council of the Muskogee Nation, 1893-99 inclusive. Muskogee, Creek Nation, 1900.

McKellop, Albert Pike. *Constitution and Laws of the Muskogee Nation.* Muskogee, Creek Nation, 1893.

Perryman, Legus C. *Constitution and Laws of the Muskogee Nation.* Muskogee, Creek Nation, 1890.

Proceedings of Intertribal Councils

"Journal of the General Council of the Indian Territory," *Chronicles of Oklahoma,* III. Oklahoma City, 1925.

Journal of the Second Annual Session of the General Council of the Indian Territory. Lawrence, Kansas, 1871.

Journal of the Third Annual Session of the General Council of the Indian Territory. Lawrence, Kansas, 1872.

Journal of the Fourth Annual Session of the General Council of the Indian Territory [copy]. Oklahoma Historical Society Archives, Oklahoma City.

Journal of the Adjourned Session of the Sixth Annual General Council of the Indian Territory. Lawrence, Kansas, 1875.

"Okmulgee Constitution," *Chronicles of Oklahoma,* III. Oklahoma City, 1925.

Proceedings of the International Territorial Convention. [Probably published at Muskogee, Creek Nation, 1885.]

4. Other Documents

Acts of the General Assembly of the State of Georgia, 1826. Milledgeville, Georgia, 1826.

Matthews, James M. (editor). *Statutes at Large of the Provisional Government of the Confederate States of America.* Richmond, 1864.

Ross, William P. *Indian Territory.* Washington, 1879.

III. Compilations of Source Material

Caughey, John Walton. *McGillivray of the Creeks.* Norman, Oklahoma, 1938.

Richardson, James D. *Messages and Papers of the Presidents,* VII. New York, 1909.

IV. Court Records

Federal Reporter, XLVII, LXIII, CXV. St. Paul, 1892-1902.
Indian Territory Reports, I-III. Parsons, Kansas, 1900-02.
United States Court of Claims Reports, LXXVIII. Washington, 1934.

United States Reports, CXXXV, CCXLVIII. New York, 1890-1919.

V. Books in the Creek Language

Buckner, H. F. *The Gospel According to John.* Marion, Alabama. n. d.

Fleming, John. *I stutsi in Naktsokv (The Child's Book).* Union Mission, Cherokee Nation, 1835.

Loughridge, Robert M., and David M. Hodge. *English and Muskokee Dictionary.* St. Louis, 1890.

Robertson, W. S., and David Winslett. *Nakcokv Kerretv Enhvteceskv (Muskokee or Creek First Reader).* Philadelphia. n. d.

VI. Accounts by Travelers and White Residents

Adair, James. *History of the American Indians.* London, 1775.

Bartram, William. *Travels Through North and South Carolina, Georgia, East and West Florida, the Cherokee Country, the Extensive Territories of the Muscogulges or Creek Confederacy, and the Country of the Chactaws.* London, 1792.

Beadle, J[ohn] H[anson]. *The Undeveloped West.* Philadelphia, 1873.

Bourne, Edward Gaylord (editor). *Narratives of the Career of Hernando de Soto,* I, II. New York, 1922.

Catlin, George. *North American Indians,* II. Edinburgh, 1926.

Farnham, Thomas J. *Travels in the Great Western Prairies, the Anahuac, and Rocky Mountains* (Reuben Gold Thwaites, *Early Western Travels,* XXVIII), I. Cleveland, Ohio, 1906.

Foreman, Grant (editor). *A Traveler in Indian Territory* (Journal of Ethan Allen Hitchcock, 1841-42). Cedar Rapids, Iowa, 1930.

Gregg, Josiah. *Commerce of the Prairies* (Reuben Gold Thwaites, *Early Western Travels, XX*), II. Cleveland, Ohio, 1905.

Hall, Basil. *Travels in North America in the Years 1827 and 1828,* III. Edinburgh, 1829.

Hawkins, Benjamin. *A Sketch of the Creek Country in the Years 1798 and 1799* (Collections of the Georgia Historical Society, Vol. III, Part 1). Savannah, 1848.

————. *Letter (No. 1 of Documents Accompanying the President's Communication to Congress the 8th Day of December, 1801).*

Hodgson, Adam. *Letters from North America,* I. London, 1824.

Irving, Washington (George C. Wells and Joseph B. Thoburn, editors). *A Tour on the Prairies.* Oklahoma City, 1926.

Lang, John D., and Samuel Taylor, Jr. *Report of a Visit to Some of the Tribes of Indians Located West of the Mississippi River.* Providence, 1843.

Latrobe, Charles Joseph. *The Rambler in North America,* I. London, 1836.

Loomis, A. W. *Scenes in the Indian Country.* Philadelphia, 1859.

McCoy, Isaac. *History of Baptist Indian Missions*. Washington, New York, 1840.

Methvin, J. J. "Legend of the Tie Snakes," *Chronicles of Oklahoma*, V. Oklahoma City, 1927.

Möllhausen, Balduin. *Diary of a Journey from the Mississippi to the Coasts of the Pacific . . .*, I. London, 1858.

Morse, Jedidiah. *Report to the Secretary of War of the United States on Indian Affairs*. New Haven, 1822.

Robertson, Alice M. "The Creek Indian Council in Session," *Chronicles of Oklahoma*, XI. Oklahoma City, 1933.

Schoolcraft, Henry Rowe. *Archives of Aboriginal Knowledge*, V. Philadelphia, 1868.

Stuart, James. *Three Years in North America*, II. Edinburgh, 1833.

Swanton, John R. (editor). "The Green Corn Dance" (Account by John Howard Payne, 1835), *Chronicles of Oklahoma*, X. Oklahoma City, 1932.

Turner, C. W. "Events Among the Muskogees During Sixty Years," *Chronicles of Oklahoma*, X. Oklahoma City, 1932.

VII. Contemporary Periodicals

1. Missionary Publications

Indian Record. Muskogee, Creek Nation, 1886-87.

McCoy, Isaac. *The Annual Register of Indian Affairs Within the Indian Territory*, Nos. 3 and 4. Shawanoe Baptist Mission House, Indian Territory, 1837, and Washington, 1838.

Missionary Herald, XXVI-XXXIII. Boston, 1830-37.

2. Magazines

Niles' Weekly Register, III-LXXIV. Baltimore, Washington, 1812-48.

Williams, A. M. "A Grand Council at Okmulgee," *Lippincott's Magazine*, XXIV. Philadelphia, 1879.

Wilson, Ella B. *Parsons' Memorial and Historical Library Magazine*. St. Louis, 1885.

3. Newspapers

Cherokee Advocate. Tahlequah, Cherokee Nation, 1870-71, 1873-75, 1880-84.

Indian Chieftain. Vinita, Cherokee Nation, 1883.

Indian Journal. Muskogee, Eufaula, Creek Nation, 1876-95.

Indian Progress. Muskogee, Creek Nation, 1875.

Muskogee Daily Phœnix. Muskogee, Oklahoma, 1919.

Muskogee Phœnix. Muskogee, Creek Nation, 1893-1901.

SECONDARY MATERIAL

I. Books

Abel, Annie Heloise. *The American Indian as Participant in the Civil War.* Cleveland, Ohio, 1919.

———. *The American Indian as Slaveholder and Secessionist.* Cleveland, Ohio, 1915.

———. *The American Indian Under Reconstruction.* Cleveland, Ohio, 1925.

Debo, Angie. *And Still the Waters Run.* Princeton, New Jersey, 1940.

Foreman, Carolyn Thomas. *Oklahoma Imprints.* Norman, Oklahoma, 1936.

Foreman, Grant. *Advancing the Frontier.* Norman, Oklahoma, 1933.

———. *Down the Texas Road.* Norman, Oklahoma, 1936.

———. *Fort Gibson.* Norman, Oklahoma, 1936.

———. *Indian Removal.* Norman, Oklahoma, 1932.

———. *Indians and Pioneers.* Norman, Oklahoma, 1936.

———. *Pioneer Days in the Early Southwest.* Cleveland, Ohio, 1926.

———. *The Five Civilized Tribes.* Norman, Oklahoma, 1934.

Gatschet, Albert S. *A Migration Legend of the Creek Indians.* Philadelphia, 1884.

Harman, S. W. *Hell on the Border.* Fort Smith, Arkansas, 1898.

Holmes, John. *Historical Sketches of the Missions of the United Brethren for Propagating the Gospel Among the Heathen from Their Commencement to the Year 1817.* London, 1827.

McKenney, Thomas L., and James Hall. *History of the Indian Tribes of North America,* I, II. Philadelphia, 1855.

McLendon, S. G. *History of the Public Domain of Georgia.* Atlanta, 1924.

Mohr, Walter H. *Federal Indian Relations 1774-1788.* Philadelphia, 1933.

O'Beirne, H. F., and E. S. *The Indian Territory: Its Chiefs, Legislators, and Leading Men.* St. Louis, 1892.

Pickett, Albert James. *History of Alabama and Incidentally of Georgia and Mississippi from the Earliest Period.* Birmingham, Alabama, 1900.

Tracy, Joseph, and others. *History of American Missions to the Heathen from Their Commencement to the Present Time.* Worcester, 1840.

Wyeth, Walter N. *Poor Lo.* Philadelphia, 1896.

II. Publications of Government Agencies and Learned Societies

Royce, Charles C. "Indian Land Cessions in the United States," *Eighteenth Annual Report,* Bureau of American Ethnology, Part 2. Washington, 1899.

Speck, Frank Gouldsmith. "Ceremonial Songs of the Creek and Yuchi Indians," *Anthropological Publications of the University Museum,* Vol. I, No. 2. University of Pennsylvania. Philadelphia, 1911.

———. "Ethnology of the Yuchi Indians," *Anthropological Publications of the University Museum*, Vol. I, No. 1. University of Pennsylvania. Philadelphia, 1909.

———. "The Creek Indians of Taskigi Town," *Memoirs of the American Anthropological Association*, Vol. II, Part 2. Lancaster, Pennsylvania, 1907.

Swanton, John R. *Early History of the Creek Indians and Their Neighbors* (*Bulletin No. 73*, Bureau of American Ethnology). Washington, 1922.

——— (editor). "Notes on the Creek Indians," *Bulletin No. 123*, Bureau of American Ethnology. Washington, 1939.

———. "Religious Beliefs and Medical Practices of the Creek Indians," *Forty-second Annual Report*, Bureau of American Ethnology. Washington, 1928.

———. "Social Organization and Social Usages of the Indians of the Creek Confederacy," *Forty-second Annual Report*, Bureau of American Ethnology. Washington, 1928.

III. Magazine Articles

Foreman, Grant. "Early Post-Offices of Oklahoma," *Chronicles of Oklahoma*, VI. Oklahoma City, 1928.

———. "The Five Tribes and the Prairie Indians," *Daily Oklahoman*. Oklahoma City, July 21, 1935.

Gardner, James H. "One Hundred Years Ago in the Region of Tulsa," *Chronicles of Oklahoma*, XI. Oklahoma City, 1933.

Gregory, James R. "Early Creek History," *Sturm's Statehood Magazine*, I. Tulsa, Creek Nation, 1905.

Sapulpa, William A. "Sapulpa," *Chronicles of Oklahoma*, IV. Oklahoma City, 1926.

Index

the road to disappearance

A HISTORY OF THE CREEK INDIANS

Two hundred years ago, when the activities of the white man in North America were dominated by clashing imperial ambitions and colonial rivalry, the Creek Confederacy rested in contentment under the reign of native law. No one in their whole world could do the Creeks harm, and they welcomed the slight white man who came with gifts and promises to enjoy the hospitality of their invincible towns. Within one hundred years the great Confederacy had been broken, dissembled, and removed west of the Mississippi.

In *The Road to Disappearance*, Angie Debo tells for the first time the full Creek story from its vague anthropological beginnings to the loss by the tribe of independent political identity, when during the first decade of this century the lands of the Five Civilized Tribes were divided into severalty ownership. Her book is an absorbing narrative of a minority people, clinging against all odds to native custom, language, and institution. It is the chronicle of the internal life of the tribe—the structure of Creek society—with its folkways, religious beliefs, politics, wars, privations, and persecutions. Miss Debo's research has divulged many new sources of information, and her history of the Creeks since the Civil War is a special contribution because that period has been largely neglected by the historians of the American Indian.

"The vitality of our race still persists," said a Creek orator. "We have not lived for naught. . . . We have given to the European people on this continent our thought forces—the best blood of our ancestors having intermingled with that of their best statesmen and leading citizens. We made ourselves an indestructible element in their national history. We have shown that what they believed were arid and desert places were habitable and capable of sustaining millions of people. . . . The race that has rendered this service to the other nations of mankind cannot utterly perish."

This book is Volume 22 in *The Civilization of the American Indian Series.*

The Author

Angie Debo received her Ph.D. from the University of Oklahoma and lives in Marshall, Oklahoma. She has long been a student of Indian history, and is the author of *Geronimo: The Man, His Time, His Place*; *A History of the Indians of the United States*; and *The Rise and Fall of the Choctaw Republic*, all published by the University of Oklahoma Press.

University of Oklahoma Press
Norman, Oklahoma 73019